D1446267

HUMAN
RIGHTS
WATCH

WORLD REPORT

2006

EVENTS OF 2005

Co-published by Human Rights Watch and Seven Stories Press

Printed in the United States of America

ISBN-10: 1-58322-715-6 · ISBN-13: 978-1-58322-715-2

Front cover photo: *Oiparcha Mirzamatova and her daughter-in-law hold photographs of family members imprisoned on religion-related charges. Fergana Valley, Uzbekistan.* © 2003 Jason Eskenazi

Back cover photo: *A child soldier rides back to his base in Ituri Province, northeastern Congo.* © 2003 Marcus Bleasdale

Cover design by Rafael Jiménez

Human Rights Watch

350 Fifth Avenue, 34th floor
New York, NY 10118-3299 USA
Tel: +1 212 290 4700, Fax: +1 212 736 1300
hrwnyc@hrw.org

1630 Connecticut Avenue, N.W., Suite 500
Washington, DC 20009 USA
Tel: +1 202 612 4321, Fax: +1 202 612 4333
hrwdc@hrw.org

2-12 Pentonville Road, 2nd Floor
London N1 9HF, UK
Tel: +44 20 7713 1995, Fax: +44 20 7713 1800
hrwuk@hrw.org

Rue Van Campenhout 15,
1000 Brussels, Belgium
Tel: +32 2 732 2009, Fax: +32 2 732 0471
hrwatcheu@skynet.be

9 rue Cornavin
1201 Geneva
Tel: +41 22 738 0481, Fax: +41 22 738 1791
hrwgva@hrw.org

Markgrafenstrasse 15
D-10969 Berlin, Germany
Tel.:+49 30 259 3060, Fax: +49 30 259 30629
berlin@hrw.org

www.hrw.org

Human Rights Watch is dedicated to protecting the human rights of people around the world.

We stand with victims and activists to prevent discrimination, to uphold political freedom, to protect people from inhumane conduct in wartime, and to bring offenders to justice.

We investigate and expose human rights violations and hold abusers accountable.

We challenge governments and those who hold power to end abusive practices and respect international human rights law.

We enlist the public and the international community to support the cause of human rights for all.

HUMAN RIGHTS WATCH

Human Rights Watch conducts regular, systematic investigations of human rights abuses in some seventy countries around the world. Our reputation for timely, reliable disclosures has made us an essential source of information for those concerned with human rights. We address the human rights practices of governments of all political stripes, of all geopolitical alignments, and of all ethnic and religious persuasions. Human Rights Watch defends freedom of thought and expression, due process and equal protection of the law, and a vigorous civil society; we document and denounce murders, disappearances, torture, arbitrary imprisonment, discrimination, and other abuses of internationally recognized human rights. Our goal is to hold governments accountable if they transgress the rights of their people.

Human Rights Watch began in 1978 with the founding of its Europe and Central Asia division (then known as Helsinki Watch). Today, it also includes divisions covering Africa, the Americas, Asia, and the Middle East. In addition, it includes three thematic divisions on arms, children's rights, and women's rights. It maintains offices in Berlin, Brussels, Geneva, London, Los Angeles, Moscow, New York, San Francisco, Tashkent, Toronto, and Washington. Human Rights Watch is an independent, nongovernmental organization, supported by contributions from private individuals and foundations worldwide. It accepts no government funds, directly or indirectly.

ACKNOWLEDGMENTS

A compilation of this magnitude requires contribution from a large number of people, including most of the Human Rights Watch staff. The contributors were:

Adam Abelson, Fred Abrahams, Brad Adams, Ranee Adipat, Christopher Albin-Lackey, Emily Allen, Fadi al-Qadi, Joe Amon, Krishna Andavolu, Ana Arana, Assef Ashraf, Amy Auguston, Genine Babakian, Jo Becker, Clarissa Bencomo, Andrea Berg, Nehal Bhuta, Ben Billa, Michael Bochenek, Carroll Bogert, Matilda Bogner, Peter Bouckaert, Sebastian Brett, Widney Brown, Celeste Bruff, Jane Buchanan, Maria Burnett, Helena Cardenas, Corinne Carey, Holly Cartner, Ximena Casas, Kirsten Christiansen, Jonathan Cohen, Sara Colm, Lance Compa, Andrea Cottom, Zama Coursen-Neff, Tanya Cox, Steve Crawshaw, Sara Darehshori, Jennifer Daskal, Meg Davis, Farida Deif, Quetzal Del Real, Fernando Delgadom, Rachel Denber, Alison des Forges, Richard Dicker, Corinne Dufka, Alison Epting, Tinbete Ermyas, Jamie Fellner, Solmaz Firoz, Eloise Fluet, Juan Fogelbach, Bill Frelick, Loubna Freih, Hannah Gaertner, Georgette Gagnon, Jessica Galeria, Nicholas Galletti, Arvind Ganesan, Meenakshi Ganguly, Marc Garlasco, Hadi Ghaemi, Allison Gill, Eric Goldstein, Fanny Gomez, Steve Goose, Ian Gorvin, Laura Gosa, Gretchen Gosnell, Rachel Greenwald, Inara Gulpe-Laganovska, Ali Hassan, Malcolm Hawkes, Peggy Hicks, Chris Huggins, Bogdan Ivanisevic, Vanessa James, Chloe Junge, Tiseke Kasambala, Elise Keppler, Juliane Kippenberg, Joanna Klonsky, Manu Krishnan, Sergio Latorre, Lance Lattig, Leslie Lefkow, Iain Levine, Mie Lewis, Trevor Lippman, Marisa Lloyd, Diederik Lohman, Allison Lombardo, Lucy Mair, Anjana Malhotra, Tom Malinowski, Anne Manuel, Joanne Mariner, Nora Masciole, Géraldine Mattioli, Nobuntu Mbele, Maria McFarland, Fiorella Melzi, Charmain Mohamed, Marianne Mollman, Hania Mufti, Sahr MuhammedAlly, Jennifer Nagle, Laura Negron, Anna Neistat, Katherine Newell Bierman, Amber Norris, Karem Paola, Shayna Parekh, Alison Parker, Lizzie Parsons, Wendy Patten, Alexander Petrov, Sunai Phasuk, Suzannah Phillips, Carol Pier, Vitalii Ponamarev, Lutz Prager, Jo-anne Prud'homme, Tarek Radwan, Dorit Radzin, Keramet Reiter, Sophie Richardson, Jemera Rone, Jim Ross, Claudia Sandoval, Barbara Sartori, Joe Saunders, Rebecca Schleifer, Kay Seok, Bede Sheppard, Acacia Shields, Veena Siddharth, John Sifton, Anna Sinelnikova, Param-Preet

Singh, Eugene Sokoloff, Mickey Spiegel, Vera Spirovski, Jem Sponzo, Karen Stauss, Joe Stork, Jonathan Sugden, Jude Sunderland, Agus Sutikno, Veronika Szente Goldston, Peter Takirambudde, Tamara Taraciuk, Tony Tate, Wilder Tayler, Tej Thapa, Gwendolyn Thomas, Robert Thompson, Bill Van Esveld, Anneke Van Woudenberg, Nisha Varia, José Miguel Vivanco, Janet Walsh, Ben Ward, Saralena Weinfield, Stephanie Welch, Joanna Weschler, Lois Whitman, Sarah Leah Whitson, Christophe Wilcke, Daniel Wilkinson, Christian Wlaschütz, Minky Worden, Elijah Zarwan, Sam Zia-Zarifi.

Joe Saunders, Ian Gorvin, and Iain Levine edited the report; Manu Krishnan coordinated the editing process. Layout and production were coordinated by Andrea Holley and Rafael Jiménez, with assistance from Veronica Matushaj, Amha Mogus, and Jagdish Parikh.

Ranee Adipat, Assef Ashraf, Nicolette Boehland, Celeste Bruff, Matthew Collins-Gibson, Thodleen Dessources, Hannah Gaertner, Yael Gottlieb, Erie Kaneko, Vanessa Kogan, Erin Mahoney, Katie Naeve, Jennifer Nagle, Jo-anne Prud'homme, Anna Sinelnikova, Eugene Sokoloff, and Rania Suidan proofread the report.

For a full list of Human Rights Watch staff, please go to our website:

www.hrw.org/about/info/staff.html.

TABLE OF CONTENTS

INTRODUCTION

By Kenneth Roth

"Practice what I preach, not what I do" is never terribly persuasive. Yet the U.S. government has been increasingly reduced to that argument in promoting human rights. Some U.S. allies, especially Britain, are moving in the same disturbing direction, while few other powers are stepping in to fill the breach.

This hypocrisy factor is today a serious threat to the global defense of human rights. Major Western powers historically at the forefront of promoting human rights have never been wholly consistent in their efforts, but even their irregular commitment has been enormously important. Today, the willingness of some to flout basic human rights standards in the name of combating terrorism has deeply compromised the effectiveness of that commitment. The problem is aggravated by a continuing tendency to subordinate human rights to various economic and political interests.

The U.S. government's use and defense of torture and inhumane treatment played the largest role in undermining Washington's ability to promote human rights. In the course of 2005, it became indisputable that U.S. mistreatment of detainees reflected not a failure of training, discipline, or oversight, but a deliberate policy choice. The problem could not be reduced to a few bad apples at the bottom of the barrel. As evidenced by President George W. Bush's threat to veto a bill opposing "cruel, inhuman, and degrading treatment," Vice President Dick Cheney's lobbying to exempt the Central Intelligence Agency ("CIA") from the bill, Attorney General Alberto Gonzales's extraordinary claim that the United States is entitled to subject detainees to such treatment so long as the victim is a non-American held overseas, and CIA Director Porter Goss's defense of a notorious form of torture known as water-boarding as a "professional interrogation technique," the U.S. government's embrace of torture and inhumane treatment began at the top.

Late in 2005, increasing global attention to the U.S. policy of holding some terror suspects as "ghost detainees"—indefinitely, incommunicado, and without charges at undisclosed locations outside of the United States—further damaged U.S. credibility.

Key U.S. allies such as Britain and Canada compounded the leadership problem in 2005 by seeking to undermine certain critical international rights protections. Britain sought to justify sending terrorist suspects to countries that torture, and Canada worked aggressively to dilute key provisions of a new treaty on enforced disappearances.

These governments, as well as other members of the European Union, also continued to subordinate human rights in their relations with others whom they deemed useful in fighting terrorism or pursuing other goals. That tendency, coupled with the European Union's continued difficulty in responding firmly to even serious human rights violations, meant that the E.U. did not compensate for this diminished human rights leadership.

Fighting terrorism is central to the human rights cause. Any deliberate attack on civilians is an affront to fundamental values of the human rights movement. And acts of terrorism took an appalling toll in 2005. In Iraq attacks on civilians occurred nearly every day, killing thousands, while other terror attacks claimed the lives of civilians in Afghanistan, Britain, Egypt, India, Indonesia, Israel, Jordan, Nepal, Pakistan, Thailand, and the United Kingdom. But the willingness to flout human rights to fight terrorism is not only illegal and wrong; it is counterproductive. These human rights violations generate indignation and outrage that spur terrorist recruitment, undermine the public cooperation with law-enforcement officials that is essential to exposing secret terrorist cells, and cede the moral high ground for those combating the terrorist scourge.

Among other pressing challenges in 2005 were the Uzbekistan government's massacre of hundreds of demonstrators in Andijan in May; the Sudanese government's consolidation of ethnic cleansing in Darfur, in western Sudan; continued severe repression in Burma, North Korea, Turkmenistan, and Tibet and Xinjiang in China; tight restrictions on civil society in Saudi Arabia,

Syria, and Vietnam; persistent atrocities in the Democratic Republic of Congo ("DRC") and the Russian republic of Chechnya; and massive, politically motivated forced evictions in Zimbabwe.

Although the United States responded to several of these developments, its impact was seriously undercut by its diminished credibility. The effect was most immediate on issues of torture and indefinite detention (indeed, the administration rarely even raised concerns about torture by other countries and would have been labeled a hypocrite if it had), but even when the administration spoke out in defense of human rights or acted commendably, its initiatives made less headway as a result of the credibility gap. European and other powers, meanwhile, had their own credibility problems or did far too little to correct the balance. The result was a global leadership void when it came to defending human rights.

Sadly, Russia and China were all too happy to fill that void by building economic, political, and military alliances without regard to the human rights practices of their partners. China's rise as an economic power, and Russia's determination to halt democratizing trends in the former Soviet Union, meant that many governments around the world confronted a political landscape significantly realigned to the detriment of human rights protection. China's and Russia's disregard for human rights in their foreign relations created, in turn, further pressure for Western governments to do likewise for fear of losing economic opportunities and political allies.

Against this bleak backdrop, certain bright spots could still be found in the global system for defending human rights. Sometimes the major Western powers still managed to stand up for human rights, as in Burma, North Korea, and Sudan. Other times, governments from the developing world stepped in. India, for example, played a constructive role in opposing the king of Nepal's takeover of the government in February and his crackdown on political parties and civil society (although India continued lending support to Burma's murderous generals). The Association of Southeast Asian Nations (ASEAN) did better with Burma, successfully pressuring it to relinquish its 2006 chairmanship because of its disastrous human rights record. Mexico took the lead in convincing the United Nations Commission on

Human Rights to maintain a special rapporteur on protecting human rights while countering terrorism. Kyrgyzstan stood up to intense pressure from its powerful neighbor, Uzbekistan, to rescue all but four of 443 refugees from the Andijan massacre, and Romania accepted the rescued refugees for temporary resettlement pending long-term relocation.

Still, governments from the developing world were hardly consistent themselves in defending human rights. Some of them took the lead, for example, in undermining the U.N. Commission on Human Rights and trying to prevent the emergence of an improved successor, the proposed U.N. Human Rights Council. Others prevented the U.N. General Assembly from condemning ongoing ethnic cleansing in Darfur. Moreover, even those that showed a genuine commitment to human rights lacked the influence to make up for reduced Western backing.

At the multilateral level, there was also some good news to report in 2005. The International Criminal Court advanced with the filing of its first indictments—on Uganda—and the U.N. Security Council's first referral to it of a case—Darfur. A U.N. committee concluded negotiations on a new convention to combat enforced disappearances, and fifteen African countries adopted a new protocol on the rights of women. A summit of world leaders at the United Nations endorsed a Canadian-sponsored concept of a global "responsibility to protect" people facing mass slaughter, and took preliminary steps toward strengthening the organization's human rights machinery, but as this report went to press in late November, major questions remained about the fate and definition of the proposed Human Rights Council.

Torture and Inhumane Treatment: A Deliberate U.S. Policy

International human rights law contains no more basic prohibition than the absolute, unconditional ban on torture and what is known as "cruel, inhuman, or degrading treatment." Even the right to life admits exceptions, such as the killing of combatants allowed in wartime. But torture and inhumane treatment are forbidden unconditionally, whether in time of peace or war, whether at the local police station or in the face of a major security threat.

Yet in 2005, evidence emerged showing that several of the world's leading powers now consider torture, in various guises, a serious policy option.

Any discussion of detainee abuse in 2005 must begin with the United States, not because it is the worst violator but because it is the most influential. New evidence demonstrated that the problem was much greater than it first appeared after the shocking revelations of abuse at Abu Ghraib prison in Iraq. Indeed, the sexual degradation glimpsed in the Abu Ghraib photos was so outlandish that it made it easier for the Bush administration to deny having had anything to do with it—to pretend that the abuse erupted spontaneously at the lowest levels of the military chain of command and could be corrected with the prosecution of a handful of privates and sergeants.

As Human Rights Watch noted in last year's World Report, that explanation was always inadequate. For one thing, the abuse at Abu Ghraib paralleled similar if not worse abuse in Afghanistan, Guantánamo, elsewhere in Iraq, and in the chain of secret detention facilities where the U.S. government holds its "high value" detainees. For another, these abuses were, at the very least, the predictable consequence of an environment created by various policy decisions taken at the highest levels of the U.S. government to loosen constraints on interrogators. Those decisions included ruling that combatants seized in the "global war on terrorism" were unprotected by any part of the Geneva Conventions (not simply the sections on prisoners of war); adopting a definition of torture that rendered the prohibition virtually meaningless; not prosecuting offenders until the Abu Ghraib photos became public, even then refusing to permit independent scrutiny of the role of senior policy makers; and making the claim, still not repudiated, that President Bush had commander-in-chief authority to order torture.

Still, it is one thing to create an environment in which abuse of detainees flourishes, quite another to order that abuse directly. In 2005 it became disturbingly clear that the abuse of detainees had become a deliberate, central part of the Bush administration's strategy for interrogating terrorist suspects.

President Bush continued to offer deceptive reassurance that the United States does not "torture" suspects, but that reassurance rang hollow. To begin with, the administration's understanding of the term "torture" remained unclear. The United Nations' widely ratified Convention against Torture defines the term as "any act by which severe pain or suffering, whether physical or mental, is intentionally inflicted on a person." Yet as of August 2002, the administration had defined torture as nothing short of pain "equivalent...to that...associated with serious physical injury so severe that death, organ failure, or permanent damage resulting in a loss of significant body function will likely result." In December 2004, the administration repudiated this absurdly narrow definition, but it offered no alternative definition.

The classic forms of torture that the administration continued to defend suggested that its definition remained inadequate. In March 2005, Porter Goss, the CIA director, justified water-boarding, a sanitized term for an age-old, terrifying torture technique in which the victim is made to believe that he is about to drown. The CIA reportedly instituted water-boarding beginning in March 2002 as one of six "enhanced interrogation techniques" for selected terrorist suspects. In testimony before the U.S. Senate in August 2005, the former deputy White House counsel, Timothy Flanigan, would not even rule out using mock executions.

Moreover, President Bush's pronouncements on torture continued to studiously avoid mention of the parallel prohibition of cruel, inhuman, or degrading treatment. That is because, in a policy first pronounced publicly by Attorney General Alberto Gonzales in January 2005 Senate testimony, the Bush administration began claiming the power, as noted above, to use cruel, inhuman, or degrading treatment so long as the victim was a non-American held outside the United States. Other governments obviously subject detainees to such treatment or worse, but they do so clandestinely. The Bush administration is the only government in the world known to claim this power openly, as a matter of official policy, and to pretend that it is lawful.

The administration was so committed to this policy that, in October, Vice President Dick Cheney presented the sad spectacle of the nation's second highest ranking official imploring the Congress to exempt the CIA—the part of the U.S. government that holds the "high value" detainees—from a legislative effort to reaffirm the absolute ban on cruel, inhuman, or degrading treatment.

While proclaiming the power to subject some detainees to "inhuman" treatment, President Bush somehow managed with a straight face still to insist that his administration would treat all detainees "humanely." He never publicly grappled with this obvious contradiction, and in August, it became clear why. The former deputy White House counsel, Timothy Flanigan, revealed in Senate testimony that, in the administration's view, the term "humane treatment" is not "susceptible to a succinct definition." In fact, he explained, the White House has provided no guidance on its meaning.

The Bush administration's effort to prevent Congress from unambiguously outlawing abusive treatment was hardly an academic matter. Lt. Gen. Michael V. Hayden, the deputy director of national intelligence and one of those who oversees the CIA, explained to human rights groups in August that U.S. interrogators have a duty to use all available authority to fight terrorism. "We're pretty aggressive within the law," he explained. "We're going to live on the edge."

A Compromised U.S. Defense of Human Rights

Needless to say, this embrace of abusive interrogation techniques—not as an indirect consequence of official policy but as a deliberate tool—has significantly weakened the U.S. government's credibility as a defender of human rights.

In 2005, even the exception proved the rule. An important success story in late 2004 and early 2005 was the Orange Revolution in Ukraine, where U.S. pressure for reform and support for Ukrainian civil society and political pluralism played a positive role. The United States was able to help in part because Eastern Europe is one of the few parts of the world where the United States, because of its long history of opposing Soviet domination, is still acknowledged and admired as a credible proponent of democracy and human rights. When the Ukrainian government tried to undermine support for the democratic opposition by linking it to U.S. actions, many ordinary

Ukrainians paid no heed. The same dynamic no longer obtains in many parts of the world.

In the Middle East, for example, the Bush administration stepped up efforts to engage Arab countries on a range of rights issues, something that no past U.S. administration has done. The limited pressure it brought to bear helped create more space for some dissidents and genuinely independent political and civic organizations. But its success was circumscribed by its own human rights record.

One indication of that credibility problem was that when the Bush administration tried to promote certain rights, the poverty of its own record meant it largely had to avoid the term "human rights." Instead, it supported "democracy" and "freedom"—important goals, but ones that do not encompass the full range of human rights protections and are notably devoid of reference to international legal standards that might inconveniently bind the United States.

The Bush administration is not the first U.S. government to misuse such concepts. The Reagan administration, as early as 1982, trumpeted "democracy" and "freedom" in places like El Salvador. Death squads raged at the time, but the Salvadoran government's willingness to hold elections qualified it, in the Reagan administration's view, for a pass on its human rights record.

The Bush administration's efforts in 2005 remained similarly focused mainly on the electoral realm. In Egypt, U.S. officials raised a range of political rights issues. The administration, for example, usefully pressed President Hosni Mubarak to allow competitive presidential elections for the first time. When the Egyptian government imprisoned the leading opposition candidate, Ayman Nour, on trumped-up charges, U.S. Secretary of State Condoleezza Rice cancelled a February visit to Egypt. Deputy Secretary of State Robert Zoellick warned that the administration would withhold $200 million in U.S. aid until Egypt released Nour. President Bush at the time "embraced" President Mubarak's decision to hold competitive elections and criticized beatings of dissidents by ruling-party vigilantes. Secretary Rice even went so far as to urge replacement of Egypt's decades-old emergency rule, the legal backdrop for many of Egypt's worst abuses, with the rule of law.

But the Bush administration's own record of mistreating detainees forced it to limit the kind of democracy it promoted. Other than the State Department's legally mandated once-a-year human rights report, the administration made no public protest (and no known private protest) about the Egyptian government's extensive and well documented use of torture. As one State Department official told Human Rights Watch, "how can we raise it when the Bush administration's policy is to justify torture?"

A similar dynamic was evident with respect to Saudi Arabia. The U.S. Congress conducted hearings on religious freedom in Saudi Arabia and discussed the Saudi Accountability Act, which seeks to compel compliance with anti-terrorism measures and a ban on hate speech. But, with one notable exception, discussed below, there was rare mention of such unseemly topics as domestic repression through torture and arbitrary arrest of Saudi dissidents, let alone such matters as executions, floggings, and routine discrimination against and denial of justice to Saudi women and migrant workers.

In Iraq, where the United States also made promotion of democracy the cornerstone of its efforts, U.S. authorities in November helped uncover and shut down an Iraqi Interior Ministry secret detention and torture center in Baghdad, but the administration's actions won it little praise in light of its own practices in Iraq and elsewhere.

British Complicity with Torture

The United States is the only major Western democracy to openly espouse detainee abuse by its own interrogators, but Britain has adopted policies that would make it complicit in torture. In 2005, Prime Minister Tony Blair proposed sending terrorist suspects to governments that have a history of torturing such people—a policy that the United States had already adopted, in a practice sometimes referred to as "extraordinary rendition."

The U.N. Convention against Torture prohibits without exception sending anyone to a country "where there are substantial grounds for believing that he would be in danger of being subjected to torture." Yet, following precedents set by the Bush administration, the Blair government proposed sending terrorist suspects to places such as Libya, Jordan, Algeria, Morocco, and Tunisia—all governments with notorious records of torturing radical Islamists.

The fig leaf offered to cover this complicity with torture had two parts. First, the British government proposed signing memoranda of understanding in which the government receiving a suspect would promise not to mistreat him. General agreements of this sort were reached with Libya and Jordan and were in the works as of late 2005 with other North African countries. Second, the agreements allowed for monitors to periodically check how detainees were being treated.

But these agreements, known as diplomatic assurances, are not worth the paper they are written on. All the governments in question have ratified the Convention against Torture—a major multilateral treaty—yet routinely flout it. Why would they pay greater heed to a bilateral agreement which, because of the embarrassment of non-compliance, neither the sending nor the receiving government has any incentive to enforce?

The monitoring will not help either. Round-the-clock monitoring might deny torturers an opportunity to ply their trade, but the Blair, like the Bush, government contemplates only periodic monitoring. Occasional monitoring would permit a general sense of how detainees across an entire institution are treated, as the International Committee of the Red Cross obtains during its prison visits, because detainees can benefit from safety in numbers to report abuses anonymously and thus minimize the risk of retaliation.

But episodic visits cannot protect an isolated detainee. Indeed, they are cruel. Imagine the awful dilemma of an isolated torture victim receiving a monitor. Does the victim pretend he was never mistreated, denying the shattering experience of torture? Or does he report his mistreatment, knowing that the account will be traced right back to him and, in retaliation, he might be returned to the torture chamber? No detainee should be made to face that dreadful choice. For such reasons, the U.N. Committee Against Torture ruled in May that Sweden violated the anti-torture convention by relying on diplomatic assurances to send a terrorism suspect, Ahmed Agiza, to Egypt, a country with a long record of torturing Islamic radicals. Agiza was, predictably, tortured.

This plan's incompatibility with international law led the British government to try to change the law. At the U.N. General Assembly in New York, the British delegation, working with the United States, objected to a resolution affirming that diplomatic assurances do not relieve governments of the duty never to send suspects to countries that are likely to torture them. At the European Court of Human Rights in Strasbourg, the British government contended that this duty should be balanced against security needs—that an absolute prohibition should be made conditional. Britain encouraged other European governments to join it in this retrograde position.

Canada's Ambivalent Position

The Canadian government, to its credit, held probing, public hearings in 2005 into the role played by Canadian officials in Washington's shipment of Maher Arar, a Canadian citizen of Syrian extraction, to Syria, where Syrian authorities predictably tortured him—despite the U.S. government's claim to have received assurances from Syria that it would not mistreat him. In this respect, Canada showed significantly greater concern with a single act of possible complicity in torture than the U.S. government has shown about its systematic use of torture. Yet a Canadian law permits the detention and expulsion of immigrants and refugees on national security grounds to countries where they risk torture. The Supreme Court of Canada was due to review the constitutionality of this law in early 2006 to determine whether it infringes the Canadian Charter of Rights and Freedoms. The U.N. Human Rights Committee, in reviewing Canada's record, said that such transfers "can never be justified," echoing concerns expressed in May by the U.N. Committee against Torture when it reviewed Canada's compliance with the torture convention.

Detention

The Bush administration continued in 2005 to detain large numbers of people without charge or trial and without regard to the laws of armed conflict. Sometimes it forcibly "disappeared" them into one of its secret overseas detention facilities, making them highly vulnerable to torture. Under customary laws of war and the Geneva Conventions, a state can detain enemy combatants without trial until the end of an armed conflict. But the Bush administration extended that principle beyond recognition. It continued to detain former Taliban soldiers even though the war with the Afghan government, on whose behalf they had fought, ended at least by June 2002 after the government of Hamid Karzai formally took office. It continued to snatch suspects from places far from any traditional battlefield—Italy, Macedonia, Bosnia, Tanzania, the United States—without regard to their criminal-justice rights.

Under the administration's theory, it can, on its own say-so, without any judicial review, seize anyone anyplace in the world and hold him until the end of the "global war against terrorism," which may never come. That radical theory shreds the most basic due process protections. However, in November 2005, when it appeared that the U.S. Supreme Court might test this theory in the case of Jose Padilla, a U.S. citizen arrested in the United States and held for more than three years as an enemy combatant, the Bush administration suddenly decided to charge him criminally, in an apparent effort to avoid judicial review.

Other governments have not made such extreme claims, but they nonetheless have sought to detain terrorist suspects without trial—often on the basis of secret evidence of dubious reliability. Canada uses "security certificates" to detain indefinitely non-citizens said to present a threat to national security. Britain and Australia introduced legislation in 2005 allowing for "control orders" to subject suspects to house arrest and other restrictions without trial for renewable one-year periods. The British government also sought to extend the period that terrorism suspects can be detained without charge from fourteen days (already the longest in Europe) to ninety days. Parliament rejected the proposal but appeared willing as of late November to double the detention period to twenty-eight days. These policies further discredited these governments as human rights defenders. At this writing, for example, Jordan reportedly was modeling a draft anti-terrorism law on recent British legislation.

Counterterrorism as an Excuse for Silence

The same calculus that led the Bush administration to adopt policies of abusive interrogation and arbitrary detention—the belief that human rights can be sacrificed in the name of fighting terrorism—led it to disregard the promotion of democracy, let alone human rights, with respect to governments that it viewed as allies in its "global war against terrorism."

Pakistan was a case in point. Responding to a question about his broken promise to step down as army chief by the end of 2004, General Pervez Musharraf, the Pakistani president, said to the *Washington Post* in September 2005, "Let me assure you that President Bush never talks about when are you taking your uniform off." The Bush administration offered no public refutation. President Bush did criticize General Musharraf for refusing in June to grant a visa to Mukhtar Mai, a victim of a retaliatory gang rape. But when Musharraf during the same interview in September suggested that Pakistani women get themselves raped to "get a visa from Canada or citizenship and be a millionaire," the State Department offered only weak platitudes about "encouraging leaders around the world to speak out about the fact that violence against women is unacceptable." By contrast, Canadian Prime Minister Paul Martin formally objected to the remarks when he met with Gen. Musharraf later that month. "I stated unequivocally that comments such as that are not acceptable and that violence against women is also a blight that besmirches all humanity," Martin said.

The Bush administration gave a mixed response when, in May, the Uzbekistan government of President Islam Karimov massacred hundreds of protesters in Andijan. On the one hand, the State Department protested the killings, insisted on an international investigation, and helped arrange to airlift to safety 439 refugees who had survived the slaughter. On the other hand, Defense Secretary Donald Rumsfeld resisted calls to withdraw U.S. forces from the Karshi-Khanabad (K2) military base—a re-supply point for operations in Afghanistan and a foothold in former Soviet Central Asia—despite the inappropriateness of partnering with a military force that massacres its own people. Instead, Karimov beat Rumsfeld to the punch in July when he asked the United States to leave the base.

After its ouster from Uzbekistan, the U.S. still had an opportunity to make a human rights point: it could have withheld the $23 million in back rent owed for the base as a way of signaling its displeasure with Uzbekistan's ongoing internal crackdown. Instead, in November, the Pentagon decided to pay, apparently because of its hope that doing so might convince Uzbekistan authorities to allow it to maintain overflight rights. Also in November, the State Department refused to list Uzbekistan as a "country of particular concern," despite its extensive violation of religious freedom, and to co-sponsor a resolution condemning Uzbekistan before the U.N. General Assembly. These mixed messages continued a pattern started in 2004, when the State Department rescinded $18 million in U.S. aid on human rights grounds, only to watch Gen. Richard Meyers, then chairman of the Joint Chiefs of Staff, visit Tashkent and award $21 million in new assistance. This groveling before Karimov proved futile when, in late November 2005, he denied NATO members the sought-after use of Uzbekistan's land or airspace to support Afghanistan operations.

The Bush administration was also weak on Russia in 2005. Secretary Rice, like her predecessor, Colin Powell, periodically spoke about Russian abuses—the torture and enforced disappearances that have characterized the conduct of Russian forces in Chechnya and President Vladimir Putin's disturbing consolidation of political power at the expense of the legislature, the media, the private sector, and, increasingly, nongovernmental organizations. But President Bush, who was uniquely well positioned to influence Russian President Putin, spoke about such concerns only in broad platitudes. Receiving President Putin at the White House in September, President Bush mentioned their joint work "to advance freedom and democracy in our respective countries and around the world" but nothing about any specific human rights abuse in Russia. At the same time, President Bush praised the Putin government as "a strong ally…fighting the war on terror," noting that the two governments "have a duty to protect our citizens, and to work together and to do everything we can to stop the killing."

The Bush administration in November waived congressionally imposed restrictions on arms sales to Indonesia. The restrictions had been imposed following the Indonesian military's atrocities in East Timor in 1999, yet the administration lifted them without any senior Indonesian military official having been held accountable for these crimes. Even though President Susilo Bambang Yudhoyono was democratically elected, the Indonesian military remains unreformed. The administration seemed intent nonetheless on rewarding Indonesia for its role in combating terrorism.

In Egypt, where as already noted the administration expressed support for some basic freedoms but overlooked torture and arbitrary detention, even its vision of competitive elections was limited. While it spoke out in advance of the presidential election and helped secure the release of Nour, leader of the liberal Ghad Party, it ignored sustained government and government-inspired attacks on the party in the run-up to November parliamentary elections. The administration's behavior during the parliamentary elections was even worse, possibly in part reflecting its displeasure at the success in those elections of independent candidates associated with the banned Muslim Brotherhood, Egypt's leading opposition political group, which won dozens of seats in early rounds. As events unfolded, White House and State Department officials repeatedly passed up opportunities to criticize mounting government-inspired violence, ballot-stuffing, and vote-buying. And the administration at no point questioned or criticized the Egyptian government's continuing ban on the Muslim Brotherhood.

Similarly, while the administration deserves credit for seeking and helping win the release of three jailed Saudi political reformers in 2005 (the notable exception mentioned above), it put no real pressure on the Saudi royalty to democratize beyond a token, extremely circumscribed municipal election that excluded women voters and candidates. It cited Saudi Arabia for restrictions on religious practice and tolerance of trafficking in sex workers and laborers but waived the application of sanctions. When President Bush welcomed then-Crown Prince (now King) Abdullah to his Texas ranch in April, the administration said that it "applauds" the municipal elections and "looks for even wider participation in accordance with the Kingdom's reform program." In the joint statement, however, Saudi Arabia merely "recognize[d]" the freedoms that make elections meaningful; it did not vow to protect them in law or abide by them. President Bush added nothing on the subject.

When Secretary Rice visited Riyadh in June, she offered none of the strong language used in Cairo the previous day about "the right to speak freely. The right to associate. The right to worship as you wish. The freedom to educate your children—boys and girls. And freedom from the midnight knock of the secret police." By November, at the inauguration of the first Saudi-U.S. strategic dialogue in Riyadh, democracy, human rights and political reform had safely retreated from the public eye to bilateral discussions behind closed doors. Instead, the public emphasis was on Saudi cooperation on fighting terrorism and limiting the price of oil.

The Bush administration did somewhat better with respect to China. Although trade and security concerns featured prominently on Washington's agenda for Beijing, the U.S. government did offer at least rhetorical support for human rights. During a meeting at the United Nations in September, President Bush gave Chinese President Hu Jintao a list of political prisoners of concern to the United States, but the Chinese government released none of them. Indeed, it cracked down on dissidents in advance of President Bush's November visit to Beijing, eliciting a protest from Secretary Rice. During that visit, President Bush highlighted the issue of religious freedom by visiting a Protestant Church, but the church was a state-sanctioned one, not one of the unapproved "house churches" that are the subject of Chinese persecution. President Bush did express his "hope" that the Chinese government "will not fear Christians who gather to worship openly," but it is unclear whether that plea was meant to embrace the secretive meetings sometimes required for worship in house churches.

Before arriving in China, President Bush spoke of the rise of freedom and democracy in Asia, including China. He said: "The people of China want more freedom to express themselves, to worship without state control, to print Bibles and other sacred texts without fear of punishment." Once he arrived in China, President Bush settled for citing as progress that President Hu had mentioned the term "human rights" in his remarks.

The willingness to sacrifice basic human rights principles in the name of fighting terrorism hit a new low around the issue of enforced disappearances. "Disappearances" occur when governments seize people without acknowledging their detention, leaving them highly vulnerable to torture or execution, and their families in a painful limbo, knowing nothing of the fate or whereabouts of their loved ones.

A long-term effort at the United Nations to complete a treaty outlawing "disappearances" reached a milestone with the adoption of a draft by a working group of the Commission on Human Rights. Several Latin American governments sponsored the effort, including Argentina, Chile, Mexico, and Uruguay, because they had suffered a devastating plague of "disappearances" in the 1970s and 1980s. France also played an important leadership role. To their disgrace, the United States and Russia strongly opposed the effort, not least because each had begun using forced disappearances itself—Russia in Chechnya, where young men suspected of being rebels or their allies routinely "disappear" after their arrest by Russian forces, and the United States in the secret detention facilities that it maintains in allied countries, where twenty-six people are known to have "disappeared" and some dozen others are suspected held. Canada contributed to this shameful opposition, not because it is known to forcibly "disappear" people, but apparently because Prime Minister Martin, eager to improve relations with the United States that had been strained under his predecessor, decided to run interference for one of his neighbor's unsavory practices.

The European Union

Washington was not the only cause of the global leadership void on human rights. The European Union might have filled the gap, but instead it continued to punch well below its weight, due in part to institutional disarray and in part to competing priorities.

The need to achieve consensus among twenty-five members was part of the problem. The proposed new constitution would have streamlined foreign policy decisions, easing the need for unanimity among its members as well as strengthening the E.U.'s chief foreign policy representative. However, the constitution suffered a major setback when voters rejected it in referenda held in France in May and the Netherlands in June.

The continuing need for unanimity, combined with an opaque decision-making process and a lack of leadership among E.U. members, produced a dynamic that favored muted responses toward human rights violations in third countries. However, with regard to E.U. accession countries, a transparent process coupled with the ability of any single member to block progress for an aspiring state tended to raise the bar on human rights. Positive pressure for improvement was thus exerted, most notably on Turkey.

When it came to external protests or interventions, however, the E.U.'s decision-making procedures tended to work the other way. When E.U. governments had already agreed to common pressure, as in the arms embargo imposed on China following the Tiananmen Square massacre of 1989, their consensus rules favored perpetuation of the status quo, even though France and Germany, among others, sought to end the embargo. More commonly, though, in the case of new initiatives, E.U. procedures favored weak responses.

The E.U. managed to achieve consensus and play a positive role by sponsoring critical resolutions at the United Nations on human rights in the DRC, North Korea, Sudan, Uzbekistan, and Turkmenistan. But the E.U. generally failed to give teeth to its human rights protests by effectively using its many trade and cooperation agreements to press for human rights improvements in countries benefiting from massive E.U. assistance and trading privileges.

For example, the E.U. continued to see its relationship to the Middle East and North Africa primarily in terms of trade and economic assistance. Most governments in the European-Mediterranean Cooperation Area have concluded agreements with the E.U. that require respect for human rights and the rule of law. Yet the E.U. rarely, and never publicly, enforced these human rights conditions by, for example, detailing concrete, country-specific steps that a government should take to put it on a positive trajectory, let alone outlining a timeframe for required reforms and spelling out the consequences of non-compliance.

A good illustration was the Egypt-E.U. Association Agreement, which entered into force in June 2004. The E.U. has yet to invoke the clause premising the entire agreement on "respect for human rights and democratic principles." The same could be said of E.U. agreements adopted with Tunisia in 1999 and Israel in 2000. E.U. governments are the largest donors to the North Africa region, giving them plenty of potential influence, but they seldom used it in 2005. Conveniently, the E.U. tended to claim instead that trade and quiet diplomacy on human rights would yield more liberal regimes, but that left the region's simmering civil society movement for reform without the overt backing of the powerful E.U.

With respect to Africa, the European Union did not hesitate to act against a pariah state such as President Robert Mugabe's in Zimbabwe. There, it adopted a series of punitive measures, including an arms embargo, freezing of assets, a visa ban, and suspension of all non-humanitarian aid. Key European governments also continued to supply peacekeeping troops in the Ivory Coast and logistical support to African Union troops in Darfur. But the E.U. did not act with similar forcefulness when it came to abuses by governments with which it maintained closer relationships. In Angola, Ethiopia, Rwanda, and Uganda, for example, the E.U. condemned abuses but did not put the governments on notice that they were in serious breach of their human rights obligations, including those written into the agreement that regulates European assistance to such countries. In this respect, the E.U. seemed increasingly to favor the status quo in Africa.

Individual European governments were not better in their own policies toward Africa. Britain's Prime Minister Blair invited Ethiopian Prime Minister Meles Zanawi as one of only two African heads of state or government on Blair's Commission for Africa, but Britain was silent about Meles's repression of his political opposition. Similarly, Belgium continued strong support for Rwandan President Paul Kagame despite his government's repression at home and responsibility for atrocities in the neighboring DRC. Meanwhile, although the French government maintained its troop presence in the Ivory Coast, its policy of "tactical disengagement" from much of the rest of the African continent posed potential dangers for human rights protection. On a continent where better human rights protection frequently depends on greater external commitment, the decline of French willingness to engage raised the specter of more hardship in francophone African countries such as the DRC, Guinea, and the Ivory Coast. This diminished European activism on Africa paralleled China's increasing engagement with the continent on terms that attached no importance to human rights.

One positive exception to the E.U.'s disregard for other government's binding human rights commitments with it came in the case of Uzbekistan. It took more than four months, but in October, the E.U. finally decided to partially suspend its partnership and cooperation agreement with Uzbekistan because of President Karimov's refusal to permit an international inquiry into the Andijan massacre. This was the first time the E.U. had suspended any such agreement on human rights grounds—an important precedent on which to build but also a sad commentary on the lack of seriousness with which the E.U. typically has treated the legally binding human rights requirements in all such agreements.

The E.U. also took the lead in the successful effort to condemn Uzbekistan before the U.N. General Assembly. In addition, the E.U. imposed an arms embargo on Uzbekistan and a visa ban on a dozen senior officials believed to have played a role in the massacre—though, incomprehensibly, not on President Karimov himself. Germany also allowed the Uzbek interior minister, Col. Gen. Zakirjan Almatov, one of those believed to have ordered the Andijan massacre, to enter Germany for medical treatment despite the travel ban. As the point of the travel ban was to deny such people the privilege of precisely this kind of visit, the German behavior called into question whether the sanctions were really part of a coherent strategy for seeking change in Uzbekistan.

Apart from its trade and aid relationships, the E.U. in recent years has begun to play a positive role in mounting overseas field operations in conflict zones.

By current count, there are at least nine active European Security and Defence Policy missions. The E.U. helped secure a peace accord to end the vicious conflict in Aceh and provided monitors to oversee its implementation, including respect for human rights. It provided police to oversee the border crossing at Rafah following the Israeli disengagement from the Gaza Strip. And it provided rule-of-law assistance in places such as Georgia and the DRC.

Given the E.U.'s difficulty speaking in a common voice, the member states might have treated the E.U. common position on external human rights matters as a floor rather than a ceiling—as the minimum they would do for human rights rather than the maximum. That might have especially been the case with respect to such important countries as Russia, China, the United States, and Saudi Arabia—all countries with which E.U. members have active individual foreign policies in addition to their common position. For the most part, though, the lack of human rights leadership toward these countries that stymied effective common action was also visible in bilateral dealings.

The E.U. position on Russia in 2005 made the U.S. defense of human rights seem vigorous. Business, energy, and other political interests dominated E.U. concerns, abetted by an unseemly competition among British Prime Minister Blair, French President Chirac, and former German Chancellor Schroeder to proclaim the closeness of their relationship with Russian President Putin. Germany, for example, was preoccupied with negotiating the construction of a gas pipeline from Russia, which was agreed to in September, and sought Russia's support for its bid for a permanent seat on the U.N. Security Council. Schroeder, who reportedly met with Putin thirty-seven times during the years he was chancellor, continued to make little public reference to Russia's human rights record. France sought to maintain warm relations to facilitate cooperation on the Security Council, especially with regard to the Middle East.

At an E.U.-Russia summit in October hosted in London by the British presidency, the assembled leaders, according to the E.U.'s account, merely "addressed in a constructive spirit internal developments in the E.U. and

Russia, including the situation in Chechnya and the forthcoming elections there," and "welcomed" an E.U. decision to provide financial assistance to the North Caucasus as "a further sign of E.U. willingness to cooperate in the region." There was no hint in this embarrassingly positive statement that the central problem in Chechnya was Russia's refusal to end atrocities by its forces. Along similar lines, the E.U. failed to sponsor a resolution critical of Russia's rights record in Chechnya at the U.N. Commission on Human Rights.

With respect to China, business and other political interests again dominated. For example, France and Germany pressed to lift the arms embargo toward China that had been imposed in protest of the Tiananmen Square massacre, even though no progress had been made in holding accountable those officials who ordered the killing, and the Chinese government refused to provide information about the number killed, injured, and arrested. The embargo stayed in place because of strong American security objections, supported by Czechoslovakia, Denmark, Finland, the Netherlands, Poland, and Sweden, among others. Britain initially supported the U.S. position, reversed its position under pressure from France and Germany, and then reversed its position again after Chinese threats against Taiwan made lifting the embargo untenable. In November, Germany, under its new chancellor, Angela Merkel, came out in favor of continuing the embargo, leaving little prospect for the embargo to be lifted in the foreseeable future. Meanwhile, the E.U. continued to refuse to sponsor a resolution on China at the U.N. Commission on Human Rights.

As for Saudi Arabia, German Chancellor Schroeder visited it without public mention of political reforms. British Prime Minister Blair conducted his visit secretly. The British government pressed hard for Saudi Arabia to buy arms from British manufacturers while remaining virtually silent on the kingdom's abysmal human rights record. France received Crown Prince Abdullah, an occasion that President Chirac used to speak in glowing terms about "reforms," calling them "an ambitious program of transformation." He praised the above-noted municipal elections, with their circumscribed scope and absence of women voters or candidates, as well as "recent developments in the Consultative Council," which had merely expanded from 120 to 150 members, all appointed, with no women and only a minor increase in minority representation (from two to four seats).

As for trans-Atlantic relations with the United States, the E.U. understandably was eager to repair the damage done by disagreements triggered by the invasion of Iraq, but its strategy seemed to include largely ignoring U.S. rights transgressions. For most of the year, the E.U. collectively utterly failed to raise concerns about the U.S. practice of "disappearing" terrorist suspects. The sole exceptions were national investigations opened in Italy, Germany, and Sweden into the CIA's role in seizing or luring suspects from their soil and sending them to Egypt or Afghanistan. The E.U. became more assertive only in the face of broad public outrage triggered by evidence that was made public in November suggesting the United States had maintained secret detention facilities near airports in Poland and Romania. Only then did several national parliaments and prosecutors launch investigations, the European Commission opened an informal inquiry, and the E.U. foreign ministers requested clarification from the United States about CIA activities on E.U. territory. The Council of Europe began a formal inquiry and the council's secretary-general sent a rare formal request for information about the matter to all forty-five member states.

After successfully securing custody of its nationals held in Guantánamo, Britain went so far as to become an apologist for the United States. Britain's 2005 human rights report spoke of "five substantial [U.S.] inquiries" into prisoner abuse which "concluded that the incidents of abuse were the result of the behaviour of a few sadistic individuals and a failure of oversight by commanders, rather than the result of US policy or procedures." In fact, as noted, U.S. *policy* has been to subject detainees to cruel, inhuman, and degrading treatment, if not torture. Meanwhile, none of the dozen self-investigations into past abuses launched by the Bush administration was independent, let alone substantial: only one examined the role of senior Pentagon officials, and it was run by members of Defense Secretary Rumsfeld's own Defense Policy Board Advisory Committee; only one looked at the role of the CIA, and it was run by the CIA's own inspector general; and none looked at the role of senior White House officials. The Bush administration opposed creating an independent, bipartisan panel on interrogation abuses similar to the September 11 Commission and refused to appoint a special prosecutor, even though Attorney General Alberto Gonzales, as a central architect of the administration's interrogation policy, had an obvious conflict of interest.

Closer to home, the E.U. threatened to flout human rights standards in its own treatment of refugees and migrants. International refugee law requires that a government give any asylum-seeker a fair determination of his claim and protect him from return to persecution or torture. But in an effort to deter asylum-seekers from seeking refuge in Europe, the E.U. pursued policies that would shift to neighboring countries—such as Libya and Ukraine—responsibility for processing asylum claims, hosting refugees, and managing migration, despite these countries' demonstrated lack of capacity to protect even the basic rights of asylum-seekers and migrants in their territories, let alone to provide a fair determination of asylum claims. Libya, for example, does not even have laws by which its judiciary could assess claims for asylum.

The Nefarious Role of Russia and China

Just as nature abhors a vacuum, so governments fill leadership voids. In this case, Russia and China have been all too eager to assert themselves in the absence of firm Western leadership on human rights, but their interventions have been anything but helpful. Uzbekistan illustrates the problem. Less than two weeks after the Uzbekistan government's massacre of protestors in Andijan in May, China welcomed Uzbek President Karimov to Beijing for a state visit, complete with a 21-gun salute. Not to be outdone, in November, just as Uzbekistan was completing a show trial to supposedly demonstrate that its troops never committed a massacre in Andijan, Russia invited Karimov to Moscow to initial a mutual-defense pact. In July, the secretary general of the Shanghai Cooperation Organization, which includes China, Russia, and several Central Asian countries, blamed the Andijan massacre on "terrorists" rather than Uzbekistan's own security forces, while Presidents Putin and Hu announced billion dollar economic packages for Uzbekistan.

Russia has been playing a similar role throughout the former Soviet Union. Fearful of the democratic currents that led to the overthrow of once-allied governments in Georgia, Ukraine, and Kyrgyzstan, Russia threw its active support behind such abusive partners as Presidents Alexander Lukashenko of Belarus and Ilham Aliev of Azerbaijan. For example, Russia maintained that the fraudulent November 2004 presidential election in Ukraine was free and fair, with Putin calling then-Prime Minister Viktor Yanukovich to congratulate him on his "victory" soon after the voting ended. Following the November 2005 parliamentary elections in Azerbaijan, which were said to be won by Aliev's party, President Putin described them as "successful" even though the Organization for Security and Cooperation in Europe ("OSCE") found that the elections failed to meet international standards for democratic elections.

Russia also has tried to diminish the positive influence of the OSCE, which has played a central role in pressing for free and fair elections throughout the former Soviet Union, in favor of a greater emphasis on security issues. Russia has suggested that such OSCE "human dimension" operations as the Office for Democratic Institutions and Human Rights and the Office of the High Commissioner for National Minorities should be dealt with by "consensus" among member states, which would empower Moscow to veto any initiative it did not like. Russia also threatened in October to use a procedural maneuver that effectively would halt rapid progress toward a credible U.N. Human Rights Council to replace the discredited U.N. Commission on Human Rights.

As for China, its economic growth and quest for natural resources combined with its stated policy of "non-interference in domestic affairs" led to its bolstering of corrupt and repressive regimes in Africa, Latin America, and Asia, to the disadvantage of the people of these regions. Willing to do business with anyone, the Chinese government threw an economic lifeline to such highly abusive governments as those of Sudan and Zimbabwe. In purchasing oil and making massive oil-backed loans, Beijing also closed its eyes to corruption on the part of unaccountable governments such as Angola. This massive infusion of cash helped Angola resist anti-corruption measures sought by the International Monetary Fund. China provided financial and military support to the Sudanese government even as it was engaged in massive ethnic cleansing in Darfur, while Beijing successfully watered down U.N. Security Council resolutions threatening sanctions against Khartoum for its Darfur atrocities. The most deprived people of Africa suffered further because Beijing, in its dealings with their governments, showed such indifference to their plight.

Increasingly China is a donor as well, but without the concomitant pressure to respect human rights that, at least theoretically, accompanies Western aid. As President Hu put it: "Providing African countries with aid without any political strings… is an important part of China's policy towards Africa." China's view that human rights conditions constitute unjustified political interference significantly reduces the chance that its aid will benefit those people who need it most.

Darfur and the African Union

The continued deployment of African Union troops into Darfur in 2005 unquestionably saved lives. However, the belated decision by the A.U.—a new, still poorly equipped organization—to allow Western countries to provide logistical and other support meant that many lives that could have been saved were lost. The contingent of seven thousand A.U. troops and civilian police that by October had finally been deployed in Darfur was not nearly large enough to create the conditions of security needed for some two million forcibly displaced people to return home safely.

Much of the continued violence in Darfur was due to the Sudanese government, most notably its refusal to disarm, demobilize, and end the impunity with which its proxy militia, the "Janjaweed," operates in Darfur. The Sudanese government also placed many obstacles in the path of the A.U. force, such as refusing for months to allow the A.U. to import armored personnel carriers for the protection of its troops and civilians. However, the A.U. itself must share part of the blame. Its interpretation of its mandate was anemic—it showed too little willingness to move aggressively when necessary to protect people. By insisting on handling Darfur itself, moreover—a wish that the international community, preoccupied elsewhere, was all too willing to grant—the A.U. relieved more powerful governments of any immediate pressure to deploy their own troops.

The U.S., Canadian, and European governments played supportive roles in Darfur. Officials spoke repeatedly about the continuing killing and rape and sent emissaries regularly to Khartoum and Darfur, but preoccupation with Iraq and Afghanistan made the contribution of U.S., E.U., or NATO troops a political non-starter. As a result, Western governments and the international community as a whole left Darfur in the hands of A.U. troops and failed to take the opportunity to forcefully implement the newly endorsed international "responsibility to protect" civilians at grave risk. By year's end, there was still no prospect that the forcibly displaced residents of Darfur would be able to return home safely and that "ethnic cleansing" would be reversed.

If the A.U. cannot quickly field the substantially larger force needed to uphold a full protective mandate and to make possible the safe return of displaced people, the international community has a duty to send in troops to reinforce the A.U. military and civilian presence, if necessary under a U.N. flag. Meanwhile, the international community must put intense pressure on the Sudanese government to permit a larger force, if necessary involving non-African troops, and to stop obstructing the protective work of those forces that are deployed. In a troubling sign, the African Union itself defused that pressure by helping to block a vote in November at the U.N. General Assembly that would have condemned Sudan for its continuing responsibility for atrocities in Darfur.

At this writing, the African Union was facing a substantial additional challenge with respect to Darfur: its next scheduled summit was to be held in January 2006 in Khartoum, with Sudan seeking the A.U. presidency. If Sudan's President El Bashir indeed were to lead the A.U., its mission in Darfur would face unsustainable contradictions, and civilians in Darfur would be at greater risk than at any time since the A.U. first deployed there. Allowing a murderous government such as Sudan's to lead the A.U. would make a travesty of the A.U.'s stated commitments to human rights and undermine the credibility it needs to work effectively throughout the continent.

In creating the African Union, African nations compare favorably with nations in regions such as Asia and the Middle East that continue to lack any comparable multilateral mechanism for addressing conflict and promoting human rights. At the same time, the A.U. continues to suffer from the cronyism and lack of principle that plagued its predecessor, the Organization of African Unity. The A.U. made modest interventions in Burundi, Togo, Zimbabwe, and the DRC in 2005. Initially acting effectively in Togo, the A..U., and especially Nigerian President Olusegun Obasanjo, condemned a coup in February and threatened to impose sanctions when Faure Gnassingbe tried to have himself installed as president upon his father's death without an election. However, when elections were held some two months later, the A.U. failed to condemn well documented intimidation, violence, and massive vote-rigging.

The A.U., supported by a United Nations peacekeeping force, facilitated a significant improvement in Burundi, where a vicious civil war has substantially waned. On the other hand, the A.U. has managed only to dispatch emissaries to President Mugabe of Zimbabwe, without putting meaningful pressure on him, even as, beginning in May, he ordered the politically motivated destruction of thousands of homes in urban shantytowns, creating a humanitarian crisis. In the DRC, the A.U. has spoken of addressing the politically sensitive issue of foreign combatants in the country but has yet to act. In the Ivory Coast, the A.U. has downplayed issues of justice and accountability that are likely to prove essential to a lasting peace. Meanwhile, certain powerful leaders, such as Prime Minister Meles Zenawi of Ethiopia, escaped A.U. pressure altogether, even as he, unwilling to accept opposition gains in the country's first contested elections in May, led the police to kill scores of demonstrators and arrest thousands of opposition supporters.

International Justice

The emerging system of international justice made important strides in 2005, helping to fill some of the gaps left by waning governmental support for human rights. Most notably, the International Criminal Court ("ICC") publicly revealed its first indictments in October. The targets were Joseph Kony and four other leaders of the Lord's Resistance Army ("LRA"), the notorious Ugandan rebel group that has built a military force by kidnapping children and forcing them to commit all manner of atrocities. The indictments encountered predictable objections from those who said they would disrupt the Ugandan peace process, but most observers judged the peace process moribund anyway—more a device for the LRA to bide time and regroup than a conscientious effort to reach an agreement with the Ugandan government. Indeed, by further delegitimizing the LRA leadership, the indictments will arguably hasten an end to the war by making it politically more difficult for the Sudanese government to continue to harbor the LRA in southern Sudan, particularly as Khartoum cedes power there to the Sudan People's Liberation Army as part of the separate Sudanese peace process.

The ICC received a major boost in March when the U.N. Security Council gave it jurisdiction over atrocities committed in Darfur. The major obstacle to Security Council action was the United States, given the Bush administration's ideological hostility to the court because of the court's theoretical power to prosecute a U.S. citizen for genocide, war crimes, or crimes against humanity committed on the soil of a government that had ratified the ICC treaty. Germany began the process of overcoming that resistance by leading the effort at the Security Council in September 2004 to establish a U.N. commission of inquiry into the ethnic cleansing in Darfur. The commission recommended in January 2005 that the Security Council refer the situation in Darfur to the ICC.

The Bush administration struggled to suggest alternatives to the ICC, from adding a chamber to the overworked International Criminal Tribunal for Rwanda to the unlikely prospect of creating from scratch a brand new African Criminal Court. Washington viewed these alternatives as preferable because, even if less effective, they were less likely to have jurisdiction over Americans. Strong backing for the ICC from many of its African members, as well as the E.U. and particularly France, helped to move beyond these inferior options. Britain also played a useful role in the negotiations. Faced with a choice between granting effective immunity to the killers in Khartoum and accepting ICC jurisdiction over Darfur, the Bush administration, along with China, abstained on the ICC resolution at the Security Council, allowing the resolution to be adopted. Russia voted in favor of the resolution. That vote means that the ICC henceforth has become a realistic option for prosecuting even tyrants whose governments have not ratified the ICC treaty.

Yet the Bush administration continued to take extraordinary steps to avoid any prospect that the court would exercise jurisdiction over a U.S. citizen. Washington continued to blackmail governments to accept bilateral immunity agreements in which they promise never to send an American to the ICC. And it insisted that non-ICC states parties have exclusive jurisdiction over their nationals in Darfur.

The ICC was never the appropriate tribunal to try Saddam Hussein and his henchmen in the deposed Iraqi government, because they committed the bulk of their crimes before July 1, 2002, when the ICC's jurisdiction took effect. Yet fear that new international tribunals might legitimize multilateral justice was part of the reason that the Bush administration insisted on trying the former Iraqi leadership before an Iraqi-led tribunal. The administration stuck stubbornly to that decision in 2005, even though the Iraqi Special Tribunal found itself plagued with problems, including its susceptibility to political interference by the new Iraqi government, its members' lack of experience with complex trials, the troubling deficiencies in its adopted procedures, and its difficulty in safeguarding the participants in its proceedings. An internationally led tribunal, such as the mixed international-national tribunal used in Sierra Leone, could have overcome most if not all of these difficulties.

Meanwhile, the international Yugoslav tribunal made enormous progress in securing the arrest of indicted suspects. U.S. and E.U. pressure on Serbia yielded the surrender of fourteen people who had been indicted but remained at large between October 2004 and April 2005. With that influx of defendants, 131 suspects had appeared before the tribunal, while only nine suspects remained fugitives, although those at large included such leading figures as the Bosnian Serb wartime army chief, Ratko Mladic, the Bosnian Serb wartime president, Radovan Karadzic, and Croatian General Ante Gotovina.

The Rwandan tribunal also significantly picked up the pace of its prosecutions in 2005, although it continued to focus exclusively on the genocide and, disturbingly, still had not issued indictments for atrocities committed by the Rwandan Patriotic Front ("RPF"). Spain stepped into this void by launching investigations into some dozen RPF officers. Similarly, Belgium indicted Hissene Habre, the dictator of Chad in the 1980s, whose mass murder and torture are not covered by any existing international tribunal. After having promised repeatedly that he would extradite Habre if the latter was indicted by Belgium, Senegal's President Abdoulaye Wade suffered a failure of will in November and instead sent the matter to the African Union to resolve.

As for the Special Court for Sierra Leone ("SCSL"), its most important defendant, former Liberian President Charles Taylor, continued to enjoy a comfortable exile in Nigeria. In June 2003, the SCSL unveiled an indictment of Taylor for his role in supporting the barbarous Revolutionary United Front rebels, known for murder, rape, and hacking off the limbs of their many victims during the Sierra Leone civil war.

Nigerian President Obasanjo did a service by providing Taylor refuge in August 2003 to ease him out of Liberia without further bloodshed. But as the U.N. Security Council reaffirmed in November 2005, that refuge was meant to be only temporary. Pleas for Obasanjo to deliver Taylor for trial were also made in the course of 2005 by the European Parliament, in February; the U.S. Congress, in May; the U.N. high commissioner for human rights, in July; and the Mano River Union, consisting of Guinea, Liberia, and Sierra Leone, also in July.

More than two years since Taylor's flight from Liberia, however, President Obasanjo stubbornly refused to hand him over to the SCSL. Obasanjo said that he would abide by a request from a democratically elected Liberian government to deliver Taylor for trial, but that approach passed the buck to a new government that legitimately may fear retaliation by Taylor's many violent allies in Liberia. It is to be hoped that Liberian President Ellen Johnson-Sirleaf, newly elected in November, will make such a request, but if Obasanjo were a true statesman, he would take the heat himself rather than hide behind the new Liberian president. The African Union, for its part, should encourage such a move, but rather than seeking a victory for justice and the rule of law—ostensible goals of the African Union—some A.U. leaders in

2005 seemed more worried about setting a precedent that someday might facilitate their own prosecution.

Justice made little progress in East Timor. Due to a lack of political and financial support, the U.N. tribunal there shut down in May, six years after it was established. The tribunal did manage to prosecute and convict a significant number of East Timorese militia members, but the majority of the Indonesians indicted, including General Wiranto, the former Indonesian defense minister and armed forces commander, remained at large in Indonesia with no prospect of trial. In the meantime, both the U.N. Security Council and U.N. Secretary-General Kofi Annan, caving into Indonesia as a regional power and important counterterrorism ally, continued to sit on a report commissioned by the secretary-general that had recommended keeping the tribunal alive. The report had also recommended the establishment of an international criminal tribunal if Indonesia continued to be uncooperative on the justice front, but the Security Council returned the report to the secretary-general without taking action.

The United Nations

Any analysis of the United Nations' human rights role must divide the institution into its two essential parts. On the one hand are the Secretariat and its associated operational agencies, on the other hand is a series of conference halls where the nations of the world meet to address a broad range of issues.

Kofi Annan is clearly the most committed to advancing human rights of any secretary-general the organization has known. For example, through his personal interventions on Darfur (including at least sixteen statements on the situation in 2005), Annan struggled to keep attention focused on the ongoing crisis and to prompt further remedial action. His human rights work was aided by Louise Arbour, a strong and principled high commissioner for human rights, whose work to establish a monitoring mission in Nepal and to report on violence in Uzbekistan was particularly helpful.

Also in 2005, a new report on human security published by the University of British Columbia made a compelling case that international efforts to address conflicts are saving lives. Failures to address human rights crises naturally continued to capture headlines, but in many places, such as Liberia, where fighting has been curbed and successful elections were held, international intervention helped to end the killing and launch law-abiding democratic governments. The rapid expansion of U.N. preventive diplomacy and peace-keeping missions suggests that a multilateral response to crises sometimes can overcome the leadership void among some of the most powerful U.N. members. However, major-power leadership is likely to remain essential to make meaningful the U.N. summit's endorsement of a "responsibility to protect" civilians at grave risk.

As for the United Nations as a governmental forum, the results were mixed at best. On the positive side, it finally became accepted wisdom that the U.N. Commission on Human Rights had become a shameful embarrassment that discredits the entire organization. With a large number of its fifty-three seats occupied by highly abusive governments, the Commission functioned less to advance human rights than to ensure paralysis, thereby shielding from criticism almost any government (other than Israel), no matter how abusive.

Unfortunately, this growing consensus led to little more than a pronouncement that the Commission must be replaced by a more effective Human Rights Council. As of late November, there was still no agreement on how that Council should be constituted. Most important, much dispute remained about how to improve the quality of the Council's membership.

Much of the problem with the Commission's membership lay with the practice of allowing each region to dictate which governments would occupy its allocated seats without any input from the rest of the world. Each region would typically nominate a "clean slate"—the same number of nominees as available seats—rendering moot the later U.N. election. Because the composition of these slates was thus left to backroom deals, the human rights qualifications of the candidates often played little role in the nomination process. Indeed, because highly abusive governments often placed more importance on avoiding condemnation by the Commission than did rights-respecting governments, they took the horse-trading more seriously and thus tended to prevail.

There are various possible solutions to end this race-to-the-bottom. Most obvious would be to insist that each region nominate more candidates than its allocated slots—perhaps double the number—thus ensuring a real choice when elections occur. Requiring a candidate-by-candidate vote—rather than a vote for an entire slate—would allow the rest of the nations of the world at least the possibility of voting down inappropriate candidates. Requiring candidates seeking election to the Council to secure a two-thirds majority of U.N. member states would make it much less likely that the worst abusers could be elected. Reserving a small number of "at large" seats, available on a first-come-first-served basis to any region that has successfully filled all of its allocated seats, would provide an incentive for upgrading further the quality of the candidates.

The difficulty in resolving these issues and moving forward with creation of a new Human Rights Council left the embarrassing prospect that the Commission, an institution now utterly discredited, might meet again in March and April—not simply to oversee a transfer of responsibilities and disband, but to conduct regular business. Such a collective failure of political will would only provide new ammunition to critics of the United Nations.

The major summit of world leaders convened at the United Nations in September to commemorate the organization's 60th anniversary was, in many respects, a disappointment. Its most important contribution was giving an official imprimatur to the Canadian-sponsored concept of a "responsibility to protect" people at risk of large-scale loss of life, even though much work remains to implement that commitment, such as creation of a quick-reaction stand-by force. In tacit endorsement of Kofi Annan's vision that human rights should join security and development as one of three pillars of the U.N. system, the summit also pledged to greatly increase the budget of the Office of the High Commissioner for Human Rights. Efforts to condemn terrorism in all of its forms ran aground on perennial attempts by some to justify deliberate attacks on civilians in cases of national liberation or fights against occupation, and on efforts of many Western governments to exempt the concept of state-sponsored terrorism.

John Bolton, the new U.S. ambassador to the United Nations, played a particularly unhelpful role during the summit negotiations. As the negotiations were concluding, the newly arrived ambassador introduced hundreds of last-minute amendments including many designed to exempt the United States from any binding obligations. The extremism of his interventions opened the door for other governments to indulge their worst tendencies, and seemingly agreed upon compromises, including on many aspects of the Human Rights Council, came undone.

Much blame fell as well on the various obstructionist governments, such as Cuba, Algeria, Zimbabwe, Belarus, Pakistan, Russia, and Venezuela, who profited from the disarray to undermine any initiative that might improve enforcement of human rights standards.

The summit also failed to agree on any plan to expand the U.N. Security Council, including by adding some number of new permanent seats to reflect shifts in power since the 1940s. The competition for those permanent seats proved particularly counterproductive for human rights enforcement, since some of the leading contenders—Germany, Japan, Nigeria, South Africa— were eager not to do or say anything that might offend potential supporters. South Africa's and Nigeria's reluctance to make enemies had a notably deleterious effect on the African Union's human rights activities.

Conclusion

Encouraging as some developments in 2005 were, they could not obscure the many compromises in the defense of human rights that have arisen in the context of the fight against terrorism. There is no doubting that terrorism today poses a serious threat. All governments have a duty to take effective steps to counter this deadly danger. Yet the seriousness of the threat does not justify the flouting of human rights standards to which the response of certain governments has given rise. Many governments have experienced serious security threats, from invasion to civil war, that put the lives of their citizens at risk. The current threat of terrorism is different only in that citizens of the major Western powers appear prominently among the victims. After preaching for many years that all governments should respond to security threats within the constraints of human rights law, these Western governments should hardly be surprised that hypocrisy alarms ring loudly when they cite security concerns to defend their own human rights transgressions.

Because of the enormous influence of Western governments, and because of their importance as major parts of the global defense of human rights, this official hypocrisy has substantially harmed the human rights cause. It diminishes the persuasive power of these governments when they do rise on behalf of human rights, as it undermines the effective strength of the international standards that they transgress. That these human rights compromises are unnecessary—that they undermine rather than advance the campaign against terrorism—makes the behavior of the major Western powers all the more tragic. There is an urgent need for enlightened leadership—for governmental leaders who still embrace human rights to stand up, reject this misguided approach to fighting terrorism, and reaffirm that even in the face of a serious security threat respect for human rights is good for all.

Washington's role in the ongoing degradation of human rights leadership is especially dangerous. Now that responsibility for the use of torture and inhumane treatment can no longer credibly be passed off to misadventures by low-level soldiers on the night shift, it is time for the Bush administration to acknowledge the wrongfulness of its interrogation policies and to embrace respect for human rights as a moral, legal, and pragmatic imperative. Pressure will be needed, both from the citizens of the United States and from friends and allies around the world. For the good of the human rights cause, and for the security of those at risk of terrorist strikes, reevaluation and reversal of Washington's shameful policies are essential.

This Report

This report is Human Rights Watch's sixteenth annual review of human rights practices around the globe. It summarizes key human rights issues in sixty-eight countries, drawing on events through November 2005.

Each country entry identifies significant human rights issues, examines the freedom of local human rights defenders to conduct their work, and surveys the response of key international actors, such as the United Nations, European Union, Japan, the United States, and various regional and international organizations and institutions.

The volume begins with separate essays on the social responsibilities of corporations and effective HIV/AIDS prevention. The first essay argues that momentum is building for enforceable human rights standards for corporations and concludes that corporate executives would do well to begin engaging the debate now to ensure that the rules eventually adopted create a level playing field for all firms. The second essay details how abuses of marginalized populations are fueling the global HIV/AIDS pandemic and notes that in several countries moralistic approaches to prevention programs are replacing the science-based, human rights-informed responses that work best. It makes the case that, to succeed, prevention programs must be premised on basic respect for individuals and their rights.

This report reflects extensive investigative work undertaken in 2005 by the Human Rights Watch research staff, usually in close partnership with human rights activists in the country in question. It also reflects the work of our advocacy team, which monitors policy developments and strives to persuade governments and international institutions to curb abuses and promote human rights. Human Rights Watch publications, issued throughout the year, contain more detailed accounts of many of the issues addressed in the brief summaries collected in this volume. They can be found on the Human Rights Watch website, www.hrw.org.

As in past years, this report does not include a chapter on every country where Human Rights Watch works, nor does it discuss every issue of importance. The failure to include a particular country or issue often reflects no more than staffing limitations and should not be taken as commentary on the significance of the problem. There are many serious human rights violations that Human Rights Watch simply lacks the capacity to address.

The factors we considered in determining the focus of our work in 2005 (and hence the content of this volume) include the number of people affected and the severity of abuse, access to the country and the availability of information about it, the susceptibility of abusive forces to influence, and the importance of addressing certain thematic concerns and of reinforcing the work of local rights organizations.

The World Report does not have separate chapters addressing our thematic work but instead incorporates such material directly into the country entries. Please consult the Human Rights Watch website for more detailed treatment of our work on children's rights, women's rights, arms and military issues, academic freedom, business and human rights, HIV/AIDS and human rights, international justice, refugees and displaced people, and lesbian, gay, bisexual, and transgender people's rights, and for information about our international film festival.

Kenneth Roth is executive director of Human Rights Watch.

PRIVATE COMPANIES AND THE PUBLIC INTEREST: WHY CORPORATIONS SHOULD WELCOME GLOBAL HUMAN RIGHTS RULES

By Lisa Misol

It has been a decade since Ken Saro-Wiwa was convicted in an unfair trial and executed with eight others in retaliation for protesting Shell Oil's operations in Nigeria. That same year, 1995, the international spotlight fell on American clothier "The Gap" for deplorable working conditions in its supplier factories in El Salvador.

Both companies paid a price: Shell soon faced a lawsuit (still pending) in a U.S. court for alleged complicity in the executions; The Gap confronted nationwide picketing of its stores, which ended only when the company agreed to the demands of anti-sweatshop activists.

These were watershed moments. Many multinational corporations, worried about the costs and consequences for their brand names if they were blamed for the human rights impact of their business practices, woke up and took notice. In response to their critics, some of the companies in the line of fire adopted human rights policies. Others, seeing the writing on the wall, pre-emptively did the same. Many prominent companies have now adopted voluntary codes of business conduct that include respect for basic human rights.

Because voluntary commitments are insufficient in themselves to prevent corporate involvement in human rights abuses, there have been increasingly frequent calls for binding standards. Indeed, regulations already have begun to emerge in some sectors on some issues, but coverage and enforcement is spotty, far short of the kind of comprehensive framework many believe is necessary. Multinational corporations have long responded to calls for any kind of binding human rights standards with the claim that self regulation or voluntary guidelines are enough. But there are signs that this opposition may be beginning to change.

In private, some multinational executives have started to question whether industry's antagonism to regulation makes sense when it comes to human rights. They realize that only binding standards can ensure a level playing field and that, increasingly, the choice facing them is not between adopting voluntary codes of conduct and doing nothing. It is a choice between continuing to compete on an uneven, ever-shifting playing field and participating in the creation of universally binding and enforceable rules that apply equally to all companies.

For most corporations, having clear, consistent rules would be preferable to being subjected to unfair competition and a confusing mix of standards that provides little guidance to companies and little comfort for victims of human rights abuse.

This essay argues that enforceable global standards are desirable, inevitable, and, contrary to received wisdom, good for business.

The Drive for Corporate Social Responsibility

Pressure from campaigning organizations in the fields of environmental protection and human rights helped spur the movement toward greater corporate responsibility. Today, Corporate Social Responsibility (CSR) is a burgeoning field, encompassing corporate ethics, workplace issues, and environmental as well as human rights concerns.

Growing numbers of nongovernmental organizations (NGOs) are monitoring corporate practices against basic standards, including human rights. The news media also increasingly scrutinize corporate conduct. Ethically-minded investors and consumers are demanding more from the companies with which they do business. CSR advocates now find greater numbers of sympathetic listeners in government and corporate headquarters.

In part the ground is shifting because of the impact of globalization on businesses. Companies now commonly operate in a wide variety of locations, not just in their own country or in like-minded locales. Their products and brand names reach all corners of the globe, as do the news media that follow their activities. In some of the countries that host their operations, the clout of multinational corporations rivals or exceeds that of the national government.

There is no sign that these trends are letting up. In the current environment, public advocacy for CSR can only be expected to increase and to spotlight more and more instances of corporations implicated in abuse.

There is plenty to focus on. Workers the world over still struggle to assert their rights in the face of company indifference and government inaction. Harmful child labor, unsafe conditions, and discrimination—not to mention the deprivation of workers' rights to free association and collective bargaining—remain all too common throughout both the developed and developing world.

In areas of violent conflict and instability, the pursuit of profits without human rights safeguards can fuel a range of abuses, including torture, forced labor, war crimes, and crimes against humanity. All too often, companies cozy up to local armed groups to get access to lucrative resources, or buy smuggled goods from killers who use the proceeds to purchase weapons.

In response to increasing public attention to the role corporations can play in facilitating human rights abuse, recent years have seen a proliferation of voluntary initiatives on corporate social responsibility. A number of CSR initiatives explicitly address human rights, along with environmental and other issues. By way of illustration, some 2,300 global companies have endorsed the United Nations Global Compact, a modest voluntary commitment to abide by ten ethical principles, including respect for human rights. Voluntary corporate commitments to human rights, however, can be demonstrably inadequate, as the following example shows.

Limitations of Voluntary Guidelines: The Congo Gold Example

We are cursed because of our gold. All we do is suffer.
There is no benefit to us.

CONGOLESE GOLD MINER

Companies operating globally face many challenges: managing across borders, navigating different regulatory regimes, protecting their brands, and dealing with shifting expectations. For companies active in zones of weak governments, the challenges are still greater. These companies must cope with questions about security, immense poverty, and lack of a functioning state, to name just a few. Frequently voluntary guidelines are simply not enough to ensure respect for human rights in these environments. A report published by Human Rights Watch in June 2005 on the abuses taking place in the gold fields of the Democratic Republic of Congo illustrates the limitations of such voluntary commitments by one of the world's largest gold producers, AngloGold Ashanti, part of the international conglomerate Anglo American.

Northeastern Congo is home to one of Africa's largest unexplored goldfields. It is also a region in a desperate state. Torn apart by years of war, the Congolese economy is shattered, and more than three million of its citizens are dead. The desire to control Congo's rich mineral resources—including gold, diamonds, and other precious minerals—has been central to the war that started in 1998. Brutal killings continue, despite a fitful peace process and a shaky transitional government launched in June 2003. Those unfortunate enough to live in mineral-rich areas have suffered some of the worst atrocities.

In this volatile environment, AngloGold Ashanti decided to explore for gold. The company set up a project camp in Mongbwalu, a gold town ruled by the murderous Nationalist and Integrationist Front (FNI), and developed links with its leaders to gain access to the gold-rich area. The situation on the ground must have been clear. FNI combatants controlled all road and airport access into the town, flaunted their guns in the streets, forced people to work in the gold mines, and conducted killing sprees in nearby villages.

Human Rights Watch documented in detail the links between AngloGold Ashanti and the local warlord, showing how the FNI armed group responsible for these atrocities gained financial and logistical support, and, most importantly, political credibility from its ties to the company.

Significantly, AngloGold Ashanti has a corporate code of conduct that includes human rights standards and public commitments to corporate social responsibility. Its commitments are viewed by many other companies as cutting edge. AngloGold Ashanti executives should have ensured that their operations in Congo complied with those commitments and did not adversely affect human rights. They do not appear to have done so.

In response to the Human Rights Watch report, AngloGold Ashanti said it regretted any payments made to the armed group, that the payments were minimal, and that such support was not part of company policy. The company undertook a high level review of its activities in Congo to determine how, and if, it could operate in such an environment with integrity. It also publicly pledged to cease all payments to abusive armed groups in Congo and to pull out of the mine site if the groups attempted to extort funds in the future. As one company executive later put it, "we learned too late not to 'do as in Rome.'"

The activities of AngloGold Ashanti in Congo show the limitations of voluntary guidelines and illustrate the need to move beyond rhetoric. If binding standards had been in place, AngloGold Ashanti would have been induced to devise stronger mechanisms to prevent such an ill-advised and ultimately detrimental relationship with abusive warlords in the Congo, secure in the knowledge that its potential corporate competitors would be held to the same standards.

Towards Binding CSR Standards

Companies are increasingly aware that human rights problems are bad for business. Human rights issues are having a decided impact on how companies do business. In a survey of the world's 500 largest companies, more than a third of respondents reported that human rights concerns had caused them to drop a proposed investment, and nearly a fifth said they disinvested from a country for that reason.

In a number of areas, steps have been taken to move beyond purely voluntary CSR standards. Leading companies have worked to reflect their human rights commitments in corporate practices. In some industries, particularly apparel, companies have agreed to not only codes of conduct, but also independent monitoring to increase the odds that they and their suppliers will live up to their word. The Fair Labor Association has a monitoring process that provides one example.

To a limited extent, enforceable regulations have also begun to emerge, though their reach is spotty. Some stock indices, such as FTSE 4Good, require qualifying companies to comply with basic ethical standards. Certain international financial institutions make similar demands of their loan beneficiaries. For instance, the International Finance Corporation, the private-sector lending arm of the World Bank Group, has said it will require companies to live up to the Voluntary Principles on Security and Human Rights, which provide for human rights protections and some company disclosures about payments. Companies that are complicit in serious human rights abuses risk liability under laws such as the U.S. Alien Tort Claims Act. In extreme cases, corporate executives could even face prosecution by the International Criminal Court. And individual governments, sometimes prompted by trade agreements, increasingly demand that trading partners regulate certain corporate conduct.

Moreover, public expectations already constrain the behavior of some large corporations. This is mostly the case for major companies based in countries with an active civil society and vigorous news media. In such countries, political leaders often respond to demands for corporate responsibility by endorsing standards for business conduct. These measures, in turn, provide a yardstick against which watchdog groups judge the behavior of the companies based there.

In each of these cases, however, constraints on corporate behavior are limited to those companies that fall under the regulatory or public eye, leaving other businesses free to break the rules. The first point to be made is that global rules would level the playing field. As things stand, more responsible companies sometimes lose economically for doing the right thing or face competitive disadvantages based on the standards applicable to their home country.

A company executive, speaking anonymously under Chatham House rules, acknowledged the difficulty of trying to operate ethically in difficult environments when there are no clear rules and other companies do not feel so constrained. As he put it, "Any regulation is better than no regulation."

A second point is that companies eager to get ahead of the curve may be signed up to a dizzying number of CSR guidelines, codes of conduct, and voluntary commitments. Complying with these initiatives in their global operations can be time consuming and expensive, especially where monitoring and reporting mechanisms are built in. Rather than having to navigate so many divergent codes and make sense of emerging liabilities, it would be in the interest of these companies to operate under simpler, enforceable rules that eliminate ambiguity.

The current patchwork of rules hardly creates a fair competitive environment: it is piecemeal in its coverage and unpredictable in its enforcement. Different initiatives identify and interpret human rights standards differently, leading to divergent expectations. From the point of view of a corporate executive who needs to plan and manage risks, that should be an unsettling thought.

The Problem of "Rogue" Companies

A compelling reason for prominent or far-sighted businesses to back binding human rights standards derives from the fact that public pressure tends to focus on highly visible companies, especially ones that have a brand or image to protect. Relatively few companies are so prominent that their behavior is under regular scrutiny from activists and the press. That gives an unfair advantage to less well-known competitors who can operate under the radar screen of public attention.

Well-known companies, worried about the harm that misconduct could cause their reputation, must assume the costs of meeting broadly recognized standards of corporate conduct. For example, a big company might have to accept paying higher wages associated with employing adults rather than children or permit trade unions to operate freely in its factories. By contrast, a no-name company, confident that the public will not notice its misdeeds, may not feel compelled to act as responsibly.

The gold industry again provides an illustration of this. Warlords in Congo, working together with their local business allies, used the proceeds from the sale of gold to gain access to money, guns, and power. Operating outside of legal channels, they worked together with a network of gold smugglers to funnel gold out of Congo to Uganda, destined for global gold markets in Switzerland and elsewhere, where it was bought by multinational companies.

One such company that bought gold from this network was Metalor Technologies, a leading Swiss gold refinery. Metalor knew, or should have known, that gold bought through this network came from a conflict zone in Congo where human rights were abused on a systematic basis. The company claimed it actively checked its supply chain to verify that acceptable ethical standards were being maintained. Yet during five years of buying gold from the network, no serious questions were raised.

After discussions and correspondence with Human Rights Watch and just prior to the publication of the Human Rights Watch report, Metalor announced it would suspend its purchases of gold from Uganda. Fearing possible repercussions for their business, other Swiss gold refineries followed Metalor's lead. The trade in "tainted gold" from northeastern Congo immediately slowed; warlords and their business allies were finding it difficult to find clients for their ore. But the halt was only temporary. In less than two months, other gold refineries less concerned about their reputation stepped into the void. The trade moved from Switzerland to Dubai.

Concerned about the ramifications of pressure from campaigning groups, the gold jewelry industry wants to counter concerns over "tainted gold." Following in the footsteps of the diamond industry, which has sought to disassociate itself from "blood diamonds," the jewelry industry aims to set standards for responsible practices, including human rights standards, that will protect its consumer market. To do so they will need to tackle those within the industry who act irresponsibly. This will be tough, if not impossible, to carry out on a voluntary basis. Pitching "clean" products becomes hard when unscrupulous competitors can still play dirty. Attention to the misdeeds of no-name companies can sully the reputation of an entire industry—damaging even larger established brands.

Only enforceable rules, applicable to all companies regardless of prominence, can avoid this double standard.

The Way Forward

Social responsibility is not the first issue for which corporations have begun to recognize the advantage of enforceable standards with broad reach. A similar dynamic emerged after the U.S. government's adoption in 1977 of the Foreign Corrupt Practices Act, which made it illegal for companies operating in the United States to bribe foreign officials. The U.S. law was adopted in the wake of a domestic corporate scandal but, once in place, put U.S. companies at a competitive disadvantage because their foreign competitors remained free to continue securing business through bribery. In response, U.S. firms pressed for—and got—a multilateral treaty to even out the competitive environment.

After years of complaints, the Organization for Economic Cooperation and Development (OECD) in 1997 adopted a treaty requiring all its member states to criminalize such bribery. The OECD's thirty members account for some two-thirds of the world's goods and services and 90 percent of global private capital flows. China remains outside the treaty, but as its companies increasingly operate overseas its exclusion will become legally less tenable.

The OECD already has set out corporate social responsibility standards. Its Guidelines for Multinational Enterprises have been endorsed by a total of thirty-nine countries, including nine non-OECD members. The adhering countries are home to ninety-seven of the world's top one hundred multinational companies. The OECD Guidelines are voluntary but do have an implementation process run by governments, and are widely used to judge corporate conduct. For example, a U.N. expert panel publicly chastised a number of Western companies operating in Congo for failing to comply with the OECD Guidelines. In addition, NGOs have lodged formal complaints against some of these companies under OECD procedures.

OECD member countries, following on the anti-bribery effort, should move to make their CSR standards binding. They should adopt a treaty under which they agree to enact laws similar to the OECD Guidelines that would be enforceable under national criminal or civil codes, carrying penalties such as fines or, in extreme cases, imprisonment. Like anti-bribery laws, this national legislation would bind any company operating in that nation's jurisdiction.

In addition, the United Nations, which has already drafted non-binding norms on corporate conduct, might provide a forum to negotiate a universally applicable treaty. U.N. discussions on business and human rights have tended to be highly polarized, but a new approach may emerge. In 2005 the United Nations' human rights body launched a two-year process to examine these issues. The Commission on Human Rights created a mandate for a high-level expert, appointed in July 2005 by the U.N. Secretary-General, to raise awareness of the human rights responsibilities of companies, look at the tough issues that have blocked progress to date, and map a way forward. An advantage of this U.N.-led process is that it is explicitly focused on human rights and brings together governments, companies, and concerned civil society groups from around the world.

The U.N. mandate—if focused appropriately—has the potential to move beyond a purely voluntary approach toward effective human rights protection that combines elements of voluntarism with enforcement potential on core rights issues. It carries risks as well. Unless human rights are taken as the point of departure, the process could degenerate into a consensus around weak "standards" that are lower than those derived from human rights law and principles.

Though any such agreements or treaties will take time, it is crucial to begin to move down that road. The next few years offer a valuable opportunity to break the current impasse on the corporate accountability debate. Already, many corporations are engaged with other stakeholders in various processes to debate and refine CSR standards. These companies are working on several fronts to develop CSR standards and widen their application within and across different industries.

Given the momentum behind the CSR movement, the continuing proliferation of different standards, and the problem of an unequal playing field, it is clear that business has a vital interest in helping to define human rights norms. By doing so, it can help ensure that the resulting requirements are clear, practicable, and fair. Industry also has a direct stake in seeing that these requirements are applied to all companies, regardless of where they are based, and that they are effectively implemented and enforced. Ultimately, that means making the rules universal and mandatory.

Sometimes it pays to take the initiative. For hard-headed businesspeople, the smart move is to face up to global human rights standards early and make them work by making them stick.

Lisa Misol is a researcher with the Business and Human Rights Program at Human Rights Watch.

Some of the arguments and language used in this essay first appeared in a Financial Times opinion article ("Rules on Corporate Ethics Could Help, Not Hinder, Multinationals," June 21, 2005) by Human Rights Watch Executive Director Kenneth Roth. Anneke Van Woudenberg, senior researcher in Human Rights Watch's Africa Division, contributed material for the Congo case study.

PREVENTING THE FURTHER SPREAD OF HIV/AIDS: THE ESSENTIAL ROLE OF HUMAN RIGHTS

By Joseph Amon

AIDS is no longer [just] a disease. It is a human rights issue.

NELSON MANDELA

After twenty-five years, the global AIDS pandemic is still expanding. More than forty million people are living with HIV/AIDS. In 2005, five million people were newly infected, and three million died of AIDS. Between 2003 and 2005, the number of people living with HIV in East Asia rose by more than 25 percent, and the number of people living with HIV in Eastern Europe and Central Asia rose by more than one-third. However, sub-Saharan Africa remains by far the worst-affected region.[1] Countries such as Lesotho and Swaziland, with nearly one in three adults infected, are openly presented as possibly being the first countries to "die" of AIDS.

Why has the epidemic spread so inexorably across the globe? Why have countries failed to act—or acted so ineffectually—to stop the epidemic from progressing? It has been acknowledged for almost as long as HIV has been recognized that HIV/AIDS is fundamentally tied to human rights abuses.[2] But such acknowledgment has had surprisingly little impact on the global response to the epidemic, and this failure explains, to a large extent, why we have made so little progress.

Worldwide, vulnerability to HIV/AIDS is linked to populations marginalized by society because of their gender, race/ethnicity, sexual orientation, or social or economic class. Human rights are central both to our understanding of the dynamics of the disease and to how we must combat it.

HIV/AIDS is commonly thought to be related to "economic, social, and cultural rights" (such as the right to health care), as opposed to "civil and political rights," such as freedom of expression and association and due process of law. However, many of the human rights abuses that most increase HIV risk—violence and discrimination against women and marginalized populations as well as people living with HIV/AIDS, harassment and imprisonment without due process of outreach workers and at-risk populations seeking HIV/AIDS information or services, and censorship of health information—are abuses of civil and political rights. The fact that these abuses have a concrete impact on the health of individuals underscores what has been called the "indivisibility" of human rights norms—the notion that civil and political rights and economic, social, and cultural rights are mutually reinforcing and derive from a single principle: the fundamental dignity of each human being.

While there is widespread, though by no means universal, recognition that social stigma can fuel the epidemic, and that the characteristics of HIV infection do not warrant intrusive restrictions on liberty, all too often these basic understandings are not reflected in law or in concrete policy terms. Equally important, there is uneven (at best) appreciation of the broader human rights issues that contribute to the continuing spread of the disease. Most perversely, some of the critical lessons about stopping HIV/AIDS, learned painfully and acted on with positive results in the 1980s and 1990s, are now being disregarded. Even while treatment options are expanding, responses to HIV/AIDS in many places are getting further from the kind of science-based, human-rights informed response that has been proven to stop the spread of the disease. Left unaddressed, human rights abuses will undermine both HIV/AIDS prevention and treatment.

Mobilizing Communities, Increasing Awareness (1981-1999)

Although the first AIDS case was diagnosed in 1981, little global recognition of the disease or response to the epidemic was seen before 1986 when, at the World Health Assembly, Uganda's health minister declared that his country had an enormous problem with AIDS and needed help. The Minister and the Assembly called on the World Health Organization (WHO) to act. In September 1986, a WHO program for prevention and control of AIDS was formed, which, in February of 1987, became the Global Programme on AIDS (GPA).

By January 1990, the GPA was working in 123 countries to develop national AIDS prevention plans. The national programs that emerged from these plans emphasized public education and information on how HIV is and is not transmitted, and encouraged people to avoid unprotected sex. This was the main function of these first programs: urgent public education in the face of widespread denial—by governments as well as populations—that AIDS was a "local" problem.

Starting in the mid-1980s in the United States, Europe, and Australia, and throughout the 1990s in Uganda, Thailand and Brazil, a handful of pragmatic programs focused on equipping vulnerable populations with prevention information and services. Many of these programs implicitly incorporated human rights principles and produced impressive results.

In the United States, Europe, and Australia, outreach and education programs were initiated by new organizations created by men who have sex with men (MSM) and injecting drug users (IDU) who were concerned about the vulnerability of their peers. These programs emphasized reducing the number of sexual partners, condom distribution, and needle and syringe exchange, often in the face of great stigma and risk of criminal prosecution. As these programs became more established, some local government health departments extended cooperation and funding.

In Uganda, a national program was developed based upon a grassroots community dialogue explaining the new disease and emphasizing partner reduction ("zero grazing"). Community groups and religious institutions spoke out about the disease, and initiated programs of home-based care for those falling sick. In 1988, partly in response to a WHO review, Uganda made several key changes in its program including increasing the resources dedicated to HIV/AIDS prevention; decentralizing information, education, and communication activities; encouraging stronger community-based organizations and efforts; and increasing outreach programs to the illiterate and the poor.

In 1990 in Thailand, after the Ministry of Health revised the estimated number of HIV-infected persons from 1,700 to 150,000, a program emphasizing mass education and 100 percent condom use in brothels was established.

In Brazil, HIV/AIDS prevention programs made aggressive efforts to reach sex workers (including by organizing national sex worker conferences) and

MSM with HIV information and instructions on how to use condoms and negotiate condom use with partners. Broader messages to the general population were conveyed through the mass media to "humanize" the disease and fight stigma and discrimination.

Although taking different approaches, these programs were all initiated by individuals from the most affected communities, supported by local or national governments (often through financing as well as new legislation), and based on the dignity and autonomy of each individual. The programs quickly saw results. In New York, HIV prevalence among white MSM at STD clinics decreased from 47 percent to 17 percent between 1988 and 1993. In Uganda, adults reported increased condom use and decreased numbers of sexual partners, while youth reported delayed onset of sexual behaviors. Uganda saw the start of a downward trend in HIV prevalence, peaking in the early 1990s at over 15 percent and decreasing to 6-7 percent by 2003. In Thailand, decreases were seen in the number of men reporting commercial sex, while increases were reported in condom use. HIV prevalence declined to 1.5 percent in 2003. In Brazil, the percentage of young people who reported using condoms the first time they had sex increased from less than 10 percent in 1986 to more than 60 percent in 2003, and national HIV prevalence among pregnant women remained below 1 percent.

Despite these visible successes, in communities where outreach efforts were less focused—for example among drug users in Thailand, Hispanic MSM in New York City, or poor slum dwellers in Brazil—considerably less success was noted.

Nonetheless, these comprehensive programs, remarkable for their mobilization of resources, political will, engagement with the community, and respect for human rights, were seen as models for expanding the HIV/AIDS response worldwide.

Through the mid-1990s emphasis was also put on understanding the epidemic as a *multi-dimensional* problem, requiring a *multi-sectoral* response. This strategy emerged in part because HIV/AIDS was expanding unchecked with massive social and economic consequences and in part because of difficulties generating the resources required to fight the epidemic properly. Concerned officials and donors sought to leverage resources simultaneously from multiple sources including ministries of education, agriculture and industry.

Then, from the mid to the late-1990s, international efforts to fight HIV/AIDS foundered and splintered. The earlier focus and success in places like Thailand and Uganda were not replicated elsewhere, and the global leadership at WHO waned. Fast-growing epidemics were recognized virtually everywhere. Bilateral programs expanded, as did the prominence (and budget) of the World Bank, but these developments were unable to keep pace with the increasing demands of the pandemic. Increased attention was placed on the biomedical aspects of HIV/AIDS, including vaccine development and the use of anti-retroviral drugs to treat people living with HIV/AIDS and reduce the risk of mother-to-child HIV transmission.[3]

Expanding Resources, Narrowing Approaches: Moralizing the Epidemic (2000-2005)

In June 2001, a historic U.N. General Assembly Special Session (UNGASS) on HIV/AIDS for the first time generated global acknowledgement of the pandemic as not only a public health crisis but also a threat to societies and international security. The special session put virtually all of the world's leaders on record as endorsing a set of specific global targets in combating HIV/AIDS, while its formal declaration explicitly underscored the links between poverty, underdevelopment, and illiteracy to the spread and impact of HIV/AIDS. It also recognized that stigma, silence, discrimination, and lack of confidentiality undermined prevention and care efforts, and that gender equality and the empowerment of women and girls were fundamental to reducing vulnerability. The Declaration affirmed that access to medication in the context of pandemics such as HIV/AIDS was fundamental to the realization of the right to health.

Specifically, governments pledged: "by 2003, to enact, strengthen or enforce as appropriate, legislation, regulations and other measures to eliminate all forms of discrimination against, and to ensure the full enjoyment of all human rights and fundamental freedoms by people living with HIV/AIDS and members of vulnerable groups, in particular to ensure their access to, inter alia, education, inheritance, employment, health care, social and health services, prevention, support and treatment, information and legal protection, while respecting their privacy and confidentiality; and develop strategies to combat stigma and social exclusion connected with the epidemic."[4]

While this effort arguably increased the political will to address HIV/AIDS, the most important change in this era was perhaps the increased allocation of resources committed to fighting the epidemic. In 2001, the Global Fund to fight HIV/AIDS, TB and Malaria was created. Three years later, the United States Leadership against AIDS, Tuberculosis and Malaria Act of 2003 (the U.S. Global AIDS Act) and the U.S. President's Emergency Plan for AIDS Relief (commonly known as PEPFAR) were enacted. The same year, a revitalized WHO announced an ambitious plan to get three million people on anti-retroviral treatment by the end of 2005.

But these declarations and commitments of new resources, while seeming to recognize the central importance of combating the human rights violations underlying the epidemic, have addressed them in only limited ways. The integration of prevention and treatment programs has splintered. Science-based prevention programs increasingly are being replaced by conservative, moralistic sexual abstinence campaigns that stigmatize those living with AIDS and deny people information about condoms. Treatment programs have made some headway but still do not reach many affected populations and still do not recognize critical obstacles that rights-based approaches would help overcome. In 2003, one-half of all governments in sub-Saharan Africa had yet to adopt legislation specifically outlawing discrimination against people living with HIV/AIDS and only one-third of countries worldwide had adopted legal measures specifically outlawing discrimination against populations especially vulnerable to HIV/AIDS.

Throughout the 1990s the dominant approach to HIV prevention among young people was comprehensive sex education, which teaches abstinence as a healthy choice for young people but also provides information about condoms and safer sex. As a part of the PEPFAR program, comprehensive sex education programs are being replaced by programs that emphasize "abstinence only" until marriage, which censor or distort information about condoms and safer sex. The U.S. Global AIDS Act requires that 33 percent of HIV prevention spending go to "abstinence-until-marriage" programs.[5] Abstinence-only proponents commonly rely on fear-based messages, making unsubstantiated claims about the psychological effects of pre-marital sex and exaggerating the failure rate of condoms. These programs often suggest that condoms are appropriate only for those who "fail" at abstinence or marital fidelity and "choose to engage in high-risk sex"—contributing to an environment of shame and stigma which discourages the use of condoms even for sexually active youth and among adults with multiple, concurrent partners.[6]

Another example of HIV/AIDS policies turning their back on proven, evidence-based approaches that respect human rights is the restriction in the U.S. Global AIDS Act requiring that organizations receiving U.S. anti-AIDS funding have a policy "explicitly opposing prostitution" and barring the use of funds to "promote or advocate the legalization or practice of prostitution."[7] This approach recalls the efforts by Senator Jesse Helms in 1987 to block federal HIV/AIDS education funding to groups that "promote" homosexuality.

The U.S. requirements not only coerce organizations into adopting a particular ideology as a condition of receiving HIV/AIDS funding, but also negate the ability of outreach organizations to approach sex workers with the non-judgmental and non-moralistic attitude that has been shown to be effective with these communities. Empowering women marginalized in prostitution to participate in public life and to challenge the rights abuses that impede their struggle against HIV/AIDS has been a documented success in the efforts against AIDS. Far from addressing the harms associated with sex work, the U.S. requirements are likely to alienate sex workers and to fuel public opprobrium against them, further driving sex workers underground and away from life-saving services. In addition, the lack of guidance from the U.S. government regarding just what it means to "oppose prostitution" casts a shadow of uncertainty over HIV prevention programs and places a chilling effect on organizations wishing to conduct outreach and HIV prevention with sex workers in a respectful, non-judgmental manner.[8]

U.S. restrictions on needle exchange and other "harm reduction" programs and U.S. law enforcement interference with grassroots HIV prevention work are additional examples of the disastrous effect of replacing science-based approaches with narrowly defined moralistic ones.[9] The sharing of hypodermic syringes accounts for the majority of new HIV infections in much of Eastern Europe, Central and Southeast Asia, and Latin America: needle exchange programs are a matter of life and death. Needle exchange programs, moreover, are perhaps the best studied HIV prevention intervention in the world. Rigorous evaluations consistently show that providing sterile syringes and information about sterile drug injection to people who use drugs reduces HIV risk without increasing rates of drug use.[10] Although the effectiveness of sterile syringe programs has been endorsed by the World Health Organization, the Joint United Nations Program on HIV/AIDS, the U.S. National Institutes of Health, the U.S. Institute of Medicine, and other leading public health bodies,[11] the United States remains the only country in the world to ban the use of federal funds for needle exchange. Recently, it has begun to aggressively export this standard internationally.

The U.S. has blocked resolutions at the United Nations that would recognize the human rights of injection drug users;[12] sought to obstruct the work of UNAIDS and the U.N. Office on Drugs and Crime in promoting harm reduction and needle exchange in countries hard-hit by HIV/AIDS;[13] and encouraged national governments to adopt criminal law approaches to drug use rather than recognizing that epidemics of drug addiction and HIV/AIDS are public health threats requiring humane, rights-based responses.[14]

With the expanded resources now available for HIV/AIDS, it is finally possible to imagine HIV treatment programs joining HIV prevention efforts in an integrated, rights-respecting continuum of services. Unfortunately, moralistic approaches to HIV prevention which place new obstacles in the way of reaching populations that most need information and services hinder such a comprehensive approach. Restrictive and moralistic U.S. policies also endanger one of the most ardently promoted and potentially life-saving approaches to HIV prevention and treatment: expanded HIV testing.

Expanding access to HIV testing is a critically important step in improving responses to the epidemic. When accompanied by effective counseling and accessible post-test services—including comprehensive prevention (information and condoms) and treatment and care—expanded HIV testing can encourage more people to protect themselves and their partners, and to seek care which can prolong their lives.

Expanded HIV testing can take many forms, however. It is all too common for HIV testing to be mandatory for certain populations—prisoners and military recruits, for example. In many countries, moreover, even HIV testing outside such institutional settings is sometimes conducted without consent and test results sometimes are not given to the person who was tested.

In medical settings, two different approaches have recently been promoted: "routine offer" HIV testing—with an "opt-in" emphasis—proposes that every individual in the health care setting be offered an HIV test. By contrast, "opt-out" HIV testing attempts to increase the number of individuals consenting to an HIV test by requiring that individuals be tested unless they specifically decline the test. In some settings, protocols require individuals to decline the test three times before their refusal is accepted, and before they are entitled to receive medical care.

The newest approach to expanded HIV testing, however, goes beyond these approaches by seeking to bring HIV tests out of the medical setting and into communities. On December 1, 2005, the Ministry of Health of Lesotho and the WHO announced an unprecedented effort in the fight against HIV/AIDS: a village-to-village campaign to test every Mosotho (resident of Lesotho) aged twelve and older for HIV by the end of 2007.[15] This program was launched in Lesotho because it has one of the highest HIV prevalence rates in the world, with approximately one in three adults infected. With Lesotho facing a projected massive population loss from migration as well as mortality and a decrease in life expectancy from fifty-two to thirty-four years between 2000 and 2005, observers fear that Lesotho will collapse and fail—the first country to "die" of AIDS.

Village-to-village HIV testing recalls the great public health campaigns of thirty years ago, such as the worldwide eradication of smallpox through case detection, isolation, and mass vaccination. Because of the inextricable link between HIV/AIDS and human rights abuse, however, this method of HIV testing also carries the potential for spreading stigma and, with it, discrimination and other human rights violations. HIV/AIDS, a disease with a long and silent incubation period, with transmission caused by intensely personal behaviors (sex, childbirth, drug use), and with disproportionate prevalence among the most marginalized populations in society, is strikingly different from smallpox, and must be treated as such.

Historically, the largest concerns around HIV testing were ensuring that testing was voluntary, that it was confidential, and that adequate counseling was provided. These concerns were of primary importance in a context where few resources existed for people who tested positive, and where people believed to be living with HIV/AIDS faced serious and often life-threatening violence and abuse (women facing domestic violence as well as MSM and marginalized populations generally). It was hoped that if individuals learned their HIV serostatus, they would adopt behaviors that would either reduce their risk of infection if they were HIV-negative, or reduce the risk that they would transmit the virus to others if they were HIV-positive. In some cases, where counseling was adequate, and decisions were truly voluntary, these programs were shown to work.[16]

In the past few years, as significant resources have been committed to expanding access to anti-retroviral drugs throughout the world, treatment that can alleviate suffering and postpone death has become a real possibility for hundreds of thousands of people living with AIDS. In this context, HIV testing has become increasingly critical to expanding access to treatment, and, in turn, is helping to transform HIV/AIDS from a death sentence to a manageable chronic disease. These changes have led to a justified re-evaluation of HIV testing principles, and have led many people in the public health community to push for a different approach.[17] Specifically, they emphasize the "right" to know one's HIV serostatus and have called for dramatic increases in the numbers of people tested.

But much of the call for this type of expanded approach rests upon two assumptions: 1) that mass HIV testing will lead to positive changes as people change their behaviors and seek treatment; and 2) that few human rights abuses will result from this approach. There is little evidence to support these assumptions.

Studies in sub-Saharan Africa have found between 3.5 percent and 14.6 percent of women report abuse following the disclosure of their HIV test result. The highest rates of negative outcomes have been reported by women tested in antenatal clinics, and the lowest rates by women tested at voluntary counseling and testing sites. Women who are tested at antenatal clinic sites do not have a chance to think about testing or prepare themselves or their partners for testing. Therefore they are both less likely to disclose results to their partners and also are more likely to be victims of violence when they do.

The Lesotho operational plan for universal access to HIV testing states that "every household will be offered an HIV test" and that "communities will choose how HIV testing and counseling will be carried out for [their] members." Independent oversight "to guarantee the rights of community members" will be provided by a three-person committee in each health center catchment area, with each center providing "at least a biannual written report." The government is also creating a national telephone hotline.[18]

Public health officials argue that it is unfair to criticize the lack of evidence in support of village-to-village testing in light of the public health crisis facing Lesotho. That argument would be justified if this were the only approach available. But it is not. The other available alternative—concerted, large-scale promotion of voluntary HIV counseling and testing—has not been tried.

The Lesotho plan will only be as successful as the government's ability to get people to participate, as well as its ability to provide comprehensive HIV prevention information and necessary medicines. However, without better protections for human rights and without concerted efforts to reduce the stigma of HIV/AIDS within Lesotho, there is little hope for widespread, truly voluntary participation. Even if large numbers of people are tested, the Lesotho plan allocates only 3,000 Maloti (U.S.$465) out of a total of 75,593,250 Maloti (U.S.$11.7 million) to support post-test referrals and services.[19]

The Lesotho plan, like many calls for expanded HIV testing, focuses almost exclusively on individual behavior change and does not adequately take into account the structural barriers—violence, abuse, and interference with life-saving information and services—that prevent individuals most vulnerable to infection from taking measures to reduce their HIV risk.

Efforts to expand HIV testing should not put public health experts on one side and human rights proponents on the other. Both recognize that people have a right of access to HIV testing as part of the broader right to health care enshrined in the International Covenant on Economic, Social, and Cultural Rights. Informed consent and confidentiality requirements, protections against violence and discrimination, and measures to combat stigma need not be barriers to expanded HIV testing.

The 1984 Siracusa Principles on the Limitation and Derogation of Principles in the International Covenant on Civil and Political Rights, moreover, illustrate that, where there is a perceived conflict between critical public health needs and human rights imperatives, governments should proceed rationally and deliberately. Public health policies can infringe rights if they are sanctioned by law, serve a legitimate public health goal, are necessary to achieve that goal, are no more intrusive or restrictive than necessary, and are non-discriminatory in application. The International Guidelines on HIV/AIDS and Human Rights, issued as non-binding policy guidance to governments by the Office of the High Commissioner for Human Rights (OHCHR) and the Joint United Nations Programme on HIV/AIDS (UNAIDS) in 1996, affirm that HIV testing of individuals "should only be performed with the specific informed consent of that individual" except where specific judicial authorization is granted to perform a mandatory test.

Too often, expanded HIV testing programs forget their goal is not simply to get a large number of people tested once. "Knowing your HIV status" is a dynamic issue with repeat testing required, as adolescents become adults, as an individual's behavior (and risk) changes, or (as is especially true for women and girls in many parts of the world) as their own behavior stays the same but their partner's behavior changes. Mass HIV testing programs may be able to test large numbers of people once, but only programs that protect individual rights will encourage people to seek follow-up treatment services and help people reduce their risk behaviors and their vulnerability to HIV infection over time.

A Different Approach: Protecting Human Rights

Over the course of the HIV/AIDS epidemic, too little has been done to change laws and practices that violate human rights, putting individuals at risk of infection and disease and impeding access to HIV information and services for those who need it most. Changing these laws is not only a moral imperative, but is also key to the sustained success of prevention, testing, and treatment programs.

In sub-Saharan Africa, for example, nearly 60 percent of individuals living with HIV infection are women. This disproportionate burden is due less to a specific biologic susceptibility to infection, and more to their lack of basic human rights. Women and girls are put at risk by economic vulnerability resulting from discrimination and lack of legal protections; sexual violence, including in institutions such as schools, prisons, and workplaces; domestic violence, including marital rape; violations of property and inheritance rights; and, in some countries, harmful traditional practices such as exorbitant bride price, widow inheritance, and even ritual sexual "cleansing." Governments, which have an obligation to stop such violations and abusive practices, too often tolerate them.

Responding to the HIV/AIDS epidemic requires addressing such vulnerabilities directly, not indirectly through general education campaigns or HIV testing. In Zimbabwe, an estimated 700,000 people lost their homes, livelihood, or both when, in May 2005, the government unleashed Operation Murambatsvina (Cleanse the Filth), a campaign of forcible evictions and demolitions in urban areas throughout the country. Six months into the crisis, hundreds of thousands of people remained displaced throughout the country. Among other things, the massive displacement disrupted access to life-saving therapies for individuals with HIV and TB, encouraging the emergence of multi-drug resistant strains, and it created the conditions—displacement, destitution, lack of legal protections—which are known to spur the epidemic. This was recognized by UNAIDS representatives when, in November 2005, they cautioned that recent declines in HIV prevalence in Zimbabwe "could start rising again if underlying vulnerabilities, which contribute to unsafe sexual behaviour and fuel the epidemic, are not sufficiently addressed. Such vulnerabilities include gender inequality, poverty and population mobility."[20]

Stigmatizing attitudes and discrimination by health care providers continue to hinder access to HIV testing and treatment in many places. In other places, violence, or the fear of violence, prevents many people from obtaining HIV/AIDS testing and treatment. In Uganda, despite long-standing and well run programs, service providers have reported that women come to them secretly, fearing that their husbands will beat them if they seek HIV testing or medical attention. Jane Nabulya, a Ugandan woman, said that she secretly tested for HIV in 1999 when she found out her husband had AIDS. She explained: "I was scared to tell him that I had tested HIV-positive. He used to say [of] the woman who gives him AIDS, 'I will chop off her feet.' I have never told him."[21]

Conclusion

The response to the HIV/AIDS epidemic by governments and multilateral agencies must recognize and respect human rights. In parts of the world today, the lack of an adequate response to the epidemic—whether due to denial of the existence or extent of the epidemic, misappropriation of resources, or hostility to those individuals infected or those populations most at-risk of infection—represents a basic violation of the right to health. In other countries, HIV education, prevention, and treatment programs are inaccurate or inequitable.

All individuals, including those most marginalized, must enjoy access to accurate information about HIV/AIDS and have equal access to HIV/AIDS programs. HIV testing in particular—as the entry point for access to anti-retroviral drugs and important services—must be accessible to all. But efforts to expand HIV testing, and to put in place "routine" testing, must not become coercive, must recognize the rights of the individuals being tested, and must provide linkages to both prevention and care.

Across the globe, people who test positive for HIV have been denied employment, fired from their jobs, kicked out of hospitals, denied both HIV specific and general medical treatment, harassed and assaulted by community members who find out their status, and sometimes even killed. Because human rights abuses fuel the HIV epidemic, HIV/AIDS programs must explicitly address, and find ways to mitigate, these abuses.

Combating the rights abuses that put vulnerable populations at risk of HIV is essential to turning around the AIDS crisis. Concrete policy measures are urgently needed and can have immediate and long-term impact. New laws can be put in place, or enforced if they already exist, to protect women's equal rights in the areas of inheritance, sexual violence, domestic violence and spousal rape, marriage, division of property upon divorce, land use and ownership, and access to housing and social services.

Programmatic reforms, designed to address human rights violations, should ensure that national HIV/AIDS programs include measures to combat dis-crimination and violence against people living with HIV/AIDS, with particu-lar attention to marginalized populations. Efforts should also be made to pro-vide human rights training for judges, police, and other officials; improve data collection relating to police abuse and domestic violence, women's prop-erty rights, and sexual abuse of girls; ensure that anti-retroviral drug distribu-tion systems recognize the challenges marginalized populations face in accessing treatment; and ensure that HIV test results and other patient infor-mation is kept confidential. Public education campaigns on the human rights of people living with HIV/AIDS in local languages and using appropriate media should be intensified.

It is sometimes suggested that paying attention to human rights is somehow so costly and time consuming that it should really be considered optional during a public health crisis. However, there is no reason that public health and human rights be considered in opposition to one another. In responding to the global HIV/AIDS epidemic, only programs that start with a basic respect for individuals, and their rights, will be successful. Those programs which adopt strategies in the name of efficiency or ideology and which fail to respect human rights will ultimately fail.

Joseph Amon directs the HIV/AIDS Program at Human Rights Watch.

[1] U.N. Joint Progamme on HIV/AIDS (UNAIDS), *AIDS Epidemic Update: December 2005* (Geneva: United Nations, 2005), http://www.unaids.org/epi2005/doc/EPIupdate2005_html_en/epi05_00_en.htm#TopOf Page (retrieved November 21, 2005).

[2] Jonathan Mann, who headed the first Global Programme on HIV/AIDS at the World Health Organization (WHO), recognized early in the epidemic the importance of linking HIV/AIDS and human rights, especially to ensure that those at risk would not be stigmatized in using services. See Jonathan M. Mann, "Human rights and AIDS: The future of the pandemic," in Jonathan M. Mann, Sofia Gruskin, Michael A. Grodin, and George J. Annas, eds., *Health and Human Rights: A Reader* (New York and London: Routledge, 1999).

[3] HIV can be transmitted from an HIV-infected mother to her child during pregnancy, labor, and delivery, or through breastfeeding. The administration of antiretroviral drugs to HIV-infected pregnant women and to her infant shortly after birth greatly reduces the risk of mother-to-child HIV transmission.

[4] United Nations General Assembly, "Declaration of Commitment on HIV/AIDS," June 27, 2001.

[5] U.S Global AIDS Act, 22 U.S.C. §§ 7672(b)(3), 7673(a); see also Office of the United States Global AIDS Coordinator, "The President's Emergency Plan for AIDS Relief. U.S. Five Year Global HIV/AIDS Strategy," February 2004.

[6] For further information about U.S.-funded abstinence-only-until-marriage programs, see Human Rights Watch, "The Less they Know, the Better: Abstinence-only HIV/AIDS Programs in Uganda," vol. 17, no. 4(A), March 2005; Human Rights Watch, "Ignorance Only: HIV/AIDS, Human Rights and Federally Funded Abstinence-Only Programs in the United States: Texas: A Case Study," vol. 14, no. 5(G), September 2002.

[7] U.S. Global AIDS Act, 22 U.S.C. § 7631(e, f) (2003); see also Letter from Human Rights Watch, et al., to President Bush opposing mandatory "anti-prostitution pledge," May 18, 2005, http://hrw.org/campaigns/hivaids/hiv-aids-letter/; Rebecca Schleifer, "United States: Funding Restrictions Threaten Sex Workers' Rights," *HIV/AIDS Policy and Law Review*, vol. 10, no. 2, August 2005.

[8] Two separate lawsuits have been filed in U.S. courts challenging the "anti-prostitution pledge" requirements as violating fundamental rights to health and to free expression. See Rebecca Schleifer, "Challenges filed to U.S. Anti-AIDS Law Anti-prostitution Pledge Requirement," *HIV/AIDS Policy and Law Review* (forthcoming) (describing cases); "Prostitution Loyalty Oath," http://www.genderhealth.org/loyaltyoathsuit.php (website links to court pleadings filed in cases).

[9] See Human Rights Watch, "Injecting Reason: Human Rights And HIV Prevention For Injection Drug Users; California: A Case Study," vol. 15, no. 2(G), September 2003.

[10] See studies cited in "Injecting Reason," pp. 10-17.

[11] See, e.g., World Health Organization, Joint United Nations Program on HIV/AIDS, and United Nations Office on Drugs and Crime, "Policy Brief: Provision of Sterile Injecting Equipment to Reduce HIV Transmission" (2004); Joint United Nations Program on HIV/AIDS, "Intensifying HIV prevention: UNAIDS policy position paper," August 2005, p. 23; U.S. National Institutes of Health, *Interventions to Prevent HIV Risk Behaviors: Consensus Development Statement*, February 11-13, 1997; Institute of Medicine of National Academy of Sciences, *No Time to Lose: Getting More from HIV Prevention* (2001).

[12] Transnational Institute, "The United Nations and Harm Reduction – Revisited: An unauthorized report on the outcomes of the 48th CND session," Drug Policy Briefing No. 13, April 2005.

[13] Ibid.; see also, Letter from Antonio Maria Costa, Executive Director, United Nations Office on Drugs and Crime, to Robert B. Charles, Assistant Secretary, International Narcotics and Law Enforcement Affairs, U.S. Department of State, November 11, 2004.

[14] See, e.g., Jole Baglole, "Vancouver Drug Facilities Draw Ire of U.S. Officials," *Wall Street Journal*, April 1, 2003.

[15] "Lesotho launches groundbreaking HIV campaign on World AIDS Day," WHO website: http://www.who.int/mediacentre/news/releases/2005/pr64/en/index.html (retrieved December 1, 2005).

[16] See: The Voluntary HIV-1 Counseling and Testing Efficacy Study Group, "Efficacy of VCT in individuals and couples in Kenya, Tanzania, and Trinidad: A Randomised Trial," The Lancet, vol. 356, July 8, 2000, pp 103-112; M.H. Merson, J.M. Dayton, K. O'Reilly, "Effectiveness of HIV prevention interventions in developing countries," AIDS, September 2000, vol. 14, supp. 2, pp. S68-84; and C.A. Liechty, "The evolving role of HIV counseling and testing in resource-limited settings: HIV prevention and linkage to expanding HIV care access," Current HIV/AIDS Report, December 2004, vol. 1(4), pp. 181-5.

[17] See, e.g., Kevin De Cock et al., "A serostatus-based approach to HIV/AIDS prevention and care in Africa," The Lancet, vol., 367 (2003), pp. 1847–49; Kevin De Cock, et al., "Shadow on the continent: public health and HIV/AIDS in Africa in the 21st century," The Lancet, vol. 360 (2002), pp. 67-72.

[18] Lesotho Ministry of Health and Social Welfare (STI, HIV & AIDS Directorate and Partners), "'Know Your Status' Campaign Operational Plan 2006-7; Gateway to comprehensive HIV prevention, treatment, care and support; Universal Access to HIV Testing and Counseling," December 1, 2005.

[19] This figure refers to the total budget for Strategic objective 7: "Strengthen post-test services for both HIV positive and HIV negative people" as specified in Lesotho Ministry of Health and Social Welfare (STI, HIV & AIDS Directorate and Partners), "'Know Your Status' Campaign Operational Plan 2006-7; Gateway to comprehensive HIV prevention, treatment, care and support; Universal Access to HIV Testing and Counseling," December 1, 2005.

[20] UNAIDS, "HIV rates decline in Zimbabwe," November 21, 2005, http://www.unaids.org.zw/default.htm (retrieved November 21, 2005).

[21] Human Rights Watch, "Just Die Quietly: Domestic Violence And Women's Vulnerability to HIV In Uganda," August 2003, vol. 15, no.15(A), p. 29

DEMOCRATIC REPUBLIC OF CONGO

The Curse of Gold

HUMAN
RIGHTS
WATCH

"We are cursed
because of our
gold. All we do
is suffer."

CONGOLESE GOLD MINER

WORLD REPORT
2006

AFRICA

ANGOLA

The slow pace of post-war reconstruction and reconciliation in the wake of Angola's twenty-seven year civil war, which ended in 2002, continued in 2005. While important electoral legislation was approved by the national assembly, much remains to be done to create an environment in which free and fair elections can take place and to extend civil and political rights to all Angolans. The government continues to violate Angolans rights to freedom of expression, association, and assembly. Persistent delays remain in rebuilding roads, schools, and other infrastructure in the rural provinces. The consistent lack of full transparency in the government's use of ever-increasing oil revenues remains a further impediment to enjoyment of human rights and reconstruction in Angola. Abuses against civilians by the Angolan military and political tension in the province of Cabinda remain causes for concern.

Preparations for 2006 Elections

In early 2005, the Angolan government and opposition political parties negotiated a "package" of electoral laws that would form the legal basis for parliamentary and presidential elections in 2006. Despite some opposition, the National Assembly, dominated by the Movement for the Popular Liberation of Angola (*Movimento Popular de Libertação de Angola*, MPLA) voted in favor of the legislative package on April 26, 2005. The original legislation barred President Jose Eduardo Dos Santos from seeking reelection, but the Supreme Court later overruled this provision. The National Union for the Total Independence of Angola (*União Nacional para a Independência Total de Angola*, UNITA) and other opposition groups called for legislative and presidential elections to take place simultaneously in 2006, but these dates have still not been set. Statements by the ruling party in late 2005 that "Angola is not ready" and that "elections must not be rushed" have raised the level of uncertainty as to the likelihood of elections being called for 2006. Disagreement over the composition of the National Electoral Commission, in which the governing MPLA named seven of the eleven members, has delayed preparations for elections.

Opposition parties raised other problems with the electoral process, notably issues pertaining to electoral registration, electoral education, and political party financing. Media reports in 2005 that the MPLA might use surplus money arising from oil sales to finance its political campaign received widespread attention. Voter registration reportedly began in some areas loyal to the ruling party before the establishment of the national, provincial, and local electoral commissions, and was tightly controlled and monitored by the MPLA and its members. Official voter registration was delayed due to lack of infrastructure and capacity outside the capital, complications related to the identification of Angolan citizens, many of whom are returning refugees without national identity cards, and political disagreements over the electoral commissions. The national registration process is now slated to begin in January 2006.

Rede Eleitoral (Electoral Network), a coalition of civil society organizations working for free and fair elections, advocated for disarmament and reintegration of former combatants and civic education of the police in response to reports that much of the rural population still fear that the elections may turn violent. The lack of access to information and limits on freedom of expression, especially in rural areas, are also significant obstacles to free and fair elections.

The lack of resources, conflict over land rights, and rising frustration among ex-combatants due to the slow pace of reintegration have contributed to increased political tension throughout Angola. The paucity of development and reconstruction funding flowing to rural areas, especially areas that heavily support the opposition, increased the perception that the central government is corrupt and uninterested in reconciliation. In one incident, UNITA accused the MPLA of involvement in the destruction of its local headquarters in Moxico province and of attacking party supporters on April 5, 2005. The incidents were apparently in response to the discovery of a land mine on the runway of the Lumbala N'guimbo airport, which was blamed on UNITA.

Freedom of Expression, Association and Assembly

Press freedom remains a concern in Angola, both for journalists in private and government-owned news outlets. While a much-debated national media law was stuck in parliament for the greater part of 2005, the government continued to maintain control of the airwaves in rural areas. Radio Ecclesia, a privately-owned Catholic radio station, continued to seek permission to broadcast outside Luanda. While this permission was not forthcoming, Radio Ecclesia's popular news program began playing on Vatican Radio in November, allowing the station to be heard outside Luanda. Several incidents demonstrated the tendency of the government to limit free speech. Angolan National Radio suspended a popular radio talk show after its host criticized the government in an interview on Radio Ecclesia. In April, the Deputy Minister for Information warned journalists at the state-owned daily newspaper "Jornal de Angola" not to criticize the government or give too much print space to the opposition.

Restrictions on the right of people to assemble peacefully were imposed on several occasions in 2005. On August 25, Carlos Almeida, a senior member of the opposition Party to Support Democracy, was jailed for 45 days for staging an unauthorized protest outside parliament. He was protesting his party's exclusion from the National Electoral Commission. In mid-July, the government of the province of Cabinda refused, without explanation, the request of a number of NGOs to hold a rally in favor of a peaceful solution to the conflict.

Tensions in Cabinda

While the government repeatedly stated that the armed conflict against the Front for the Liberation of the Cabinda Enclave (FLEC) in the oil-rich province of Cabinda had ended, it continued to maintain a massive military presence in the enclave. Fears of military escalation increased in July as local authorities reported that a new Angolan army offensive against FLEC in Cabinda was underway to crush the armed insurgency. The army has denied that it stepped up the military campaign, but abuses committed by armed forces personnel do not seem to have subsided. Violations connected to the military continued to be reported in 2005, including the brutal murder on April 14 of a three-year old girl and allegations that the army kidnapped and tortured members and sympathizers of Mpalabanda, a local human rights NGO, in July. The commander of the armed forces in Cabinda claimed that justice in these cases has been served. Asked to comment on the acts of indiscipline committed by soldiers under his command, General Marques Banza admitted that "there might have been isolated cases of indiscipline here and there, and in those instances we have known how to mete out punishment."

Reports that the Angolan government is in discussion with oil companies to grant exploration rights for drilling on-shore, as opposed to off-shore where most of the oil is currently produced, could exacerbate tensions in Cabinda, and lead to a continued military presence to ensure unfettered access to these resources.

Since March 22, 2005, there has been significant popular opposition to and protest over the Catholic Church's naming of an "Angolan" bishop to preside over Cabinda. When the Archbishop of Angola traveled to Cabinda on July 18, he was met at the airport by protests which turned violent. The violence continued as he tried to hold mass and he was forced to leave. Relations between the Vatican and the local population and Catholic priests have remained tense, with both Cabindans and the local Catholic clergy accusing the Vatican of not favoring the interests of the enclave. One priest was briefly detained by the military, and the Angolan Catholic Church suspended two popular Cabindan priests in August and shut down the Immaculate Conception Church in Cabinda. The governor of Cabinda accused Mpalabanda of being involved in orchestrating the protests.

Return and Resettlement

The United Nations High Commissioner for Refugees said that 2005 would be the last year that the agency would facilitate repatriation of refugees from neighboring countries; starting in 2006, it will focus solely on reintegrating those already repatriated. This will leave approximately 130,000 Angolan refugees still living in neighboring countries. It is unclear whether these refugees will independently return to Angola or remain in the countries where they are presently located. However, the repatriation of refugees from Zambia, which began in May, and the Democratic Republic of Congo (DRC), was delayed due to poor infrastructure and a lack of social services such as education and health in the rural areas of the Angolan interior. Rumors circulating in refugee camps in Zambia that a shortage of food and medicine exists in Angola kept many from returning home. The United Nations Children's Fund reported in late August that rural areas in Angola do not have access to sufficient drinking water and U.S.$440 million needs to be invested to change the situation. The population has yet to receive any benefit from increasing oil revenues that have come with skyrocketing oil prices. Some refugees also reportedly fear that they will be forcefully incorporated into the army. Returns from the DRC were also delayed due to the outbreak of the Marburg virus epidemic in Uige province in Angola.

Key International Actors

International pressure on Angola to improve its record on transparency and human rights has not been very effective. A U.S.$2 billion credit line granted to the government of Angola by the Chinese Export-Import bank has allowed the ruling party to reject calls for greater transparency. The Angolan government also rejected several reports critical of the human rights situation in Angola, including the report by Hina Jilani, the U.N. special rapporteur for human rights defenders.

Donor countries have indefinitely postponed the holding of a donors conference to help fund reconstruction efforts in Angola, largely due to the failure of the Angolan government to come to an agreement with the International Monetary Fund (IMF) on setting up a Staff Monitored Program, the main precondition to holding a donors conference. Despite many in-country visits by IMF staff and directors, an agreement does not look likely in 2005. Huge gains in oil revenues resulting from soaring international oil prices have not been accounted for by the government. The international donor community is reluctant to provide development aid because the Angolan government has largely failed to improve financial accountability and transparency, especially in the oil sector.

While the influence of international actors such as the IMF has waned, the role of regional actors, such as member states of the Southern African Development Community (SADC), will increase in the run-up to elections. The government has not made encouraging statements with respect to allowing international observers to monitor the elections in 2006. SADC member states and other regional actors will need to take a firmer stance in ensuring that free and fair elections are conducted in a climate of improved enjoyment of human rights. However, SADC's endorsement of blatantly unfair elections in Zimbabwe in 2005 is cause for concern.

BURUNDI

In 2005 Burundians went to the polls for the first time in twelve years, choosing a president, Pierre Nkurunziza, who declared his commitment to establishing the rule of law in a country marked by years of widespread human rights abuses. His government took office under a new constitution that guarantees power-sharing between the Hutu and Tutsi ethnic groups and among political parties. The constitution, adopted by over 90 percent of voters at a February 28, 2005 referendum, also requires that 30 percent of parliamentary seats be reserved for women, the first time they have held this much power in the legislature.

The new government seeks to end an ongoing war with the Forces of National Liberation (FNL), a guerilla group that controls territory around Bujumbura, the capital. Some FNL combatants split from the rest of the group in October 2005, claiming to want peace, but they appear to number only about one hundred. According to some in this group, other FNL under Agathon Rwasa killed seven of those seeking peace.

During 2005, soldiers and rebel combatants killed, raped, abducted, and robbed civilians in hundreds of incidents, although none on the scale of massacres in previous years. Some of these abuses were committed by FNL combatants and by soldiers of Nkurunziza's movement, the National Council for the Defense of Democracy-Force for the Defense of Democracy (CNDD-FDD), as they struggled to control territory near Bujumbura.

As skirmishes between FNL and government soldiers increased in September and October, soldiers summarily executed five civilians and detained and tortured others in Kanyosha commune, all suspected of ties with the FNL. Intelligence agents also detained dozens of persons from the Kinama neighborhood of Bujumbura and beat some of them in the weeks just after Kinama voters had preferred candidates from the Burundian Front for Democracy (FRODEBU) to those of the CNDD-FDD.

Hundreds of soldiers, former rebel combatants, and members of a government-sponsored militia, Guardians of the Peace, ended military activities.

Without any prospect of employment, some turned to crime. The many cases of armed robbery, sometimes resulting in death of the victims, and rape drew attention to the incapacity of the police and judicial systems. Nkurunziza promised that no one would be above the law, but as of late 2005 his government had yet to propose ways to deal with current crime or with the widespread crimes committed during the war, including those committed by combatants from his own force.

Peaceful Installation of the New Government

Burundians last voted in 1993 when they chose Melchior Ndadaye as president, the first Hutu elected to this position. Military officers from the Tutsi-dominated army assassinated Ndadaye soon after, touching off a twelve-year war where hostilities between Hutu (85 percent of the population) and Tutsi (14 percent of the population) colored partisan and regional struggles for power.

In addition to winning the presidency in 2005, the CNDD-FDD easily carried both the legislative and communal elections, significantly reducing the power of the parties that had controlled the previous government. Except for one limited effort by the FNL to disrupt voting, the polling was generally peaceful. In a welcome innovation, Burundian radio stations cooperated to cover polling throughout the country—their reports of calm encouraged voters to go vote. Although relatively few incidents marred voting, there were numerous reports of harm or threats by CNDD-FDD loyalists against supposed opponents during the pre-electoral period.

In contrast to neighboring Rwanda which dealt with Hutu-Tutsi hostility by eliminating ethnic categories, Burundi acknowledges ethnic groups and, under its new constitution, guarantees 40 percent of governmental and administrative posts and 50 percent of places in the armed forces to Tutsi. The new system also reserves three parliamentary seats for Twa, a minority who comprise less than 1 percent of the population. The CNDD-FDD has also tried to counter ethnic hostilities by recruiting Tutsi into its ranks, previously largely Hutu.

A Disappointing Beginning

After applauding a new government and the presidential promises for protecting human rights, Burundians have been disappointed to see officials continuing old abuses. Under the guise of searching out FNL supporters, soldiers beat and then executed four civilians in Kanyosha on October 1 and another on October 5. Intelligence agents detained dozens of persons associated with FRODEBU and beat some of them, particularly after the September local elections. Among the victims were three recently elected officials and the husband of another.

Demobilization and Disarmament

Early in 2005, the forces of the CNDD-FDD and the former Burundian Armed Forces were integrated into the new National Defense Force (FDN). There was no vetting to eliminate officers or soldiers implicated in past violations of human rights or international humanitarian law, some of whom continued in positions of responsibility. More than 16,000 former combatants have been demobilized but many of them rejoined the new army. Groups comprising several thousand Guardians of the Peace and other militia have been disbanded and their members demobilized. Dissatisfied with delays in disbursing the payments of U.S. $100 that they are supposed to receive, former militia took to the streets several times, most recently in October 2005. Only a few hundred militia members have turned in firearms to the authorities; many weapons and grenades, in some cases distributed by the authorities themselves during the war, remain in civilian hands, posing a risk of future violence.

Justice

The national judicial system, reformed in 2003, functions poorly, in part because of lack of resources and in part because of incapacity and corruption of personnel. Popular disillusionment with the failure to arrest and try criminals has led to an increase in lynchings of suspects. One man said to have thrown a grenade in a house in Kamenge, Bujumbura, in July 2005, was beaten to death by a crowd, as was a man accused of sorcery in Nyabiraba commune, Gitega, in January. But in an exceptional break with past patterns of impunity, the Court of Appeals found senior security and prison officials guilty of the November 2001 murder of Dr. Kassy Malan, then head of the World Health Organization in Burundi. In a May 2005 decision, the court sentenced four of them to death and nine others to jail terms.

Throughout 2005, Burundians debated how to ensure accountability for the many violations of international humanitarian law committed during the war and previous periods of large-scale ethnically-based killing,, such as those which occurred in 1972 and 1988. The United Nations Security Council, charged by the Arusha Accords with assisting in this matter, recommended a reconciliation commission and a special trial chamber in the Burundian judicial system (resolution 1606, June 2005), both to be staffed by Burundian and international personnel. Late in 2005 the Burundian government, apparently reluctant to confront the complexities of delivering justice, had yet to negotiate details of these arrangements with the U.N.

Land and the Return of Refugees

Over fifty thousand Hutu refugees returned to Burundi from Tanzania in 2005, bringing to over 230,000 the number of returnees since 2002. Many had fled during the violence in 1993 and most of these returnees have reclaimed their former holdings. Local commissions, operating under a national office, are intended to resolve any conflicting claims. Although the commissions are not fully operational, land disputes remained scattered and local throughout 2005. Land disputes may increase with the return of 200,000 refugees still outside Burundi, some of whom fled in 1972 and have lost title to their land by an absence of longer than thirty years.

In April 2005 thousands of Rwandans fled to Burundi saying they feared false accusations and unfair trials in the Rwandan people's courts. Some also said they fled rumors of massacres planned by officials. Burundian authorities initially welcomed them but later cooperated with Rwandan authorities in forcing the refugees to return involuntarily to Rwanda, in violation of international conventions. In October Burundian and Rwandan officials agreed to repatriate another 3,000 Rwandans, against their will if necessary.

Key International Actors

The United Nations Operation in Burundi (ONUB) along with key regional leaders—particularly South Africa, Uganda, and Tanzania—played major roles in moving the various political parties through the transition period and to the installation of the new government. Tanzania continues attempts to broker a peace agreement with the FNL. Although ONUB troops have only occasionally been able to protect Burundians from violence, the ONUB human rights division has efficiently documented and publicized many human rights abuses, exerting significant pressure towards improvements in the police and judicial systems. The U.N. Security Council delayed responding to Burundian calls for help in establishing justice for crimes committed during past periods of ethnic violence, but it now appears ready to partner with Burundi in this important effort.

In September, the U.N. secretary general called for an international mechanism, including regional and African Union representatives, to support further reforms and disarmament. Many international donors offered financial assistance, including Belgium, which provided an emergency grant of some 2 million euros to pay salaries of administrative staff in September 2005.

CÔTE D'IVOIRE

During 2005, the political impasse between the Ivorian government and northern-based New Forces rebels resulted in a steady increase in human rights abuses by Ivorian security forces, the rebels, and militias associated with both sides. Throughout the year there were persistent reports of extrajudicial executions, torture, arbitrary detentions, extortion and looting, and of recruitment and use of child soldiers by all sides. Two deadly outbreaks of ethnically motivated violence resulted in some one hundred deaths. 2005 saw no meaningful efforts by the Ivorian government, rebels or the international community to combat the pervasive culture of impunity in the country.

Efforts to end the political-military crisis saw the failure of a third internationally negotiated peace accord, the African Union-brokered Pretoria Agreement, signed in April 2005. To avoid a constitutional crisis following the end of incumbent Gbagbo's five-year term, the African Union (A.U.) in October proposed a plan calling for Gbagbo to remain in office for up to one year. The new plan —which was not signed by the warring factions—also calls for the appointment of a new prime minister acceptable to all parties who would help ensure the implementation of crucial reforms including laws relating to nationality and naturalization and the powers and composition of the Independent Electoral Commission. However, while the plan was later endorsed by the United Nations Security Council, it was rejected by the rebels and opposition political parties.

At year's end, the apparent disenfranchisement of the rebels from the political process—as well as internal divisions along ethnic lines within the Ivorian security forces—led to serious concerns about either a renewal of armed conflict or a coup d'etat. The prospect of a renewed military offensive by either side raises serious human rights concerns given the government's prominent use of ill-disciplined militias and hate media to incite violence against perceived opponents. The extent to which the rebel leadership maintains effective command and control over its forces and the extent to which U.N. peacekeepers could protect vulnerable groups of civilians are also of concern.

As the political crisis deepens, the institutions that once provided benefits to ordinary Ivorians— the public education system, healthcare services, and the judicial system— continued to deteriorate, resulting in serious hardship particularly in the rebel-held north. Some four thousand French troops monitor a buffer zone or "Confidence Zone." between the government-controlled south and the rebel-controlled north of the country. A six thousand-strong United Nations peacekeeping mission, the United Nations Operation in Côte d'Ivoire (UNOCI), established in April 2004, is deployed country-wide. The issues at the heart of the Ivorian conflict—the exploitation of ethnicity for political gain, competition over land and natural resources, and corruption—remain unresolved.

Abuses by State Security Forces

During 2005, scores of summary executions were carried out by the police, army, and the Central Command Security Operation Force (CCOS) —a new security force of about 1700 men created by Presidential decree in July to ensure security in Abidjan. The majority of these executions appeared to target northerners, West African immigrants and other perceived rebel sympathizers, though the government maintained that the executions took place in the course of combating common crime. The police, army, CCOS and, to a lesser extent, armed militias engaged in systematic and widespread extortion, racketeering and intimidation of businessmen, street traders, and motorists among others. Perceived rebel sympathizers were believed to be particularly targeted. Army officers regularly engaged in the cross border recruitment of Liberians, including former child combatants, to fight with Ivorian pro-government militias. In July 2005, a group of armed soldiers from the Ivorian Republican Guard stormed the Abidjan offices of state broadcaster RTI and instructed directors not to broadcast footage of opposition members.

Abuses by Pro-government Militias and Groups

In 2005, pro-government militias and groups, sometimes working together with state security forces, intimidated and at times attacked opposition party members, journalists and human rights activists aligned with pro-opposition newspapers and United Nations peacekeepers. A violent pro-government student group, the Students' Federation of Cote d'Ivoire (FESCI), committed serious abuses, including torture and rape, against students perceived to be supporting the opposition. In July 2005, the pro-government Young Patriot militia burned opposition newspapers, threatened to kill newspaper vendors, surrounded and threatened the offices of opposition newspapers, and forced their way into a public TV station. U.N. peacekeepers and civilian staff were, on several occasions, intimidated, surrounded, and prevented from patrolling and conducting investigations in government-controlled areas.

Abuses by the Forces Nouvelles

New Forces rebels systematically extort money and pillage goods, including livestock and foodstuffs, from civilians in villages both under their control and within the buffer zone. Suspected government collaborators and spies were on several occasions tortured and summarily executed by rebel leaders. In the north, rebel commanders arbitrarily dispense justice, in turn leading to severe violations of human rights: numerous individuals accused of common crimes are arbitrarily detained within prisons, informal detention centers and military camps for often extended periods of time. The Dozos, a traditional tribally based civil defense group now working in coordination with the New Forces, has also committed serious violations including extortion, arbitrary detention, torture and rape.

Intercommunal Conflict over Land

During 2005 there were at least two violent episodes of inter-communal conflict between indigenous groups and immigrant farm workers in the cocoa and coffee plantation areas of the west. The causes of the violence are multi-faceted and involve a complex interplay of economic factors, disputes over land rights, the proliferation of armed militias, and the political manipulation of ethnicity. In February 2005, sixteen people were killed and thousands displaced in clashes sparked by an attack by pro-government militia on the rebel-held village of Logouale. In May and June 2005, at least seventy people were killed and thousands more displaced in a spate of revenge killings in and around the town of Duékoué.

Accountability

Throughout 2005, neither the government nor the rebel leadership took concrete steps to discipline, investigate or hold accountable those responsible for ongoing crimes, much less past atrocities which took place during the 2000 election violence, 2002-2003 civil war, and violent crackdown on an opposition demonstration in March 2004.

For their part, the United Nations Security Council and African Union resisted the adoption of concrete efforts to either hold perpetrators accountable through prosecutions or to restrain the actions of alleged human rights violators through the imposition of travel and economic sanctions. The U.N. Security Council has yet to make public or discuss the findings of the Commission of Inquiry report into serious violations of human rights and international humanitarian law since September 2002, which was handed to the UN Secretary General in November 2004. The report contained a secret annex listing people accused of human rights abuses who could eventually face trial. Similarly, the Council refused to implement travel and economic sanctions authorized under resolution 1572, which was passed in November 2004. This resolution authorized the use of sanctions against Ivorians who violated human rights, broke the arms embargo, indulged in hate speech, or blocked the peace process.

While the prosecutor for the International Criminal Court announced in January 2005 that he would send a team to Cote d'Ivoire to lay the groundwork for a possible investigation into war crimes, he had at year's end yet to do so. The prosecutor was acting on an ad hoc request to the ICC by the Ivorian government made in September 2003.

Key International Actors

No one country, international body or individual appeared willing or able to exert sufficient influence to move the two sides towards a peaceful resolution to the political and military crisis. Throughout the year key international players were exasperated with the lack of progress in the implementation of yet another peace accord. However, the African Union, which during 2005 took the lead in peace negotiations, was loath to use and maintained effective veto power over the only leverage tool available — United Nations economic and travel sanctions. Key international players were equally unprepared to take measures to combat impunity although the United Nations on numerous occasions expressed concern about ongoing violations. This reluctance—in the name of undermining future prospects for peace—appeared to embolden the perpetrators and fed into the intransigence of the Ivorian government and New Forces.

Following the failure of the parties to fully implement the Pretoria Agreement, there was no consensus as to which would be the most suitable body to play the role of negotiator during the coming year: The A.U.-appointed envoy, South African President Thabo Mbeki, was deeply mistrusted by the rebels who accused him of being too close to the government. Key members of the Economic Community of West African States (ECOWAS)—Burkina Faso and Mali—were blamed by the government for supporting the rebels. France, who has been accused of favoritism by both sides, and the United Nations deferred to the African bodies. In response, the African Union created the International Working Group (IWG)—to be chaired by Nigeria's Foreign Minister and composed of senior officials from Benin, Ghana, Nigeria, Niger, South Africa, France, United States, Britain, the International Monetary Fund, World Bank, European Union, African Union and regional body ECOWAS—to monitor the implementation of future commitments.

While the United Nations Security Council appeared frustrated with both parties to the conflict, it was reluctant to take a leadership role in pushing for accountability or sanctions. However, in June 2005, it authorized an increase of some 850 more troops.

DEMOCRATIC REPUBLIC OF CONGO

Crippled by continuing conflict among its four main component parties, the transitional government of the Democratic Republic of Congo (DRC) ended two years in power with much of the eastern region still not under its control. Faced with overwhelming logistical problems, the transitional government postponed elections scheduled for June 30, 2005 and will likely hold them in the first half of 2006. Security services committed election-related abuses throughout 2005, including the January shooting in Kinshasa of dozens of demonstrators protesting elections delays and the later detention of political activists for months without charge elsewhere in the country. Focused on assuring elections, few Congolese or outsiders worked effectively to curb ongoing violence against civilians or to address crucial post-conflict challenges, such as delivering justice for the many grave violations of international humanitarian law committed in Congo in the last decade.

Unconvinced that elections will bring results they favor, some belligerents to the war that officially ended in 2002 have kept their troops from being integrated into the new national army, as stipulated in the final peace accords. In late 2004 and in 2005 troops from the former Congolese Rally for Democracy-Goma (RCD-Goma) refused integration and fought the national army in several clashes in the eastern DRC. Armed groups which remained outside the peace process also fought each other, the national army and the U.N. peacekeeping force known as MONUC. Representatives of one such group, opponents of the Rwandan government known as the Democratic Force for the Liberation of Rwanda (FDLR), announced that they would disarm and return to Rwanda, but only a few hundred did so in 2005.

In 2005, combatants from armed groups as well as government soldiers deliberately killed, raped, and abducted civilians and destroyed or looted their property in repeated attacks, particularly in eastern Congo. A feeble justice system failed to prosecute these recent crimes and did nothing to end impunity for war crimes and crimes against humanity committed during the previous two wars. The September 2005 discovery of mass graves from 1996

DEMOCRATIC REPUBLIC OF CONGO

Civilians attacked in North Kivu

HUMAN
RIGHTS
WATCH

in the eastern region of Rutshuru served as a reminder of the unpunished mass slaughter of civilians in Congo in the last decade.

Government Soldiers and Armed Groups Target Civilians

The government failure to integrate troops of former belligerent groups into the national army and to properly train and pay its soldiers underlay some military abuses. Military abuses such as those that occurred in December 2004 in North Kivu where government soldiers and combatants refusing integration fought and killed at least one hundred civilians, many of them targeted on an ethnic basis, were repeated elsewhere in 2005. In Walungu, South Kivu, government soldiers raped civilians and looted property during operations against the FDLR in late 2004 and early 2005. In Equateur, poorly paid and undisciplined troops went on a rampage in July 2005, killing, raping, and stealing from civilians.

As government soldiers tried to take control of Ituri and parts of North and South Kivu, Maniema and Katanga in late 2004 and 2005, both they and the combatants fighting them committed grave violations of international humanitarian and human rights law. In Ituri, which experienced widespread violence against civilians in previous years, more than fifteen thousand members of armed groups agreed to lay down their weapons, but others who refused to disarm increased attacks on MONUC peacekeepers and government soldiers. In February 2005 nine peacekeepers were killed in an ambush north of Bunia, the main town. Combatants refusing disarmament took control of areas near the towns of Boga and Kilo in August and September 2005, forcing thousands of civilians to flee their homes.

In North Kivu, where authorities illegally distributed hundreds of firearms to civilians in late 2004, there was little progress in 2005 in recuperating the weapons, some of which were used by civilians to harm, rob, or intimidate others.

Foreign Armed Groups

The continuing presence of Ugandan and Rwandan rebel combatants in eastern Congo threatens regional stability by providing a pretext for intervention by the Rwandan or Ugandan governments. In mid-2005 the Ugandan government facilitated a meeting of Ituri combatants who forged a new alliance to fight the Congolese government and MONUC. Under pressure from the international community, the Ugandan government later expelled these 'warlords' from Uganda, but took no action to arrest them. In September 2005 Uganda threatened to invade Congo after some rebel Lord's Resistance Army (LRA) troops, opposed to the Ugandan government, briefly crossed into the Congo.

In March 2005, under pressure from their former backers in the Congolese transitional government, FDLR rebels said they would give up military struggle and return to Rwanda. Most FDLR combatants stayed in Congo but split into several factions. One such group, calling itself the "Rastas," killed, kidnapped for ransom, and raped civilians around Walungu, South Kivu. The African Union proposed sending a force to disarm the FDLR but by late 2005 had not put any troops in the area.

Civil and Political Rights

In January and June 2005, security forces killed dozens of men, women, and children protesting electoral delays in Kinshasa, Mbuyi Mayi, Goma and other towns. In May 2005, the national security service arrested over one hundred people, primarily from southern Katanga, supposedly suspected of planning a Katangan secession attempt. They detained some for months without charge. In hundreds of cases throughout the country, police and other agents of security services arbitrarily detained and tortured citizens with the intent of extorting payment from them. Authorities arrested and closed the operations of journalists who criticized those in power, such as a television station of Vice President Jean-Pierre Bemba, who is likely a chief challenger of President Kabila in the up-coming elections. In another case the Information Ministry in January 2005 ordered certain broadcasters to discontinue political programming and live phone-in programs. In July,

DEMOCRATIC REPUBLIC OF CONGO

Seeking Justice

The Prosecution of Sexual Violence in the Congo War

HUMAN
RIGHTS
WATCH

authorities arrested a Kinshasa editor after his newspaper reported that a government minister had misappropriated U.S. $300,000.

Illegal Exploitation of Resources

As in the past armed groups profited from the illegal exploitation of resources and fought to control rich mining areas and lucrative border posts. In gold-rich Ituri, for example, armed groups fought over mines at Kilo and Bambu in September 2005. Local organizations as well as international observers report growing corruption and fraud by officials linked to the exploitation of resources. Multinational companies sought to sign new mining deals or revitalize old ones, further complicating efforts to ensure effective national control over resources. A Congolese parliamentary commission investigating contracts signed during the war years for the exploitation of minerals and other resources reported many irregularities and recommended ending or renegotiating the contracts, a measure awaiting action by parliament.

Threats to Human Rights Groups

Congolese human rights activists face significant intimidation and violence, abuses that are rarely punished. After Pascal Kabungulu, a prominent activist, was assassinated in Bukavu in July 2005, two soldiers were arrested in connection with the killing, but their commander forced authorities to release them. In June 2005, the national security service arrested a well-known activist in Lubumbashi, saying he was linked to the May secession attempt in Katanga. When other activists protested his arrest, six of them were arrested and mistreated while in detention. Activists and members of civil society in North Kivu received anonymous threats and visits by armed men to their homes in January 2005, after they denounced war crimes committed by local troops and the distribution of weapons to civilians by provincial authorities. Four felt so threatened that they fled the country.

Delivering Justice

Despite national and international proclamations about the importance of accountability for past crimes, numerous persons suspected of violations of international human rights and humanitarian law continue to occupy posts of national or local responsibility, including in the newly integrated army. In exceptional cases, authorities responded to international pressure by arresting several armed group leaders from Ituri in early 2005 and by issuing arrest warrants for other military figures who resist government control. The prosecutor of the International Criminal Court (ICC) is investigating war crimes and crimes against humanity in Congo, an effort that may eventually bring some major perpetrators to justice.

Key International Actors

MONUC peacekeepers were posted outside of urban areas in early 2005, helping to deter human rights violations in some places. But MONUC troops are still too few to protect civilians throughout the country. In September 2005, the Security Council authorized deployment of an additional 841 MONUC police during elections and provided a further three hundred peacekeepers.

The United States, the United Kingdom, and South Africa are working to keep the peace process from collapse, helping resolve disagreements among partners in the national government and seeking a solution to disarming the FDLR. Focused on making elections happen, donors have not yet addressed how to assure political space or deliver justice after elections.

ERITREA

The Eritrean government's tyranny became more ruthless in 2005. Rule by force and caprice remains the norm, as the government aggressively moves to intimidate the population and to isolate it from the outside world.

The border dispute with Ethiopia continues to fester and is used by the government to justify repressive policies. The government of Eritrea seriously interfered with the United Nations' ability to monitor troop movements along the border in 2005 and threatened to resume war unless Ethiopia accepts an independent Boundary Commission decision which it considers favorable.

Arrests, Imprisonment and Torture

Suppression of Political Dissent and Opinion, Arbitrary Arrest, and Illegal Detention

No political party other than the People's Front for Democracy and Justice (PFDJ) is allowed to exist in Eritrea and no national elections have been held since the country won its independence from Ethiopia in 1993. Using the excuse that Eritrea remains at war, the government has refused to implement the 1997 constitution, drafted by a constitutional assembly and ratified by referendum, that respects civil and political rights.

The government has arrested thousands of citizens for expressing dissenting views, practicing an "unregistered" religion, avoiding endless military conscription, attempting to flee the country, or on suspicion of not fully supporting government policies. Mass arrests began in September 2001 with the detention of eleven leaders of the PDFJ who questioned President Isayas Afewerki's erratic and autocratic leadership. The government arrested publishers, editors and reporters and closed all independent newspapers and magazines. The arrests continued in 2005 and included three leaders of government-affiliated labor unions, the only unions allowed to operate in the country.

97

Most of those arrested are held indefinitely in incommunicado detention. None are formally charged, given access to lawyers or brought to trial. Some prisoners are released but are warned not to talk about their imprisonment or treatment. Some manage to escape and flee the country. As of September 2005, the World Food Program reported that ten thousand fleeing Eritreans are in refugee camps in Ethiopia, two hundred of whom fled since January, with two hundred to three hundred more arriving monthly.

Prison Conditions and Torture

Prisoners are often held in secret prisons, including underground cells. Because of the large number of arrests, less prominent prisoners are packed into cargo containers or in other overcrowded prisons. In addition to psychological abuse, solitary confinement and abysmal conditions, escapees report the use of physical torture. Prisoners are suspended from trees with their arms tied behind their backs, a technique known as *almaz* (diamond). Prisoners are also placed face down, hands tied to feet, a method of torture known as the "helicopter."

Military Conscription Roundups and Arrests

Eritreans between the ages of eighteen and forty-five must perform two years of compulsory national service. In practice, however, the time for service is repeatedly prolonged. There are frequent *giffas* (sweeps) to round up "evaders"—some of whom have already fulfilled their lawful obligations. The government often uses national service as retribution for perceived criticism of government policies. Those accused of evading service are frequently tortured. Conscripts are often used for public works projects, such as road building. There have been persistent reports that they are also used as laborers on party, military, and officers' personal farms.

In September 2005, the Italian newspaper *Corriere della Sera* published photographs taken by a diplomat in Asmara who witnessed a killing by security forces of a young man wounded during a giffa. According to the diplomat, a security agent shot the man at close range, execution-style, while the victim lay in the road. The government denied the diplomat's account and photographs, quoting several persons who lived in the area who asserted that the only body in the street was that of a drunk.

In mid-2005, the government for the first time made hundreds of arrests of family members of children who had not reported to the military training camp at Sawa for their final year of high school or who otherwise did not report for national service. Although the government issued denials, foreign diplomats confirmed the arrests.

Three separate immigration decisions in 2005, by an appellate court in the United States (*Nuru v. Gonzales*, 404 F.3d 1207 (9th Cir.), the European Court of Human Rights (*Said v. the Netherlands*, Application no. 2345/02), and the United Kingdom Immigration Appeal Tribunal (Appeal No: Eritrea CG [2005]UKIAT 00106), granted asylum to Eritreans fleeing conscription on the grounds that national service is used as a measure of political repression and that anyone forcibly returned to Eritrea is likely to be tortured.

Religious Persecution

The government closed all religious institutions in May 2002 except for those affiliated with the Eritrean Orthodox, Roman Catholic, Eritrean Evangelical (Lutheran) churches and Sunni Muslim mosques. Members of Pentecostal Christian churches are arrested for possession of Bibles or for attending communal worship. In 2005, the government intensified its persecution of adherents of unregistered religions by raiding wedding parties at private homes. Some clergy of a modernizing wing of the Eritrean Orthodox church were also arrested in 2005. Many of those arrested are beaten or tortured during their arrest or while in captivity.

Jehovah's Witnesses have been especially mistreated. Some have been detained for a decade for refusing to participate in national military service even though the official penalty is incarceration for no more than three years. The Eritrean government defends its practices on the ground that the unrecognized churches have failed to register, but some religious groups applied for registration in 2002 and have not been registered. The government announced in April 2005 that it soon would register the Seventh Day Adventist denomination, but as of November 2005, it had not done so.

In September 2005, the United States imposed sanctions after having earlier designated Eritrea as a "country of particular concern" for its religious persecution.

Suppression of Human Rights Groups

Neither domestic nor international human rights organizations are allowed to operate in Eritrea. Indeed, almost no domestic civil organizations are allowed to function except as an appendage to the government or to the PDFJ. In June 2005, the government imposed new restrictions on non-governmental organizations (NGOs) providing assistance to the country. The restrictions require annual registration and prohibit any NGO with less than U.S.$2 million in capital (if foreign) or U.S.$1 million (if domestic) from being registered.

No non-governmental sources of information exist except word-of-mouth. Foreign broadcasts are periodically jammed.

Relations with Ethiopia

The 1998-2000 war with Ethiopia ended with an armistice agreement by which Eritrea and Ethiopia agreed to binding arbitration of their border. An international peace-keeping force, U.N. Mission in Eritrea-Ethiopia (UNMEE), maintains troops and observers along the twenty-five-kilometer-wide armistice buffer line between the two countries. The force and the zone are based on the armistice agreement that suspended the conflict.

In 2003, Ethiopia announced its rejection the decision of the independent Boundary Commission, largely because it awarded the village of Badme, the flashpoint for the war, to Eritrea. The Eritrean government uses the possibility of renewed conflict as a justification for postponing elections, prolonging national service, and for its repressive policies. Eritrea has lashed out against the international community for not compelling Ethiopia to implement the border commission decision. Eritrea insists that the border be demarcated without conditions and Ethiopia insists that, while it accepts the Boundary Commission's decision in principle, demarcation can proceed only after bilateral discussions. No serious international pressure has been applied to Ethiopia to honor its commitments.

In 2005, President Issayas threatened to resume the war if the impasse is not resolved. In October 2005, the government declared that UNMEE helicopters and night patrols could no longer be used to monitor the border. By November, both Eritrea and Ethiopia had substantially increased troop levels and armament near the border.

Key International Actors

In January 2005, the African Union adopted a 2003 African Commission on Human and Peoples' Rights report finding Eritrea's arrest of the eleven government officials in 2001 and their continued incarceration in violation of the African Charter on Human and Peoples' Rights. In April, the Inter-Parliamentary Union unanimously concluded that continued detention was a gross violation of fundamental rights under Eritrean and international law, and inferred from the conflicting justifications given by the government that the accusations against the eleven were groundless.

The international community's assistance consists of food and other humanitarian assistance. The European Union announced in 2003 that it would provide Eritrea an unstated sum under the European Initiative for Democracy and Human Rights, in addition to a ? 96 million five-year aid package (until 2007) for social and economic development. The European Union said that its assistance would depend on the government's willingness to improve civil liberties but has taken no action to withdraw assistance in the face of government intransigence.

With minor exceptions, the United States withholds non-humanitarian assistance to Eritrea because it has refused to release two American embassy local employees arrested in 2001. (After four years, no charges have been filed against them.) In August 2005, Eritrea arrested two more local embassy staff, allegedly for human trafficking. In early summer, the government demanded that the U.S. Agency for International Development cease operations in the country without offering a reason, other than that the government was uncomfortable with HIV/AIDS programs and wanted assistance to be provided directly to the government. In September, the United States imposed a partial denial of arms-export licenses on Eritrea for its religious persecution. This sanction is more symbolic than real because the United States exports few arms to Eritrea. The Eritrean ministry of defense issued a statement calling the sanction part of a U.S. Central Intelligence Agency plot to "instill chaos" in Eritrea and to rescue the Ethiopian government. Despite the official U.S. position of keeping its distance, high-level U.S. Defense department officials frequently visit and praise the Eritrean government for fighting terrorism.

ETHIOPIA

The aftermath of Ethiopia's landmark May 2005 parliamentary elections has laid bare the deeply entrenched patterns of political repression, human rights abuse and impunity that characterize the day-to-day reality of governance in much of the country. This dispiriting reality has come as a shock to many international observers who had viewed the electoral process with a great deal of optimism. The run-up to the May elections witnessed displays of openness and genuine political competition unprecedented in Ethiopia's long history. But many Ethiopians experienced these limited openings in a context still dominated by heavy-handed government efforts to suppress and punish any form of political dissent. Worse, the aftermath of the May elections has been marred by seemingly intractable controversy and displays of government brutality that threaten to reverse the gains yielded by the electoral process.

Post-election Uncertainty and Violence

Official tallies in the weeks following the May 15 voting indicated that opposition parties had made enormous gains in parliament but had fallen well short of obtaining a majority. The largest opposition coalition, the Coalition for Unity and Democracy (CUD), refused to accept those results, alleging that it had been robbed of outright victory by widespread government fraud. The government, in turn, has accused the CUD of conspiring to overthrow the government by force. At the time of writing, a full five months after the elections, it is still unclear whether the CUD will take its seats in parliament.

These tensions exploded in early June, when protests broke out in Addis Ababa in defiance of a government ban on public assemblies. Police and military forces responded with excessive force, killing at least thirty-six unarmed civilians and wounding more than 100. Security forces then arrested several thousand opposition supporters throughout the country. In November negotiations between the government and leading opposition parties broke down, sparking a fresh wave of protests. Ethiopian security forces again reacted with brutality, killing at least 46 people and arresting more than

4000 in Addis Ababa and other towns. The government then ordered the arrest of several dozen opposition politicians, journalists, editors and civil society activists. Ethiopian authorities have indicated that several among them are likely to face charges of treason, which carries a potential sentence of death under Ethiopian law.

Political Repression

Government officials and security forces in much of Ethiopia make routine use of various forms of human rights abuse to deter and punish dissent. For more than a decade, authorities in the country's vast Oromia region have used exaggerated concerns about armed insurgency and "terrorism" to justify the torture, imprisonment and sustained harassment of their critics and even ordinary citizens. Student protests in 2004 at Addis Ababa University and in secondary schools throughout Oromia led to the arrest of hundreds of students, many of whom were mistreated while in custody. Ever since the protests and throughout 2005, regional officials in Oromia have gone to oppressive lengths to monitor and control the speech and conduct of students and teachers alike.

In rural areas in Oromia, local officials often threaten to withhold vital agricultural inputs such as fertilizer from impoverished farmers if they speak out against them or their policies. In other cases, local officials selectively enforce harsh penalties for the non- repayment of debts to justify the imprisonment of their critics or the seizure of their property. In the months prior to the May 2005 elections, regional officials in Oromia created new quasi-governmental structures used to subject the rural population to intense levels of surveillance and to impose restrictions on farmers' freedoms of movement, association and speech.

Abuses Committed by the Ethiopian Armed Forces

The Ethiopian government has taken no meaningful action to address widespread atrocities committed by Ethiopian military forces in the remote southwestern region of Gambella. Federal authorities have refused even to investigate human rights abuses so severe that they may rise to the level of

በኢትዮጵያ ጉ: 3 የዋጐተ: ስ፳፯

ANUAKS MASSACRED IN GAMBELLA TOWN
AND OTHER PART OF THE REGION FROM
DECEMBER 13-15/2003,

እ፡ ኦኩሊኝ: ፍጓዉ
OKULLY NYEGWO

እ፡ ምሮኬሎ አኳይ
m/rokello AKWAY

እ፡ ኦቻላ ኢሳኾ
OCHALLA ISAKO

ጐ/ር ፬የሮ ኦኪዲ
OWAR-OKIDI

ETHIOPIA

Targeting the Anuak

Human Rights Violations and Crimes against Humanity
in Ethiopia's Gambella Region

HUMAN
RIGHTS
WATCH

crimes against humanity and continue to allow the authors of those crimes the enjoyment of near-total impunity.

In December 2003, military personnel joined civilian mobs in a rampage through indigenous Anuak neighborhoods in Gambella town, murdering as many as 424 Anuak civilians. In the months that followed, Ethiopian military forces subjected Anuak communities throughout the region to widespread and systematic acts of murder, rape, torture, arbitrary imprisonment and the destruction of entire villages. The immediate trigger for these abuses was a series of attacks in 2004 by Anuak civilians against civilians on other ethnic groups in the area.

A government-sponsored Commission of Inquiry set up to investigate the December 2003 violence in Gambella town resulted in a whitewash, and since then the government has refused even to investigate any of the abuses that have taken place throughout the region since early 2004. Reports of ongoing abuses continued to emerge from Gambella in 2005, albeit on a smaller scale than the violence in late 2003 and 2004.

Security forces frequently arrest civilians in other parts of Ethiopia, claiming they are members of the Oromo Liberation Front in Oromia state or the Ogaden National Liberation Front and Al-Itihad Al-Islamiya in Somali state. Few of those arrested are brought to trial. Some are released; others are kept in arbitrary detention for prolonged periods, often without a hearing or cause shown, sometimes incommunicado. Frequent reports of extrajudicial executions and torture emerge from Somali region, but access to the region has been restricted by the military to such a degree that these reports are impossible to confirm.

Restrictions on the Press

Many independent journalists, editors and publishers continue to endure harassment and intimidation, and criminal penalties for a range of speech-related penalties remain on the books. In June 2005, the Ministry of Information revoked the licenses of five Ethiopian journalists working for the

Voice of America and Radio Deutsche-Welle because it disapproved of their coverage of the elections and the post-election controversy.

Judicial Delay

The courts in Ethiopia often step in to order the release of government critics jailed on trumped-up charges of treason or armed insurrection. However, judicial action often occurs only after unreasonably long delays, both because of the courts' enormous workload and because of excessive judicial deference to bad faith police requests for additional time to produce evidence. In addition, courts have shown themselves far less likely to contest prolonged pretrial detention in high-profile cases that have the attention of high-level federal officials.

Fourteen years after the overthrow of the former military government (the Derg), several thousand of its former officials remain jailed awaiting trial, charged with genocide, crimes against humanity, and major felonies. Former dictator Mengistu Haile Mariam, on trial in absentia, remains a guest of the Mugabe government in Zimbabwe, with little chance of being held accountable for his abuses so long as he remains there.

Local Human Rights Defenders

Ethiopia has only one large, nationwide human rights organization, the Ethiopian Human Rights Council (EHRCO). Government officials routinely accuse the organization of working to advance an anti-government political agenda and its staff and ordinary members are often subjected to harassment and intimidation by local officials and members of the security forces. In June 2005, three EHRCO investigators were arrested and taken to military detention camps because of their efforts to document the human toll of the government's post-election crackdown. All three were subsequently released but were threatened with future criminal proceedings.

Another human rights organization, the Human Rights League, reopened its offices in March 2005 after winning a protracted court battle against government efforts to ban its operations. It remains to be seen whether the organization will be allowed to operate free of government interference.

Key International Actors

Ethiopia is considered an essential partner of the United States in its "war on terrorism," and Washington has generally been unwilling to apply meaningful pressure on the Ethiopian government over its human rights record. The U.S. suspects Islamic extremist groups are hiding in bordering areas of Somalia, and sometimes inside Ethiopia itself. The U.S. military, operating primarily out of a base in Djibouti, cooperates closely with the Ethiopian armed forces in counterterrorism efforts and capacity building work. The United States is also the largest donor of bilateral aid in Ethiopia.

Other Western donors have also been reluctant to criticize Ethiopia's human rights record and have in many respects actually embraced the Ethiopian government as something of a model for Africa. UK Prime Minister Tony Blair invited Ethiopian Prime Minister Meles Zenawi to play a leading role on Blair's Commission for Africa, which was charged with finding solutions to some of the continent's most intractable problems. There is no indication that donors' unusually robust criticism following the post-election crackdown in Addis Ababa will translate into a sustained willingness to be more vocal in demanding that the federal government respect human rights.

The United Nations Mission in Ethiopia and Eritrea (UNMEE) maintains approximately 3300 troops and military observers along the twenty-five kilometer-wide armistice buffer line between the two countries. In September 2005 the Security Council voted to extend UNMEE's mandate through March 2006, as tensions remain high between the two countries (see Eritrea chapter).

LIBERIA

The completion in October and November 2005 of presidential and parliamentary elections marked a major step towards the consolidation of Liberia's transition from a near-failed state rife with human rights abuses to a democratic state governed by the rule of law. The elections followed a 2003 peace agreement which ended three years of internal armed conflict and the deployment in 2003 of some fifteen thousand United Nations peacekeepers.

At year's end there were solid grounds for optimism including the disarmament of more than 101,000 combatants; the return home of tens of thousands of civilians who had fled during the war; the recognition by both Liberia and the international community of the role corruption played in fomenting armed conflict; and the ability of journalists and civil society to function after years of being silenced, persecuted and targeted. A Truth and Reconciliation Commission empowered to recommend prosecutions for the worst offenders was also established. However, the human rights situation remained precarious as a result of frequent criminal acts in the face of inadequate police and civil authorities; striking deficiencies within the judicial system; financial shortfalls for programs to train demobilized combatants; and continued regional instability, most notably in neighboring Côte d'Ivoire. Moreover, there was little progress on ensuring accountability for past atrocities.

Ongoing Insecurity and Related Abuses

During 2005, United Nations peacekeepers and civilian police consolidated their control throughout all major Liberian towns leading to significant improvements in protection for civilians. However, serious institutional deficiencies within the national police force and judicial system remain. The illegal occupation of rubber plantations by former rebel leaders who refused to recognize the legitimacy of the Liberian Transitional Government of Liberia (NTGL), rioting by ex-combatants mostly in response to delays in reintegration programs, as well as the emergence of vigilante groups formed to combat rising crime in the face of an incompetent police force were worrying developments in 2005. There are ongoing risks associated with the election or appointment into public office of individuals known to have committed human rights abuses in the past. A former faction leader, several individuals subject to United Nations sanctions for their engagement in activities aimed at undermining security in Liberia and the sub-region, and a few former high-level military commanders against whom there are credible allegations of responsibility for serious human rights abuses were elected into office in the 2005 elections. The abusive records of these persons raises concerns that they may in the future resort to force and other extra-legal measures to undermine the rule of law in Liberia. As well, unidentified individuals made verbal and, in some cases, physical threats against human rights defenders believed to be providing information to the Special Court for Sierra Leone. Throughout 2005, there were consistent reports of former president Charles Taylor interfering in Liberian political affairs and fomenting instability in the region.

Disarmament of Former Combatants and Re-recruitment into Regional Conflicts

From 2003-2005, more than 101,000 individuals were disarmed and demobilized. The disarmament exercise was criticized for not having strict admittance criteria and for letting in numerous individuals who were not real combatants, a factor which contributed to the shortfall of funds from international donors to support education or skills training programs. At years end, this shortfall left some 43,000 ex-combatants outside of the reintegration program. During 2005, the dearth of training and education programs, particularly along the border with neighboring Cote d'Ivoire, contributed to re-recruitment by the Ivorian government and rebel forces, of hundreds of ex-combatants, including children. According to interviews with Liberian fighters, the majority went to fight alongside militias associated with the Ivorian government. In 2005, two periods of intense recruitment occurred: at the beginning of March and September 2005, in anticipation of future attacks on Ivorian rebel-held positions.

WEST AFRICA

Youth, Poverty and Blood

The Lethal Legacy of West Africa's Regional Warriors

HUMAN
RIGHTS
WATCH

Rule of law

Liberia's history of armed conflict and human rights abuses reflect profound and deep-rooted weaknesses in institutions which should guarantee the rule of law. In 2003, the U.N. Security Council mandated the United Nations Mission in Liberia (UNMIL) to assist in the restructuring and training of the police, army and judiciary. 2005 saw some progress in the rehabilitation of these institutions. However, serious problems in reform of the Liberian police force, delays in demobilizing the former army, and lack of donor support to rebuild the decimated judicial infrastructure stalled progress in establishing the rule of law.

Liberian National Police

One feature of the restructuring of the Liberian police was a vetting procedure to screen out applicants alleged to have committed serious violations of human rights and international humanitarian law. The civilian component of UNMIL administered the vetting that took place in 2004 and 2005. The vetting process appears to have been disorganized, inefficient, and most likely ineffective in screening out human rights abusers. Problems with the process included the lack of clear criteria for the elimination of potential human rights abusers, the failure to allocate adequate human resources to conduct thorough and systematic background checks on applicants, and inadequate involvement of Liberian human rights groups and the general population in the process. Meanwhile, countrywide, the newly trained and vetted Liberian police continue to engage in unprofessional and at times criminal behavior including extortion.

The Liberian Army

The United States has the lead in recruiting and training a new Liberian army of some two thousand soldiers. In early 2005, the US contracted the project to a privately owned security company, DynCorp. The restructuring exercise is running months behind schedule and is set to begin in late 2005. Although DynCorp has a detailed plan to screen recruits for past human rights abuses, it remains to be seen whether this plan will be successfully implemented.

Judiciary

In 2003, UNMIL proposed an ambitious strategy to rebuild the justice system. In 2005, however, reforms progressed at an alarmingly slow pace. The judiciary remains severely dysfunctional: only half of 145 magistrate positions are staffed, and of these none holds a law degree. Only five of Liberia's fifteen circuit courts are operational. Of grave concern is that only 3% of all inmates in Liberia's prisons and holding cells are convicted felons. The 97% remaining are being held in pre-trial detention, often for extended periods of time.

Even when judicial authorities have been assigned to a courtroom, the dearth of prosecutors and public defenders undermines the quality of justice dispensed. Judges and other staff often fail to fulfill their duties, sometimes by neglecting to attend proceedings. Magistrate and local tribal courts often try, sentence, fine and imprison people for criminal and civil matters that are outside their jurisdiction. Frequent reports exist of judicial authorities releasing suspects charged with criminal offenses after having received a bribe, or soliciting money from them to stop the case from proceeding to a higher court. Prisons and detention centers continue to operate far below international standards with overcrowded cells and lack of food and water for detainees.

Truth and Reconciliation Commission

On June 10, 2005, an act establishing the Liberian Truth and Reconciliation Commission (TRC) was signed into law. The TRC is mandated to investigate gross human rights violations and economic crimes that occurred between January 1979 and October 14, 2003. It is empowered to recommend amnesty in cases not involving serious violations of international humanitarian law and to recommend prosecution for the most serious cases. The TRC was set to begin work in early 2006.

Accountability for Past Abuses

Neither the Liberian government nor the international community have developed a concrete strategy to bring perpetrators of serious war crimes and crimes against humanity committed during Liberia's armed conflicts to justice. However, throughout 2005 there was public debate on whether to prosecute these individuals: civil society leaders stressed the importance of perpetrators of gross violations facing justice for their crimes while Liberian transitional government officials and the international community maintained that prosecutions could undermine efforts to consolidate the peace. While the TRC is empowered to recommend prosecution for the most serious cases, there was no indication as to whether or not TRC commissioners would act on this power and, if they did, whether the Liberian judicial system would be able and willing to try these crimes.

Corruption

Corruption in the public and private sectors of Liberian society has long been endemic, and is widely recognized as having contributed to the country's political instability and ensuing armed conflicts. Throughout 2005, there were numerous scandals and allegations made against members of the NTGL including the manipulation of contract bidding, the looting of state coffers, and the misappropriation of development aid. The international community financed audits of the Central Bank and other state-owned enterprises and proposed a hard-hitting three-year anti-corruption plan—the Governance and Economic Management Assistance Programme (GEMAP)—which was approved by the NTGL in September 2005. The plan provides for foreign financial experts to be placed in and empowered to co-sign all financial and operational matters within the National Bank of Liberia, the Finance Ministry, and several other revenue generating agencies. It also calls for the establishment of an independent anti-corruption commission. However, the original proposal for using foreign judges to adjudicate cases was dropped.

Key International Actors

International actors, notably the United Nations and Economic Community of West African States (ECOWAS) were committed to full implementation of the 2003 Accra Peace Accords, which included the completion of elections in October 2005. ECOWAS took the lead inn resolving internal disputes within the NTGL. Throughout 2005, the international community's top priorities were ensuring that the election exercise was a success and putting in place mechanisms to fight corruption. However, other key rule of law issues, including the imperative to rebuild Liberia's fractured judicial system and the merits of pursuing justice for the past atrocities, received little attention.

Despite mounting international pressure, the Nigerian government, which offered former president Charles Taylor a safe haven in 2003, refused to hand him over to the Special Court for Sierra Leone, which indicted him for war crimes connected with his support for rebels in Sierra Leone. The United States continued to be the largest donor to both reconstruction efforts and the United Nations peacekeeping mission in Liberia. In June 2005, the U.N. Security Council voted to reapply the largely successful arms embargo and travel ban against individuals involved in previous attempts to destabilize the region, and to continue sanctions on the sale of diamonds and timber.

NIGERIA

Nigeria's most serious human rights problems remain unresolved. The government has largely failed to tackle the impunity that often attaches to serious human rights abuses, particularly abuses committed by the security forces and government officials. No one has yet been brought to justice for the massacre of hundreds of people by the military in Odi, Bayelsa state, in 1999, and in Benue state, in 2001, and members of the Nigerian police force are very rarely held accountable for widespread abuses including torture and murder. While the federal government has made some efforts to tackle corruption, it remains a pervasive problem even as the vast majority of Nigerians continue to live in extreme poverty. Widespread corruption leads directly to violations of social and economic rights and exacerbates other causes of violence and intercommunal tension.

In recent years, Nigeria has repeatedly been shaken by devastating outbreaks of intercommunal violence that are often fueled by government mismanagement and political manipulation. Many unresolved tensions are likely to be made even more explosive by intense political competition surrounding landmark presidential primaries in 2006 and general elections in 2007. Concerns exist that many politicians may resort to the same violent tactics in the upcoming elections that undermined the legitimacy of the last nationwide polls in 2003.

Intercommunal Violence

Intercommunal violence along ethnic, religious and other lines has claimed thousands of lives since the end of military rule in 1999. While 2005 saw no large-scale outbreaks of communal violence comparable to the worst incidents of recent years, smaller local-level clashes, for example in Kwara, Delta and Edo states, during which scores of people were believed to have died, occurred throughout 2005. Human Rights Watch estimates that between two thousand and three thousand people have been killed in outbreaks of intercommunal violence in Plateau State alone since 2001, including seven hundred people in 2004.

NIGERIA

Revenge in the Name
of Religion

The Cycle of Violence in Plateau and Kano States

H U M A N
R I G H T S
W A T C H

The continuing tensions underlying Nigeria's endemic intercommunal clashes— including conflicts over citizenship rights, environmental and population pressures, basic state failure to provide needed services, religious extremism, economic decline, corruption and cynical political manipulation of intercommunal divisions— are as complex as they are volatile. But Federal and State government officials in Nigeria have generally failed to heed warning signs that might allow them to prevent episodes of violence and have failed to respond effectively to violence when it occurs. Security forces are often notably absent when violence erupts, and widespread impunity for human rights violations contributes to the cycle of violence and emboldens perpetrators. For example, since the 2004 violence in Plateau and Kano, those responsible for instigating and planning the attacks appear to have escaped justice.

Conflict in the Niger Delta

The oil-rich Niger Delta in the south of the country remains the scene of recurring violence between members of different ethnic groups competing for political and economic power, and between militia and security forces sent to restore order in the area. Violence between ethnic militias often occurs within the context of clashes over control of the theft of crude oil. The violence is aggravated by the widespread availability of small arms, a problem which exists throughout Nigeria but is particularly acute in the Delta. Despite a robust military and police presence in the region, local communities remain vulnerable to attack by militias, criminal gangs, and the security forces themselves. Oil companies rarely speak out publicly about such abuses; indeed, some of their own practices have contributed to ongoing conflict in the region.

Federal policy towards conflict in the Delta has vacillated between heavy-handed attempts at imposing order and attempts to bring reconciliation. In September 2005 federal authorities arrested Niger Delta People's Volunteer Force (NDPVF) leader Asari on charges of treason; that same month, U.K. police arrested Bayelsa state Governor Diepreye Alamieyeseigha in London on charges of money laundering. This contrasted sharply with the government's response to violence in 2004, during which rival militias waged running battles that devastated villages around Port Harcourt in Rivers State. Alhaji Dokubo Asari's NDPVF staged a brazen attack on neighborhoods controlled by a rival militia in Port Harcourt itself. At the time, Nigerian President Olusegun Obasanjo responded by calling those two rival militia leaders to Abuja in September 2004, where he brokered a ceasefire.

The two arrests in 2005 led to a sharp rise in tensions throughout the Niger Delta, largely because both men claim to be standard-bearers for the cause of self-determination and resource control for the Delta's ethnic Ijaw population. Ijaw militants briefly seized control of a Chevron flow station in response to Asari's arrest and threatened future violence unless Asari is released. That reaction underscored how little the government has done to address the underlying causes of violence in the region. Most glaringly, the end of military rule in 1999 has not led to effective efforts to deliver material benefits or basic security to impoverished Delta communities living atop the country's vast oil reserves.

Abuses by Police

During 2005, as in years before, torture, ill-treatment, extra-judicial killings, arbitrary arrest and detention and extortion by the police, often perpetrated by or with the knowledge of senior police, remained widespread and routine. Impunity from prosecution remains the biggest single obstacle to combating this problem. In June 2005 six people were killed at a police checkpoint in Abuja. In response to a nationwide outcry over the killings, federal authorities took the highly unusual step of bringing five police officers to trial on charges of homicide. According to statistics provided by the Nigerian police, several thousand "armed robbery" suspects have been killed by the Nigerian police in recent years. The police have also killed scores of people in custody or in the course of routine duties such as traffic control. There is no independent mechanism to ensure that abuses by the police are addressed or even properly investigated. Since the end of military rule there have been no successful prosecutions against Nigerian police officers alleged to have committed torture.

NIGERIA

"Rest in Pieces"

Police Torture and Deaths in Custody in Nigeria

HUMAN
RIGHTS
WATCH

In August 2005, President Obasanjo publicly acknowledged that Nigerian police officers have committed murder and torture. It remains to be seen whether this statement will be followed up with a serious push for badly needed reforms.

Human Rights Concerns in the Context of Shari'a

Since 2000, Shari'a (Islamic law) has been extended to give Shari'a courts jurisdiction over criminal cases in twelve of Nigeria's thirty-six states. In Katsina state two men were put on trial in Shari'a court on charges of sodomy in 2005; if convicted they could be sentenced to death by stoning. Shari'a has provisions for sentences that amount to cruel, inhuman and degrading treatment, including death sentences, amputations and floggings. No executions or amputations have taken place since early 2002 and capital sentences have generally been thrown out on appeal, but Shari'a courts continue to hand down death sentences.

Many trials in Shari'a courts fail to conform to international standards and do not respect due process even as defined by Shari'a legislation; defendants rarely have access to a lawyer, are not informed about their rights, and judges are often poorly trained. The manner in which Shari'a is applied discriminates against women, particularly in adultery cases where standards of evidence differ based on the sex of the accused.

Freedom of Expression and Attacks on Civil Society

Despite significant gains in civil liberties since the end of military rule, several restrictions on freedom of expression remain. Throughout 2005 Federal Police and State Security Service (SSS) forces continued to harass and occasionally detain publishers, editors and journalists in 2005. In at least two such cases in 2005, security forces raided newspaper offices in response to articles that accused politically prominent individuals, including the wife of President Olusegun Obasanjo, of corruption.

There have also been numerous cases of arrests, detention, ill-treatment, intimidation and harassment of critics and opponents of the government.

Security forces have harassed and intimidated civil society activists from the Niger Delta and members of the Movement for the Actualization of the Sovereign State of Biafra (MASSOB), an Igbo self-determination group, in several different incidents throughout 2005.

Indicted War Criminal Charles Taylor and his Exile in Nigeria

In another example of Nigeria's failure to tackle impunity, former Liberian President Charles Taylor, indicted by the Special Court for Sierra Leone for war crimes, crimes against humanity and other serious violations of international humanitarian law, was granted asylum in Nigeria in 2003 and continues to live in exile in Calabar, Nigeria. Despite mounting international pressure from African countries, the United Nations, the European Union and the United Sates, and a wide array of international African civil society groups, Nigeria continues to refuse to surrender him to the court.

Key International Actors

Under President Obasanjo, Nigeria continues to enjoy a generally positive image in the eyes of foreign governments. The country has enhanced its regional and international significance through the leading role played by Obasanjo in the African Union, his efforts to broker peace in the Darfur region of Sudan and his role in calming tension during the February 2005 political crisis in Togo. This, combined with Nigeria's economic significance as a major oil producer, creates an unwillingness on the part of key governments, notably the United Kingdom and the United States, and intergovernmental organizations such as the African Union and the Commonwealth, to publicly criticize Nigeria's human rights record, despite abundant evidence of serious human rights problems and little action on the part of the government to address them.

RWANDA

In 2005 Rwanda expanded its system of people's courts (gacaca jurisdictions) from one tenth of the territory to the whole country. Established to try crimes from the period of the 1994 genocide, the jurisdictions were supposed to draw their legitimacy from popular participation, but many Rwandans did not trust them and boycotted the sessions. Some judges ignored gacaca rules by jailing hundreds of persons in preventive detention or for false or incomplete testimony. Since few appellate gacaca courts exist yet, most of those jailed have no recourse. As the jurisdictions started pre-trial inquiries throughout Rwanda, some 10,000 Rwandans fled to surrounding countries, many saying they feared false accusations and unfair trials.

Throughout 2005, authorities pursued the elusive goal of national unity, continuing earlier campaigns against "divisionism" and "genocidal ideology." On occasion they equated "genocidal ideology" with dissent from government policies or with opposition to the Rwandan Patriotic Front (RPF), the dominant party in the government.

In September 2005 the government published a law on land tenure, the result of several years of debate. Although guaranteeing Rwandans (and foreign investors) the right to own land, the law also grants government far-reaching powers over land use, potentially subjecting owners to loss of land without compensation.

Gacaca Jurisdictions

Meant to combine customary practices of conflict resolution with punitive justice, gacaca jurisdictions began on a pilot basis in 2002. Many jurisdictions failed to win public trust for various reasons: hundreds of judges were themselves accused of crimes; some witnesses refused to speak or to speak truthfully; and the jurisdictions were prohibited from examining crimes by RPF soldiers, leading to perceptions that they delivered one-sided justice. Authorities reformed the jurisdictions in 2004, simplifying the structure and reducing the number of judges on each panel, but these changes had barely been implemented when officials announced plans for further reforms in

September 2005. Pilot jurisdictions have tried fewer than three thousand cases. Trials have yet to begin in most of the country and will be further delayed by the proposed reforms. In 2005 authorities said that an estimated 761,000 persons (just under one half of the adult Hutu male population at the time of the genocide) would be accused of crimes. Officials aim to complete trials by 2007, an unrealizable goal at the current rate of proceedings. The reforms put the system under closer administrative control; e.g., instead of the popular assembly drawing up lists of accused persons, administrative agents now do so. Local officials are permitted to fine and otherwise sanction citizens who do not attend required sessions.

In September 2005, the national prosecutor's office arrested Guy Theunis, a priest, journalist, and human rights activist, and submitted the case it had prepared against him to a gacaca jurisdiction. As in many gacaca cases throughout the country, evidence was insubstantial, yet judges decided Theunis, a Belgian citizen, should be tried for inciting genocide and sent him back to prison. Belgium asked that the case be transferred to Belgian hands. He was returned to Belgium in late November 2005 for possible prosecution.

In July authorities provisionally released nearly twenty thousand detainees who had confessed to genocide or who were elderly, ill, or who had been minors in 1994. This brought to nearly forty-five thousand the number released since 2003, all of whom will supposedly stand trial. Genocide survivors, who feared new attacks or attempts to impede justice by those released, protested the decision.

In September some 750 persons convicted of genocide began performing community service labor as part of the sentence to be served for their crimes. For administrative convenience, all were brought to work in one place, contravening the original intent—to compensate for damage done in locations where the crimes had been committed—of the labor service program.

Most of the 10,000 Rwandans who fled in 2005 crossed into Burundi, where they were initially welcomed. But later, Burundian authorities cooperated with Rwandan officials to return them to Rwanda against their will. Widely criticized by international partners for violating international refugee conventions, Burundian authorities nonetheless decided in October to send back three thousand other Rwandans still in Burundi.

Other Judicial Issues

In a landmark decision in May 2005, the High Court issued a writ of habeas corpus for the first time. When authorities failed to produce the person named in the order, the court held a minister, the national prosecutor, and national police commissioner in contempt, but vitiated the decision by concluding that the court had no authority to impose penalties on the officials. Authorities continued to detain persons without charge in violation of Rwandan law, including Col. Patrick Karegeya, an officer once close to President Paul Kagame, who was held for five months. In March an appeals court affirmed the conviction of newspaper editor Charles Kabonero for defaming an official and increased his penalty to a one-year suspended jail term and a hefty fine. It failed to affirm a promising lower court ruling limiting "divisionism" to certain forms of public action, thus missing the opportunity to restrict future use of this vague charge against others. In May the High Court found opposition politician Leonard Kavutse guilty of inciting "divisionism" and sentenced him to two years in jail. It ignored Kavutse's claim that he had confessed after being tortured, and excused authorities who had detained him illegally. In late October the Supreme Court began hearing an appeal in the cases of former President Pasteur Bizimungu and seven others, convicted of inciting violence and other charges in trials marked by insubstantial evidence and many due process violations.

Divisionism and "Genocidal Ideology"

Following 2003 and 2004 parliamentary reports attacking political opponents of the RPF and several nongovernmental organizations (NGOs) for "divisionism" and "genocidal ideology," the Senate in 2005 commissioned a study, as yet unpublished, to identify such ideas among international NGOs and scholars. Officials interrogated and intimidated two former presidential candidates after radio broadcasts in which they voiced doubts about gacaca. As high-level officials focused on "genocidal ideology" in speeches and ceremonies, Rwandan and international NGOs tailored their activities to avoid confrontation with authorities. Human rights organizations, particularly hard hit by 2004 attacks, avoided taking stands likely to draw official ire. Authorities refused official recognition to the Community of Indigenous Peoples in Rwanda (CAURWA), which defends the rights of the Batwa minority (some 30,000 people), saying its ethnic focus violated the constitution. Officials interrogated and detained journalists who criticized the government and seized one issue of a newspaper, refusing to allow its distribution.

New Land Law

The long-awaited land law issued in 2005 is meant to transform a jumble of small, fragmented, and minimally productive plots into a more prosperous system of larger holdings producing for global, as well as for local, markets. National authorities are to determine how land holdings will be regrouped, which crops will be grown, and which animals will be raised. Farmers who fail to follow the national plan may see their land "requisitioned," with no compensation, and their land would be given to others. Such centralized control of land use, characteristic of some colonial and post-colonial regimes, marks a radical departure for Rwanda.

The law legitimates "land sharing" which requires land owners to give a part of their land without compensation to others designated by authorities. Some farmers who resisted the policy when it was begun in the 1990s were punished by fines or jail sentences; the policy remains the source of many disputes. The law also affirms the policy of obligatory grouped residence under which persons living in dispersed homesteads must move to government-established "villages" (*imidugudu*). When implemented on a large-scale in the late 1990s, authorities in some cases used force, fines, and prison terms to make Rwandans relocate. At least two imidugudu were created in northwestern Rwanda in 2005, leading to land loss for local farmers. The law claims to accept the validity of customary rights to land, but rejects the customary use of marshlands by the poor and abolishes important rights of prosperous landlords (*abakonde*) in the northwest, the home region of the previous regime.

Key International Actors

In late 2004 the United Kingdom and Sweden suspended aid to discourage Rwandan interference in the Democratic Republic of Congo but took no similarly strong stands on human rights issues. Although the United States criticized shrinking political space at the end of 2004, other donors rarely voiced public agreement with this assessment. In 2005, some donors funded civil society programs meant to promote human rights but failed to provide corresponding political support.

Generally applauded for its economic growth (with little recognition of the dramatically widening gap between rich and poor), Rwanda reached the completion point for Heavily Indebted Poor Countries, as designated by the World Bank and International Monetary Fund, and was rewarded with $1.4 billion dollars in multilateral debt relief, followed shortly after by forgiveness of some $90 million owed to the Paris Club nations.

Rwanda, one of the first countries to undergo assessment by the peer review mechanism of the New Partnership for African Development (NEPAD), received a generally favorable report but was criticized for refusing recognition to CAURWA, mentioned above. In response, Rwanda agreed to discussions with CAURWA, but with no result by late in the year. Increasingly important in Africa-wide politics, Rwanda provided troops for the African Union peacekeeping force in the Sudan.

SIERRA LEONE

While the end of Sierra Leone's brutal armed conflict in 2002 brought an end to the gross violations of human rights that characterized the eleven-year armed conflict, there is growing recognition by the international community and Sierra Leonean civil society that the government has done little to address the issues that gave rise to the conflict—endemic corruption, weak rule of law, and the inequitable distribution of the country's vast natural resources. The government's refusal to do more to address crushing poverty in the face of high unemployment among young adults and continuing insecurity within the sub-region renders Sierra Leone vulnerable to future instability. 2005 also saw a rise in attacks against the Sierra Leonean press.

Persistent inadequacies in the police and judiciary continue to undermine improvements in implementing the rule of law in Sierra Leone. However, through the efforts of the United Nations-mandated Special Court for Sierra Leone, significant progress continues to be made in achieving accountability for war crimes committed during the war. Meanwhile, the government was resistant to implementing key recommendations made by Sierra Leone's Truth and Reconciliation Commission and has yet to appoint commissioners to the National Human Rights Commission, established by parliament in 2004.

In anticipation of the complete withdrawal of U.N. peacekeepers set for December 2005, and in recognition of Sierra Leone's continued institutional weaknesses within the security, judicial and governance sectors, the U.N. Security Council in August 2005 approved the establishment of a peacebuilding mission to be called the U.N. Integrated Office for Sierra Leone (UNIOSL). The mission's mandate will begin in January 2006 following the complete withdrawal of the once-17,000-strong peacekeeping mission. The priorities of UNIOSL will focus on fighting corruption, improving transparency, establishing the rule of law and assisting in preparations for the 2007 general elections.

SIERRA LEONE

Justice in Motion

The Trial Phase of the Special Court for Sierra Leone

HUMAN
RIGHTS
WATCH

Accountability for Past Abuses

Throughout 2005, the Special Court for Sierra Leone (SCSL), established in 2002 to bring justice for victims of atrocities committed during the war, continued to make progress. The appointment of judges in January 2005 to the second trial chamber enhanced the court's overall efficiency, and at year's end, three trials of nine accused from all three warring factions were proceeding simultaneously The court also uses innovative practices to promote fair trial rights to protect witnesses who testify and to make the court accessible to Sierra Leoneans. Some concerns remain about the court's performance, including instances of disclosure of identifying information about protected witnesses, delays in rendering decisions on motions, and few initiatives designed to have impact with the national judicial system.

Despite mounting international pressure from African countries, the United Nations, the European Union and the United States, Nigeria continues to resist surrendering Charles Taylor to the Special Court, which in 2003 indicted him on seventeen counts of war crimes. Initially dependent on voluntary financial contributions, the Special Court has also struggled to operate effectively in an uncertain funding environment. Despite voluntary contributions by government and a subvention grant provided by the UN General Assembly, the Special Court does not have adequate funds to complete its work nor carry out critical activities such as ensuring longer-term protection for witnesses. The court is currently seeking $25 million to cover operations for 2006. International donors have so far pledged only approximately $10 million.

The Truth and Reconciliation Commission

In mid-2005, the report of the Truth and Reconciliation Commission (TRC) was finally released to the public. The report contains several significant findings and recommendations. It notes that decades of corrupt rule by Sierra Leone's political elite largely created the conditions which led to the civil war. The recommendations include judicial reforms, measures to increase the transparency of the mining industry, steps to improve good governance and accountability, and the abolition of the death penalty.

In June 2005, months after promising to respond to the TRC report, the government of Sierra Leone published its proposals for the implementation of the report's recommendations. However, the Government's "white paper" was widely criticized by civil society groups as being vague and noncommittal. Concretely, they said it failed to establish a timeline for implementing measures like reparations for war victims, was largely devoid of concrete steps to improve governance or address corruption, and in some cases rejected recommendations, such as the abolition of the death penalty.

Attacks against Journalists and Members of Civil Society

In 2005, several attacks were reported against Sierra Leonean journalists. In May 2005 Harry Yansaneh, acting editor of the independent daily *For Di People*, was severely beaten by individuals allegedly acting on the orders of ruling party parliamentarian Fatmata Hassan Komeh. Yansaneh died two months later as a result of his injuries. After widespread condemnation by Sierra Leonean civil society and the international community, an inquest was launched and several people, including Komeh and two others were arrested and charged with manslaughter. In May 2005, two journalists from the private weekly *The Trumpet* were detained and charged with "seditious libel," and, in September 2005, the Deputy Editor of the *Awareness Times* was attacked by members of an opposition political party.

Corruption

Corruption within both the public and private sectors in Sierra Leone remains widespread and continues to rob the public of funds needed to provide vital services such as education, water, and healthcare. As in previous years, 2005 saw few convictions for corruption-related offenses. In 2000, largely under pressure from international donors, the Anti-Corruption Commission (ACC) was established to investigate charges of corruption. However, since the power to refer cases for prosecution rests with the attorney general who is appointed by the president, the ACC has been subject to political manipulation: in practice, only cases involving lower level officials are referred for prosecution. Efforts to correct this weakness were boosted in

2005 when the power to recommend prosecution was expanded to include two foreign prosecutors. It is hoped that this, together with the three judges from Commonwealth countries who have since 2003 been attached to the Sierra Leone High Court to hear corruption related cases, will contribute to the independence of the ACC.

Efforts to Establish the Rule of Law

Despite considerable international donor aid intended to improve the judiciary, striking deficiencies remained evident throughout 2005. These included extortion and bribe taking by court officials; insufficient numbers of judges, magistrates and prosecuting attorneys; inadequate remuneration for judiciary personnel; and extended periods of pre-trial detention and sub-standard conditions within detention centers. The system of local courts presided over by traditional leaders or their officials and applying customary law, which is often discriminatory particularly against women, is the only form of legal system accessible to an estimated 70 percent of the population. Local court officials frequently abuse their powers by illegally detaining persons and charging high fines for minor offenses, as well as by adjudicating criminal cases beyond their jurisdiction. At years end, there were ten men on death row following a December 2004 conviction for treason in connection with a 2003 coup attempt; however, no executions were carried out.

Sierra Leone Army and Police

The Sierra Leone Army and police have over the years been the source of considerable instability, corruption, and human rights violations and have enjoyed near-complete immunity from prosecution. During 2005, the police continued to exhibit unprofessional and at times illegal behaviour. This included widespread extortion from civilians, including the mounting of checkpoints to obtain money from passing vehicles and the arbitrary arrest and detention of suspects. The police were widely criticized for initially failing to take action in response to the beating of the journalist Yansaneh. The Commonwealth Police Development Task Force (CPDTF) has, since 1998, been responsible for restructuring and retraining the police and maintains that low salaries and inadequate resources remain key challenges.

Efforts by the British-led International Military Advisory and Training Team (IMATT), which since 1999 has worked to reform, restructure, and rehabilitate the Republic of Sierra Leone Armed Forces (RSLAF), have led to considerable improvements in the professionalism and accountability within the force. However, shortages of equipment, fuel, and communications equipment continue to undermine their operations. In 2005, there were a few reports of abuses, extortion, and indiscipline by the army, and the RSLAF leadership demonstrated some commitment to discipline and sanction soldiers for offenses committed.

Trafficking in Persons

The trafficking of persons, particularly women and children, was a growing problem in 2005. In response, the Parliament passed legislation criminalizing the practice, and the government conducted some investigations into and closure of suspected venues employing trafficked individuals. Numerous children are trafficked from the provinces to work in diamond mines, as commercial sex workers, and in street labor, in both Sierra Leone and neighboring countries.

Key International Actors

In spite of providing billions of dollars in assistance to Sierra Leone since the end of the armed conflict in 2002, international donors have been largely reluctant to criticize the ongoing problems of corruption and bad governance, which both undermine Sierra Leone's recovery and make it vulnerable to future instability. They have also been unwilling to leverage Sierra Leone's dependency on aid to pressure the government to address corruption and governance issues.

The United Kingdom has for the last several years spent some U.S. $60 million per year on rebuilding and restructuring the army, police, and judiciary. The United States in 2005 spent some U.S.$9 million on reconstruction, military education, training and other types of development aid, including on improving the control and management of the diamond sector.

SUB-SAHARAN AFRICA

Letting Them Fail

Government Neglect and the Right to Education
for Children Affected by AIDS

HUMAN
RIGHTS
WATCH

SOUTH AFRICA

As South Africa enters its eleventh year of democracy, its challenge lies in implementing policies in line with the country's far-reaching and progressive constitution. Areas of particular concern relate to the rights of detained and accused persons, excessive use of force by police, the rights of refugees and asylum seekers, and access to education on commercial farms.

Police

The decrease in 2005 in the number of deaths in police custody and as a result of police action is welcome. Reforms in policing particularly in the conduct of arrests and detention had a positive effect. By April 2005, 652 deaths involving law enforcement had been reported—down from 714 by March 2004. Of these 652 cases, 286 occurred in police custody and included deaths by suicide, natural causes, and injuries sustained prior to detention. The remaining 366 deaths were the result of law enforcement action, including fatalities incurred in the course of arrests, beatings in detention, and shooting of innocent bystanders.

Of concern is a gradual increase in the number of cases of inappropriate use of force by the police—a matter that has been raised and investigated by the Independent Complaints Directorate (ICD), an independent oversight body. Increasingly, police have been involved in violent confrontations with communities protesting against a lack of services. In May, police used rubber bullets to control residents of an informal settlement of Happy Valley, Kommetjie who were protesting against tardy delivery of housing and basic services. On September 21, in a protest against the local municipalities' slow response to a typhoid outbreak in Botleng, Delmas, the police used rubber bullets against protestors, injuring at least six people. On July 12, police used teargas and rubber bullets to disperse a peaceful demonstration to protest against the lack of progress in the dispensing of antiretroviral medication for the treatment of HIV/AIDS in Queenstown, Eastern Cape.

In June, the ICD completed its investigation into the death of a seventeen-year-old boy following the firing of rubber bullets on peaceful protestors of eNtabazwe—a township previously designated for Africans—outside Harrismith on August 30, 2004. It recommended that the state should prosecute the police officers who fired at the protesters. These officers are due to stand trial on February 6, 2006. The ICD urged that police officers should not use lethal ammunition such as birdshot and buckshot to manage protestors. The United Nations Basic Principles on the Use of Force and Firearms by Law Enforcement Officials provides that police shall, as far as possible, use nonviolent means before resorting to the use of force and firearms. Whenever the lawful use of force and firearms is unavoidable, police must exercise restraint in such use and act in proportion to the seriousness of the offense and the legitimate objective to be achieved, and also minimize damage and injury.

Prisons

The entry into force of sections addressing the treatment of prisoners in the Correctional Services Act 111 of 1998 on July 31, 2004 provides a framework to safeguard the human rights of prisoners. Overcrowding in South Africa's prisons remains high. As of September 30, 2005, 155,770 prisoners were being held in facilities that should accommodate 113,825. The number of sentenced prisoners decreased from 133, 764 in March 31, 2004 to 110, 971 in September. The number of pre-trial prisoners dropped from 52, 326 as of January 31, to 44, 799 in September 31, 2005. This marginal drop from the previous year is due, in part, to the early release of 31, 865 qualifying prisoners between May and August. Despite these steps, overcrowding continues to threaten the health and living conditions of prisoners and impedes rehabilitation efforts. Sexual assaults and gang violence are a further threat to the safety of prisoners. The Inspecting Judge of Prisons—an independent oversight body—has raised concerns at the high prison population, and has recommended the early release of prisoners who are too poor to afford bail in order to reduce the number of inmates. As of March 31, 2005, 13,880 detained prisoners—about a third of the pre-trial population—could not afford bail.

Following, in part, a constitutional court order requiring the substitution of the death sentence in May 2005, sixty-three inmates were no longer imprisoned under the death sentence. As of September 30, forty three prisoners were awaiting the substitution of their sentences.

Children in Detention

Juveniles continue to be incarcerated while awaiting trial despite international legal requirements that child offenders not be detained except as a last resort. Notably, however, the number of children awaiting trial in detention has dropped significantly from between two to three thousand in March 2004 to 1227 as of September 30, 2005. The total number of children in detention is 2314. International standards stipulate that juveniles should be held in separate quarters from adults; however, this is not always the case in South Africa. Children in detention are reportedly victims of sexual abuse, violence, and gang related activities. The Child Justice Bill, deliberated in the South African Parliament 2005, proposes a restorative justice approach in an attempt to move children out of the criminal justice system. The bill establishes one-stop child justice centers.

Rights of Refugees and Asylum Seekers

Since the inception of the 1998 Refugees Act, which formally protects the rights of asylum seekers and refugees in line with international law, South Africa has witnessed a steady increase in the number of asylum seekers. In 2003 the asylum seeker and refugee population was 110, 643. By the end of 2004, this number had increased to 142,907. 32, 600 new asylum applications were lodged with the Department of Home Affairs in 2004. The implementation of the Refugees Act remains problematic. Delays in the refugee status determination process, inconsistency in application of a court decision allowing for the right to work and study for asylum seekers;, corrupt practices and inadequate procedures for unaccompanied minors seeking asylum render protections for asylum seekers inadequate. The number of applications for asylum pending at the end of 2004 was 115,220, while only 27,683 applications had been granted refugee status. These administrative difficulties can present a risk of unlawful arrest and possible deportation for asylum seekers. South Africa deported a total of 167,137 foreign nationals in 2004. Between

January and September 30, South Africa deported 156, 893. The majority of the deportees are from Southern Africa.

Violence against Women and Children

Violence against women and children is widely recognized as a serious concern in South Africa: 55,114 rapes and attempted rapes were reported to the South African police between April 2004 and March 2005 (though the real number is almost certainly significantly higher.) This is an increase from the previous year over a similar period. The South African Parliament considered the Sexual Offenses Bill to remove anomalies from the existing law by broadening the definition of rape and focusing on the victim rather than the perpetrator with respect to violence against women in 2005. Police and the court officials continue to receive training in handling cases of violence against women and children. The government established fifty-two sexual offenses courts to adjudicate and focus specifically on cases related to gender violence by end 2004.

Social and Economic Rights

South Africa has a number of good policies intended to safeguard social and economic rights. However, the government continues to face challenges in a number of areas including land reform, provision of services such as health care and education in rural areas, and broadly finding a solution to poverty (between 40 and 50 percent of the population can be considered poor). 2005 saw several demonstrations against poor delivery of services in impoverished communities in the Western Cape, Free State, Eastern Cape and Gauteng provinces.

People living in rural areas continue to face difficulties in accessing their rights to health care and social services. For example, although access to public schooling for children is widely available and enrollment continues to increase, conditions of schools in poor areas remain inadequate. Insecure buildings, lack of water, and unhygienic sanitation facilities are some of the conditions pupils face. Physical access to education in rural areas remains difficult for a number of rural learners. Walking distances can reach thirty kilometers each day to and from school, exposing learners to dangers such as sexual violence and contributing to high dropout rates. With respect to public schools on farms, there has been marginal progress in concluding contractual agreements between government and farm owners. These contracts delineate the roles and responsibilities of each party in providing education. Since 1997, when legislation was enacted providing for these contracts, only approximately half these schools have such contractual agreements. The lack of contracts hinders children's abilities to receive a quality education. A government ministerial committee on rural education released a report in May that makes a number of key recommendations to improve schooling in rural areas. The national Department of Education indicated that it was preparing a policy document on the recommendations. The South African Human Rights Commission—an independent statutory body—conducted public hearings on the right to a basic education in October 2005.

Key International Actors

In the promotion of human rights, democracy and peace, South Africa continues to play a key role in Africa under the auspices of the African Union. South Africa has provided troops in peace support operations, supported post-conflict reconstruction and led mediation efforts in the Democratic Republic of Congo, Burundi, Darfur, western Sudan and Côte d'Ivoire respectively.

The South African government began a national consultative process of the African Peer Review Mechanism (APRM)—a self-monitoring, voluntary mechanism—as agreed to by the African Union and Government Implementation Committee of the New Partnership for Africa's Development to review the country's practice of democracy, governance and social and economic development in September. The APRM country review team will consider this report when it visits South Africa in 2006.

SUDAN

The January 9, 2005 Comprehensive Peace Agreement ending the twenty-one-year civil war between the Sudanese government and southern rebels has brought little significant improvement to Sudan in the area of human rights. Implementation of the agreement was delayed by several factors, including the sudden death of southern rebel leader Dr. John Garang. As part of the agreement, the Sudanese government lifted the state of emergency though-out Sudan (with the exception of Darfur and the east) but attacks on villages in Darfur continued, and killings, rape, torture, looting of civilian livestock and other property took place on a regular basis. Arbitrary arrests and detentions, executions without fair trials, and harassment of human rights defenders and other activists remained a feature of Sudanese policy in both Darfur and other areas of Sudan. For the first time, however, the U.N. Security Council made use of its power to refer the situation of Darfur to the International Criminal Court (ICC) in March 2005. .

The Crisis in Darfur

In 2005, indiscriminate and targeted killings, rape, forced displacement, and looting of civilians of the same ethnicity as the rebel groups in Darfur continued to occur at the hands of government-backed militias or "Janjaweed" although on a lesser scale than in 2003-2004. An upsurge of attacks occurred in September and October 2005, including targeted attacks on international aid workers and members of the African Union Mission in Sudan (AMIS), tasked to monitor the April 2004 ceasefire agreement and protect civilians under imminent threat. Government-supported militias also attacked civilian villages and an internally displaced persons camp in Aro Sharow, West Darfur.

This violence contributed to the inability of the two million internally displaced people, living precariously in camps, to return home. Subject to attack when leaving the camps, displaced person remained confined in them, dependent on international humanitarian aid. Women and girls particularly

Sudan

Entrenching Impunity

Government Responsibility for International
Crimes in Darfur

HUMAN
RIGHTS
WATCH

were victims of sexual attacks in any remote area when going for water, fire-
wood or fodder, or to take their wares to market.

Sudanese government policy towards the displaced communities continued to
be marked by suspicion and abusive policies such as frequent arbitrary
arrests, detentions of displaced leaders on an ethnic basis and increasing
harassment and intimidation of humanitarian aid agencies assisting the displaced persons. In some areas, women who complained about rape to the
police were humiliated and threatened; some unmarried women and girls
were accused of adultery solely on the basis of their unwanted pregnancy and
unwed status.

The Sudanese government took no concrete steps to implement a 2004
Security Council resolution demand to disarm and disband its allies, the
Janjaweed. Government militia allies, to whose abuses civil servants turned a
blind eye, and army troops committed abuses with impunity, encouraging
further lawlessness. In June 2005, the Sudanese government set up a tribunal,
the "Special Criminial Court on Events in Darfur," purportedly to try individuals guilty of abuses. However, as of October 2005, of six cases tried by
the new tribunal, none concerned major crimes associated with the conflict.
No medium or high-level government officials or militia leaders were suspended from duty, investigated, or prosecuted for serious crimes in Darfur.

The two main rebel movements—the Sudan Liberation Army (SLA) and the
Justice and Equality Movement—were responsible for numerous abuses,
including attacks on civilians, commercial vehicles and aid workers, abductions of civilians, looting of livestock and the use of child soldiers. A splinter
faction of the JEM captured more than thirty ceasefire monitors from the
African Union Mission in Sudan in October then released them after a few
days.

As the year wore on, the rebel movements were increasingly plagued by
internal splits, partly on an ethnic basis, and with increasing fragmentation.
Reports of abuses by certain rebel factions grew, particularly by those factions
controlling the Jebel Marra region.

Southern Sudan

A long-awaited peace agreement, the result of almost three years of negotiations, was signed between the Sudanese government and the southern-based Sudan People's Liberation Movement (SPLM) on January 9, 2005, allowing autonomy for the southern region for six and a half years, followed by a referendum on self-determination for the south. The agreement also provided for elections at national, regional, state and local levels after four years. It also provided that half the government revenues of oil produced in southern Sudan be allocated to the southern regional government.

The north-south peace agreement, however, had major human rights defects, including the absence of any mechanism to ensure accountability for abuses committed during the twenty-one year war waged mostly in southern Sudan.

John Garang's death in a helicopter accident on July 30 provoked a massive response among southerners in Khartoum, Malakal, and Juba. Khartoum saw the worst of the communal violence that followed: three days of ethnically-motivated attacks by southerners and northerners resulted in more than 130 deaths and more than 800 wounded. The Sudanese government reportedly arrested more than 1,500 people, most of whom were almost immediately released.

While it is too early to judge his potential for bringing democratic changes to the southern Sudan, Garang's successor and long-time deputy, Gen. Salva Kiir, had been a low-profile leader within the Sudan People's Liberation Army (SPLA) for reforms to promote accountability within the movement. One early indication is favorable: Gen. Salva Kiir instructed that the selection process for legislators to both the regional and national assemblies be opened up to public participation, as there was no time to organize elections. Southerners rushed to take part. While many obstacles exist to the creation of a southern government that is transparent and accountable and enforces human rights, this early willingness to let people choose their representatives is a good sign. They already enjoy more human rights than do their northern fellow citizens, in that the presence of security forces in the southern garrison towns is lessened and there has been more free speech, free press and free assembly in the south than for decades. The national army, however, has not withdrawn from the south but under the peace agreement it has about two years to complete this process.

Attacks on Human Rights Defenders

Human rights defenders and other activists remained under serious threat of arbitrary arrest and detention in 2005. A prominent human rights defender based in Khartoum, Dr. Mudawi Ibrahim Adam, the chairperson of the Sudan Social Development Organization (SUDO), was arrested twice—in January and May 2005—and charged with "crimes against the state." Articles 51, 52, 53, and 58 of the Sudanese Criminal Code, which include "crimes against the state" and espionage, were often used used to intimidate individuals speaking out about abuses, including international humanitarian aid workers working in Darfur. More than twenty international or national aid workers were arbitrarily arrested, detained, or threatened by Sudanese police and security forces in Darfur in the first six months of the year alone.

Key International Actors

Throughout 2005, international policy towards Sudan vacillated between condemnation and appeasement. This reflected the varying interests at stake, such as the implementation of the north-southern peace agreement, ending the atrocities in Darfur, and even regional counterterrorism efforts. The U.S. government was a prime example of this policy schizophrenia. U.S. officials vociferously condemn the continuing attacks, but the U.S. Central Intelligence Agency invited Sudanese security chief Salah Ghosh, a likely indictee before the ICC for war crimes committed in Darfur, to Washington in April 2005 to discuss Sudanese-U.S. counterterrorism interests.

Divided interests regarding Sudan were prevalent not just bilaterally among western governments, but also within the United Nations Security Council. The single most important achievement of the Security Council was the historic referral of Darfur to the ICC on March 31, 2005. In June the ICC announced that it would investigate the crimes in Darfur. In a second March 2005 resolution, the Security Council established a sanctions committee to identify individuals who violated an arms embargo on Darfur and who committed abuses; the sanctions would not apply retroactively. Despite the continuing abuses in Darfur throughout 2005, however, the Security Council was prevented from enacting stiffer sanctions due to resistance from China and Russia, two of its five permanent members. In November Sudanese authorities roughed up two visiting members of the sanctions committees' panel of experts.

The African Union played an increasingly prominent role in Darfur. In April 2005 the AU requested, and the Sudanese government agreed, to a further deployment to total 7,700 military and police for AMIS' expanded mission. Donors pledged U.S. $291 million for the project, including logistical assistance for this deployment from NATO, the E.U., the U.N., the U.K., the U.S., Canada, France and others. AMIS' peace support efforts in Darfur had mixed results. Although AMIS troops contributed to some measure of improved security and civilian protection in those areas where they were deployed, the mission was plagued by continuing logistical and financial problems. The AU's efforts at mediating peace talks on Darfur were not as successful; sharp leadership clashes within the SLA, which had the most forces in the field of all the rebel groups, left the group unable to make decisions at the negotiating table.

UGANDA

Uganda failed to make progress on human rights and its international reputation suffered in 2005. The conflict in northern Uganda claimed victims daily and more than 1.5 million people continued to languish in displaced persons camps, vulnerable to abuses by the brutal Lord's Resistance Army (LRA) and an undisciplined government army, the Uganda Peoples' Defence Forces (UPDF). The Ugandan government arrested on treason and rape charges the front-running challenger to twenty-year incumbent President Yoweri Museveni, only three weeks after he returned from exile. Dr. Kizza Besigye, the candidate for the opposition Forum for Democratic Change, was charged with twenty-two others; when fourteen of those were granted bail, government Joint Anti-Terrorism Task Force agents in black suits entered the court building and prevented all present from leaving. The chief justice denounced the "rape" of the courthouse. Other political opponents and journalists were threatened and put in jail for criticizing the government, and some, accused of rebel collaboration or treason, were tortured in illegal detention centers.

The War in Northern Uganda

The nearly twenty year long conflict in northern Uganda continues to victimize the population in the three districts of the Acholi, more than 90 percent of whom are in displaced persons camps and are not free to return home. The rebel LRA committed killings of civilians, torture, mutilations and sexual abuse, including rape and forced "marriages" of girls to rebel commanders, and abducted thousands of children and brutalized them, forcing them to serve as child soldiers. Despite repeated assurances by the government that it has won the war against the rebels, the LRA continues to launch brutal attacks, often in response to such government assurances. Three separate attacks on aid workers in northern Uganda probably by the LRA resulted in the death of two individuals on October 26 and the injury of four others. In November the LRA, appeared to threaten to target foreigners, causing most international nongovernmental relief organizations to temporarily withdraw their staff.

Uganda

Uprooted and Forgotten

Impunity and Human Rights Abuses in Northern Uganda

HUMAN
RIGHTS
WATCH

Peace talks between the Ugandan government and the LRA, mediated by
Betty Bigombe, a former government minister from the north, broke down
in early 2005 and fighting was renewed. The violence escalated after the
main LRA negotiator, Brigadier Sam Kolo, defected to the government side
in mid-February 2005.

The LRA continued to launch attacks against civilians in northern Uganda
from its bases in southern Sudan, and increasingly attacked Sudanese in
Sudan. In September 2005, some four hundred LRA rebels crossed to the
West Bank of the Nile in southern Sudan and, attacking Sudanese villages
along the way, crossed into northeastern Democratic Republic of Congo
(DRC) where they were interviewed by the UN Mission in DRC
(MONUC). The Ugandan government renewed threats to enter the DRC to
deal with the LRA but did not act following widespread condemnation of any
action that would further destabilize northeastern DRC. The LRA appeared
to withdraw from DRC back into southern Sudan within the month, however, and resumed attacks on civilians, killing two demining workers and one
relief worker south of Juba.

Soldiers and officers of the Ugandan army, which is deployed in or near
every displaced persons camp in northern Uganda, engaged in abuses in
2005, beating, raping and even killing civilians with near total impunity.

After more than a year's investigation, the International Criminal Court
(ICC) issued sealed arrest warrants for five LRA leaders in October, asking
the Ugandan, Sudanese and DRC governments to enforce them. The five
include Joseph Kony, leader of the LRA, and Vincent Otti, the second-in-
command. Joseph Kony is to be tried on twelve counts of crimes against
humanity and twenty-one counts of war crimes, including murder, inducing
rape, intentionally directing an attack against a civilian population and forced
enlisting of children. The ICC was criticized by some civic and religious
leaders in northern Uganda for scuttling the peace process.

Political Freedoms

Bowing to growing international pressure to democratize Uganda and wean the country off the Movement system of "no-party" politics, the government organized a referendum on July 28 asking voters whether they wanted to open up political space for parties to compete for power in elections scheduled for March 2006. The main opposition coalition boycotted the referendum, complaining that the decision by President Yoweri Museveni—who has been president since 1986— to push through a constitutional amendment in June that removed presidential term limits, allowing him to run for a third term, undermined any efforts at democratic reform. A majority of voters cast their ballots in favor of multi-party politics, but the turnout was low.

Opposition politicians critical of the government faced increased threats to their safety and freedom with the stakes rising higher as the March 2006 presidential election date approached. On April 20, 2005, two opposition members of Parliament, Ronald Reagan Okumu and Michael Nyeko Ocula, were arrested by the Criminal Investigations Division of the police and charged with the 2002 murder of a councilman. Both MPs are from Gulu district in northern Uganda, are vocal defenders of human rights and critics of the government's conduct in the war against the LRA and are prominent opponents of Museveni's third term.

Okumu and Okulu were released on bail on May 17, but a number of other members of the political opposition have been arrested on politically motivated capital charges such as treason, including the chairman of the opposition group Forum for Democratic Change in Rukungiri district in southwestern Uganda.

In late October, Kizza Besigye, the failed candidate against Museveni in the 2001 presidential election, returned to Uganda from his four-year exile in South Africa, despite hints that he might be jailed as a member of the "armed opposition." He won the nomination by the FDC as their presidential candidate and began to draw large crowds while campaigning in the north and in the southwest—his as well as President Museveni's home area.

He was arrested three weeks after his return, on November 14, for a 1997 rape and for involvement in the LRA and another armed movement, the People's Redemption Army (PRA), based in DRC; unlike the LRA, the PRA has not launched any attacks inside Uganda. The arrest prompted demonstrations by his supporters that were met with tear gas; one person was killed.

During the entire bail hearing for fourteen of his co-defendants in court in Kampala, on November 16, the court was surrounded and controlled by thirty military commandos and two senior police commanders and several agents in civilian clothes. The judiciary denounced this as "utterly despicable" and a "day of infamy." The presence of commandos in court during the hearing of a petition was "simply unprecedented in the annals of this or any other High Court. They unleashed an incredible chilling effect on the administration of justice in this country," the Principal Judge of Uganda's High Court said.

Freedom of Expression

Uganda enjoys a relatively vibrant free press, especially in Kampala. However, journalists who criticized the government on politically sensitive topics still faced intimidation and arrest. Following the July 30 death of Sudanese First Vice-President John Garang, many Ugandans speculated that the Ugandan government was to blame for Garang's death, although the two had been close allies. Garang died when traveling in President Museveni's presidential helicopter; the helicopter crashed at night in the rain in southern Sudan as he was on his way back from a meeting with Museveni. President Museveni said that such speculation was a threat to national security and would not be tolerated. When popular radio talk show host Andrew Mwenda suggested that Garang's death was the result of the Ugandan government's incompetence, Mwenda was charged with sedition and jailed on August 12.

KFM radio, which broadcasts Mwenda's call-in show, was shut down for a week and the independent newspapers the Daily Monitor and the Weekly Observer, which ran a column by Mwenda, also faced closure. Mwenda was released on bail after three days and returned to his radio show, but the arrest casts a shadow on less prominent journalists in Uganda, especially in the politically charged run-up to elections.

Torture

The use of torture as a tool of interrogation has featured prominently in human rights violations by Ugandan security and military forces. Official and ad hoc military, security and intelligence agencies of the Ugandan government have illegally detained and tortured suspects, often in unofficial and illegal "safe houses," seeking to force confessions of links to rebel groups. Torture and prolonged incommunicado detention, sometimes as long as two years, in military barracks has been used against common criminals as well. Despite a number of high profile cases and the work of the Ugandan Human Rights Commission, a government body, verifying the use of torture, no one was punished for it. In May, the UN Committee against Torture published a report which found that these practices were still prevalent in Uganda in 2005. It called on the government of Uganda to end impunity for violators of human rights and urged it to abolish "safe houses."

HIV/AIDS

The Ugandan government was lauded internationally for implementing successful HIV prevention programs in the 1990s. But the country adopted U.S.-funded "abstinence-only" programs that jeopardize Uganda's successful fight against HIV/AIDS, with the support of conservative religious groups inside Uganda and the First Lady. These programs included the removal of critical HIV/AIDS information from primary school curricula, including information about condoms, safer sex, and the risks of HIV in marriage—in violation of the public's right to accurate health information. Over the past year, access to condoms in Uganda has been reduced dramatically due to government recalls and new taxes and quality-testing requirements on imported condoms, causing a shortage of condoms previously made freely available in government health clinics. Stephen Lewis, U.N. special envoy for HIV/AIDS in Africa, in August said the Bush administration's policy of promoting abstinence prevention programs and cuts in federal funding for condoms have contributed to a condom shortage in Uganda and undermined the country's HIV/AIDS fight.

UGANDA

The Less They Know, the Better

Abstinence-Only HIV/AIDS Programs in Uganda

HUMAN
RIGHTS
WATCH

Key International Actors

The international donor community has been slow to respond to the nine-teen-year human rights crisis in northern Uganda, and for many years fund-ing for the humanitarian crisis was far from what was necessary. In 2005, agencies such as UNICEF and the United Nations Office for the Coordination of Humanitarian Affairs moved to expand protection and human rights monitoring in the north and the U.N. Office of the High Commissioner for Human Rights' announced plans to deploy human rights monitors to the same region.

Donor governments were more critical of the backward movement on politi-cal reform in Uganda. Those that once praised Museveni withheld aid in 2005 in response to the lack of progress on democratic reform, symbolized by the third term constitutional amendment and plans for President Museveni to run again. Fears were that this would cause the entrenchment of a one-party state. Uganda is dependent on foreign aid to finance 40 percent of its budget.

In May Britain withheld U.S. $9.5 million in aid, accusing the Ugandan gov-ernment of poorly handling the political transition. Ireland also withheld U.S. $3.5 million. In July Norway also withheld U.S.$4 million for what Norwegian Ambassador Tore Gjos stated was his government's displeasure at "mishandling of the democratic process." The Ugandan government blamed the aid cuts on a negative campaign by the opposition who urged donors to freeze aid to the Uganda. These measures, while symbolic (aid was only "withheld", not cancelled), pressured the government to hold a referendum on a multiparty system, but the National Resistance Movement still con-trolled all government institutions.

Several prominent critics of Uganda, including former U.S. ambassador Johnny Carson, urged Museveni not to run again. A leaked unpublished World Bank consultancy report described widespread corruption, nepotism, and cronyism that permeate Uganda's institutions, and urged the Bank to cut its aid to Uganda. The Global Fund to fight AIDS, tuberculosis and malaria temporarily suspended its programs to Uganda due to "serious mismanage-ment" of funds on August 24, then restored the funding later in the year.

ZIMBABWE

The continuing erosion of human rights in Zimbabwe was highlighted in 2005 by Operation Murambatsvina, the government's program of mass evictions and demolitions which began in May, and, which, according to the United Nations, deprived 700,000 men, women and children of their homes, their livelihoods, or both throughout the country. The evictions and demolitions occurred against a background of general dissatisfaction in many of Zimbabwe's urban areas over the political and economic situation in the country. The country is currently spiraling into a huge economic and political crisis.

The government continues to introduce repressive laws that suppress criticism of its political and economic policies. In August, parliament passed the Constitutional Amendment Act, which gives the government the right to expropriate land and property without the possibility of judicial appeal, and to withdraw passports from those it deems a threat to national security.

Mass Forced Evictions and Demolitions

The government's policy of forced evictions and demolition of homes and informal business structures carried out in Zimbabwe's urban areas with little or no warning violated the rights of hundreds of thousands of Zimbabweans. Police used excessive force to destroy houses and structures and in some cases police armed with guns and truncheons, threatened and assaulted people. The evictions and demolitions led to widespread homelessness, lack of freedom of movement, loss of livelihood and minimal access to food, water, health care, education, and justice for hundreds of thousands of Zimbabweans. Tens of thousands of homes, and hundreds of informal business properties as well as legal housing and business structures were destroyed without regard for the rights or welfare of those who were evicted. The scale of destruction was unprecedented, and the victims were mainly the poor and vulnerable in Zimbabwe's cities and towns including widows, children, elderly and chronically ill persons. The evictions led to the disruption

ZIMBABWE

Evicted and Forsaken

Internally displaced persons in the aftermath
of Operation Murambatsvina

HUMAN
RIGHTS
WATCH

of anti-retroviral therapies and treatment of opportunistic infection for those living with HIV/AIDS.

Thousands of people remain homeless and displaced by the evictions with no shelter and little or no access to food, water and medical assistance. To date noone has received any housing under the Zimbabwe government's Operation Garikai program, ostensibly initiated to provide accommodation to all persons made homeless by the evictions. The Zimbabwean government has not investigated reports of excessive use of force by the police or brought the perpetrators to justice.

Blocking of Humanitarian Assistance

The government's refusal to cooperate with a United Nations emergency appeal for the hundreds of thousands affected by the evictions worsened their plight. On August 29, the U.N. Under-Secretary General for Humanitarian Affairs Jan Egeland condemned the lack of cooperation from the government with regard to mitigating the effects of the evictions, and accused it of hampering efforts to aid those affected. The government continues to obstruct the provision of humanitarian assistance by local and international humanitarian agencies to internally displaced and evicted populations. On October 31, 2005, the U.N. Secretary General Kofi Annan made a heartfelt appeal calling on the government to allow U.N. agencies and other humanitarian agencies access to help those made homeless by Operation Murambatsvina.

In addition, an estimated 2.9 million people across Zimbabwe were in need of food aid by the end of September. However, despite the serious food shortages, the government of Zimbabwe refused to make a formal appeal for food aid from the World Food Program.

The humanitarian situation has also been exacerbated by Zimbabwe's failing economy. In September 2005, inflation reached 359.8 percent and unemployment was at 80 percent. Although some reports suggest that the rate of HIV infections has recently decreased, the issue of HIV/AIDS is still of critical concern with almost 1.8 million people infected with HIV/AIDS (more than 20 percent of all adults) and nearly one million children orphaned. The government was saved from expulsion from the International Monetary Fund in September when it managed to repay a total of U.S. $135 million in debts.

Elections

There has been no thaw in relations between the opposition and the ruling party. Tensions between the two main parties were heightened by the result of parliamentary elections which took place in March 2005. The ruling Zimbabwe African National Union-Patriotic Front won the elections but the opposition Movement for Democratic Change (MDC) declared that the elections were not free and fair. In the run up to the elections, Human Rights Watch documented a series of human rights violations, including political intimidation of opponents by ruling party supporters, electoral irregularities, and the use of repressive legislation by the government. Local civil society organizations, international organizations, including Amnesty International and International Crisis Group, and the international community including the European Union (E.U.), and the governments of the United Kingdom and the United States widely criticized the elections. The African Union (A.U.), the Southern African Development Community and South African observer teams, however, endorsed the election results. Senate elections were scheduled to take place on November 26, and triggered serious divisions within the MDC over whether or not to participate in the elections. The disagreements subsequently led to the expulsion of 26 members from the party, who decided to contest the elections against the wishes of other party members and leader Morgan Tsvangirai.

Repressive Legislation and Human Rights Defenders

The situation of human rights defenders and journalists in Zimbabwe remains precarious. The Constitutional Amendment Act has been added to a raft of laws that restrict the human rights of those who criticize the government and try to protect human rights in Zimbabwe. Apart from allowing the government to expropriate land and property without recourse to the courts, the act also allows the government to withdraw passports from those it deems to be a threat to security, thus restricting the rights to freedom of movement of any government critics or human rights defenders.

Human rights groups continue to work in a highly restrictive environment. The government uses repressive laws such as the Public Order and Security Act to restrict the right to freedom of assembly, association, and expression of civil society activists and the opposition. Although President Robert Mugabe did not sign the restrictive Non-Governmental Organization Act into law, its existence has had a detrimental effect on the ability of human rights groups to operate freely, as they fear that the Act may be revived and lead to their shutting down.

Key International Actors

In response to the mass forced evictions, in May 2005 U.N. Secretary General Kofi Annan appointed a special envoy, Anna Tibaijuka, to investigate. Her strongly-worded report, released on July 22, concluded that the evictions were carried out in an "indiscriminate and unjustified manner" and recommended that those found responsible for the evictions be brought to justice. The government of Zimbabwe strongly refuted the U.N.'s findings and claimed that the evictions were lawful and that the U.N. had exaggerated both the scale of the evictions and the numbers of persons affected.

Western governments, in particular the governments of the United States, United Kingdom, and other European Union governments, also condemned the mass evictions. Many African governments once again refused to publicly condemn human rights violations in Zimbabwe and chose to remain silent on the issue of the evictions. The South African government indicated that it would await the U.N. report on the crisis before responding but did not do so. Although the South African government has expressed some concern with the human rights conditions in Zimbabwe, it continues to exercise a policy of 'quiet diplomacy' in its dealings with the government, an approach which has to date yielded few tangible results.

Attempts by African governments and the African Union to address Zimbabwe's human rights crisis have so far yielded little. In August, the government of Zimbabwe refused to accept the A.U. appointment of former president Joachim Chissano as an envoy to broker talks between the ruling party and the opposition MDC, claiming that such talks would not be taking place. The commendable effort by African Union Commission Chair Alpha Oumar Konare to appoint a special envoy to investigate the evictions was blocked by the Zimbabwe government, which refused to grant the envoy permission to investigate, until he was forced to leave the country on July 7, 2005. The Zimbabwe government claimed that the African Union had failed to follow protocol in sending the envoy to investigate the evictions. The Southern African Development Community also failed to discuss Zimbabwe at its annual summit in August. In general, there has been a lack of sustained attention from African governments to the crisis in Zimbabwe.

The United Kingdom and other E.U. governments have provided some humanitarian aid to address the crisis caused by the evictions. However, donors have become increasingly frustrated by the government's obduracy in dealing comprehensively with the humanitarian crisis caused by the evictions. The government's refusal to sign a U.N. emergency appeal to help those affected by the evictions and to make a formal appeal for food aid added to already existing tensions with western governments.

Western governments, in particular the United Kingdom and the United States, have failed to convince other influential governments (especially those in the South) to take a stronger stand on Zimbabwe at forums such as the U.N. Security Council. China, Russia and other African countries state that Zimbabwe does not warrant discussions at the Security Council because they claim it is not a threat to international peace or security.

CUBA/UNITED STATES

Families Torn Apart

The High Cost of U.S. and Cuban Travel Restrictions

HUMAN

RIGHTS

WATCH

WORLD REPORT
2006

AMERICAS

ARGENTINA

Violence in Argentina's overcrowded prisons worsened in 2005. Guard brutality, which has been especially well documented in Buenos Aires province, is widespread and shows no signs of diminishing.

Prosecutors continue to investigate the systematic violations of human rights committed under military rule (1976-1983). In June 2005, in an historic decision, the Supreme Court declared the "Full Stop" and "Due Obedience" laws to be unconstitutional, removing the remaining legal obstacles to these trials.

Prison Conditions

According to the Provincial Commission of Memory, a governmental body, three prisoners were killed every week in Buenos Aires province through March 2005, triple the level of violence in 2004. Prisoners in other provinces also suffer from overcrowding, deplorable conditions, and inmate violence. Eight people were killed, including five prisoners, two guards, and a police officer, in a prison riot in February 2005 in a prison in Córdoba province. Built to hold fewer than one thousand inmates, the prison was holding over 1,700 at the time. Two months later, thirteen inmates died in an inter-prisoner clash in the *Instituto Correccional Modelo* in the city of Coronda, Santa Fe province. According to official reports, eleven died of gunshot wounds, and two were burned alive.

A third deadly riot claimed thirty-two lives in October after a fire broke out in the Magdalena prison in Buenos Aires province. While the fire was started by clashing prisoners, some reports allege that fire extinguishers in the prison did not function and firefighters never entered the prison to battle the blaze.

The vast majority of inmates in Argentine prisons have not yet been tried. As of February 2005, only 11 percent of inmates in the province of Buenos Aires had been sentenced. Pretrial detention facilities are grossly inadequate. According to the Center for Legal and Social Studies (CELS), a respected human rights organization, 5,951 detainees in Buenos Aires province were

ARGENTINA

Decisions Denied

Women's Access to Contraceptives
and Abortion in Argentina

HUMAN
RIGHTS
WATCH

being held in crowded police lockups in April 2005 for lack of regular prison accommodation.

In May 2005, the Supreme Court of Justice declared that all prisons in the country must abide by the United Nations Standard Minimum Rules for the Treatment of Prisoners. The court was ruling on a collective *habeas corpus* petition lodged by CELS in 2001 on behalf people held in prisons and police lockups in Buenos Aires province. In August 2004 Human Rights Watch, the International Commission of Jurists, and the World Organization against Torture presented an *amicus curiae* brief in support of the petition. In December 2004 the Supreme Court held a public hearing on the issue, the first ever in a human rights case, in which CELS, Human Rights Watch, and the provincial government of Buenos Aires participated. In addition to declaring the U.N. rules to be national minimum standards, the court required that police lockups be barred from detaining children under age eighteen or sick people.

Torture

Torture and other forms of brutality are widespread in the prison system of the province of Buenos Aires. In May 2005, prison guards in La Plata beat inmate Cristián López Toledo and shocked him with electric current in reprisal for denouncing earlier beatings to the Committee against Torture of the Provincial Commission of Memory. A forensic doctor confirmed the use of electricity from a skin sample. No effective measures have been taken to implement the committee's recommendations since the publication of its October 2004 report on abuses in the prison system.

Accountability for Past Abuses

Argentina continues to make progress in prosecuting perpetrators of grave human rights violations during the country's so-called dirty war, in which at least 14,000 people "disappeared." In June 2005, the Supreme Court declared the "Full Stop" and "Due Obedience" laws to be unconstitutional by a 7-1 majority, with one abstention. The two amnesty laws, passed in the late 1980s, granted immunity to perpetrators of torture, killings, and disappearances during military rule. Although Congress annulled the laws in 2003 and cases had been reopened, progress had been slow as investigators waited for the court to rule definitively on the constitutionality of the two laws.

Three hundred and thirty former military and police personnel are now facing human rights-related charges and about 180 are detained in prisons or military installations, or are under house arrest. Public attention has focused on two "mega-cases" involving illegal arrest and torture by the First Army Corps, and by the navy at the Navy Mechanics School (Escuela de Mecánica de la Armada, ESMA), a torture center in the capital where an estimated 5,000 people are believed to have been held in secret detention before being killed.

Forty-three alleged perpetrators have been detained in the First Army Corps case, and an additional seven are fugitives from justice. Eighteen former ESMA officers are currently under arrest. They include former naval Cap. Alfredo Astíz, now in detention in a navy installation and awaiting trial for the "disappearance" of two French nuns, Alice Domon and Léonie Duquet, among other crimes. Duquet's remains, which had been buried for twenty-eight years in an unmarked grave, were finally identified using DNA samples in August 2005. In 1990, after a trial *in absentia*, a French court sentenced Astíz to life imprisonment for this crime. Thirteen other former ESMA officers, including Jorge Acosta, alias "The Tiger," have been charged with stealing property from detainees who "disappeared."

The pace of prosecutions has been slow, mainly due to numerous appeals presented by the defendants. Despite these delays, human rights groups expect some of the cases to be tried in open court in 2006.

In March 2005, the Federal Appeals Court declared pardons issued by former President Menem in 1989 and 1990 on behalf of six former army generals to be unconstitutional. Three of the six who are still living—Carlos Suárez Mason, Juan Bautista Sasaíñ, and Jorge Olivera Rovere—are accused of human rights violations as former officers of the First Army Corps. The appellate court reached the same conclusion in another case in July. It declared unconstitutional the pardons of two vice-admirals, Antonio Vañek and Julio Torti, both charged with human rights violations at ESMA. All five are expected to stand trial in the coming months.

Reproductive Rights

Women in Argentina continue to face arbitrary and discriminatory restrictions on their reproductive decisions and access to contraceptives and abortion. Access to one of the most effective forms of contraception—female sterilization—continues to be subject to discriminatory limitations. Women are often told that they need to obtain spousal authorization, that they must have at least three children, and that they must be at least thirty-five years old to be eligible.

Many women must choose between an unwanted or dangerous pregnancy or an illegal and unsafe abortion. Approximately half a million illegal abortions occur every year in Argentina, according to the health ministry, representing 40 percent of all pregnancies.

In 2005, in an important step toward guaranteeing women's right to access to health care services, the Argentine government published national guidelines on humane post-abortion care.

Freedom of Expression

Draft legislation to extend rights of free expression and access to information made no progress in 2005. A bill approved in the lower house in May 2003, that would give Argentine citizens the right to information held by public bodies, was weakened in the Senate and is now back in the lower house. An earlier bill to make defamation of public officials punishable only by civil damages, as opposed to criminal sanctions, has also not advanced. The need for such legislation is still apparent. In June 2005 the government's media minister, Enrique Albistur, brought a criminal defamation suit against journalists and directors of the magazine *Noticias* and the publishing house Perfíl for a January article criticizing his policies on the distribution of government advertising. The minister, who had asked for the maximum three-year sentence, later withdrew the lawsuit.

Key International Actors

In December 2004, the U.N. Committee against Torture reported on Argentina's implementation of the Convention against Torture and Other Cruel, Inhuman or Degrading Treatment or Punishment. Among the committee's concerns were the high number of reports of torture and ill-treatment, the small number of convictions, the detention of children below the age of criminal responsibility, and overcrowding and poor conditions in prisons.

In April 2005, a Spanish court sentenced Argentine ex-naval officer Adolfo Scilingo to 640 years in prison for crimes against humanity. Scilingo went to Spain in 1997 to voluntarily confess his role in throwing detainees into the sea from airplanes, but subsequently retracted his admissions. Judge Baltasar Garzón is also investigating the case of Ricardo Miguel Cavallo, another ESMA agent, who was extradited from Mexico in 2003 on charges of genocide and terrorism.

In July, in proceedings before the Inter-American Commission on Human Rights, the Argentine government formally accepted partial responsibility for failing to prevent the 1994 bombing of the Jewish Argentine Mutual Association (AMIA), and for subsequently failing to properly investigate the crime. Not a single person has been sentenced for the attack, while five have been acquitted for lack of evidence.

BRAZIL

Significant human rights abuses continue in Brazil. Human rights defenders suffer threats and attacks; police are often abusive and corrupt; prison conditions are abysmal, and rural violence and land conflicts are ongoing. And while the Brazilian government has made efforts to redress human rights abuses, it has rarely held to account those responsible for the violations.

Police Violence

Brazil's intractable problems of police violence and death squads reached a grisly zenith in the early morning hours of March 31, 2005, when armed men executed twenty-nine people —including women and children—outside Rio de Janeiro. Only one person escaped. The Baixada Fluminense area, where the killings occurred, is notorious for its high murder rate and for death squads connected to the military police. In the wake of mass demonstrations by Brazilian rights groups, and a public outcry from around the world, unprecedented cooperation between state and federal authorities led to the arrest of eleven police, who are being held in police custody pending trial.

Authorities believe that the Baixada massacre was committed in retaliation for the previous detention of nine police officers accused of killing two people and leaving their bodies behind a police station in Duque de Caxias, in the Baixada region. The police, whose actions were caught on film, decapitated one of the bodies and threw the head into the station. In September 2005, rights groups requested that the Rio de Janeiro State government adopt a permanent program to reduce civilian deaths in police operations. Many deaths continue to be registered under the much-criticized category of "resisting arrest," which is often used to cover up extrajudicial executions.

Police violence is one of Brazil's most systemic, widespread, and longstanding human rights concerns, disproportionately affecting the country's poorest and most vulnerable populations. Cases of police abuse all too often end in impunity.

BRAZIL

In the Dark

Hidden Abuses Against Detained Youth in Rio de Janeiro

HUMAN
RIGHTS
WATCH

Death Squads

The Public Security Secretary of Ceará was ousted in June 2005 after military police under his command were found to be involved in death squads acting as illicit private security guards. Twelve people were accused of participating in this criminal group, and six were placed in pretrial detention in August.

Conditions of Detention

The inhumane conditions, violence, corruption, and overcrowding that have historically characterized Brazilian prisons remain one of the country's main human rights problems. National and international governmental and non-governmental sources all agree that prisons and other places of detention hold inmates in scandalously abusive conditions.

Children and adolescents confined in Brazil's youth detention facilities face similar conditions. Severe overcrowding is endemic to these facilities. In some cases, such as the Padre Severino youth detention unit in Rio de Janeiro, facilities are operating at more than twice their design capacity. Staff shortages also create real threats to the security of inmates and staff. In March 2005, clothing and food shortages, as well as a lack of opportunities for recreation and rehabilitation, led to a series of riots and escapes from youth detention facilities in São Paulo.

Rural Violence and Land Conflict

Indigenous people and landless peasants face discrimination, threats, violent attacks, and killings as a result of land disputes in rural areas. According to a report by the Pastoral Land Commission, twenty-eight people were killed in rural conflicts from January to August 2005. By not intervening to guarantee the safety of people in these contexts, and by not punishing those who have carried out attacks, authorities encourage continued violence.

On February 16, 2005, in Goiás state, two people were killed and dozens of others were wounded in a police operation to evict some 3,000 families from a 130-hectare property near a luxury apartment block. Although precautions were taken to avoid violence, state authorities later acknowledged that the police demonstrated a "lack of proper restraint" in the operation.

Impunity

Impunity is the rule in Brazil, with few human rights crimes being effectively investigated or prosecuted. In December 2004, in an effort to remedy this glaring problem, the Brazilian government passed a constitutional amendment to make human rights crimes federal offenses, a change that international organizations such as Human Rights Watch had recommended for many years. The change allows certain human rights violations to be transferred to the federal—as opposed to the state—justice system for investigation and trial. Authority to order such transfers rests with the Attorney General or the Council for the Defense of Human Rights.

In another positive step, the federal government has made efforts to open files from the military archives and has opened a reference center on political repression during Brazil's military government, which will contain documents, films, and victims' statements from the period.

In August 2005, the Supreme Court granted pretrial release to Norberto Mânica, who is accused of ordering the execution of three agents investigating slave labor, and their driver, in the city of Unaí in Minas Gerais in January 2004. None of the four men accused of the crime have been punished to date. In another controversial ruling, in September, the Supreme Court ordered that Lt. Col. Mário Pantoja be released on bail. Pantoja had been sentenced to 228 years in prison as one of those responsible for the 1996 murder of nineteen rural workers in the Eldorado de Carajás case, but he was granted a retrial, which is pending.

Human Rights Defenders

Human rights defenders face threats, intimidation, and physical attack. While the government launched the National Protection Program for Human

Rights Defenders in October 2004, the program has not been effective in shielding those brave enough to stand up for victims of human rights abuses.

A seventy-four-year-old U.S. missionary and activist, Sister Dorothy Stang, was shot dead as she walked to a meeting on February 12, 2005, in the western city of Anapu, Pará state. Sister Dorothy had worked in the region for over twenty years. She had met with federal and state officials, including members of the federal Human Rights Secretariat, to discuss death threats against rural workers just a week before she was killed.

In another prominent case, Father Paulo Henrique Machado, who had played a key role in mobilizing family members of the victims of the Baixada massacre, was shot to death on July 25, 2005, in Nova Iguaçu, just outside Rio de Janeiro. Although the Federal Program for Protection of Victims and Witnesses (Provita) was put in place in the Baixada area after the massacre, Father Machado's murder was understood as part of an effort to discourage human rights work in its aftermath.

Adamor Guedes, president of the Amazonian Association of Gays, Lesbians, and Transvestites, was stabbed to death in his home on August 28. Guedes was a recognized defender of the human rights of gay people.

Key International Actors

The European Union pledged 6.5 million Euros to Brazil's Support Program for Police Ombudsmen and Community Policing. The objective of the program is to ensure that Brazil's police forces respect human rights and find less violent methods to combat crime.

Brazil decided to turn down $40 million in U.S. global AIDS money in May 2005 because of a requirement that funding recipients condemn prostitution. Supported by public health and human rights groups, Brazilian officials insisted that anti-prostitution policies undermine efforts to stem the spread of HIV.

In March 2005, in an official report, the U.N. Special Rapporteur on the Independence of Judges and Lawyers blasted Brazil for lack of access to justice, nepotism, and discrimination based on gender and ethnicity, among other problems. Hina Jilani, the U.N. Special Representative on Human Rights Defenders, was scheduled to visit Brazil in December.

By early 2005, the first two cases against Brazil had been sent to the Inter-American Court of Human Rights. The first involved Damião Ximenes Lopes, a young psychiatric patient who was tortured to death in state custody in 1999, and the second involved Gilson Nogueira de Carvalho, a human rights lawyer in Rio Grande do Norte who was killed by a death squad in 1996.

CHILE

Chile continues to prosecute hundreds of former military personnel accused of committing grave human rights violations during the dictatorship of Gen. Augusto Pinochet. After President Ricardo Lagos pardoned a low-ranking official convicted of homicide, a debate on clemency measures, long advocated by the army commander-in-chief and the opposition parties, was restarted in Congress.

The Lagos government failed to tackle reform of the over-extended system of military justice, which still allows civilians to be prosecuted by military courts for assaults on police and even speech offenses.

After years of debate, extensive constitutional reforms have become law. They have eliminated most of the authoritarian elements of the Constitution introduced by Pinochet in 1980.

Prosecutions for Human Rights Violations under Military Rule

Progress toward holding accountable those responsible for Pinochet-era human rights violations continues, but not without challenges. On January 25, 2005, the Chilean Supreme Court ordered all judges investigating human rights violations under military rule to halt their inquiries within six months. Unless trials were begun within this time, or the parties appealed successfully for cases to be kept open, all investigations into human rights violations committed during the dictatorship were to terminate on July 25, 2005. In early May, after sustained attention by both local and international human rights groups, the court rescinded the measure.

Former dictator Augusto Pinochet still faces a series of court cases. Before criminal proceedings can begin courts have to decide, on the merits of each case, whether to strip him of immunity from prosecution as a former president. Some immunity cases in 2005 were decided in his favor, others against him. The evident inconsistencies in the different Supreme Court decisions reflected variations in the composition of the panels hearing the cases, as well as the fact that panels are not bound by past precedent.

In March 2005, the Supreme Court upheld Pinochet's immunity against charges relating to the 1974 assassination in Buenos Aires of former army commander Gen. Carlos Prats and his wife. In September and October, in contrast, the Supreme Court lifted Pinochet's immunity in the so-called Colombo Operation and Riggs Bank cases. The former involves an elaborate scheme in 1975 to cover up the abduction and murder of 119 Chilean leftists. The latter involves possible charges of tax evasion and forgery, among others. The judicial probe into these issues followed the U.S. Senate's discovery in 2004 that Pinochet had salted away millions of dollars in secret accounts at Riggs Bank in Washington. It has been alleged that the main source of Pinochet's fortune (estimated at $27 million) were rake-offs from arms trafficking.

Pinochet's lawyers continued to use his alleged mental incapacity to block prosecutions. In June, an appeals court decided that Pinochet was not fit to stand trial for nine deaths and a kidnapping associated with a scheme known as Operation Condor by which political dissidents in neighboring countries were forcibly "disappeared." In September the Supreme Court upheld the ruling. However, in November a medical team from the state Medical Legal Service concluded that Pinochet had exaggerated his symptoms and was fit enough to stand trial in the Colombo case.

In a surprise decision in August, President Lagos pardoned an army sergeant convicted of the 1982 murder of a trade unionist. Manuel Contreras Donaire (no relation to Manuel Contreras Sepúlveda, Pinochet's director of intelligence) was serving an eight-year sentence for his part in the abduction and murder of Tucapel Jiménez, the president of the public employees' union. President Lagos commuted the remainder of Contreras's sentence to be served at home. The measure, reflecting Lagos's view that low-ranking soldiers obeying orders should be treated leniently, aroused passionate debate. Opposition senators presented several bills aimed at shortening sentences for human rights violators and allowing other military prisoners to benefit automatically from pardons.

In March 2005, Paul Schaefer, founder and leader of the Colonia Dignidad, a mysterious German colony in southern Chile, was captured in Buenos Aires and swiftly deported to Chile to face child sex abuse and human rights-related charges. Schaefer and his associates enjoyed close relations with the military government, which used the colony as a detention center after the 1973 military coup. Scores of political prisoners are thought to have been held there and tortured and many "disappeared." In March and May police found three cars buried on the property similar to those owned by political prisoners who disappeared in the 1970s. In June, a huge arsenal of military weapons was discovered, as well as files containing intelligence documents about political figures and prisoners believed to have been held there.

Torture Commission

The government has continued to confront the military-era legacy of torture, even though it has not supported prosecutions for this systematic abuse. In June 2005, the National Commission on Political Imprisonment and Torture, which issued a major report in November 2004, published an addendum on 1,204 new victims. It included a chapter about the situation of eighty-six victims who were detained with their parents when they were younger than twelve years old, who were born in prison, or were in gestation when their mothers were detained. The commission classified those detained with their parents or born in detention as torture victims. Some had been used as hostages or to pressure their parents while they were being tortured.

The government's insistence that the testimonies collected by the commission must be kept secret for fifty years—even from the courts—has hindered prosecutions.

Terrorism Prosecutions of Mapuche

A court in the southern city of Temuco frustrated prosecutorial efforts to reinstate terrorism charges against five Mapuche defendants and a sympathizer whom a trial court had unanimously acquitted in November 2004. Most of the defendants' alleged crimes were against property and none posed a direct threat to life. The Supreme Court had annulled the November verdict on grounds that prosecution evidence had not been properly considered, ordering a retrial. The second trial court found in July 2005 that there was insufficient evidence to sustain charges of illicit terrorist association. An appellate court later upheld the ruling, as did the Supreme Court in November.

Restrictions on Free Expression

Chilean legal restrictions on free expression have been eased. In August 2005, Congress finally approved a bill amending the Criminal Code to eliminate provisions that penalized strongly worded criticism of the president, military officers, members of Congress, and higher court judges, a type of law known as *desacato*. Unfortunately, the text approved after a three-year debate in Congress was a watered-down version of the bill originally presented by the government. It retained desacato offenses in the code of military justice, such as the offense of sedition, and preserved the jurisdiction of military courts in such cases, even over civilians. Moreover, legislators insisted on criminalizing "threats" made against them for their views expressed in Congress or made against judges for their decisions, a prohibition that could be used in the future to penalize criticism.

Progress in the area of freedom of expression was also made in July, when the Senate rejected a proposal by the lower house to strengthen the constitutional protection of "public life," an anachronistic notion dating from the military government that shielded public officials and politicians from scrutiny. Constitutional reforms approved in August went a step further, removing from the Constitution references to public life and the crime of defamation. The reforms also established the principle that the decisions of government bodies are public.

Discrimination on the Basis of HIV Status

In August a Chilean court ordered Carabineros, the uniformed police, to pay compensation of 100 m. pesos (approx. $1,800) to a former police corporal who was fired because he was living with HIV. In the first decision of its kind, the 13th Civil Court of Santiago cited Law No. 19,779 of 2001, which states that an HIV test result may not be grounds for dismissal from employment.

Constitutional Reform

In August 2005 a package of constitutional reforms that had been under debate since the early 1990s finally became law. It abolished the position of "appointed senator," and restored the president's power to fire the commanders-in-chief of the armed forces and the uniformed police.

International Criminal Court Ratification

Despite strong advocacy by Foreign Minister Ignacio Walker, the Senate has still not approved a constitutional reform allowing Chile to ratify the Rome Statute for the International Criminal Court. Approval of the Statute has been stalled since April 2002 when the Constitutional Court, ruling on a petition by a group of opposition senators, declared the ratification bill unconstitutional.

Criminal Procedure Reform

The introduction of a new code of criminal procedure in all parts of the country has improved due process guarantees for defendants facing criminal prosecution. Legislation was passed in November 2005 toughening some of its provisions, making pretrial release more difficult to obtain.

Key International Actors

The Chilean Congress has still to implement legislation compensating the family of United Nations diplomat Carmelo Soria, who was abducted and killed by government agents in 1976. In a friendly settlement brokered by the Inter American Commission on Human Rights in March 2003 the Chilean Government agreed to pay $1,500,000 to Soria's relatives. However, after months of delay, in November 2005 the Senate Foreign Relations Committee rejected the compensation payment.

COLOMBIA

Colombia presents the most serious human rights and humanitarian situation in the region. Battered by an internal armed conflict involving government forces, guerrilla groups, and paramilitaries, the country has one of the largest populations of internally displaced persons in the world.

Colombia's irregular armed groups, both guerrillas and paramilitaries, are responsible for the bulk of the human rights violations, which in 2005 included massacres, killings, forced disappearances, kidnappings, torture, and extortion. Despite ongoing negotiations with the government, paramilitary groups repeatedly committed abuses in breach of their cease-fire declaration.

Members of the armed forces have at times been implicated in abuses, independently or in collaboration with paramilitaries. Impunity for such crimes, particularly when they involve high-ranking military officers, remains a serious problem. Ties between military units and paramilitary groups persist, and the government has yet to take credible action to break them.

Demobilization of Paramilitary Groups

2005 was marked by the passage of Law 975, a controversial package for the demobilization of armed groups that the government called the "Justice and Peace Law." The law offers reduced sentences to members of these groups responsible for serious crimes, if they participate in a demobilization process. Drafted in the context of extended negotiations with paramilitaries, the law fails to include effective mechanisms to dismantle the country's mafia-like armed groups, which are largely financed through drug trafficking. It also utterly fails to satisfy international standards on truth, justice, and reparation for victims.

Although Colombian President Alvaro Uribe signed the demobilization law in July 2005, the government has not begun applying it. The law faced several constitutional challenges, which were still pending at this writing in late November 2005.

COLOMBIA

Smoke and Mirrors

Colombia's demobilization of paramilitary groups

**HUMAN
RIGHTS
WATCH**

Even before the demobilization law was passed, the government sponsored large-scale demobilization ceremonies in which thousands of paramilitaries handed over weapons. The government portrayed these demobilizations as important steps towards peace, but there were widespread reports of continuing abuses and illegal activity by paramilitaries around the country, including the recruitment of new troops.

Little effort has been made to investigate the past crimes of demobilized paramilitaries or to collect intelligence that could be used to dismantle the groups' structures or identify their supporters and assets. Cross-checking of individuals' names against prosecutors' records resulted in only a few dozen paramilitaries being linked to ongoing investigations, given that in most investigations, the perpetrator is not identified by name but rather by alias or other factors.

Many top paramilitary commanders remain in the specially designated area of Santa Fe de Ralito, safe from arrest or prosecution. In June 2005, prosecutors ordered the arrest of top paramilitary commander, Diego Murillo Bejarano (also known as "Don Berna" or "Adolfo Paz"), for allegedly ordering the assassination of a local congressman and two other people two months before. Nonetheless, the government announced that Murillo would be allowed to demobilize and eventually receive the benefits of Law 975. The government also suspended extradition orders for Murillo and commander Salvatore Mancuso, both of whom are wanted in the United States for drug trafficking.

Impunity and Military-Paramilitary Ties

The overwhelming majority of investigations involving human rights abuses are never resolved. The problem of impunity affects crimes committed by all armed groups, as well as the military.

Units of the Colombian military continue to tolerate, support, and commit abuses in collaboration with members of paramilitary groups. In 2005, there continued to be reports of abuses by members of the Army's 17th Brigade as well as by members of the armed forces operating in the region of Chocó.

In February 2005, eight residents of the Peace Community of San Jose de Apartadó, including four minors, were brutally killed. The government's immediate reaction to the massacre, prior to any investigation, was to blame it on guerrillas and deny any military presence in the area. Yet members of the community have alleged that military and possibly paramilitary groups were involved, and there is evidence pointing to military movements near the location of the massacre. The investigation has proceeded slowly, in part due to the unwillingness of witnesses to come forward, apparently out of fear and distrust of authorities.

During the tenure of Attorney General Luis Camilo Osorio, starting in 2001, major investigations into abuses by high-ranking officers were seriously undermined. This troubling trend continued in 2005, as the Attorney General's office closed its criminal investigation into Rear Admiral Rodrigo Quiñonez's alleged involvement in the Chengue massacre, in which paramilitaries killed over 20 people.

In May 2005, the Attorney General's office also closed the investigation of General Eduardo Avila Beltran for his alleged complicity in the 1997 paramilitary massacre of 49 civilians in the town of Mapiripán. Two separate courts—military and civilian—had previously ordered the Attorney General's office to investigate Avila's role in the massacre.

Osorio's term ended in mid-2005. The new Attorney General, Mario Iguarán, has expressed an interest in working more closely with human rights groups.

Human Rights Monitors and Other Vulnerable Groups

Human rights monitors, as well as labor leaders, journalists, and other vulnerable groups are frequently threatened and attacked for their work in Colombia. Investigations into such threats and attacks generally move slowly and are rarely resolved. The problem has at times been exacerbated by high-level government officials, who in 2005 once again made public statements suggesting that legitimate human rights advocacy was aimed at promoting the interests of armed groups.

In May 2005, three prominent journalists received anonymous funeral wreaths, accompanied by notes of condolence, at their homes or offices. As reported by the OAS special rapporteur for freedom of expression in 2005, such threats and prevailing impunity for killings of journalists have a chilling effect on the media.

Monica Roa, the lead attorney in a constitutional challenge to Colombia's almost complete ban on abortion, received numerous death threats in 2005. Confidential case files and two computers were stolen from her office during a break-in.

Human rights defenders from the *Colectivo de Abogados Jose Alvear Restrepo* and other organizations were also threatened in 2005. Meanwhile, there was no obvious progress in the investigation into *Operación Dragon*, a large scheme allegedly involving retired members of military intelligence, to conduct surveillance of human rights defenders, trade unionists, and politicians in Cali..

Violations by Guerrilla Groups

After a prolonged slowdown in their armed activity, guerrillas from the Revolutionary Armed Forces of Colombia (FARC) once again increased their level of violent activity in 2005. FARC attacks on government forces were accompanied by numerous and serious abuses, including massacres of civilians and targeted killings.

In April, the FARC used gas cylinder bombs in the region of Cauca, launching them in an indiscriminate manner in the direction of residential areas. The attacks primarily affected members of indigenous communities, resulting in numerous deaths and the displacement of much of the population. Other FARC attacks targeted media, including radio stations.

Both the National Liberation Army (ELN) and the FARC continue to kidnap civilians, holding them for ransom or political gain.

Child Recruitment

At least one of every four irregular combatants in Colombia is under eighteen years of age. Of these, several thousand are under the age of fifteen, the minimum recruitment age permitted under the Geneva Conventions. Eighty percent of the children under arms belong to one of two guerrilla groups, the FARC or the ELN. The remainder fights for paramilitaries.

Internal Displacement

Colombia has the world's largest internal displacement crisis after Sudan. In the last three years alone, more than three million people, as much as 5 percent of Colombia's population, have been forcibly displaced because of the country's armed conflict. More than half of all displaced persons are children under the age of eighteen. While Colombia is among a handful of countries that have enacted legislation to protect the internally displaced, displaced families are often denied access to education, emergency healthcare, and humanitarian aid.

In 2004, Colombia's Constitutional Court held that the government's system for assisting displaced persons was unconstitutional. In September 2005, the Court found that the steps taken by the government to comply with its ruling were insufficient in terms of both resources and institutional will.

Key International Actors

The United States remains the most influential foreign actor in Colombia. In 2005 it provided close to U.S. $800 million to the Colombian government, mostly in military aid. Twenty-five percent of U.S. security assistance is formally subject to human rights conditions, but the conditions have not been consistently enforced. Certification of 12.5 percent of the assistance was delayed in the first half of 2005 due to serious setbacks and lack of progress in key investigations of military abuses, among other factors. Nonetheless, the certification was ultimately granted, with the U.S. State Department citing late progress in some specific cases.

COLOMBIA

Displaced and Discarded

The Plight of Internally Displaced Persons
in Bogotá and Cartagena

**HUMAN
RIGHTS
WATCH**

In February 2005, the member countries of the G-24 group of international donors to Colombia met in Cartagena to discuss continuing cooperation with Colombia. Members of Colombia's human rights community expressed disappointment over the resulting Cartagena Declaration, which, while reaffirming the terms of the preceding London Declaration, was viewed as weaker than the earlier document on various human rights issues.

While some European and U.S. assistance to the demobilization process seems likely, its extent and nature remained an open question as of this writing in late November 2005. The U.S. Congress approved U.S. $20 million in assistance for the demobilization process, but the aid is conditioned on full Colombian cooperation with U.S. extradition requests and on specific measures to ensure accountability and the dismantlement of paramilitary structures.

The E.U. Council of Ministers stated that Law 975 could, if effectively implemented, contribute to peace. It expressed concern, however, over the law's failure to adequately take into account international standards on truth, justice, and reparation.

The OAS Mission to Support the Peace Process in Colombia, which is charged with verifying the demobilization process, was widely criticized by victims and human rights groups. Not only has it failed to adequately monitor paramilitaries' cease-fire declaration, it has also failed to follow up on complaints of abuses, and it shows little or no independence from the government. As of November 2005, the OAS Secretary General reportedly was considering possible reforms to the Mission's structure and activities.

The Office of the U.N. High Commissioner for Human Rights is active in Colombia, with a presence in Bogotá, Medellín, and Cali. Its relations with the government are difficult due to Colombia's repeated failure to implement the office's human rights recommendations.

CUBA

Cuba remains a Latin American anomaly: an undemocratic government that represses nearly all forms of political dissent. President Fidel Castro, now in his forty-seventh year in power, shows no willingness to consider even minor reforms. Instead, his government continues to enforce political conformity using criminal prosecutions, long- and short-term detentions, mob harassment, police warnings, surveillance, house arrests, travel restrictions, and politically-motivated dismissals from employment. The end result is that Cubans are systematically denied basic rights to free expression, association, assembly, privacy, movement, and due process of law.

Legal and Institutional Failings

Cuba's legal and institutional structures are at the root of rights violations. Although in theory the different branches of government have separate and defined areas of authority, in practice the executive retains clear control over all levers of power. The courts, which lack independence, undermine the right to fair trial by severely restricting the right to a defense.

Cuba's Criminal Code provides the legal basis for repression of dissent. Laws criminalizing enemy propaganda, the spreading of "unauthorized news," and insult to patriotic symbols are used to restrict freedom of speech under the guise of protecting state security. The government also imprisons or orders the surveillance of individuals who have committed no illegal act, relying upon provisions that penalize "dangerousness" (*estado peligroso*) and allow for "official warning" (*advertencia oficial*).

Political Imprisonment

In early July 2005 the Cuban Commission for Human Rights and National Reconciliation, a respected local human rights group, issued a list of 306 prisoners who it said were incarcerated for political reasons. The list included the names of thirteen peaceful dissidents who had been arrested and detained in the first half of 2005, of whom eleven were being held on charges of "dangerousness."

Of seventy-five political dissidents, independent journalists, and human rights advocates who were summarily tried in April 2003, sixty-one remain imprisoned. Serving sentences that average nearly twenty years, the incarcerated dissidents endure poor conditions and punitive treatment in prison. Although several of them suffer from serious health problems, the Cuban government had not, as of November 2005, granted any of them humanitarian release from prison.

On July 13, 2005, protestors commemorated the deadly 1994 sinking of a tugboat that was packed with people seeking to flee Cuba. The protestors marched to the Malecón, along Havana's coastline, and threw flowers into the sea. More than two dozen people were arrested. Less that two weeks later, on July 22, another thirty people were arrested during a rally in front of the French Embassy in Havana. While the majority of those arrested during the two demonstrations have since been released, at least ten of them remain incarcerated at this writing.

Travel Restrictions and Family Separations

The Cuban government forbids the country's citizens from leaving or returning to Cuba without first obtaining official permission, which is often denied. Unauthorized travel can result in criminal prosecution. The government also frequently bars citizens engaged in authorized travel from taking their children with them overseas, essentially holding the children hostage to guarantee the parents' return. Given the widespread fear of forced family separation, these travel restrictions provide the Cuban government with a powerful tool for punishing defectors and silencing critics.

Freedom of Assembly

Freedom of assembly is severely restricted in Cuba, and political dissidents are generally prohibited from meeting in large groups. In late May 2005, however, nearly two hundred dissidents attended a rare mass meeting in

Havana. Its organizers deemed the meeting a success, even though some prominent dissidents refused to take part in it because of disagreements over strategy and positions. While barring some foreign observers from attending, police allowed the two-day event to take place without major hindrance. The participants passed a resolution calling for the immediate and unconditional release of all political prisoners.

Prison Conditions

Prisoners are generally kept in poor and abusive conditions, often in over-crowded cells. They typically lose weight during incarceration, and some receive inadequate medical care. Some also endure physical and sexual abuse, typically by other inmates with the acquiescence of guards.

Political prisoners who denounce poor conditions of imprisonment or who otherwise fail to observe prison rules are frequently punished by long periods in punitive isolation cells, restrictions on visits, or denial of medical treatment. Some political prisoners carried out long hunger strikes to protest abusive conditions and mistreatment by guards.

Death Penalty

Under Cuban law the death penalty exists for a broad range of crimes. Because Cuba does not release information regarding its use of the penalty, it is difficult to ascertain the frequency with which it is employed. As far as is known, however, no executions have been carried out since April 2003.

Human Rights Defenders

Refusing to recognize human rights monitoring as a legitimate activity, the government denies legal status to local human rights groups. Individuals who belong to these groups face systematic harassment, with the government putting up obstacles to impede them from documenting human rights conditions. In addition, international human rights groups such as Human Rights Watch and Amnesty International are barred from sending fact-finding missions to Cuba. It remains one of the few countries in the world to deny the International Committee of the Red Cross access to its prisons.

Key International Actors

At its sixty-first session in April, the U.N. Commission on Human Rights voted twenty-one to seventeen (with fifteen abstentions) to adopt a blandly-worded resolution on the situation of human rights in Cuba. The resolution, put forward by the United States and co-sponsored by the European Union, simply extended for another year the mandate of the U.N. expert on Cuba. The Cuban government continues to bar the U.N. expert from visiting the country, even though her 2005 report on Cuba's human rights conditions was inexplicably and unjustifiably mild.

The U.S. economic embargo on Cuba, in effect for more than four decades, continues to impose indiscriminate hardship on the Cuban people and to block travel to the island. An exception to the embargo that allows food sales to Cuba on a cash-only basis, however, has led to substantial trade between the two countries. Indeed, in November 2005, the head of Cuba's food importing agency confirmed that the U.S. was Cuba's biggest food supplier. That same month the U.N. General Assembly voted to urge the U.S. to end the embargo.

In an effort to deprive the Cuban government of funding, the U.S. government enacted new restrictions on family-related travel to Cuba in June 2004. Under these rules, individuals are allowed to visit relatives in Cuba only once every three years, and only if the relatives fit the government's narrow definition of family—a definition that excludes aunts, uncles, cousins, and other next-of-kin who are often integral members of Cuban families. Justified as a means of promoting freedom in Cuba, the new travel policies undermine the freedom of movement of hundreds of thousands of Cubans and Cuban Americans, and inflict profound harm on Cuban families.

Countries within the E.U. continue to disagree regarding the best approach toward Cuba. In January 2005, the E.U. decided temporarily to suspend the diplomatic sanctions that it had adopted in the wake of the Cuban government's 2003 crackdown against dissidents, and in June it extended the sanctions' suspension for another year. Dissidents criticized the E.U.'s revised position, which Spain had advocated, and which the Czech Republic, most notably, had resisted.

Ladies in White (Damas de Blanco), a group of wives and mothers of imprisoned dissidents, were among three winners of the prestigious Sakharov Prize for Freedom of Thought for 2005. The prize is granted annually by the European Parliament in recognition of a recipient's work in protecting human rights, promoting democracy and international cooperation, and upholding the rule of law. As of this writing, it was not clear whether the Cuban government would allow representatives of Ladies in White to travel to France in December 2005 to receive the prize.

Relations between Cuba and the Czech Republic continue to be strained. In May 2005, Cuba summarily expelled Czech senator Karel Schwarzenberg, who was visiting Havana to attend the dissidents' two-day meeting. On October 28, on the eighty-seventh anniversary of the establishment of independent Czechoslovakia, the Cuban authorities banned a reception that the Czech Embassy was planning to hold in Havana, calling it a "counter-revolutionary action." The Cubans were reportedly angered by the embassy's decision to invite representatives of Ladies in White to attend the function.

Venezuela remains Cuba's closest ally in Latin America. President Castro and Venezuelan President Hugo Chavez enjoy warm relations, and Venezuela provides Cuba with oil subsidies and other forms of assistance.

GUATEMALA

Nearly two decades after the return of civilian rule, Guatemala has made little progress toward securing the protection of human rights and the rule of law, essential features of a functioning democracy. Impunity remains the rule when it comes to human rights abuses. Ongoing acts of political violence and intimidation threaten to reverse the little progress that has been made toward promoting accountability in recent years.

Impunity

Guatemala continues to suffer the effects of an internal armed conflict that ended in 1996. A U.N.-sponsored truth commission estimated that as many as 200,000 people were killed during the thirty-six-year war and attributed the vast majority of the killings to government forces.

As Human Rights Watch has noted in the past, Guatemalans seeking accountability for these abuses face daunting obstacles. The prosecutors and investigators who handle these cases receive grossly inadequate training and resources. The courts routinely fail to resolve judicial appeals and motions in an expeditious manner, allowing defense attorneys to engage in dilatory legal maneuvering. The army and other state institutions fail to cooperate fully with investigations into abuses committed by current or former members. The police do not provide adequate protection to judges, prosecutors, and witnesses involved in politically sensitive cases.

Of the 626 massacres documented by the truth commission, only one case has been successfully prosecuted in the Guatemalan courts. In 2004, a lieutenant and thirteen soldiers were found guilty of the 1995 Xamán massacre in which eleven civilians were killed; they were each sentenced to forty years in prison. By contrast, the prosecution of former military officers allegedly responsible for the 1982 Dos Erres massacre, in which 162 people died, has been held up for years by dilatory defense motions.

The few other convictions obtained in human rights cases have come at considerable cost. In the case of Myrna Mack, an anthropologist who was assassinated in 1990, it took over a decade to obtain the conviction of an army colonel, Valencia Osorio, for his role in orchestrating the killing. During that time, a police investigator who gathered incriminating evidence was murdered, and two other investigators—as well as three witnesses—received threats and fled the country. Osorio, meanwhile, escaped police custody and has not served his sentence.

Attacks and Threats by "Clandestine Groups"

Over the past four years, there have been an alarming number of attacks and threats against Guatemalans seeking justice for past abuses. The targets have included human rights advocates, justice officials, forensic experts, and plaintiffs and witnesses involved in human rights cases. They have also included journalists, labor activists, and others who have denounced abuses of authority.

In January 2005, Guatemala's Human Rights Ombudsman reported a plot to assassinate Bishop Álvaro Ramazzini, who has been an outspoken voice on social and economic issues. In March, radio journalist Marielos Monzón, who had broadcast special programs on recent clashes between police and indigenous protestors, reported that an anonymous caller had told her to "[s]top defending those stinking Indians, you bitch, or we will kill you." In August, members of the Guatemalan Foundation for Forensic Anthropology received repeated death threats, apparently due to their work exhuming bodies buried in clandestine cemeteries throughout the country.

There is a widespread consensus among local and international observers that the people responsible for these acts of intimidation are affiliated with private, secretive, and illegally armed networks or organizations, commonly referred to in Guatemala as "clandestine groups." These groups appear to have links to both state agents and organized crime—which give them access to considerable political and economic resources. The Guatemalan justice system, which has little ability even to contain common crime, has so far proven no match for this powerful and dangerous threat to the rule of law.

Excessive Use of Force

While political violence is no longer carried out as a matter of state policy, members of the national police still sometimes employ excessive force against suspected criminals and others. These cases usually entail the abuse of authority by poorly trained police officers.

In January 2005, police and soldiers clashed with protestors who had blocked the passage of a mining company's vehicle in the Department of Sololá. One local resident was killed, and at least twelve people were injured, among them several police officers. In March, two men were shot and killed by army troops during a confrontation with protestors in the Department of Huehuetengo.

Workplace Discrimination

Women and girls working in Guatemala's two female-dominated industries— the export-processing (maquiladora) and live-in domestic worker sectors— face widespread sex discrimination at the hands of private employers and the government. Domestic workers are denied key labor rights protections, including minimum wage guarantees and an eight-hour workday, and have only limited rights to paid national holidays. Younger women and girls, in particular, sometimes face sexual harassment and violence in the homes where they work.

Women and girls working in the maquiladora sector, though formally pro-tected under the law, encounter persistent sex discrimination in employment based on their reproductive status, with little hope for government remedy. Guatemalan maquiladoras, many of which are suppliers for well-known South Korean and U.S.-based corporations, discriminate against women workers in a number of ways—including requiring women to undergo preg-nancy tests as a condition of employment; denying, limiting, or conditioning maternity benefits; denying reproductive health care to pregnant workers; and, to a lesser extent, firing pregnant workers from their jobs.

Despite pressure from civil society, in 2005 the Guatemalan Congress failed to pass legislation that would have regulated work conditions for domestic workers by setting minimum salary standards, limiting permissible work hours, and protecting against sexual harassment.

Key International Actors

The United Nations High Commissioner for Human Rights opened an office in Guatemala in 2005 to provide observation and technical assistance on human rights practices (a role that the United Nations Verification Mission in Guatemala (MINUGUA) had played for nearly a decade, until it closed its operations in December 2004).

No progress has been made toward implementing the 2004 agreement between Guatemala and the United Nations to establish a special commission to investigate and promote the prosecution of "clandestine groups." The Commission for the Investigation of Illegal Groups and Clandestine Security Organizations (CICIACS) grew out of a proposal developed by the Guatemalan government and local human rights groups, in consultation with members of the international community. The Guatemalan Congress has never ratified the agreement, and the country's Constitutional Court has held that several of its provisions are unconstitutional. The current government has said it would propose modifications to the initiative that would make it consistent with the court's restrictive interpretation of the Guatemalan Constitution.

The inter-American human rights system continues to provide an important venue for human rights advocates seeking to press the state to accept responsibility for abuses. In July 2005, for example, Guatemala held a public ceremony in the town of Plan de Sánchez, presided by Vice President Eduardo Stein and attended by the vice president of the Inter-American Commission on Human Rights, to accept state responsibility for the massacre of 268 villagers in 1982. The Inter-American Court of Human Rights had ordered this act of public acceptance in a 2004 judgment.

In a landmark ruling, Spain's Constitutional Court held in October 2005 that cases of alleged genocide committed during Guatemala's internal armed conflict could be prosecuted in the Spanish courts, even if no Spanish citizens were involved. Finding that "principle of universal jurisdiction takes precedence over the existence or not of national interests," the Constitutional Court granted the appeal by Guatemalan Nobel laureate, Rigoberta Menchú, whose efforts to press charges in Spain for abuses committed in Guatemala had been blocked by a lower court.

HAITI

Haiti's already bad human rights conditions worsened in 2005, its second year under an unelected interim government. Citing summary executions, mob violence, torture and arbitrary arrests, the head of the human rights section of the United Nations mission in Haiti told reporters in October that the country's human rights situation was "catastrophic." It was far from clear, as elections approached, whether free and fair polling would be possible.

Election Conditions

Presidential, legislative and local elections were supposed to take place before the end of the year, but as of November 2005 the dates remained tentative. They will be Haiti's first elections since the February 2004 ouster of President Jean-Bertrand Aristide. Delays in election preparations over the course of 2005 led to multiple postponements in the electoral schedule, but unelected Prime Minister Gerard Latortue continues to insist that the transfer of power will take place as scheduled on February 7, 2006.

Irregularities in electoral preparations, including problems in the distribution of voting materials, cast doubt on the reliability of the vote. There were also suggestions that political bias had tainted the electoral process.

Violence, Lawlessness and Instability

With waves of violence engulfing the country, especially the capital, Port-au-Prince, Haiti remains unstable and dangerous. In Port-au-Prince clashes between rival criminal gangs, including some associated with former president Aristide, result daily in civilian deaths. Armed groups of Aristide supporters have sought to spread chaos and fear in hopes that the failure of the interim government to stem the violence will lead to Aristide's return. In the provinces irregular armed groups, many made up of former members of the Haitian military, exercise de facto governmental authority. Former soldiers have set up barracks in police stations and abandoned buildings. They man check points, conduct searches, seize weapons from civilians (and, at times, from police), make arbitrary arrests, and run their own makeshift prisons. Because Haiti's government institutions are largely dysfunctional and its security forces are woefully inadequate, abuses go unpunished and violent crime rates have soared.

The U.N. multinational peacekeeping force, mandated by the U.N. Security Council to assist local authorities in maintaining order, has not succeeded in stopping violent crime. But after an almost uncontrolled spike in violence in May-June 2005, U.N. troops began taking more aggressive measures in Port-au-Prince that, to a limited extent, have helped alleviate the atmosphere of insecurity. The strengthened U.N. presence has, for example, sharply reduced kidnappings, which had reached epidemic levels. Allegations were made, however, that U.N. forces used indiscriminate force, particularly in sweeps of slum areas of Port-au-Prince.

Police Abuses

Police lawlessness is a major contributor to overall insecurity. Not only are the Haitian National Police (HNP) largely incompetent in preventing and investigating crime, they are responsible for frequent arbitrary arrests, torture, beatings, and the excessive and indiscriminate use of force against demonstrators. They also face credible allegations of extrajudicial executions and of involvement in drug trafficking and other criminal activity. Untrained and unprofessional, the police suffer from severe shortages of personnel and equipment.

Police perpetrate abuses with almost total impunity. Human Rights Watch knows of no members of the HNP who have faced criminal prosecution for their abusive conduct. But in a welcome move, the head of the Haitian National Police announced in early November 2005 that fourteen police officers would be charged for their alleged responsibility in the August killings of at least eleven people at a soccer game.

Justice and Accountability

Haiti's justice system is hardly functional, suffering from corruption, politicization and a lack of personnel, training and resources. In the provinces judges complain there are no police to execute warrants and no prisons in which to keep detainees; few crimes are even investigated. Where prisons exist, their conditions are dire, with prisoners held in dirty and crowded accommodation often lacking sanitary facilities.

Accountability for past abuses remains out of reach. Indeed, significant regress occurred in 2005, as exemplified most dramatically by the case of Louis Jodel Chamblain, formerly second in command of the paramilitary Revolutionary Front for the Progress and Advancement of Haiti (Front Révolutionnaire pour l'Avancement et le Progrès d'Haïti, FRAPH), responsible for countless abuses during the de facto military government. He had been convicted in absentia of the 1993 murder of a prominent Haitian businessman and of the 1994 Raboteau massacre, but he surrendered to judicial authorities in 2004 to exercise his right to a retrial. The convictions were reversed, and although the Haitian authorities continued to detain him for a few months on other allegations, they released him in August 2005. In a related development in early May 2005, Haiti's Supreme Court (Cour de Cassation) quashed the sentences of fifteen other former soldiers and paramilitaries who had been held responsible for the Raboteau massacre in a historic 2000 trial. The grounds for the Supreme Court ruling were extremely flimsy.

The long-term imprisonment of former Prime Minister Yvon Neptune continues to raise serious concerns. Although formal charges were finally brought against Neptune in September 2005, the apparent political grounds for Neptune's detention undermines confidence in the validity of the charges and in the fairness of any future trial.

Human Rights Defenders and Journalists

Human rights defenders, working in a dangerous, highly-politicized environment, face threats and intimidation. Haiti is a dangerous country for journalists as well, who face threats and violence for their reporting. In June 2005, after having received several kidnapping threats, prominent radio journalist Nancy Roc left the country to go into exile. A few weeks later, in mid-July, newspaper and television reporter Jacques Roche was abducted and brutally murdered by unknown assailants. Roche's body was found in a slum neighborhood of Port-au-Prince; he had been tortured and shot several times. U.N. envoy to Haiti Juan Gabriel Valdes reportedly said that Roche's death "has all the elements of a political murder."

Key International Actors

The U.N. Security Council voted unanimously in late June 2005 to extend the mandate of the U.N. Stabilization Mission in Haiti (MINUSTAH) until February 15, 2006, "with the intention to renew for further periods." The U.N. resolution also authorized the addition of more than one thousand soldiers and civilian police to bulk up the thinly-staffed peacekeeping force. The numbers mandated raised military troops to 7,500 and police to 1,897. But MINUSTAH's slow deployment of personnel and general lack of preparation for urban warfare have plagued the mission's efforts to restore security to Haiti.

In November 2005, a group of human rights attorneys filed a complaint with the Inter-American Commission on Human Rights alleging that U.N. peacekeeping forces were involved in massacres in Haiti in July and August.

The United States is Haiti's largest donor, having budgeted U.S.$407 million for Haiti in 2004-05. Canada and the European Union are also major donors. In mid-October, the E.U. unblocked ?72 million (U.S. $87 million) in aid to support Haiti's electoral process. The funds had been frozen several years previously in protest over irregularities in the 2000 legislative elections.

Haitians continue to risk their lives attempting to sail overcrowded, often leaky boats across the rough seas that separate Haiti from the United States. Many boats are intercepted by U.S. Coast Guard cutters, but some number of them are lost at sea. Haitians who reach the United States are subject to mandatory detention and expedited removal procedures.

MEXICO

Among Mexico's most serious human rights problems are those affecting its criminal justice system. Persons under arrest or imprisonment face torture and other ill-treatment, and law enforcement officials often neglect to investigate and prosecute those responsible for human rights violations.

President Vicente Fox has repeatedly promised to address these problems and has taken important steps toward doing so—establishing a special prosecutor's office to investigate past abuses and proposing justice reforms designed to prevent future ones. Unfortunately, neither initiative has lived up to its potential.

Torture, Ill-treatment, Police Brutality, and Pretrial Detention

Torture remains a widespread problem within the Mexican criminal justice system. A factor perpetuating the practice is the acceptance by some judges of evidence obtained through violations of detainees' human rights. Prison inmates are subject to abuses, including extortion by guards and the imposition of solitary confinement for indefinite periods of time. Children in some juvenile detention facilities are forced to live in squalid conditions and are reportedly subject to beatings and sexual abuse. Foreign migrants are especially vulnerable to abusive practices, including extortion, by government agents.

Over 40 percent of prisoners in Mexico have never been convicted of a crime. Rather, they are held in pretrial detention, often waiting years for trial.

In 2004, President Fox proposed reforms designed to fix features of Mexican criminal procedure that perpetuate and even encourage the use of torture by law enforcement officials. The new legislation would bar all evidence obtained illegally and allow confessions to be entered as evidence at trial only when they were made in the presence of a judge and defense counsel.

The reform package also contained measures to address the problem of preventive detention. Specifically, it would amend the Constitution to establish that criminal suspects are presumed innocent until proven guilty. The reform would allow judges to decide in each case, based on objective criteria, whether preventive detention is necessary.

Although the Senate approved several positive pieces of the reform package in July 2005, Congress has yet to vote on measures addressing the critical problems of torture and preventive detention.

Impunity

The criminal justice system routinely fails to provide justice to victims of violent crime and human rights abuses. The causes of this failure are varied and include corruption, inadequate training and resources, and a lack of political will. One prominent example is the unsolved murders of hundreds of young women and girls over the last decade in Ciudad Juárez, a city on the U.S. border in Chihuahua state. Several individuals facing charges for some of the Júarez killings have recanted confessions that they claim were coerced through torture.

A major shortcoming of the Mexican justice system is that it leaves the task of investigating and prosecuting army abuses to military authorities. As Human Rights Watch documented in a 2001 report, the military justice system is ill-equipped for such tasks. It lacks the independence necessary to carry out reliable investigations and its operations suffer from a general absence of transparency. The ability of military prosecutors to investigate army abuses is further undermined by fear of the army, which is widespread in many rural communities and which inhibits civilian victims and witnesses from providing information to military authorities. The Mexican Supreme Court had an opportunity to address the problem of military jurisdiction in a 2005 case, but in September it upheld the military's authority over cases involving army members even when the alleged crimes were committed while off-duty.

The Special Prosecutor's Office

The special prosecutor's office that President Fox established in 2001 to address past abuses has produced limited results. In November 2003, the special prosecutor won a landmark decision from the Mexican Supreme Court holding that statutes of limitations do not apply to old "disappearance" cases as long as the victims' bodies have not been found. He then obtained arrest warrants for several high-level officials, and secured custody of three of them.

But these advances have been counterbalanced by significant failures. The majority of the suspects pursued by the special prosecutor have managed to escape arrest. The special prosecutor has also made only limited progress in uncovering the fate of hundreds of people who were "disappeared" in the 1970s.

The special prosecutor's most ambitious move—the indictment of former president Luis Echeverría for genocide—was thrown out by a trial judge on grounds that the statute of limitations had expired. The special prosecutor won an appeal before the Supreme Court, which ruled in June 2005 that the statute of limitations had not expired in Echeverría's case because he had been shielded by immunity during his presidency. But the case was thrown out again by a lower court in July 2005, on the grounds that the 1971 massacre did not constitute genocide.

The special prosecutor subsequently sought to indict Echeverría again on genocide charges for a 1968 massacre of student protesters, but in September 2005 a lower court once again rejected his argument.

Labor Rights

Legitimate labor-organizing activity continues to be obstructed by collective bargaining agreements negotiated between management and pro-management unions. These agreements often fail to provide worker benefits beyond the minimums mandated by Mexican legislation, and workers sometimes only learn of the agreements when they grow discontented and attempt to organize independent unions. Workers who seek to form independent unions risk losing their jobs, as the government generally fails to protect them from retaliatory dismissals.

Freedom of Expression

Journalists have occasionally faced harassment and attacks, particularly those who have investigated drug trafficking or have been critical of state governments. In April 2005, a journalist in Tamaulipas and one in Veracruz were killed. During that same month, another journalist in Sonora disappeared, and at this writing is still missing. In June 2005, thirty-one journalists of the Oaxaca-based *Noticias* newspaper were forced to stay inside the newspaper facilities for more than a month because members of a pro-government trade union had initiated a strike outside the building. Newspaper staff maintain that the strikers did not actually work at the newspaper and aimed merely to stop the paper's publication.

Mexican defamation laws continue to be excessively restrictive and tend to undermine freedom of expression. Besides monetary penalties, journalists can be subject to criminal prosecution for alleged defamation of public officials.

Right to Education

A chronic concern in Mexico is the government's failure to ensure that tens of thousands of rural children receive primary education during the months that their families migrate across state lines to work in agricultural camps. A large number of parents choose to have their children work in the fields rather than attend school during these months. The government's failure to enforce child labor laws facilitates this choice. Although there is a federal program to provide primary schooling in the agricultural camps, the classes are generally offered in the evening when children are too exhausted from their work to study.

Electoral Rights

According to electoral laws in Mexico, presidential candidates must be nominated by political parties. Jorge Castañeda, a former foreign relations minister, challenged these laws, arguing that he should be allowed to run as an independent candidate. In August 2005, the Supreme Court refused to hear his appeal on the grounds that only political parties have standing to challenge the electoral laws.

Key International Actors

As part of a Technical Cooperation Agreement signed by President Fox, the U.N. High Commissioner for Human Rights maintains an in-country office that, in December 2003, produced a comprehensive report documenting ongoing human rights problems and providing detailed recommendations for addressing them. The Fox administration's justice reform proposal incorporates some of those recommendations while ignoring others, such as the recommendation to end military jurisdiction over cases involving human rights violations. In December 2004, the administration presented a national human rights program that outlined a wide range of policy objectives based on the report's recommendations. In 2005, the administration established a committee, with representatives from the government and civil society, to monitor the implementation of the program.

Along with the United States and Canada, Mexico is a party to the North American Free Trade Agreement and its labor side accord. The side accord commits the three countries to enforcing their laws protecting workers' rights and grants them authority to hold one other accountable for failing to meet these obligations. Under the accord, when a government of one country receives a complaint of violations committed in one of the other two, it can investigate the charges. However, because the complaint process is convoluted and enforcement mechanisms are weak, the accord has had little impact on labor rights violations in Mexico.

Mexico has maintained its leading role at the international level in pressing for human rights promotion to be considered an integral part of counter-terrorism efforts. It sponsored resolutions to that end at both the U.N. General Assembly and the U.N. Commission on Human Rights, and successfully pressed the Commission to name an independent expert on the protection of human rights and fundamental freedoms while combating terrorism.

In an important move, Mexico, after a long process, ratified the Rome Statute of the International Criminal Court in October 2005, becoming the 100th state party of the court.

PERU

Efforts to prosecute those responsible for gross human rights violations dating from Peru's armed conflict (1980-2000) have begun to show results, but they still face formidable obstacles. These include a chronic shortage of funds and resources, a lack of trained investigators, and a lack of cooperation by the armed forces.

Military courts continue to investigate human rights violations committed by military personnel during this period, even though the Constitutional Court and the Supreme Court have ruled that they lack competence to do so. Torture is an ongoing problem. Journalists face violence and harassment, particularly in provincial cities. Human rights defenders are vulnerable to threats and intimidation.

Confronting the Past

At the end of November 2005, former president Alberto Fujimori was in detention in Santiago, Chile, awaiting possible extradition to Peru on charges of corruption and human rights abuse. Arriving unexpectedly in the Chilean capital by private jet from Japan on November 6, Fujimori cleared immigration without difficulty despite an Interpol alert for his arrest. Chilean police detained him early the following morning acting on a warrant issued by the Peruvian Supreme Court. Apart from numerous accusations of corruption, Fujimori faces charges for killings and "disappearances" in the early 1990s. Before leaving Japan, where he had been in self-exile since 2000, Fujimori had announced his intention to stand as a candidate in Peru's April 2006 presidential elections.

The number of military and police personnel facing trial for human rights abuses committed during Peru's counterinsurgency campaign rose significantly in 2005. As of October 2005, 383 former and still serving officers had been charged in twenty-two cases, most of them having been forwarded to the attorney general by the Truth and Reconciliation Commission in August 2003.

In August 2005, the trial began in open court of more than fifty members of the "Colina Group," a clandestine army death squad active during the government of Alberto Fujimori (1990-2000). They are accused of numerous killings and forced disappearances, including shooting dead fifteen unarmed civilians at a fundraising barbecue in the Barrios Altos district of Lima on November 3, 1991, and kidnapping and murdering nine students and a teacher from the La Cantuta university on July 18, 1992.

Testimony showing that the squad acted under government orders is expected from three former members who confessed in court to the charges. Two of them were sentenced at the beginning of the trial.

There has also been progress in cases dating from the presidencies of Fernando Belaúnde (1980-1985) and Alan García (1985-1990). The special human rights prosecutor in Ayacucho, Cristina Olazábal, has filed charges in at least twelve cases. In July 2005, Judge Miluska Cano of the Fourth Supra-Provincial Criminal Court in Lima indicted 118 soldiers for first-degree murder, extrajudicial execution, and forced disappearance in connection with a massacre at Cayara in May 1988, in which thirty-nine civilians were killed.

These criminal investigations face serious obstacles, however. The attorney general mandated two special prosecutors to devote themselves full-time to human rights cases, but the government has provided no funds to train them, adequately equip their offices, or cover their expenses. The armed forces deny having information to identify those who served at counter-insurgency bases implicated in abuses; military prosecutors continue to carry out parallel investigations of their own apparently aimed at blocking civilian trials, and the army and police consistently fail to carry out arrest orders. According to the human rights ombudsman, courts have issued 252 warrants for the arrest of military and police personnel for human rights violations (naming 277 soldiers, sixty-four police officers, and fifteen marines). Yet only forty-three arrest warrants have been put into effect.

The government has also failed to provide effective protection for witnesses who testify in these cases. On two occasions in 2005 unidentified gunmen shot at Luis Ramírez Hinostroso, a key witness in a torture trial which began in October in Huancayo. In a similar 2004 attack, Ramírez was hit in the stomach by a bullet and had to undergo surgery.

Torture

Torture by police continues to be a problem, and judicial investigations in such cases are slow and frequently superficial. Those responsible, if convicted at all, usually receive light sentences and have to pay very small amounts in compensation. The Human Rights Commission (Comisión de Derechos Humanos, COMISEDH) a respected nongovernmental human rights group, documented sixteen cases of torture from January through September 2005. In four cases the victims died.

On a positive note, in January 2005 an Ayacucho court sentenced three soldiers to six years in jail for the torture in July 2002 of a nineteen-year-old military recruit. The recruit had been drugged and subjected to brutal sexual abuse in the Domingo Ayarza army base in Ayacucho. The three perpetrators were each ordered to pay the victim compensation of 6,000 soles (about U.S. $1,800). A military judge, Maj. José Etel Espinoza, received a three-year suspended sentence for covering up the crime. On appeal by the prosecutor, in November the Supreme Court increased the sentences to ten years and eight years, and boosted the compensation to 30,000 soles (about U.S. $9,000). This was believed to be the stiffest sentence ever imposed for torture in Peru.

Attacks on Journalists

Journalists and radio commentators in Peru's provinces are vulnerable to physical attack, intimidation, and harassment for criticizing local authorities. This pattern of abuse has been constant for many years and shows the precariousness of respect for press freedom in Peru. The Inter-American Press Association reported in March 2005 that violent attacks on journalists are on the increase in Peru.

Pucallpa, a city in the coca-growing area of the Upper Huallaga valley, is a dangerous place for radio journalists. On two occasions in February 2005, armed men broke into the *Radio Frecuencia Oriental* radio station in Pucallpa, threatening journalist Paul Garay Ramírez with a gun on the first occasion, and severely beating him on the second. Garay said that he had been reporting on corruption in local government and in labor organizations. In October, police arrested Luis Valdez Villacorta, the mayor of the province of Coronel Portillo, after an alleged hit-man confessed that Valdez hired him to murder journalist Alberto Rivera Fernández. A persistent critic of the provincial government and close colleague of Garay, Rivera was shot dead in April 2004.

Human Rights Defenders

Peru has a diverse and vibrant range of nongovernmental human rights groups that operate without governmental or legal restrictions. For years, however, some have suffered anonymous attacks, threats, and harassment.

In September 2005, Salomón Lerner, former president of the Truth and Reconciliation Commission, received death threats. While he was out of the country, his secretary received a telephone call from an individual who told her that Lerner should "consider himself dead." Previously, Lerner had received a series of insulting and anti-Semitic emails. Other commission members received insulting messages accusing them of attacking the armed forces. The threats coincided with efforts to discredit the commission following the second anniversary of publication of its report on human rights violations and abuses committed by both sides during Peru's armed conflict (1980-2000). Several critical articles appeared in the press signed by retired soldiers implicated in abuses. The commissioners faced nine lawsuits from senior retired officers who claimed that they had distorted the facts.

Also in September, COMISEDH, whose lawyers represent torture victims and relatives of the "disappeared," suffered two anonymous attacks. On September 6, someone tied a dirty lock of human hair to the door of its office in Ayacucho. A week later, unidentified armed individuals staged a nocturnal raid on COMISEDH's office in Lima, tampered with the alarm, and disabled the phone and cable connections. Before they left the building they fired shots to scare off a night-watchman. Nothing was stolen.

Prosecutors and forensic experts working on human rights cases have also received threats. Cristina Olazábal, the special human rights prosecutor in Ayacucho, received intimidating calls from anonymous callers on several occasions while she was investigating extrajudicial executions at Accomarca and the Los Cabitos military base in Ayacucho. In February and August 2005, three experts from the Medical Legal Institute (the forensic branch of the public ministry) who were participating in the Los Cabitos investigation received threatening text messages on their cell phones. Altogether, there were forty-five incidents involving attacks, threats, and intimidation against witnesses and relatives, judges, prosecutors, forensic staff, and human rights activists from January through October 2005, according to the human rights umbrella group National Human Rights Coordinating Group.

Peru's minister of justice acknowledged that the government had failed to provide adequate protection for participants in human rights trials. He promised to coordinate with the minister of the interior to investigate the attacks and increase the level of protection.

Key International Actors

The Inter-American Commission on Human Rights and the Inter-American Court of Human Rights continue to consider Peruvian cases. In March 2005, the Court ordered Peru to bring to justice those responsible for the extrajudicial execution of labor leader Pedro Huilca Tecse, who was assassinated by members of the Colina death squad in December 1992. Finally admitting responsibility for his murder, the Peruvian government agreed to pay U.S.$250,000 in compensation to his surviving relatives as well as undertake various measures of symbolic reparation.

The United States and several European countries provided funds in past years to support the work of the Truth and Reconciliation Commission. Money for the prosecutorial effort that has followed the commission's report—for office equipment, computers, transportation, and the capital cost of forensic equipment and laboratories—has come almost entirely from international donors. In 2005, the European Union pledged 483,447 Euros (U.S.$586,373) to assist prosecutors and forensic investigations.

By contrast, the United States decided to axe its program of support for judicial reform initiatives. Overall aid to Peru was cut as a result of the Bush administration's policy of partially withholding assistance to countries that refuse to sign a Bilateral Immunity Agreement to shield Americans from prosecution by the International Criminal Court.

VENEZUELA

Since winning a national referendum on his presidency in 2004, Hugo Chávez and his majority coalition in Congress have taken steps to undermine the independence of the country's judiciary by packing the Supreme Court with their allies. They have also enacted legislation that seriously threatens press freedoms and freedom of expression. Several high profile members of civil society have faced prosecution on highly dubious charges, and human rights defenders have been repeatedly accused by government officials of conspiring against the nation. Police violence, torture, and abusive prison conditions are also among the country's most serious human rights problems.

Independence of the Judiciary

The Venezuelan Congress dealt a severe blow to judicial independence in December 2004 by packing the country's Supreme Court with twelve new justices. A majority of the ruling coalition, dominated by President Chávez's party, named the justices to fill seats created by a law passed in May 2004 that expanded the court from twenty to thirty-two members. In addition to the justices named to the twelve new seats, five justices were named to fill vacancies that had opened in recent months, and thirty-two more were named as reserve justices.

The political takeover of the Supreme Court compounded the damage already done to judicial independence by policies pursued by the court itself. The court, which has administrative control over the judiciary, has failed to provide security of tenure to 80 percent of the country's judges.

Freedom of Expression

Laws passed since late 2004 have introduced onerous new restrictions on the media. The Law of Social Responsibility in Radio and Television, approved by the National Assembly in December 2004, establishes detailed regulations for the content of television and radio programs. For example, stations deemed to "condone or incite" public disturbances or publish messages "contrary to the security of the nation" are subject to heavy fines and can be ordered to suspend broadcasting for seventy-two hours; on a second offense they may forfeit their broadcasting license for up to five years. Key terms such as those quoted above are left ill-defined, inviting politically motivated application. The National Commission of Telecommunications (CONATEL) may issue "precautionary measures" prohibiting the transmission of outlawed content.

In March 2005, amendments to the Criminal Code came into force which extended the scope of Venezuela's *desacato* (disrespect) laws, and increased penalties for desacato, criminal defamation, and libel. By broadening its desacato provisions, Venezuela ignored the recommendations of the Inter-American Commission on Human Rights (IACHR) and bucked a continent-wide trend toward the repeal of this type of law.

In July, Attorney General Isaías Rodríguez ordered an investigation into whether the newspaper *El Universal* had illegally subjected his office and the country's judiciary to public contempt by publishing an editorial entitled "Justice on its Knees" (Justicia Arodillada). In October, in a welcome ruling, the Supreme Court found that the editorial in question did not in fact constitute an "institutional insult" prohibited by law. The Court noted, however, that the constitution proscribes "the use of freedom of information and opinion to destabilize democratic institutions."

Police Killings

The killing of three innocent students in the Kennedy district of Caracas on June 27, 2005, highlighted the violence and lawlessness of Venezuela's police forces. Leonardo González, Erick Montenegro, and Edgar Quintero died after police from the Directorate of Military Intelligence (DIM) and the Criminal Investigations Police (Cicpc) opened fire on their car when they were returning from the university. The police reportedly confused the students' car with a vehicle they were pursuing, and opened fire when it failed to heed an order to stop. González's body was found in the street near their car, with a bullet wound in the eye. According to an eyewitness, men in civilian clothes wearing hoods captured Montenegro and Quintero in an alley, made them lie on the ground, and shot them in cold blood. The police reportedly planted weapons on the scene to make it appear that they had been fired on first.

Hundreds of police executions have been reported over the past several years, although the problem long predates the current administration. While the Attorney General's Office and the human rights ombudsman have denounced these abuses, little progress has been made in prosecuting the police responsible or introducing the reforms necessary to combat the practice. In August 2005, the Attorney General's Office announced that it was investigating 5,520 presumed extrajudicial executions—involving 6,127 victims—committed between 2000 and July 31, 2005. Of 5,997 police and military personnel allegedly implicated, prosecutors have filed charges against 517, and at this writing only eighty-eight had been convicted (1.47 percent).

Prison Conditions

Conditions in Venezuela's prisons are notoriously abusive. Overcrowding is chronic and armed gangs maintain effective control within the prison walls. Prison riots and inmate violence claim hundreds of lives every year. In October 2005, Venezuelan Prison Watch (Observatorio Venezolano de Prisiones), a Caracas-based group, claimed that 314 prisoners were killed and 517 were wounded in violent incidents over the course of the year.

Border Security and the Right to Refugee Status

The Venezuelan and Colombian authorities continue to implement joint plans to assist hundreds of refugees who cross into Venezuela to escape violence by irregular armed groups in Colombia. Due to insecurity in the border regions, many Colombians fleeing the armed conflict head for an uncertain but safer future in Venezuela's cities. In June, a group of sixty-two people, many of them children, took refuge in a settlement of the indigenous Barí people in Zulia state. After negotiations with Barí community leaders who wanted them to leave, in September the National Commission for Refugees transported the refugees by helicopter to a safer and better equipped location

Human Rights Defenders and Civil Society

Public officials and government media have continued pursuing efforts to discredit Venezuela's nongovernmental human rights organizations. Government officials and pro- government legislators publicly accused Humberto Prado, coordinator of Venezuelan Prison Watch and a prominent critic of prison policy, of starting a prison protest. In January, Prado reportedly received anonymous threats on his mobile phone. In March, COFAVIC, a respected human rights organization, reported that official media had insinuated that the organization had taken a share of money paid by the State in reparation to the victims of police killings during the Caracazo riots of 1989, a claim the organization vigorously denied.

In August 2005, the Supreme Court rejected a petition by another human rights organization, PROVEA, to order President Chávez to retract public statements he had previously made suggesting that both groups were participating in a U.S.-backed conspiracy against the government.

During 2005 the Attorney General's Office opened a criminal investigation of one of Venezuela's most respected human rights lawyers, Carlos Ayala Corao (a former president of the IACHR and current president of the nongovernmental Andean Commission of Jurists), for an alleged role in the unsuccessful 2002 coup against Chávez. The investigating prosecutor refused to inform Ayala about the details and grounds of the accusation, and a judge backed the prosecutor when Ayala challenged the prosecutor's actions. After a concerted campaign by local and international human rights advocates, the prosecutor eventually dropped the case in October.

In July, a Caracas court ordered the prosecution of four civil society leaders on charges of treason. The court ordered that María Corina Machado, Alejandro Plaz, and two colleagues be tried on treason charges brought by a public prosecutor because their nongovernmental organization, Súmate, accepted foreign funds for a program that encouraged citizen participation in a 2004 referendum on President Chavez's presidency. They were charged under article 132 of the Venezuelan Penal Code with "conspiracy to destroy the nation's republican form of government" because Súmate received financial support from the National Endowment for Democracy (NED). According to the NED, an organization that is itself financed by the U.S. Congress, Súmate received U.S.$31,150, which was used for workshops to educate citizens regarding Venezuela's constitutional referendum process. If convicted, Machado and Plaz face up to sixteen years in prison.

Key International Actors

United States-Venezuelan relations continue to be marked by hostility and mutual distrust. The Bush administration is preoccupied by Venezuela's close trading relationship with Cuba and Chávez's friendship with Castro, as well as his perceived influence in politically unstable countries like Bolivia. Secretary of State Condoleeza Rice referred to Venezuela as a "negative force in the region" in her Senate confirmation hearing in January 2005.

Chavez's criticism of the Bush administration has always been outspoken. In a television broadcast in February, he confided that he was sure that Washington was planning to assassinate him, and threatened to respond to aggression by cutting off oil exports to the United States.

In response to the IACHR, the Venezuelan government maintained that the IACHR's analysis and recommendations regarding Venezuela in its 2003 report infringed upon the country's national sovereignty. The commission had criticized Venezuela's weak separation of powers, the concentration of power in the executive branch, and the growing participation of the armed forces in government. In its 2004 annual report, published in early 2005, the commission noted that the government's position was "incompatible with international law and with the American Convention itself."

CHINA

Devastating Blows

Religious Repression of Uighurs in Xinjiang

HUMAN
RIGHTS
WATCH

HRIC

WORLD REPORT
2006

ASIA

AFGHANISTAN

Four years after U.S. forces ousted the Taliban from Kabul, Afghanistan faces an increasingly violent insurgency in southern and southeastern areas, while in the rest of the country regional military commanders—warlords—further entrench themselves by subverting the political process and controlling the country's drug trade.

Insecurity hampers development in much of Afghanistan, one of the least developed countries in the world. Economic growth remains mostly limited to urban areas, and in particular, Kabul. Human rights abuses, poverty, and insecurity increase markedly with distance away from city centers.

Women and girls continue to suffer from discrimination and restrictions. Only 35 percent of school-age girls are in school. According to 2005 U.N. and Afghan government figures, most marriages continue to involve girls below the age of sixteen, many of them forced.

The election of a parliament completed the process initiated by the Bonn Agreement in 2001. Election day was free of serious violence or technical problems, but during the campaign period Human Rights Watch documented pervasive intimidation of voters and candidates, in particular women. Over half the members of the new parliament are linked to armed groups or have records of past human rights abuses.

In early May 2005, sixteen protesters were killed by police and army troops during violent demonstrations in several cities in response to reports of U.S. interrogators desecrating a copy of the Koran during interrogations at Guantanamo Bay.

Afghanistan again produced nearly 80 percent of the world's heroin, and narcotics production and trafficking brought in an estimated U.S. $3 billion to the Afghan economy, far and away the largest single source of income for the country and a significant source of criminality and resistance to the rule of law.

AFGHANISTAN

Blood-Stained Hands

Past Atrocities in Kabul and Afghanistan's Legacy of Impunity

HUMAN RIGHTS WATCH

Insurgency

In 2005, Taliban and other anti-government forces, some allied with Gulbuddin Hekmaytar, significantly expanded their insurgency in the predominantly Pashtun areas in southern Afghanistan. It was also the deadliest year for U.S. forces and their coalition allies in Afghanistan: more than eighty-five U.S. troops were killed, more than fifty of them as a result of hostile fire. Over 1,500 Afghan civilians died because of this political violence.

On May 7, a suicide bomber set off a bomb in a Kabul internet café, killing several Afghan civilians and a Burmese engineer working for the United Nations. Several other suicide attacks, previously rare in Afghanistan, took place, mostly in southern Afghanistan. Another alarming development was the Taliban's assassination of at least eight clergymen supportive of the central government.

The sharp increase in violence indicates that the Taliban has succeeded in regrouping, with significant assistance from across the Pakistani border. It also reflects growing resentment by local Afghans against a central government that fails to deliver on promises of development and the heavy-handed tactics employed by U.S. and coalition forces.

Insecurity

Despite the insurgency's growing strength, the majority of Afghans cited the numerous regional warlords as the greatest source of insecurity. In some remote areas, there are still no real governmental structures or activity, only abuse and criminal enterprises by warlords, many of whom were brought to power with the assistance of the United States after the Taliban's defeat.

Armed clashes between rival factions decreased in 2005, but in many areas warlords and their troops continue to engage in arbitrary arrests, illegal detentions, kidnapping, extortion, torture, murder, extrajudicial killings of criminal suspects, forced displacement, and rape of women, girls, and boys.

Women and Girls

Women and girls continue to face severe discrimination and suffer the worst effects of Afghanistan's insecurity. Conditions are better than under the Taliban, but four years later progress has been inadequate and too slow. Women who are active in public life as political candidates, journalists, teachers, or NGO workers, or who criticize local rulers, still face disproportionate threats and violence.

Women and girls are subject to both formal and informal (customary) justice mechanisms that fail to protect their rights. Violence against women and girls remains rampant, including domestic violence, sexual violence, and forced marriage. Authorities often fail to investigate or prosecute these cases. Dozens of women are imprisoned around the country for "running away" from abusive or forced marriages, or for transgressing social norms by eloping. Some are placed in custody to prevent violent retaliation from family members. Women and girls continue to confront tight restrictions on their mobility, and many are not free to travel without a male relative and a burqa.

In mid-April 2005, a twenty-nine-year-old woman was beaten to death by her own family for adultery in Badakhshan province. And on May 4, three women were found murdered in Baghlan province with notes attached to the bodies warning women not to work for nongovernmental organizations or Western aid agencies.

The most recently available figures show that in Afghanistan, one woman died every thirty minutes due to complications in pregnancy and childbirth. Maternal mortality claims 1,600 women per every 100,000 births in the country. According to the most recently available figures, only 35 percent of girls of school age attend classes, with only 10 percent of girls attending secondary school. In five Afghan provinces in the south, at least 90 percent of school-age girls do not attend school.

On October 11, Ali Mohaqiq Nasab, editor of the monthly *Haqooq-i-Zan* (Woman's Rights), was sentenced to two years in prison on blasphemy charges for allegedly offending Islam by suggesting the need for reinterpreting Islamic law to protect women's rights. His sentence was the first such conviction in post-Taliban Afghanistan. Despite significant public outcry from inside and outside Afghanistan, he remains behind bars as of the time of writing.

Parliamentary Elections and the End of the Bonn Process

On October 18, Afghanistan held elections for a lower house of parliament (the Wolesi Jirga) as well as for provincial councils. The elections marked the end of the process begun by the 2001 Bonn Agreement, which brought President Hamid Karzai to power as the president of Afghanistan and produced a new constitution for the country.

On election day, Afghans again demonstrated their eagerness for embracing a political process instead of violence; there was little systematic violence and election authorities managed to distribute ballot boxes in most of the country. Women comprised almost half the votes in several provinces, but the overall turnout was significantly lower than expected. Afghan election authorities declared the participation of 53 percent of registered voters, as compared with over 75 percent of voters in the presidential elections last year. In the south and southeast, anti-government forces opposed to the elections managed to drive down participation to nearly a third of registered voters.

Although there were no security problems in Kabul, only 36 percent of the registered voters showed up at the polls. Human Rights Watch found that voters were put off by the complexity of the ballots, disenchantment with the performance of the government and international community, and the presence of too many candidates with records of serious human rights abuses.

Human Rights Watch documented attempts by warlords to subvert the parliamentary elections. Election regulations barring candidates associated with armed factions from running for office were poorly enforced, and armed factions supported their own candidates by threatening independent candidates and intimidating voters. Women candidates, who were guaranteed at least a quarter of the parliamentary seats, faced particular challenges in reaching out to voters and campaigning; nevertheless, sixty-eight women—a slightly higher number than the 25 percent quota set aside for them—were elected to parliament.

Among the more infamous successful candidates were Abdul Rabb al-Rasul Sayyaf, Burhanuddin Rabbani, Mullah Taj Mohammad, Younis Qanooni, Haji Almas, and Mullah Ezatullah—candidates from in and around Kabul—who were all implicated in war crimes and crimes against humanity that occurred during hostilities in Kabul in the early 1990s. Even Mullah Abdul Salim "Rocketi," a notorious Taliban commander, ran and won in Zabul province.

Transitional Justice

In January 2005, the Afghan Independent Human Rights Commission published the results of its consultation with the Afghan people, which found that more than 90 percent of those polled supported efforts to obtain justice for the victims of the crimes of the past twenty-five years. In June, representatives of the Afghan government and the international community met in The Hague and agreed to pursue a plan for creating a transitional justice process, beginning with commemoration of the victims of abuses and documentation of their ordeals and then moving toward a system of accountability.

Parts of the plan were approved by President Karzai's cabinet in October, but the crucial decision on commencing an accountability process was delayed until the convening of the newly formed parliament, which is dominated by warlords.

Several cases under the doctrine of universal jurisdiction have proceeded outside the country against Afghan human rights abusers living abroad. In July, a U.K. court convicted Faryadi Zardad, a notorious warlord, of torturing Afghan civilians between 1991 and 1996 and sentenced him to twenty years in prison. Similarly, on October 14, a Dutch court convicted Hesamuddin Hesam and Habibullah Jalalzoy, both high level members of KHAD, Afghanistan's infamous communist-era intelligence service, of engaging in torture and sentenced them to twelve years and nine years in prison, respectively.

Key International Actors

U.S. and coalition forces active in Afghanistan under Operation Enduring Freedom since November 2001, continue to arbitrarily detain civilians and use excessive force during arrests of non-combatants. Ordinary civilians arrested in military operations are unable to challenge the legal basis for their detention or obtain hearings before an adjudicative body. They have no access to legal counsel. Generally, the United States does not comply with legal standards applicable to its operations in Afghanistan, including the Geneva Conventions and other applicable standards of international human rights law. At least six detainees in U.S. custody in Afghanistan have been killed since 2002. U.S. Department of Defense documents show that five of the six deaths were homicides.

In late 2003 NATO took over the U.N.-mandated International Security Assistance Force (ISAF). In 2005, some ten thousand NATO forces expanded ISAF's reach to western and central parts of the country. Areas where ISAF operates show improved security. ISAF has promised to increase its presence in the south and southeast but has not resolved how it will engage in counterinsurgency activity not previously experienced by ISAF in the relatively more peaceful parts of the country.

BANGLADESH

Political and security conditions deteriorated in Bangladesh in 2005. The country saw nearly daily bombings throughout the year. On August 17, more than 400 bombs went off simultaneously in sixty-three of the country's sixty-four districts, all of them targeted at government institutions. The country's human rights record, already of pressing concern, worsened, as Bangladesh's security forces continue to commit numerous abuses, including extra-judicial killings, excessive use of force, and custodial torture. Human rights defenders and journalists who report on the abuses continue to be harassed and intimidated. A culture of impunity, reinforced by 2003 legislation largely shielding the security forces from legal challenge, and by government praise for the Rapid Action Batallion (RAB), a specialized "anti-crime" unit responsible for many of the unlawful killings, means that abuses go largely uninvestigated and unpunished.

Authorities also continue to do little to protect the rights of religious minority communities, including Hindus and members of the Ahmadiyya community (a heterodox religious group that considers itself part of the larger Muslim world), even as Muslim extremist groups continue to target such groups. Tensions between the two main political parties, the Bangladesh National Party (BNP) and the Awami League (AL), continued, with frequent clashes between the two sides, as well as with police.

Corruption remained a serious obstacle for reform. For the fifth year in a row, Bangladesh headed Transparency International's list as the most corrupt country in the world.

Extrajudicial Killings and Custodial Torture

The BNP came into power in 2001 with an anti-crime mandate. In 2003, the government established the RAB, an elite "anti-crime" unit comprised of armed personnel from various security branches. Since the establishment of RAB, there have been consistent allegations of a surge in extrajudicial killings and custodial torture. Between January and October 2005, an estimated 300 persons were killed at the hands of the security forces, largely in so-called "encounter" killings. Of these killings, 223 were committed by the police and other law enforcement agencies, and seventy-eight by RAB. RAB often operates together with other armed units, such as the Bangladeshi Rifles, or paramilitary units such as Cheeta and Cobra.

Human rights groups and journalists have documented many of these killings and have demanded an inquiry into each death, but the government has refused. The government defends the actions of RAB by stating that, since its establishment, serious crime in Bangladesh has dropped by half. When the European Parliament issued a strong resolution in April 2005 condemning RAB, the government responded dismissively, arguing that "encounter killings" happen in all parts of the world.

RAB and other security agencies have also been accused of engaging in torture during custody and interrogation. For example, on July 15, 2005, members of RAB at Jasimuddin road, Uttara sector-7, Dhaka, and of the RAB–1 Office at Uttara in Dhaka severely tortured a young man. This man had been arrested for protesting the assault on an elderly man by plain-clothes RAB agents on the street. On July 27, 2005, the Boalia police in Rajsahi District tortured Azizur Rahman Shohel and his younger brother Atiquer Rahman Jewel. The brothers were beaten with batons and given electric shocks. Both were hospitalized. The police also reportedly asked for money from the boys' family.

The government's history of tolerating abuses is not new. Operation Clean Heart, a nationwide anti-crime operation that ran from October 2002 to January 2003, was marked by a severe disregard for the right to life and due process of law. Some sixty people were killed in eighty-eight days, three thousand were maimed or injured, and upwards of forty-five thousand were arrested. On the day the government announced the end of Operation Clean Heart, it passed an ordinance precluding lawsuits or prosecutions for human rights violations committed during this period, shielding the armed forces and police from any liability for their actions under the operation.

Persecution of Minority Communities

Bangladesh is a party to the International Covenant on Civil and Political Rights, which ensures the rights to freedom of religion and expression, but has tolerated violent assaults by extremists on religious minority communities.

In January 2004, the government placed a ban on all Ahmadiyya publications, in response to an ultimatum to the government by the Islami Okiya Jote (IOJ) and the Khatme Nabuwat Movement (KNM) to declare that Ahmadiyyas are not Muslims. The IOJ is a small coalition partners with the BNP, while the KNM, is an extreme Islamist vigilante and pressure group. The BNP government chose to save its coalition rather than defend the rights of the Ahmadiyya. A court later suspended the ban, but Islamist parties and organizations are threatening further legal challenge.

Attacks on Ahmadiyya homes and places of worship continued in 2005. Although human rights groups and journalists documented these attacks, the government to date has not prosecuted any of the responsible individuals and has not disciplined police who failed to protect victims.

Members of other religious minorities have also come under attack. Throughout 2005, there were persistent reports of abductions and forced conversions of minorities, and destruction and desecration of religious sites. There were also many reports of forced evictions of Hindus from their properties. In some cases of reported rape of Hindu girls, the police refused to pursue investigations.

Over the last few years, as religious intolerance across Bangladesh has increased, several hundred thousand Hindus, Buddhists, and Christians have fled the country.

Human Rights Defenders, Journalists, and Opposition Voices

The climate of intimidation has extended to other groups who document or speak against the government's actions. Opposition voices are increasingly at risk.

On January 27, 2005, senior AL member and former Finance Minister Shah Abu Mohamed Shamsul Kibria was assassinated. Attacks on opposition AL members are not new: Sheikh Hasina, the leader of the AL, survived a 2004 grenade and bomb blast during which twenty of AL's party members were killed. Other senior and junior AL members have been harassed and threatened.

On August 8, 2005, two human rights activists were attacked in public by persons who identified themselves as BNP members. The victims, Rabindra Ghosh and Ashok Taru Saha, were returning from conducting an investigation into a case of torture against a member of the Ahmadiyya community.

Journalists face tremendous risks in Bangladesh. For the third year running, Reporters Sans Frontieres reported that Bangladesh was the country with the largest number of journalists physically attacked or threatened with death. The government showed little interest in protecting journalists, while Islamist groups stepped up their intimidation of the independent news media.

HIV/AIDS

This is a critical moment in the fight against HIV/AIDS in Bangladesh. The number of reported cases is growing, India and neighboring countries in Southeast Asia face major outbreaks, and there is a good deal of migration across national borders. Rather than insisting on rights-based measures shown effective in combating the further spread of HIV/AIDS, the government both commits and condones rights violations likely to do just the opposite.

Sex workers and men who have sex with men—politically vulnerable groups at heightened risk of HIV infection—are regularly abducted, raped, gang-raped, beaten, and subjected to extortion by the police and by powerful criminals. Such abuses facilitate spread of the disease. The police have dealt a further blow to Bangladesh's anti-AIDS efforts by beating and arresting members of such groups who work on HIV/AIDS outreach and education among their peers. Official complaints filed by victims are largely ignored and sometimes ridiculed.

Key International Actors

Key members of the international community, such as the United States and the European Union, have expressed growing concern over the violence in the country. In particular, the international community has been pointing to the government's failure to take action against militant groups. Only after the August bombings did the government appear to take the threat seriously. It initiated a massive crackdown, which resulted in an estimated eight hundred arrests. The most significant arrestee, Mufti Abdul Hannan, reportedly has admitted to ties with violent fundamentalist international Islamic groups.

The E.U. parliament issued a strong resolution in April 2005, pointedly stating that the RAB was responsible for extra-judicial killings while engaged in anti-crime operations. The United States has recently taken the lead on expressing concern at the situation in Bangladesh. In October 2005, sixteen U.S. lawmakers raised the issue of increasing political violence and recommended sending a U.N. team to investigate the allegations. India expressed its concerns as well and, in February 2005, refused to attend the South Asian Association for Regional Cooperation summit which was to be hosted in Dhaka, citing, *inter alia*, concerns over the security situation there.

BURMA

Despite promises of political reform and national reconciliation, Burma's authoritarian military government, the State Peace and Development Council (SPDC), continues to operate a strict police state and drastically restricts basic rights and freedoms. It has suppressed the democratic movement represented by Daw Aung San Suu Kyi, under detention since May 30, 2003, and has used internationally outlawed tactics in ongoing conflicts with ethnic minority groups.

Hundreds of thousands of people, most of them from ethnic minority groups, continue to live precariously as internally displaced people. More than two million have fled to neighboring countries, in particular Thailand, where they face difficult circumstances as asylum seekers or illegal immigrants. The removal of Prime Minister General Khin Nyunt in October 2004 has reinforced hard-line elements within the SPDC and resulted in increasing hostility directed at democracy movements, ethnic minority groups, and international agencies.

Lack of Progress on Democracy or Human Rights

The junta's pledges of democratic reform and respect for human rights continue to be empty rhetoric. The 2003 "road map" for a transition to democracy in Burma has made no progress. The National Convention to discuss and promulgate principles for a new constitution has continued to flounder. The convention met again from February to March 2005, but did not include representatives from the National League for Democracy (NLD) and several other ethnic nationality political parties which won seats in the 1990 elections. At this writing, delegates handpicked by the SPDC were due to resume their convention on December 5, 2005, in Nyaunghnapin camp in Hnawby township outside Rangoon.

The SPDC continues to ban virtually all opposition political activity and to persecute democracy and human rights activists. Almost all offices of pro-democracy and ethnic nationality political parties remain closed, except for

BURMA

"They Came and Destroyed Our Village Again"

The Plight of Internally Displaced Persons in Karen State

HUMAN
RIGHTS
WATCH

the NLD headquarters in Rangoon which has been put under heavy surveillance.

Freedom of expression, assembly, and association are still not respected.

Despite the release of 249 political prisoners in July 2005, the detention and arrest of people who express their political opinions continues, including five opposition Members of Parliament elected in the 1990 elections. More than 1,100 people are currently imprisoned for their political beliefs. Daw Aung San Suu Kyi continues to be held in virtually solitary confinement without access to newspapers, telephones, or any correspondence.

Three bombs detonated in central Rangoon on May 7, 2005. Official figures put the death toll at eleven, with 162 wounded. The junta used this incident to denounce and put pressure on the exiled All Burma Students Democratic Front (ABSDF), the National Coalition Government of the Union of Burma (NCGUB) and other Thai-based anti-government groups, though no evidence was provided implicating these groups in the blasts.

Failed Reconciliation Efforts with and Continued Violence against Ethnic Groups

While seventeen ceasefire agreements have brought an end to the fighting in some areas of Burma, they have not resulted in political settlements or significant improvements in the daily lives of villagers. In 2005 there was an increase in government military presence in certain ceasefire areas, and the political concerns of ethnic communities appear to have been left unaddressed in the deliberations of the National Convention.

Some ethnic groups are now reconsidering ceasefire agreements, while some ceasefires have already broken down. The arrests of several Shan leaders, including the President of the Shan State Peace Council (SSPC) and the Chairman of the Shan Nationalities League for Democracy (SNLD) in early 2005, led to the withdrawal of the Shan State National Army (SSNA) from its ceasefire agreement with the government. Peace talks between the government and the Karen National Union (KNU) also stalled in 2005 as

Burmese forces continued to attack and destroy villages populated by Karen civilians or to uproot them from their homes to gain control over their land. Brutal and protracted fighting between the military government and various ethnic groups seeking autonomy and freedom has been consistent and ongoing.

The SPDC's campaigns of forcibly relocating minority ethnic groups has destroyed nearly three thousand villages, particularly in areas of active ethnic insurgency and areas targeted for infrastructure development. Forced relocation of entire villages continues.

The Burmese government has refused international access to areas of ongoing conflict, cutting off humanitarian assistance to internally displaced persons (IDPs) in violation of international humanitarian law. Hundreds of thousands of villagers have been forced to work as porters or laborers for little or no pay. Those who refuse to provide mandatory labor are often threatened with prosecution, or exhorted to pay a fee in lieu of their duties. Those who do not properly carry out their tasks are often shot or beaten to death. Anyone found to have made what the government deems "false complaints" to the International Labor Organization (ILO) can face prosecution. Government armed forces continue to engage in summary executions, torture, and the rape of women and girls. Children continue to be forcibly recruited by government armed forces.

Key International Actors

International efforts to assist the people of Burma have continued to meet serious obstacles and hostility from the SPDC.

The U.N. special envoy has not been allowed to visit Burma since March 2004, while the special rapporteur on human rights has not been able to visit the country since November 2003.

Amidst government-organized anti-ILO rallies, the ILO representative in Rangoon received death threats. In October 2005, the Burmese Labor Minister told the special adviser to the ILO's Director General that the government had decided to leave the ILO. The future of the ILO presence in Burma is now in doubt.

U.N. programs tasked to provide humanitarian assistance for the people of Burma continued to face challenges from bureaucratic hurdles, corruption, and extensive restrictions on both travel to project sites and the import of supplies and equipment. In 2005 the Global Fund to Fight AIDS, Tuberculosis and Malaria withdrew its U.S.$98 million program on the ground that "its grants to the country cannot be managed in a way that ensures effective program implementation."

Efforts to place the situation in Burma on the agenda of the U.N. Security Council gained momentum in late 2005 with the publication of "Threat to the Peace: A Call for the U.N. Security Council to Act in Burma," which was jointly commissioned by former president of the Czech Republic Vaclav Havel and South African Nobel Peace Prize Laureate Bishop Desmond Tutu. It called for an urgent, new, and multilateral diplomatic initiative at the United Nations Security Council to bring about change in Burma.

The United States and European Union maintained sanctions on Burma. In July 2005 the Association of Southeast Asian Nations (ASEAN), embarrassed by the junta in Rangoon and under pressure from the U.S. and E.U., successfully pressured the Burmese government to skip its turn as ASEAN's rotating chairman in 2006. ASEAN still faces difficulties in convincing the SPDC to fulfill promises made to other members on the commencement of genuine political reforms, national reconciliation, and the release of political prisoners including Daw Aung San Suu Kyi. China, India, and Thailand continued to offer economic and political support to the SPDC. Within ASEAN, Thailand continues to be the SPDC's closest ally, undercutting other international efforts to pressure Burma to reform.

To improve relations with the SPDC, in 2005 the Thai government adopted an increasingly hard-line stance towards Burmese refugees, asylum-seekers, and migrants. While continuing to put pressure on exiled pro-democracy activists and human rights advocates, the Thai government struck another major blow in March 2005 against Burmese opposition groups with a new policy requiring all Burmese refugees registered with U.N. High Commissioner for Refugees (UNHCR) to move to camps along the Burmese border, where they are cut off from the outside world. Thailand also continues to expel thousands of illegal immigrants to Burma every month. The Thai army has stated that Shan asylum seekers will not be allowed to cross the border.

CAMBODIA

2005 saw a sharp reversal in progress Cambodia had made in observing human rights and developing political pluralism since the signing of the 1991 Paris Peace Accords. The political opposition was effectively dismantled with the arrest or threat of arrest of opposition parliamentarians. Activists and journalists speaking out about fraudulent confiscation of farmers' land, illegal logging, or a controversial border treaty with Vietnam were arrested, physically attacked, threatened with death, or prosecuted and imprisoned on spurious charges of defamation. Continuing the trend from 2003, authorities dispersed public demonstrations, at times using excessive force. Impunity for perpetrators of human rights abuses continued. Political trials demonstrated the government's ongoing control, interference, and intimidation in the work of the courts. Despite an agreement between the United Nations and Cambodia to bring senior Khmer Rouge leaders to justice, it became increasingly doubtful that a tribunal established within the Cambodian court system could ensure fair and impartial trials.

Political Intimidation

The government of Prime Minister Hun Sen moved to silence dissent in 2005, targeting not only the opposition Sam Rainsy Party (SRP), but independent media, and civil society. Rights activists, union leaders, and opposition party members fled the country or went into hiding. In October Hun Sen threatened to abolish the monarchy.

The assault on the SRP began in February when the National Assembly lifted the immunity of three opposition parliamentarians. SRP president Sam Rainsy and Chea Poch fled the country and remained in self-imposed exile during the year in the face of criminal defamation suits. Cheam Channy was arrested, initially on allegations of forming an illegal rebel army, and on August 8 he was sentenced by the National Military Court to seven years' imprisonment for organized crime and fraud. The judge blatantly prevented Channy's lawyers from presenting a proper defense.

Legal action, notably prosecution for defamation or incitement, is increasingly used to obstruct the work of human rights defenders and other civil society figures. At least six critics of the controversial new border treaty with Vietnam faced criminal defamation suits initiated by Hun Sen, including Rong Chhun, president of the Cambodian Independent Teachers Association, and Chea Mony, who replaced his murdered brother, Chea Vichea, as head of the Free Trade Union Workers of the Kingdom of Kampuchea.

The Judiciary

The courts—widely viewed as corrupt, incompetent, and biased—continue to be used to advance political agendas, silence critics, and strip people of their land. In May 2005, the prime minister strengthened his control over the judiciary by placing the Supreme Council of the Magistracy (SCM)—a disciplinary body for the judiciary that is meant to be independent—under the Ministry of Justice.

In addition to the Cheam Channy case, above, a second high-profile political trial concluded at the beginning of August 2005, when two men were sentenced to twenty years' imprisonment on charges of murdering union leader Chea Vichea. The decision was based not on eyewitness testimony or forensic evidence, but on a confession—later withdrawn—extracted after one of the defendants was tortured by police.

The Cambodian Bar Association (CBA) remains subject to political manipulation and continuing controversy over its 2004 elections. In July 2005, the Appeals Court reinstated incumbent Ky Tech, supported by the ruling Cambodian Peoples Party, as CBA president following intimidation and legal wrangling aimed at ousting elected president Suon Visal.

Freedom of Association and Assembly

Threats to human rights defenders have intensified, with grass roots activists and human rights workers being subjected to harassment, intimidation, restrictions of movement, legal action, and physical violence. Authorities continue to impose restrictions on public demonstrations instituted after anti-Thai riots in 2003.

Conflicts over land rights in 2005 went hand-in-hand with attacks against activists defending those rights. The potential for unrest has intensified as villagers are increasingly dispossessed of their land, often through violence or threats by officially backed forces. In March, police and military police in Banteay Meanchey fired into a crowd of villagers protesting forced eviction from their land, killing at least five. Charges were later dropped against the police officers who allegedly fired on the villagers. Police used excessive force in dispersing other protests in 2005, including demonstrations in June by ethnic Pnong in Mondolkiri protesting land confiscation for the Wuzhishan concession, and a sit-down strike by Montagnard asylum seekers protesting deportation in July (see below).

In an ominous development for international advocates working in Cambodia, in July immigration officials refused entry to foreign staff of Global Witness, an international nongovernmental organization (NGO) that has exposed abuses in Cambodia's forestry sector. Cambodian staff members were threatened, and the group closed its Phnom Penh office.

Freedom of Expression

Opposition media was effectively silenced in 2005. Under threat of litigation, arrest, or physical attack, journalists increasingly engage in self-censorship. Only one opposition newspaper and radio station, and one independent radio station, continue to operate. In September a Radio Free Asia reporter was hit and dragged by a vehicle with government license plates while reporting on illegal logging in Ratanakiri. In October, authorities arrested Mom Sonando, director of the independent Beehive radio station, after he aired an interview with a critic of Hun Sen's policy towards Vietnam.

Prisons and Torture

Torture continues to be used by police officers, particularly those attempting to extract confessions from suspects in detention. In March 2005, police opened fire on convicts during a prison escape from CC3 prison in Kompong Cham. Nineteen prisoners and one warden were killed and many wounded. Rights groups later reported torture of prisoners believed responsible for the break.

Trafficking

Government officials, police, and military continue to operate and profit from trafficking of women and children. The Cambodian government has failed to prosecute perpetrators of a December 2004 attack on a safe house operated by the NGO Afesip, in which more than eighty trafficking victims were abducted. In a report issued in February 2005, the government stated the girls had left the shelter voluntarily.

Refugee Rights

Vietnam's repressive policies against indigenous minority Montagnards continue to generate a flow of refugees into Cambodia. A January tripartite agreement between the United Nations High Commissioner for Refugees (UNHCR), Cambodia and Vietnam was heavily criticized by international and Cambodian rights groups for authorizing forced repatriation of recognized refugees who refused resettlement abroad, and providing inadequate monitoring of returnees in Vietnam. Access by UNHCR and NGOs to asylum seekers in border areas remains difficult. Provincial authorities continue to forcibly return Montagnard asylum seekers to Vietnam, including four from a UNHCR shelter in Phnom Penh in January 2005 and ninety-four from a shelter in July. In 2005, officials harassed and threatened to arrest Cambodian villagers suspected of providing food or assistance to asylum seekers who were not yet under the protection of UNHCR.

Key International Actors

In 2005 Hun Sen warned donors not to interfere in rights issues, stating that "international pressure only keeps detainees behind bars longer." The international community appears to have heeded the warnings, offering little tangible influence on human rights issues. At the annual Consultative Group meeting in June 2005, donors pledged U.S.$504 million in aid.

In April 2005, Peter Leuprecht, then the U.N. secretary-general's special representative for Cambodia, delivered a blistering attack before the U.N. Commission on Human Rights on Cambodia's dismal human rights record. In July he condemned the use of electric batons by Cambodian police on Montagnard asylum seekers, and called for cancellation of the Wuzhishan land concession. In November, Kenyan constitutional lawyer Yash Ghai was appointed by the secretary-general to replace Leuprecht, upon the latter's resignation. During a visit in August 2005, the U.N. special rapporteur on the right to adequate housing criticized officials and military for land-grabbing. The International Labour Organization criticized the government's anti-union activity, notably its concealment of information regarding the assassination of union leaders. The World Bank exposed evidence of government corruption, and threatened in January 2005 to freeze U.S.$297 million in loans, but nonetheless continued to provide new loans.

As foreign governments pledged their required share of the U.S.$56 million budget of a Cambodia-based, internationally-assisted tribunal under Cambodian law to bring Khmer Rouge leaders to justice (as agreed in 2004), Cambodia in 2005 reneged on most of its own financial commitment of U.S.$13 million, stating it could only pay U.S.$1.5 million. Japan continued as Cambodia's lead donor and pledged a major share of funding for the Khmer Rouge Tribunal. Support for the Khmer Rouge Tribunal was also pledged by France, the United Kingdom, Australia, Canada, Norway, Germany, Netherlands, Denmark, Austria, Sweden, South Korea, Luxembourg and India.

In 2005, the European Parliament condemned the crackdown on the SRP, human trafficking, violations of freedom of expression, and Cheam Channy's imprisonment. China, one of Cambodia's most important donors and investors, refrained from commenting on domestic politics or rights abuses.

In May, Cambodia's National Assembly approved a bilateral immunity agreement with the United States that exempts U.S. citizens from the authority of the International Criminal Court, whose treaty Cambodia ratified in 2003. In response, in August, the United States lifted its ban on military aid to Cambodia. However, the United States. announced sanctions against Cambodia for lack of progress on trafficking issues.

CHINA

While many governments have praised recent developments in China, the country remains a one-party state that does not hold national elections, has no independent judiciary, leads the world in executions, aggressively censors the Internet, bans independent trade unions, and represses minorities such as Tibetans, Uighurs, and Mongolians.

The Chinese Communist Party (CCP) still has not come to terms with the 1989 Tiananmen massacre, refusing to publish information about the number of persons killed, injured, "disappeared," or arrested or to admit that the attack on peaceful protestors was a mistake.

In spite of its socialist roots, China faces serious challenges stemming from growing disparities between rich and poor, and urban and rural populations. Along with official corruption, such disparities in 2005 fueled a rise in protests and demonstrations from workers, farmers, people forcibly evicted from their homes, victims of police abuse, and HIV/AIDS activists, among others. According to official figures, there were seventy-four thousand protests in China in 2004 involving 3.5 million people, up from fifty-eight thousand protests in 2003. China's leaders' preoccupation with social stability has increased accordingly.

Government and CCP leaders have responded to the increasing social mobilization with a multi-faceted crackdown on demonstrators and their allies and with repression of means for disseminating information and organizing protests, particularly the Internet. Apprehension that so-called hostile foreign forces are bent on destabilizing China has led authorities to censor incoming and outgoing news and personal communications across borders and to impose long prison sentences on academics, intellectuals, and journalists for expressing political opinions challenging official views. Plans by some officials to ease regulations and give more room to civil society, including grassroots groups, appear to have been shelved.

There has been some progress. In March 2004, China amended its constitution to read "The State respects and protects human rights." Although the constitution is not directly enforceable, the amendment does offer some hope that human rights will be legally protected. The term human rights has now made its way into common discourse in China.

China's Legal System

New laws and regulations in 2005 detailing the parameters of permitted religious activities and limiting the formation of news organizations are the latest manifestations of China's ongoing attempt to position itself as a society ruled by law. Although improvements in some areas, particularly in commercial law, are noticeable, judicial processes are still compromised by political interference, reliance on coerced confessions, legal procedures weighted in favor of the state, closed trials, and administrative sentencing.

Convictions on charges of "subversion" and of "leaking state secrets" continue to result from vaguely-worded state security and state secrets laws. Shi Tao, an established journalist, was sentenced to a ten-year prison term in April 2005 for "leaking state secrets abroad." The secret was a directive banning journalists from reporting on the presence of overseas dissidents seeking to commemorate the fifteenth anniversary of the Tiananmen massacre. In September, Zheng Yichun was sentenced to a seven-year prison term for "incitement to subversion." Evidence included articles he had written for foreign publications and websites and for his association with the *Epoch Times*, a publication allied with Falungong, a spiritual group banned in China as a cult.

Plans to revise China's Criminal Procedure Law proceeded slowly in 2005. Long-discussed proposals to add a judicial component to reeducation through labor regulations appear to have stalled.

Restrictions on Freedom of Expression

Critics have labeled China's ever more sophisticated system of controls on the Internet the "Great Firewall of China." More than sixty individuals were imprisoned at this writing for peaceful expression over the Internet.

In early January 2005, the head of the Publicity Department of the Chinese Communist Party Central Committee signaled that controls over publishing, the Internet, and short messaging systems (SMS) would be significantly tightened to ensure social stability. In September, the Ministry of Information Industry and the State Council introduced new regulations on Internet news which prevent distribution of any uncensored version of a news event or commentary. Internet portals, e-mail systems, and SMS were all affected.

More than 103 million Internet users face sophisticated filters, registration of all personal domestic websites, and personal responsibility for all content. The government closes websites without warning. In October, two Mongolian sites and Yannan, which tracked a rural protest, were shut down.

Internet café users, after presenting identification, are issued user numbers which make it easy to track their web use. In February, education officials cut off hundreds of thousands of users by decreeing that only enrolled, on-site college students, using their real names, could access university Internet message boards.

In an increasing number of instances, global Internet companies have been complicit in the repression, insisting they must abide by the rules and regulations of the countries in which they operate. Google does not list links to sites banned in China; certain words may not be used as titles for Microsoft blogs; and Yahoo!, which three years ago signed a Public Pledge on Self-discipline for the Chinese Internet Industry, provided information that helped Chinese authorities arrest Shi Tao (see above).

New restrictions have affected traditional media. A 2005 regulation now obliges Chinese reporters not affiliated with official media outlets to secure a license, obtainable only after attending classes, passing a written examination, and submitting an essay reflecting the ideological training they received. Certain topics are taboo. In 2005, mainland journalists could not file their own stories about the death of Zhao Ziyang, former premier of China, the anti-Japanese protests, the election of a new Pope, or the incidence of bird flu in China.

Chinese assistants and activists who work for or assist foreign journalists run severe risks. In October 2005, local thugs savagely beat Lu Banglie, who worked with residents of Taishi village, Guangdong province, to unseat a village chief they accused of corruption. Lu was helping a journalist from *The Guardian*, a British newspaper.

In July 2005, the State Administration of Radio, Film, and Television banned regional broadcasters from cooperating with overseas media organizations. In August, the Culture Ministry announced that new applications for licenses to import print and electronic publications would not be accepted. To ensure censorship worked, the police announced a regional system of hotlines for reporting illegal publications.

Labor Rights

Workers in China may not form autonomous unions. Officials insist that the Party-run All-China Federation of Trade Unions (ACFTU) sufficiently ensures their rights, in spite of unsafe and unhealthy working conditions—according to official figures, sixteen million enterprises are "toxic" and over two hundred million workers suffer from 115 occupational diseases—unpaid wages, pensions lost when state-owned enterprises go bankrupt or are privatized, and forced and uncompensated overtime.

During 2005, workers repeatedly took to the streets. Some went to prison. Li Xintao, formerly a worker at the Huamei Garment Company in Shandong province, was sentenced to a five-year term in May 2005 for "disturbing public order [and] government institutions." He had tried to collect wages owed by a bankrupt state-owned enterprise. In October, police detained eight workers leading a protest against the closure of a steel plant in Chongqing.

Miners and a "floating population" of rural laborers have suffered disastrous accident rates. In spite of new policies, official figures report that 4,228 people lost their lives in 2,337 coal mining accidents from January through September 2005.

Religious Belief and Expression

The Regulations on Religious Affairs that went into effect in March 2005 codified religious policy in effect since 1982. All congregations, mosques, temples, churches, and monasteries must be registered to be legal. However, registration brings vetting and ongoing monitoring of religious personnel, seminary applicants, and publications; scrutiny of financial records and membership rolls; and veto power over group activities. Failure to register renders a group illegal and subject to closure, fines, and criminal sanctions.

Particularly troublesome are limits on large-scale religious gatherings and on the number of religious sites in a given area; acceptance of "guidance, supervision and inspection" by "relevant departments of the local people's government;" and a requirement that religious bodies "safeguard unification of the country, unity of all nationalities, and stability of society." This last requirement is vague enough to give the state control of any and all religious teachings and is rigorously enforced in the Tibet Autonomous Region, in the Xinjiang Uighur Autonomous Region, and in other areas with large concentrations of non-Han populations.

Equally troubling is increased vetting of relationships between Chinese religious bodies and their foreign counterparts. Officials continue to express fears that international religious ties are a façade for Western infiltration.

The new policies have been reflected in round-ups of non-registered Christians attending training sessions. Most are released quickly, some after paying fines. Despite statements suggesting accommodation between China and the Vatican, at this writing some forty Catholic clergy were being detained, imprisoned, or otherwise restricted from freely moving about.

Petitioners--The Xinfang System

Under China's unique petitioning system, citizens dissatisfied with decisions by local officials or courts may write letters of complaint or appear in person at petition bureaus, and they may appeal to petition offices in regional capi-

CHINA

"We Could Disappear at Any Time"

Retaliation and Abuses Against Chinese Petitioners

HUMAN
RIGHTS
WATCH

tals and even in Beijing. Repression of petitioners has increased as the number of petitions has grown.

Aggrieved parties have learned that public pressure forces officials to pay attention to issues such as corruption, forced evictions, and police abuse, and millions have taken to filing petitions. Local and regional officials whose careers and income could be jeopardized by popular expressions of discontent have, in turn, relied on ever harsher measures to disperse petitioners, frequently employing "retrievers," who use force to break up protests and forcibly return home petitioners congregating in Beijing or in provincial capitals.

Although petitions are rarely effective, the growth in number and increased presence of petitioners in major urban areas has forced central authorities to confront systemic problems. New amendments to petitioning regulations, in effect since May 1, 2005, mandate punishment for those who retaliate against petitioners and for officials who fail to carry out their duties. The same regulations, however, restrict petitioner activism.

Xinjiang and the "War on Terror"

Chinese authorities appear determined to eradicate an independent cultural identity, and the religious beliefs closely intertwined with that identity, for Uighurs, a Turkic-speaking Muslim population in China's Xinjiang Uighur Autonomous Region. The campaign, which extends to personal behavior and appearance, includes vetting of literature, destruction of mosques, and discharge of Uighur cadres unwilling to forcibly implement religious directives. Authorities also have fostered extensive Chinese migration into the region leading to economic disparities favoring the newcomers.

Under current policies, children under eighteen may not receive religious instruction and college students fear reprisals, including expulsion, for overt religious expression. "Strike Hard" campaigns subject Uighurs who express "separatist" tendencies to quick, secret, and summary trials, sometimes accompanied by mass sentencing rallies. Imposition of the death penalty is common.

After September 11, 2001, China used the "war on terrorism" to justify its policies, making no distinction between the handful of separatists who condone violence and those who desire genuine autonomy or a separate state. In fact, the authorities treat cultural expressions of identity as equivalent to violent agitation. In February 2005, Uighur writer Nurmemet Yasin was sentenced to a ten-year prison term for publishing "The Wild Pigeon," an alleged separatist tract. Korash Huseyin, editor of the journal that published the story, is serving a three-year term.

Tibet

Chinese authorities view the Dalai Lama, in exile in India since 1959, as the linchpin of the effort to separate Tibet from China and view Tibetan Buddhist belief as supportive of his efforts. Thus, the government limits the number of monasteries and monks, vets all applicants for the monkhood, interferes with the selection of monastic leaders, prohibits performance of traditional rites, and conducts ongoing reeducation campaigns centered on opposition to the Dalai Lama. In July 2005, the chairman of the Tibetan Autonomous Region announced that China would choose the next Dalai Lama.

Suspected separatists are routinely imprisoned; at this writing such individuals included two monks from Sichuan who received eleven-year prison sentences, probably in early 2005, for hoisting the banned Tibetan flag. Chinese authorities have long refused to allow access to the boy the Dalai Lama identified in 1995 as the new Panchen Lama (the second most important personage in Tibetan Buddhism), instead keeping him under virtual house arrest most likely in Beijing. In his place, Chinese authorities recognized another boy as the Panchen Lama and in June 2005 in Sichuan they ordered monks to come out in force to greet him. Authorities held several suspected "troublemakers" in preventive detention in advance of the visit.

In January 2005, Nepal abruptly closed the Tibetan Refugee Welfare Office in Kathmandu, jeopardizing a long-standing agreement under which Tibetans hoping to reach India could wait in Nepal until the office of the U.N. High Commissioner for Refugees (UNHCR) cleared them. Although

Tibetans in Nepal have met the government's conditions for replacing the office, Nepali authorities have stonewalled. Pressure from China is assumed to have been behind the closing and the refusal to accept another Tibetan organization as a replacement.

Schools in Tibet limit use of the Tibetan language and neglect to teach students Tibetan history and culture. Officials do not tolerate privately-run Tibetan schools.

HIV/AIDS

Although Chinese authorities have announced new steps to address the country's burgeoning HIV/AIDS crisis, they continue to obstruct the efforts of activists and grassroots organizations to contribute to prevention and education among vulnerable groups and to organize care-giving for those infected. Regulations have thwarted activists' attempts to register their organizations and to raise funds, while Internet censorship has restricted the kind of information available to individuals at high-risk. Activists who attempt to bring problems related to the crisis to media attention have been particularly vulnerable to harassment.

Forced Evictions

With courts offering little protection, urban and rural residents have banded together to protest collusion between developers and local officials who forcibly evict them from their urban homes or, without offering adequate compensation, sell off the land they have been farming. Residents rarely win, in part because land is not individually owned and in part because local judges owe their jobs to local government and Party leaders. A 2003 constitutional amendment that protects "lawful private property" has not brought redress.

Protest organizers, such as Song Shitai in Shanghai, face intimidation and violence. The city forcibly relocated fifty-five thousand families in 2004. With building for the 2010 World Expo already underway, the 2005 tally is expected to be even higher. In March 2005, Chinese officials announced

CHINA

Restrictions on AIDS Activists in China

HUMAN
RIGHTS
WATCH

plans to move five hundred thousand families to the outskirts of Beijing in order to protect the environment. In September, they announced that twelve "shabby" villages near 2008 Olympic sites would be demolished.

Hong Kong

When Hong Kong became a Special Autonomous Region within the People's Republic of China in 1997 under the principle of "one country, two systems," it was promised a "high degree of autonomy." The Hong Kong government's October 2005 proposal for constitutional reform, ostensibly an incremental step toward "universal suffrage," failed to mention how and when Hong Kong's citizens would achieve that goal.

There is no indication that Beijing, which reserves to itself the right to veto any proposed electoral change and to interpret the Basic Law, Hong's Kong's mini-constitution, will support any initiative to further "one-person, one-vote" democracy in Hong Kong. At the first meeting of its kind between Hong Kong's pro-democracy legislators and Guangdong provincial officials, sharp disagreement erupted over the issue.

Human Rights Defenders

China has never tolerated independent monitoring and reporting of human rights abuses. Lawyers and activists who use Chinese law to assist rights victims are particularly at risk. Since August 2005, officials in Shandong province have confined Chen Guangcheng, a blind local farmer, to his home and tolerated his repeated beatings by local thugs. Chen had been working with Beijing-based lawyers to prepare a suit against local officials who committed human rights abuses during enforcement of China's family planning policy.

Later in August, China closed down the Empowerment and Rights Institute and, for a time, restricted the freedom of Hou Wenzhou, its founder. The organization had been advising farmers and petitioners about their rights.

Yang Maodong (more commonly known as Guo Feixiong), a lawyer who assisted Taishi villagers (see above), was formally arrested on October 4, 2005. He was first detained in September on suspicion of gathering crowds to disrupt social order.

In November 2005, using a thinly veiled administrative pretext, authorities ordered Gao Zhisheng to close his law firm for one year or risk restriction on his personal freedom. Gao's firm had taken on sensitive cases involving labor issues, cyberdissidents, Falungong and religious practitioners, and the case of Yang Maodong.

HIV/AIDS activists, as mentioned above, have been routinely harassed, detained, and roughed up, but to date, officials have permitted some of their organizations to stay open so long as they operated within government-enforced strictures.

Key International Actors

China has taken an increasingly active role in international affairs in recent years, in a number of cases blocking independent U.N. investigations into country situations, asserting that the issues under discussion are "the internal affairs" of that country.

At the U.N. Security Council, China was one of several countries initially unwilling to refer the situation in the Darfur region of Sudan to the International Criminal Court in 2005. In the end, rather than veto the measure, China abstained and the referral was made. China reportedly also has used its position on the council's Sanctions Committee for Darfur to impede identification of individuals responsible for arms trade into and offensive military flights over Darfur.

China also has played an important role in blocking the Security Council from addressing systematic human rights abuses by Burma's military government. China is Burma's largest investor and supplier of economic and military aid.

In May 2005, two weeks after the Uzbek army killed hundreds of civilians in Andijan, Uzbekistan, the Chinese government greeted Uzbek's president in Beijing with a twenty-one-gun salute and failed to endorse calls for an independent international investigation into the Andijan violence. The Shanghai Cooperation Organization, composed of Russia, China, and four Central Asian states, characterized the Andijan incident as a terrorist plot.

The Chinese government refuses to cooperate with the U.N. special rapporteur on North Korea and refuses to allow the office of the U.N. High Commissioner for Refugees access to border areas where most North Koreans reside.

In 2005, the presidents of China and the United States met briefly in New York in August and in Beijing in mid-November. President Hu also met with Premier Paul Martin in Canada and with Prime Minister Tony Blair, representing the E.U., in Beijing and later in London. Although President Bush, in a speech in Kyoto, Japan on November 17, prodded China to extend political and religious freedoms and to embrace democracy, his Beijing agenda was long on economic and security concerns and short on human rights. Other Western governments' preoccupations were similar. Exchanges with China over human rights have been largely relegated to ineffective bilateral dialogues.

The United States did not table a resolution on China's human rights practices at the United Nations Commission on Human Rights in 2005, apparently in exchange for China's willingness to cooperate with U.N. human rights mechanisms, among other steps. China extended an invitation to the U.N. special rapporteur on torture in 2005 but at this writing still had not extended one to the special rapporteur on religious freedom.

Following his visit to China in October 2005, World Bank President Paul Wolfowitz singled out two non-economic factors, rule of law and participation of civil society, as important for economic development. Both are issues with important human rights aspects. The Bank expects to lend China between U.S.$1 billion to U.S. $1.5 billion a year for the next five years.

EAST TIMOR

Entering its fourth year of independence after a brutal twenty-five-year occupation by Indonesia, East Timor continued generally to make progress in human rights in 2005, although the pursuit of justice for past violations was challenged. Most notably, East Timor established a Provedor's office, similar to an ombudsman institution in other countries. In May the United Nations-established tribunal in East Timor, mandated to investigate and prosecute serious crimes by Indonesian military and militia, shut down due to a lack of international political and donor support. Two months earlier Indonesia and East Timor had announced the formation of a Commission of Truth and Friendship to address reconciliation between the two countries, with provisions for amnesty even for perpetrators of the worst crimes.

The destruction inflicted by the occupation and by Indonesian troops withdrawing following the U.N.-supervised independence referendum in 1999 continue to limit East Timor's ability to consolidate its gains. But negotiations with Australia over oil and gas revenue—although fraught with legal difficulties—may yet yield a significant revenue flow for the impoverished country.

Justice and Reconciliation

In May 2005, the U.N. tribunal in Dili (comprising the Serious Crimes Investigation Unit and Special Panels for Serious Crimes) established to investigate and prosecute serious crimes cases from 1999 (including the killings of 1,400 East Timorese), shut down. As Human Rights Watch has previously noted, important obstacles to justice remain for victims of the violence that accompanied Indonesia's rule and eventual withdrawal from East Timor. In addition to the failure to prosecute the 1999 cases, there has been no judicial accounting for previous atrocities committed during Indonesia's occupation.

During its six years in operation, the U.N. tribunal had convicted some East Timorese militia and prepared indictments against more senior militia leaders and high-level Indonesian officers. However, due to limitations on the tribunal's powers to extradite indictees from Indonesia, no senior Indonesian perpetrators had faced trial in Dili. Trials in Jakarta of senior Indonesian military officers ended in acquittals for all. Only one East Timorese militia commander was convicted, and he remains free pending appeal.

In February 2005, U.N. Secretary-General Kofi Annan announced the establishment of a U.N. commission of experts to review the prosecution of serious human rights violations committed in 1999 and make recommendations to him with regard to possible future actions. The commission's report to the Secretary-General, published in July, found that the trials in Jakarta for crimes committed in East Timor in 1999 were "manifestly inadequate," and showed "scant respect for or conformity to relevant international standards." The report cited the prosecution's failure to make substantial use of available evidence and of witnesses' statements already gathered by Indonesia's Commission on Human Rights and the U.N. tribunal investigators. The U.N. commission of experts recommended that Indonesia accept international support to strengthen its prosecutorial capacity, and advised issuing a clear six-month timetable to show progress on the commission's recommendations. The report also recommended that the U.N. Security Council extend and strengthen the parallel justice process in East Timor, given that East Timor had succeeded in prosecuting low-level militia members and preparing indictments against others. As of November 2005 neither the Security Council nor the Secretary-General had acted on any of the commission's recommendations.

In March East Timor and Indonesia established their own joint body to look into crimes committed in East Timor in 1999. The Commission of Truth and Friendship (CTF) was set up to establish agreed-upon facts regarding the events prior to and immediately after the 1999 referendum, with a view to further promote reconciliation and friendship between Indonesia and East Timor. The body was widely criticized by victims' groups and civil society in both countries for being unrepresentative of victims' wishes for justice and accountability, and for effectively promoting impunity. The U.N. commission also expressed reservations about the CTF, noting that the truth commission's terms of reference, which include amnesty provisions even for perpetrators of the worst crimes, "contradict[ed] international standards on denial of impunity for serious crimes." Five Indonesian and five East Timorese commissioners started their work in August.

The Commission for Reception, Truth and Reconciliation in East Timor (Comissao de Acolhimento, Verdade e Reconciliao de Timor Leste, CAVR) is a national, independent, statutory authority mandated by law to undertake truth-seeking, facilitate community reconciliation, report on its work and findings, and make recommendations for further action. Complementing the work of the (now-defunct) Serious Crimes Investigation Unit, the CAVR has been largely successful in its initial efforts to promote national reconciliation through national hearings on a wide range of issues, truth seeking, and public community-based reconciliation processes—an ambitious task after twenty-five years of violence in East Timor. The CAVR submitted its final report to the president in October.

As Human Rights Watch has previously noted, East Timor's judicial and criminal institutions remain weak, under-resourced, and overburdened. Consequently, many serious crimes, including rape and domestic violence, are habitually referred to traditional customary law mechanisms, which lack basic due process protections and regularly fail to provide justice for victims, especially victims of sexual violence.

Police

Although the National Police Service of East Timor (Policia Nacional de Timor-Leste, PNTL) has had full responsibility for the country's thirteen districts since January 2004, it has not had adequate training or resources to maintain law and order in a manner consistent with international human rights standards. Reports continue of excessive use of force by police when arresting suspects, and abuse and ill-treatment of detainees in police detention. Internal police disciplinary mechanisms remain weak at addressing such issues.

New Restrictions on Assembly

In late 2004 parliament passed a broadly worded Law on Freedom, Assembly and Demonstration which violates international law and the East Timorese constitution by restricting peoples' right to demonstrate and voice peaceful opposition to the head of state. The law introduces a prior notification requirement for demonstrations, despite a provision in the constitution that allows an unfettered right to hold assemblies "without a need for prior authorization."

Human Rights Defenders

East Timor's parliament elected the country's first Provedor in March 2005. The Office of the Provedor has far-reaching powers to investigate and report on complaints against government officials and institutions, including the police. However, the Office does not have the power to make enforceable decisions: It can only make recommendations to the relevant bodies such as the police, offer to act as a mediator between the complainant(s) and representatives of the public body involved, or refer a grievance to a competent jurisdiction or other recourse mechanism. Although it can undertake investigations without waiting for a citizen's complaint, and does have the power to order a person to appear for questioning, any recommendations can be disputed or ignored. The Provedor was officially inaugurated and started work in June 2005.

East Timor's nongovernmental human rights defenders operated freely and played an active role in lobbying the U.N. and government. There were no attacks on human rights defenders in 2005.

Key International Actors

The U.N. peacekeeping mission finished its mandate in May 2005, and was replaced by a smaller one-year political mission called the United Nations Office in Timor-Leste (UNOTIL). Its core function is to continue to provide capacity building support and advice to key government institutions, with particular regard to the police service and Border Patrol Units. The

U.N.'s Human Rights Unit provided training programs and technical support for East Timorese nongovernmental organizations.

In April 2005, Indonesia's President Susilo Bambang Yudhoyono made his first state visit to East Timor. A third meeting of the Indonesia-East Timor joint ministerial commission followed in July. Unresolved issues between the two countries continue to be negotiated through a series of bilateral talks, including the official border demarcation, and how to resolve the ongoing problems of East Timorese refugees and missing and separated children in Indonesia. Thousands of East Timorese students continue to attend schools and universities in Indonesia.

The World Bank has assisted East Timor since 1999 in rebuilding infrastructure, stabilizing the economy, and supporting government institutions. The Bank is supporting a multi-donor strategy to implement a National Development Plan in coordination with the government. However, as Human Rights Watch has previously noted, East Timor remains in desperate need of long-term international financial assistance. It receives its largest financial contributions from Japan, Portugal, the United Kingdom, the European Union, the United States, and Australia.

INDIA

The Congress Party-led coalition government elected in 2004 took some important positive steps with respect to human rights in 2005. It established a committee to review the Armed Forces Special Powers Act and has received a report for review. For the first time, a prime minister from the Congress Party has apologized for the 1984 anti-Sikh riots. During talks with rebel groups in September, the government promised to ensure an end to human rights abuses by troops deployed in Indian-administered Kashmir. For the first time, the Indian army in Kashmir apologized in July for its actions after troops killed three boys, mistaking them for militants. New legislation may strengthen the right to information, rights over land, and minimum employment guarantees.

Some problems persisted, however, and new problematic issues emerged. Attacks on civilians by militant groups and Indian security forces continued unabated. Not only were such killings reported from Kashmir and the northeast, but a leftist extremist movement known as Naxalites spread through central India, leading to a number of deaths, both in attacks by Naxalite armed groups and retaliatory measures by security forces. The government continued to use legislation that shields security forces from accountability—Indian military, paramilitary, and police forces have engaged in serious human rights abuses in conflict zones and yet there have been no attempts at transparent investigations or prosecutions of those responsible. Police reform was discussed, but torture during interrogation remained the norm. The Gujarat government again failed to investigate and prosecute those responsible for attacks on Muslims during the Gujarat riots of 2002. Despite legislative measures to protect marginalized groups, discrimination based on caste, social, or religious status continues widely in practice, with the failure to implement anti-discrimination policies being especially apparent after the December 2004 tsunami.

Rights of Dalits, Religious Minorities, and Indigenous Tribal Groups

Although caste-based abuses are forbidden under Indian law, and the government has embarked upon consultations to protect the rights of Dalits, other marginalized castes, and vulnerable communities, the government has failed to eradicate prejudice, particularly in rural areas. In a May 2005 report, *After the Deluge*, Human Rights Watch documented numerous instances in which higher-caste communities refused to share post-tsunami emergency relief with Dalits. Ongoing abuses against Dalits include harassment, excessive force by security forces in routine matters, mutilations, and killings by members of other castes for attempting to cross caste barriers. For example, in September 2005, more than fifty Dalit homes were burned down by the upper-caste Jat community in Haryana state.

Increasingly, caste *panchayats*, or caste-based village councils, extrajudicially punish inter-caste marriages with public lynching of couples or their relatives, murder of the bride or the groom, rape, public beatings, and other sanctions. This is particularly common if either bride or bridegroom is a Dalit.

Indigenous peoples, known as Scheduled Tribes or Adivasis, suffer from high rates of displacement. They make up 8 percent of the total population but constitute 55 percent of displaced people. This has had a serious effect on the overall development of these communities, particularly tribal children. The government continues to use the 1894 Land Acquisition Act to displace indigenous peoples from their lands without sufficient compensation. In 2005, the government proposed the Scheduled Tribes (Recognition of Forest Rights) Bill, which is designed to protect the rights of those who had been occupying forest land prior to October 1980. Activists worried that the new law could aggravate tensions between those who will and will not benefit. In addition, the draft fails to clarify access rights to common property resources such as pastures and forests, and it appears to be in conflict with earlier forest and wildlife protection laws.

Tribal groups who have converted to Christianity have been targeted for attack by extremist Hindu organizations. In June 2005, an independent people's tribunal investigating the rise of violent sectarianism in Orissa state was threatened by members of the right-wing Hindu extremist groups Rashtriya Swayamsevak Sangh and the Bajrang Dal.

Legacy of Communal Violence

The Indian government has failed to contain violent religious extremism and to prosecute those who instigate or participate in religious violence. Such failures only reinforce communal resentments.

After they were committed for retrial in another state on Supreme Court orders, hearings in two cases related to the 2002 attacks upon Muslims in the western state of Gujarat are nearing completion. Otherwise, there has still been little accountability for the deaths of more than 2,000 Muslims in Gujarat during the communal violence that erupted after a train carrying Hindu pilgrims caught fire, killing fifty-nine passengers. Human rights activists and lawyers had petitioned for fresh investigations and trials in a number of cases where it was felt that the local courts, prosecutors, and police were hostile to Muslim complainants. There continue to be delays in the investigation and prosecution of these cases. Victims insist that the perpetrators remain at large and threaten witnesses; the police claim that the perpetrators cannot be located.

In October 2005, five people were killed in the town of Mau in Uttar Pradesh in Hindu-Muslim riots. The majority Muslims in the town had objected to the celebration of a Hindu festival.

In February, a commission headed by Justice G.T. Nanavati to probe the 1984 anti-Sikh riots submitted its report to the government, and the report was placed before parliament in August. After initially refusing to take action against Congress leaders named in the report—a decision that led to widespread protests—Prime Minister Manmohan Singh apologized for the 1984 riots. Senior Congress leaders accused of involvement in organizing the anti-Sikh pogrom resigned from their posts. Separately, in respect of counterterrorism measures adopted by the police in Punjab to contain a separatist movement, the National Human Rights Commission (NHRC) in November 2004 found the state of Punjab "accountable and vicariously responsible" for its failure to protect lives, and ordered compensation of 250,000 rupees (U.S. $5800) for each of the more than 100 victims of summary execution. Thousands of other cases still remain to be investigated. Many of the families said they did not want the compensation unless those responsible were prosecuted—a step the Punjabi government appears unwilling to take, particularly with respect to assigning individual criminal responsibility.

Impunity of Security Forces

As Human Rights Watch noted in 2004, Indian security forces, including the military, paramilitary forces, and the police, routinely violate human rights with impunity. The Indian federal government rarely prosecutes army and paramilitary troops in a credible and transparent manner. The result has been an increase in serious abuses by security forces throughout the country.

Laws such as the Disturbed Areas Act and the Armed Forces Special Powers Act have spawned abuses in various parts of the country, including many deaths in custody, "disappearances," and widespread allegations of torture. Section 197 of the Criminal Code of Procedure gives security forces virtual immunity for crimes committed in the course of duty.

Kashmir Conflict

The Kashmir insurgency, which began in 1989, has displaced tens of thousands of people and seen thousands more "disappeared" at the hands of militant and government forces.

In 2005, India and Pakistan continued talks to resolve the Kashmir issue, and both sides also met with some Kashmiri rebel leaders. In April the governments launched a bus service between Indian- and Pakistani-held Kashmir to allow separated families to meet. After a devastating earthquake in October 2005, which killed tens of thousands in Pakistan-administered Kashmir, India sent relief materials and offered other assistance. Five points have been

opened up at the Line of Control, the de facto border between India and
Pakistan in Kashmir, to send relief materials and allow Kashmiris to meet and
assist their relatives affected by the earthquake.

According to the Indian government, there was a marked decline in violence
in 2005 because of the peace efforts. India withdrew some troops from
Indian-administered Kashmir and promised to continue demilitarization of
the valley if the violence is contained. The government released several
detainees in 2005 as part of a goodwill effort and as a means of addressing
human rights concerns.

Yet some human rights abuses continued and accountability remains a serious
problem. Militants killed and injured civilians in indiscriminate bomb attacks
and murdered a number of political activists, particularly those who participated in the 2005 municipal elections. Attacks and threats against moderate
Kashmiri leaders, apparently by separatist militants, have hindered the peace
process, and if such moderates continue to be murdered for their views, a
lasting solution is unlikely to be found.

Troops continue to be responsible for arbitrary detention, torture, and custodial killings. There has been a disturbing rise in extrajudicial executions.
Security forces regularly report gun battles where "foreign militants" are
killed. But there have been persistent allegations that such incidents are faked
and that alleged militants, taken into custody, are routinely executed.

Rights of Children

Despite a scheme launched in 2004 to provide universal education, millions
of children in India still have no access to education and work long hours in
the worst forms of child labor. Vulnerable communities such as Dalits and
tribal groups also have higher illiteracy and drop-out rates, and face significant discrimination in education. Many continue to be forced into becoming
soldiers in areas where there are armed conflicts. Others languish in substandard orphanages or detention centers where they endure inhumane conditions and assaults on their dignity. Recent investigations show that hundreds
of children, most of them living in remote tribal areas, died in the last few

years from causes linked to malnutrition. Children continue to be trafficked for marriage, sex work, or employment. Tens of thousands of children, many of them girls, live on the streets where they are at risk of physical abuse by police, heightened vulnerability to HIV transmission, trafficking, and recruitment into child labor.

Rights of Those Living with HIV/AIDS

The government estimates that in 2004, 5.134 million people in India were living with HIV/AIDS, though many experts suggest that the number is much higher. People living with AIDS, as well as those traditionally at highest risk—sex workers, injection drug users, and men who have sex with men—continue to face widespread stigmatization and discrimination. People with AIDS are denied employment and access to education and healthcare. Hundreds of thousands of children are living with HIV/AIDS. Many more are otherwise seriously affected when they are forced to withdraw from school to care for sick parents, are forced to work to replace their parents' income, or are orphaned (losing one or both parents to AIDS). India is still framing a promised legislation to end discrimination faced by people with HIV and their families. While the government says it is committed to preventing such abuse, there continue to be reports of hospitals and employers rejecting people living with HIV/AIDS. Despite promises by the then-minister of health in 2002 to provide free anti-retroviral treatment to 100,000 people (prioritizing children), only 7,333 people were enrolled in the government's program as of April 2005.

Attacks on Human Rights Defenders

Although the Congress-led central government has set up a National Advisory Council that includes some human rights defenders and also holds consultations with nongovernmental organizations to frame social welfare policies, human rights defenders in Indian-administered Kashmir and in Gujarat have been threatened. In Kashmir, human rights lawyers and activists have reported threats from both security forces and militants. Through the years of the conflict, several human rights defenders have been attacked, both by security forces and armed groups. Without proper accountability, it is difficult to identify those responsible. Kashmiri human rights groups seldom document abuses by militants because they fear retaliation. In 2005, some Gujarati lawyers and activists pursing justice in the 2002 riot cases continued to receive anonymous, threatening phone calls.

Key International Actors

As a test of its growing capabilities, India refused offers of help with immediate relief and rescue after the December 2004 tsunami, and, in fact, assisted other affected countries. The Indian government has since received substantial assistance from international donors for the rehabilitation of tsunami survivors.

Ties between the United States and India have strengthened through increasing trade, joint military exercises, training of U.S. troops by Indian counterinsurgency experts, and Washington's 2005 promise to provide India with assistance to develop its nuclear energy program. Prime Minister Singh visited the U.S. in July 2005, and, in a joint statement, both countries said they were "committed to the values of human freedom, democracy and rule of law." Through the new U.S.-India Global Democracy Initiative, both committed to assist countries that seek to build institutions and resources that strengthen the foundations to make democracies credible and effective.

Despite such commitments, India has not used its increasing influence with smaller neighbors—achieved through significant amounts of financial and military aid—to press for better compliance with human rights standards. The notable exception is Nepal—there, its suspension of military assistance and engagement with political parties after the February 2005 coup by the king has been important in promoting the restoration of democracy.

INDONESIA

The December 2004 earthquake and tsunami overshadowed all other issues in Indonesia in 2005. While the disaster helped propel an August 2005 peace agreement for Indonesia's northwest Aceh province, Indonesia struggled to cope with the massive rehabilitation and reconstruction needs posed by the crisis. The Indonesian military continued to commit human rights violations in Papua, and impunity reigned in other parts of Indonesia. There were disturbing signs of a return to intimidation of the press and criminalization of dissent. In September Indonesia's parliament finally ratified the two main international human rights covenants, on civil and political rights, and economic, social and cultural rights. Three bombs killed at least twenty-three people in Bali in October, in an attack similar to that of October 2002.

Aceh: Tsunami and Subsequent Peace Agreement

The tsunami devastated Aceh, which lies only ninety miles from the epicenter of one the worst natural disasters in recent history. Over 127,000 people were killed there in the span of minutes; an additional thirty-seven thousand are still missing and presumed dead. More than half a million displaced continue to rely on outside help for basic necessities. Aftershocks, including the March 28, 2005 Nias Island quake, which killed at least 905 people and displaced almost 107,000, continue to traumatize the populations in Aceh and North Sumatra. It will take years for Aceh to recover from the physical, emotional, and human toll of the earthquake and tsunami.

In August 2005, the government of Indonesia and the Free Aceh Movement (Gerakan Aceh Merdeka, GAM) signed a comprehensive peace agreement after thirty years of devastating armed conflict. In August and September, approximately 200 monitors from the European Union and the Association of Southeast Asian Nations (ASEAN) arrived in the province to observe the initial implementation of the agreement, which includes the release of all GAM prisoners convicted of treason, a disarmament program, and a significant reduction of government troops in the province. The agreement also covers the planned establishment of an ad hoc court in Aceh to hear cases of human rights violations. As of November, the ceasefire and implementation of the peace agreement appeared to be holding, with prospects for a sustainable peace in the region stronger than ever.

Papua

There was a significant build-up of troops in Papua, the easternmost part of the country, with reports of widespread displacement of civilians, arson, and arbitrary detention in the central highlands region. In August a reported 10,000 Papuan protestors held the largest ever demonstration in the province over the failure of the government to implement special autonomy as mandated in a 2001 agreement. In October the government finally set up the Papuan Peoples Council (MRP) in accordance with provisions in the 2001 Act on Papuan Special Autonomy and a subsequent government regulation.

To date there has been no judicial accounting for atrocities committed in Papua in 2000. In September 2005 two police officers standing trial for the December 2000 killing in Papua of three students and the torture of up to 100 civilians were acquitted by a human rights court in Sulawesi.

Papua has the highest HIV prevalence in Indonesia, and discrimination against people living with HIV/AIDS is widespread.

Terrorism

Indonesia faces a domestic terrorist threat, with more than 200 civilians killed since 2002 in bomb attacks targeting Western interests. Indonesia is addressing this threat through criminal prosecutions and a slowly improving police force, although the perpetrators of some of the attacks remain at large.

Abu Bakar Bashir, believed by many to be the spiritual head of the terrorist organization Jemaah Islamiyah, was convicted in March 2005 of criminal conspiracy behind the 2002 Bali bombings. Due to poor conduct of the prosecution, he was acquitted of the more serious charge of planning a terrorist attack. He received a sentence of only thirty months, which was further shortened to twenty-five-and-a-half months in an August 2005 Independence Day sentence reduction.

Impunity and the TNI

The Indonesian armed forces (Tentara Nasional Indonesia, TNI) continue to violate international human rights and humanitarian law with impunity. Military operations in Papua and Aceh are characterized by undisciplined and unaccountable troops committing widespread abuses against civilians, including extrajudicial executions, torture, forced disappearances, beatings, arbitrary arrests and detentions, and drastic limits on freedom of movement. Torture of detainees in police and military custody is also widespread across the country; some of the detainees tortured are children. Indonesia's executive and judicial branches regularly fail to address such abuses.

September 30, 2005, marked the fortieth anniversary of the alleged coup attempt that precipitated former Indonesian President Soeharto's rise to power. The Indonesian Communist Party remains banned for allegedly plotting the coup attempt, and former members or supporters continue to suffer discrimination. At least half a million people were killed in anti-communist purges after the coup attempt, and hundreds of thousands more were imprisoned without charge or trial. To date there has been no accountability for atrocities committed in 1965 and 1966. There has also been no legal accounting for the majority of atrocities committed during Soeharto's more than three decades in power, or for the violence instigated by pro-Soeharto forces in a failed attempt to stave off his 1998 fall from power.

Trials for the 1984 killing of civilians by Indonesian security forces at Tanjung Priok, Jakarta, finished in July 2005 with the appeals court overturning the convictions of twelve of the fourteen defendants. The other defendants had been acquitted the previous year amid reports of political interference and witness intimidation.

Despite significant international pressure and interest, trials of senior Indonesian officers in Jakarta failed to give a credible judicial accounting for atrocities committed in East Timor in 1999 (see East Timor chapter).

Freedom of Expression

Although political space for dissent increased enormously after the fall of President Soeharto, the June 2005 conviction and six-month sentence for a student in Bali for burning a portrait of President Susilo Bambang Yudhoyono illustrates how broadly-worded laws limiting freedom of expression are still used by authorities to target outspoken critics.

After the fall of Soeharto, Indonesia for a time was considered a center of media freedom in Southeast Asia. However, the trend more recently has been toward a more restrictive environment characterized by extensive restrictions on, and intimidation of, journalists in Aceh, and ongoing use of criminal defamation laws to target journalists and editors who criticize public figures.

In May 2005 two newspaper editors, Darwin Ruslinur and Budiono Syahputro, were each sentenced to nine months in jail after a judge found them guilty of defaming a local Golkar Party leader in Lampung, Sumatra. In April an appeals court upheld a one-year prison sentence for Bambang Harymurti, the editor of the prominent independent Jakarta news magazine *Tempo*, for an allegedly defamatory article about a well-connected businessman.

Freedom of Religion

In July 2005 Indonesia's Council of Ulemas issued a *fatwa* against the Ahmadiyah, prompting a series of attacks against their places of worship. Founded in 1889 by Mirza Ghulam Ahmad, the Ahmadiyah identify themselves as Muslims but differ with other Muslims as to whether Mohammad was the "final" monotheist prophet; consequently, some other Muslims perceive the Ahmadiyah as heretics. The police regularly failed to respond to the attacks, and at the time of writing no charges had been brought against any perpetrator. By November 2005 at least two local regencies in Java had banned all Ahmadiyah religious activity in those areas, in direct violation of Indonesian constitutional religious freedom guarantees.

INDONESIA

Always on Call

Abuse and Exploitation of Child Domestic Workers in Indonesia

HUMAN
RIGHTS
WATCH

Indonesian Migrant Workers

Over a million Indonesians work abroad, sending home remittances critical to the country's economy. Women comprise over 75 percent of these migrant workers.

In addition to problems these workers encounter while abroad (see the Malaysia and Saudi Arabia chapters), many women domestic workers confront a wide range of human rights abuses during recruitment, pre-departure training, and return to Indonesia. These abuses include being confined in locked, overcrowded training centers for months on end, and many fall deeply into debt to pay exorbitant agency fees. Some girls and women seeking employment become victims of human trafficking.

Indonesia has taken some positive steps to address this issue, but 2004 migrant workers legislation is deeply flawed. Indonesian officials have not vigorously implemented necessary protections, such as effectively monitoring and prosecuting labor agencies or fighting corruption.

Child Domestic Workers in Indonesia

At least 688,000 children, mainly girls, are estimated to work as domestics in Indonesia. Typically recruited between the ages of twelve and fifteen, often on false promises of decent wages and working conditions, girls may work fourteen to eighteen hours a day, seven days a week, and earn far less than the prevailing minimum wage. In the worst cases, child domestics are paid no salary at all and are physically and sexually abused. Domestic workers in Indonesia are not recognized as workers by the government, and are excluded from the nation's labor code, which affords basic labor rights to workers in the "formal" sector such as a minimum wage, overtime pay, an eight-hour work day and forty-hour work week, weekly day of rest, vacation, and social security. The Ministry of Manpower does not monitor the "informal" sector, and no effective mechanisms exist for domestics to report cases of abuse. The exclusion of all domestic workers from these rights denies them equal protection of the law and has a discriminatory impact on women and girls, who constitute the vast majority of domestic workers.

Human Rights Defenders

On September 7, 2004, one of Indonesia's most outspoken and respected human rights defenders, Munir Said Thalib, died under suspicious circumstances on a plane to the Netherlands. The autopsy report, released in November 2004, concluded that Munir had died from arsenic poisoning.

In December 2004 President Yudhoyono established, by presidential decree, an independent fact-finding team to investigate Munir's killing. The team's unpublished report identified Garuda airlines pilot Pollycarpus Priyanto as a leading suspect in the case, and linked him to senior employees of the Garuda airline and high-ranking intelligence officials. On August 9, 2005, the trial of Pollycarpus began at the Central Jakarta District Court. Pollycarpus was charged with committing or participating in the planned murder of Munir, either alone or in collaboration with two other named suspects. However, the indictment against Pollycarpus made no mention of the fact-finding team's report or findings. The trial is ongoing at this writing.

The fact-finding team also issued a summons to retired army Lt. Gen. Hendropriyono, the head of Indonesia's State Intelligence Body at the time of the murder. He refused to comply with the summons, and subsequently filed criminal defamation charges against two respected human rights defenders, Usman Hamid (the head of Kontras) and Rachland Nashidik (the head of Imparsial), who were members of the fact-finding team.

In Aceh, human rights defenders still suffer threats and intimidation from security forces and GAM when monitoring and investigating human rights abuses.

Key International Actors

In February 2005 the United States lifted long-running restrictions and resumed full International Military Education and Training (IMET) for Indonesia. First imposed following the massacre of civilians at Santa Cruz cemetery in East Timor in 1991, the restrictions had remained in place pending Indonesia's cooperation with the FBI in an ongoing investigation into the killing of two Americans and one Papuan in Papua in August 2002. In November the U.S Congress voted to maintain some restrictions on U.S military assistance to Indonesia in foreign military financing, pending progress in accountability for human rights violations, and increased civilian control over the military.

Indonesia's relationship with the United States continues to focus on joint efforts to fight terrorism. The United States has made it clear that cooperation in the "war on terror" is more critical than human rights to normalization of the U.S.-Indonesia relationship.

In February 2005 U.N. Secretary-General Kofi Annan announced the establishment of a commission of experts to review the prosecution of serious human rights violations committed in East Timor in 1999, given Indonesia's failure to do so effectively. After initially being refused visas to enter the country, the commission traveled to Jakarta in May 2005. The commission's report to the secretary-general, published in July, found that the trials in Jakarta for crimes committed in East Timor in 1999 were "manifestly inadequate," showing "scant respect for or conformity to relevant international standards," primarily due to a lack of commitment on the part of the prosecution, and a lack of expertise, experience and training. The commission recommended that Indonesia accept international support to strengthen its prosecutorial capacity, advising that the Indonesian government be given a clear six-month timetable to show progress on the commission's recommendations. At the time of writing neither the U.N. Security Council nor the secretary-general had acted on any of the commission's recommendations.

The Consultative Group on Indonesia (CGI) meeting, an annual conference of Indonesia's largest donors convened by the World Bank, continues to pledge significant sums, although donors are increasingly conditioning assistance on good governance and legal reform.

MALAYSIA

Malaysia made only marginal progress on human rights in 2005. Although the government of Prime Minister Abdullah Badawi publicized the findings and 125 recommendations of the government-appointed Royal Commission to examine police abuse, and prosecuted two Malaysians for abusing Indonesian domestic workers, significant obstacles to human rights remain. These include the use of antiquated preventive detention laws that allow for arbitrary detention without charge or trial of persons who are a threat to national security and public order, restrictions on religious freedom, and abuses against refugees and migrants.

Detention without Trial

Under the Internal Security Act (ISA), the government is holding over one hundred detainees without charge or judicial review in violation of international standards prohibiting arbitrary detention and the right to a prompt and fair trial. The government has used the ISA to silence critics and political opponents of the ruling United Malay National Organization (UMNO). After September 11, 2001, the ISA was used to arrest people accused of associating with militant Islamist groups. In 2005 it was also used to detain individuals allegedly involved in counterfeiting and forging documents.

This unchecked system of detention is conducive to abuse of detainees. On December 8-9, 2004, prison guards beat and humiliated more than twenty-five ISA detainees, some of whom have been detained for three years, in Kamunting Detention Center in Perak state. The beatings occurred after detainees in one cellblock resisted the unannounced search of their cells conducted as part of an official effort to impose a more rigid disciplinary regime, and the beatings extended to detainees in cellblocks that did not resist the inspection. No official investigation into the incident is known to have taken place, and no personnel involved in the abuse have been disciplined.

In September 2005, nine ISA detainees who had been in detention for four years for alleged ties with Islamist militant groups had their detention renewed for another two years. Subsequently, in November 2005, three of

MALAYSIA

Detained Without Trial

Abuse of Internal Security Act Detainees in Malaysia

HUMAN RIGHTS WATCH

The poster reads, "Free ISA detainees who have been jailed for four years."

them were released. One was released unconditionally, whereas two remain under a restricted residence order requiring them to report to the police once a week and forbidding them to leave their residential districts.

Malaysia's use of preventive detention laws extends to criminal suspects whom the police find difficult to prosecute due to lack of evidence. Under the 1969 Emergency Public Order and Prevention of Crime Ordinance (Emergency Ordinance) the government is authorized to detain individuals who are a threat to public order without charge or trial. A detainee is initially held incommunicado for sixty days and denied access to counsel. The minister of internal security may then order such a person to be detained for two years, renewable indefinitely. Demonstrating how government authorities can show scant respect for judicial orders, in May 2005 forty-eight out of fifty-six Emergency Ordinance detainees released on *habeas corpus* petitions were rearrested, on orders of the Ministry of Internal Security, within days of their release, on the same charges and without any additional evidence against them.

More than one thousand persons are detained under the Emergency Ordinance, at the Simpang Renggam Rehabilitation Center in Johor state. In November 2004 over four hundred of these detainees began a hunger strike to protest the conditions and the length of their detention. The Malaysian Bar Council visited the detention center that month and found overcrowded cells and detainees in need of immediate medical attention. In June 2005, the Parliamentary Caucus on Human Rights—comprised of members of parliament from the ruling party and the opposition—visited Simpang Renggam and also concluded that the detention center was overcrowded and unhealthy. Human Rights Watch was denied access to the facility, but investigations through interviews with former detainees revealed inhumane conditions of confinement, including overcrowded cells, inedible food infested with worms, limited access to fresh air or exercise, and unhygienic living conditions.

The Royal Commission recommended the repeal of the Emergency Ordinance because the "law had outlived its purpose" and had "facilitated the abuse of fundamental liberties," namely, deprivation of liberty without trial.

Restrictions on Religious Belief

Islam is the official religion of Malaysia, and ethnic Malays by definition must be Muslim. Faiths of other ethnic groups are protected under the constitution. Under Shar'ia law, applicable only to Muslims and enforced at the state level, Malays wishing to renounce Islam (apostasy) to profess other faiths or beliefs, and Muslims who hold beliefs that "deviate" from Sunni Islam, are subject to criminal sanctions.

In July 2005 a mob of masked persons launched a pre-dawn attack on a six-acre commune of the Sky Kingdom religious sect in Terengganu state. The commune's inhabitants were predominantly Malaysian followers of Ayah Pin (Ariffin Muhammad), who claims to be the reincarnation of the holy figures of Buddhism, Christianity, Hinduism and Islam. The mob damaged religious structures, homes, and vehicles. Malaysian police failed to arrest anyone involved in the attack.

In August 2005 forty-five members of the Sky Kingdom were charged with violating Islamic precepts under section 10 of the Terengganu Shariah Criminal Offenses Enactment of 2001. If convicted, they could be fined and jailed for up to two years.

Crackdown on Migrants and Refugees

In March 2005, the Malaysian government began expulsions under "Operation Firm," following through on plans announced in 2004 to round up and deport some 1.2 million undocumented migrant workers. Preceding this was a four-month amnesty during which four hundred thousand undocumented migrants returned home without being penalized under the immigration law. At the time of this writing, more than nine thousand undocumented migrants, mostly Indonesians who did not repatriate, are being held in detention centers awaiting trial for immigration violations, which are punishable by caning, heavy fines, or imprisonment.

Refugees, abused migrant workers, and trafficking victims were also rounded up during "Operation Firm." At the request of the United Nations High

Commissioner for Refugees (UNHCR), Malaysian authorities in May 2005 released over five hundred refugees and persons of concern who had been arrested under the 2002 Immigration Act. As of August 2005, 973 persons of concern were detained in prison and immigration detention centers, and 222 of them were being prosecuted for immigration violations.

The exodus of undocumented workers from Malaysia created labor shortages in the agricultural, construction, manufacturing, and service sectors, forcing the government to import workers from Burma, India, Pakistan, and Sri Lanka. In May 2005 the government allowed formerly illegal workers from Indonesia and other countries who had left under the amnesty to return and seek work. In July the minister of home affairs announced plans to absorb sixty thousand asylum seekers, mainly Rohingyas and Chin from Burma, Achenese from Indonesia, and Moro from the Philippines, into the labor force.

Malaysia is not a signatory to the 1951 Convention on the Status of Refugees, and in 2005 it deported over twenty Rohingya refugees to Burma. In contrast, it has allowed 131 Thai Muslims fleeing Thailand's southern Narathiwat province, which has been gripped with violence, to remain in Malaysia since August 2005. The Malaysian government has stated that it will not repatriate them unless it receives assurances from the Thai government that they will not be harmed.

Migrant Domestic Workers

In 2004 Human Rights Watch documented pervasive human rights abuses against domestic workers, including excessively long work hours, lack of rest days, unpaid wages, and physical and sexual abuse. Migrant domestic workers continue to be excluded from Malaysia's Employment Act of 1955, which would entitle them to one rest day per week and an eight-hour work day. In May 2004, the Malaysian government signed a Memorandum of Understanding (MOU) with Indonesia regarding migrant workers, but excluded domestic workers. Despite assurances by the governments in 2004 that they would create an MOU within three months to provide greater legal protection to domestic workers, they have yet to do so.

In June 2005 Malaysian courts sentenced a Malaysian man to twenty years in jail for beating to death his Indonesian domestic worker, and another employer received a twelve-year prison term for raping his Indonesian domestic worker.

Human Rights Defenders

Malaysian human rights defenders operate with little intimidation from the Malaysian government. However, human rights advocate Irene Fernandez continued to be on bail pending the outcome of her appeal against a 2003 conviction under Malaysia's restrictive press laws for "maliciously publishing false news," for which she had been sentenced to a year in prison. Fernandez had been arrested in 1995 when Tenaganita, a nongovernmental organization she headed, published a report documenting beatings, sexual violence, and inadequate food and water in Malaysia's immigration detention camps. Fernandez was awarded the 2005 Right Livelihood Awards, known as the alternative Nobels.

Key International Actors

The United States, once a critic of Malaysia's misuse of the ISA, has stopped voicing its disapproval. In June 2005 Malaysian Inspector General of Police Tun Sri Mohamed Bakri Omar, in asserting that governments have valid grounds to enact laws that restrict human rights, cited the U.S. Patriot Act and the United Kingdom's Prevention of Terrorism Act 2005 as justifications for Malaysia's continuing to detain individuals indefinitely without charge. Malaysian cabinet minister Datuk Mohamed Nazri told Human Rights Watch in July 2005 that the U.S. no longer criticizes Malaysia's use of the ISA because of U.S. detention practices at Guantánamo Bay.

NEPAL

The human rights situation in Nepal worsened markedly in 2005. On February 1 King Gyanendra staged a coup against the civilian government, which he claimed was a necessary step to tackle the nine-year-old Maoist insurgency. Security forces arrested all leaders of major political parties. Authorities severed all communications links within Nepal and with the outside world. Many civil and political rights, including freedom of movement and freedom of assembly, were suspended.

Approximately three thousand political, human rights, and student activists were detained for months after the coup. The crackdown forced many human rights defenders to leave the country and others to curtail their work. After months of internal bickering, the political parties in September 2005 organized a series of protests against the king's usurpation of power. However, a renewed clampdown on the press towards the end of 2005 demoralized the political opposition and the otherwise vibrant and defiant media.

Despite the king's promise to resolve the civil war, the conflict continued with the same brutal intensity until September 2005, when the Maoists declared a unilateral ceasefire. The government said that it doubted the sincerity of the ceasefire and at this writing had not reciprocated. In spite of renewed commitments to abide by international standards, both sides continue to engage in serious violations of international humanitarian law. The establishment of a U.N. human rights office has generated some hope that the tide of abuses might be curtailed through vigorous monitoring and public censure of violations.

Abuses Associated with the February Coup

The royalist government has further clamped down on civil and political rights since February 1, 2005. The government prevents political parties and trade and student unions from operating freely, the media is restricted, and individuals have almost no recourse to the law. Extrajudicial killings, illegal detentions, and "disappearances" continue to be instigated by the Royal

Nepalese Army (RNA) while the Maoists continue to engage in extortion, murder, forced displacement of civilians, and abductions. While these abuses existed before the coup, the ability of human rights defenders and the media to document abuses is now more difficult.

New laws and institutions have been designed to anchor the government's new restrictions in place. In the months after the takeover, the king maintained emergency powers through legislative changes that solidified control over key institutions, such as the National Human Rights Commission (NHRC), civil service, and media. The Human Rights Commission Act was amended to allow the king to change the composition of the NHRC appointment committee, undermining its independence and neutrality. Human Rights Watch found that the government and the RNA have consistently hampered the work of the judiciary and NHRC, despite cosmetic steps designed to give a contrary impression. Strict media regulations have prohibited the broadcasting of any news critical of the king and the royal family. FM radio stations, often the only source of news for most Nepalis, have been banned from broadcasting news. A code of conduct restricting the activities of national and international social organizations was introduced in November. The code of conduct is another legal tool which can be used to curtail the work of human rights NGOs and any other critic of the government.

The king's refusal to cede any authority to political parties has polarized the parties and reduced any chance of dialogue. The government has reacted violently to peaceful demonstrations instigated by the increasingly frustrated parties. As a result, the parties have reached out to the Maoists in a bid to isolate the king, which has resulted in the government labeling of them as "terrorists."

Abuses Associated with the Civil War

Both sides continue to commit abuses against civilians. Assisting or refusing to assist either side puts villagers at risk of reprisals by the army or the Maoists. Both sides use civilian militias, and the RNA has provided support for Village Defense Forces. The threat posed by these militias was starkly

demonstrated in Kapilvastu where mobs associated with the Village Defense Force went on a three-day rampage in retaliation for a Maoist attack on two village officials. At least 46 people were killed, most of them unarmed civilians, and a 14-year-old girl was raped. Six hundred private houses were burned and destroyed.

In 2005 Nepal continued to have the largest reported number of enforced "disappearances" in the world. In almost all cases, the disappeared persons were last seen in the custody of government security forces in informal places of detention, making it virtually impossible for family members and lawyers to locate or gain access to them. While the NHRC declared that it had good access to detention centers after the coup, interviews with NHRC members revealed that they had to give prior written notice of visits, and that detainees were removed prior to the visits. The ICRC, which has faced similar obstacles, decided in May to halt its inspection of places of detention.

While there has been a limited degree of compliance with habeas corpus orders, individuals are frequently rearrested without charges immediately upon release. The army staged a few high profile courts martial in 2005, but even individuals convicted of egregious crimes received light sentences. In the Doramba case, the major responsible for the company which summarily executed nineteen captured Maoists received just two years of imprisonment. In the widely publicized case of the torture and killing of fifteen-year-old Maina Sunuwar by government soldiers, a military tribunal only found only three army officers guilty of negligence and sentenced them to six months in prison; the court then set the men free for time served in pre-trial detention. The RNA's human rights cell, instead of investigating these cases, has engaged in a concerted campaign to denounce those, including the NHRC, who have documented and investigated allegations of war crimes. In September 2005 the U.N. special rapporteur on torture visited Nepal and said that torture and ill-treatment is systematically practiced in Nepal by the police, armed police, and the RNA in order to extract confessions and to obtain intelligence. In the case of the Maoists, he found "shocking evidence of torture and mutilation" in order to extort money, punish non-cooperation, and intimidate others.

Maoist Abuses

The Maoists continue to perpetrate serious abuses. These include summary executions of civilians, often preceded by torture, in many cases in front of villagers and family members. The Maoists have assassinated or executed suspected government informants, local political activists and non-Maoist party officials, local government officials and civil servants, and individuals who refuse extortion demands from the Maoists. The Maoists have also executed off-duty army and police officers, often capturing them when they go to their villages to visit family members. In April and May the Maoists carried out several summary executions in Nawalparasi, Kapilvastu, and Chitwan districts. In June, the Maoists detonated a bomb that exploded in the path of a civilian bus carrying 150 passengers, claiming as justification the presence of armed soldiers on the bus. At least thirty-nine civilians were killed. Basic civil and political rights such as freedom of speech and association are essentially nonexistent in Maoist-held areas.

The Maoists regularly abduct students from schools for political indoctrination. Most students are released, although some remain behind in what the Maoists describe as "voluntary" recruitment. In April 2005 Maoists carried out attacks on several schools as part of a campaign for the closure of all private schools. Hundreds of schools across the country remain closed due to threats by Maoists.

There are reports of the Maoists using children in combat, particularly as spies, couriers, and messengers. Human Rights Watch interviewed a twelve-year-old year old girl who was forcibly abducted and forced to cook for a Maoist unit. In spite of vehement denials by Maoists, journalists who have traveled through Maoist-controlled areas describe meetings with children being trained in their camps and engaging in front-line combat.

Violence and Discrimination Based on Gender and Sexual Orientation

Gender-based violence—including domestic violence, sexual assault, and trafficking into forced labor and forced prostitution—remains pervasive and deeply entrenched in Nepal. Legal discrimination continues to prevent women from equal property, marriage, and divorce rights and from passing citizenship to their children or foreign spouses. There is no domestic violence law, and several limitations in the rape and sexual offense laws prevent victims from seeking redress through the justice system.

Nepali authorities continue to turn a blind eye to a persistent pattern of police abuse of *metis* (biological males who cross-dress), men suspected of having sex with men; women suspected of having sex with women;, and HIV/AIDS outreach workers. In other cases, police have deliberately failed to protect such individuals against abuses.

Humanitarian Concerns

The conflict and coup led to increased concerns about the humanitarian situation in 2005, the primary concern being the rising numbers of internally displaced persons (IDPs). Recent IDPs have tended to be poor, often lower caste people, fleeing threats from either Maoists or security forces. Many have fled from the hills to urban centers in the Terai or India.

Nepal continues to host over one hundred thousand refugees from Bhutan and has failed to make progress in finding a durable solution to the fifteen-year impasse. The office of the U.N. High Commissioner for Refugees is planning to withdraw assistance in 2005, leaving the fate of the refugees uncertain. This population is at high risk of statelessness. Tibetan refugees also were affected by the January 21 closure of the Tibetan Refugee Welfare Office (TWRO), ostensibly because it was not registered. Only Nepali nationals are permitted to register an organization.

Key International Actors

On April 11, 2005, the Government of Nepal and the U.N. Office of the High Commissioner for Human Rights (OHCHR) reached an agreement to establish an office in Nepal to monitor and investigate abuses of human rights by both parties to the conflict. The office has a mandate to independently monitor the human rights situation as well as support the NHRC and civil society organizations. On September 16, the High Commissioner issued a report on the office's activities in Nepal which provided an overview of the human rights situation. The report charged the government with extra-judicial executions, disappearances, arbitrary arrests, and curbs on the rights of free speech, assembly, and association.

With the exception of Chinese and Pakistani officials, who called the King's actions an internal matter for Nepal, international reaction to the King's takeover was uniformly critical. The United States., United Kingdom, and India recalled their ambassadors following the coup. Several other governments issued statements condemning the King's actions. All major arms-supplying countries suspended lethal assistance.

In late 2004, the U.S. Congress passed provisions linking further security assistance to Nepal with government efforts to resolve disappearances, comply with *habeas corpus* orders, cooperate with the NHRC, and take steps to end torture by security forces. The U.S. has determined that these conditions have not been met.

Donors have had difficulty implementing their programs given the security situation and the political uncertainty. The government has also acknowledged lower levels of development spending due to the security situation. Since February 1, 2005, most donors have opted to focus on direct service delivery rather than budgetary support.

NORTH KOREA

The regime of leader Kim Jong Il, the subject of an intense personality cult, is among the world's most repressive. North Korea (The Democratic People's Republic of Korea, DPRK) in 2005 stepped back from the previous year's efforts and made little progress in human rights: the country's dismal human rights conditions, including arbitrary arrests, pervasive use of torture, and lack of due process and fair trials, remain of grave concern. There is no organized political opposition, labor activism, or independent civil society. There is no freedom of information or freedom of religion. Basic services, such as access to health care and education, are provided according to a classification scheme based on the government's assessment of an individual's and his/her family's political loyalty.

In September 2005, North Korea asked the World Food Programme (WFP) to switch its emergency food aid to long-term development aid, despite the agency's concerns that such a change was premature and could negatively affect the most vulnerable sections of the population. In a meeting with United Nations Secretary-General Kofi Annan, Vice Minister of Foreign Affairs Choe Su Hon indicated North Korea would rather forego Western food aid than have to discuss human rights with donors. North Korea also asked Western aid organizations to wind down their operations by the end of the year. As of this writing, North Korea is not showing any signs of reversing the decision. China and South Korea, the two largest donors, continue to provide food and other aid directly to North Korea.

The move came after North Korea took a few positive steps seemingly in response to international criticism of its human rights record. It deleted a provision in its Penal Code that allowed arbitrary application of laws, adopted the principle of "no criminality unless prescribed by law," and invited two members of the U.N. Committee on the Rights of the Child to Pyongyang.

Absence of Political Pluralism, Freedom of Information and Freedom of Religion

The ruling Workers' Party controls the parliament, which has only symbolic authority, and all other smaller parties are pro-government and state-controlled. State elections are held periodically, but all candidates are state candidates. Voting is openly monitored by state officials, and results in an almost 100 percent turnout and 100 percent approval rate. There is no organized political opposition in North Korea. The norm for actual or perceived "political crimes" is collective punishment of entire families, including young children. Offenses related to the personality cults of Kim Jung Il and his late father and predecessor Kim Il Sung are subject to particularly cruel punishment. There are no independent nongovernmental organizations of any kind.

All media are either run or controlled by the state, and all publications are subject to official censorship. Recent North Korean escapees have said, however, that some North Koreans in the northern border area have been watching Chinese TV and even South Korean soap operas on DVDs smuggled from China, defying risks of harsh punishment. North Korea fears that exposure to images of a free and wealthy South Korean society could lead to "ideological contamination" and "subversive behavior."

North Korea does not allow practice of religious faith outside a small number of churches and temples that it uses for state propaganda.

Discrimination in Education, Jobs, and Health Care

North Korea's politically determined classification system restricts nearly all aspects of education, labor, and health care. Membership in the Workers' Party, which is imperative to an individual's professional success, is restricted to people whose political background fits certain criteria. Although all North Korean children are required to attend school for eleven years, it is generally children of the elite who are allowed to advance to college and hold prominent occupations. Access to medical care is also strictly based on the classification system, as hospitals admit and treat patients depending on their social background. Many North Korean citizens, especially children, suffer from diseases that can be easily treated. The numerous trade unions in all industrial sectors are controlled by the state. Strikes and collective bargaining are illegal, as are all independently organized labor activities.

Detention, Torture, and Execution

No legal counsel is provided or allowed to criminal suspects, and many of them are tortured or mistreated during the interrogation process. All prisoners are subjected to forced labor and face cruel, inhuman, and degrading treatment; many die in prison because of mistreatment, malnutrition, and lack of medical care. Torture appears to be endemic. Under North Korea's penal code, premeditated murder and so-called anti-state crimes such as treason, sedition, and acts of terrorism are punishable by death. During the food crisis in the 1990s, North Korea began executing people accused of crimes related to economic difficulties, such as stealing grain from agricultural cooperatives. Numerous eyewitness accounts by North Korean escapees have detailed how executions are carried out publicly, often at crowded marketplaces, and in the presence of children.

North Koreans in China

According to a South Korean refugee relief organization, Good Friends, the number of North Koreans in the three northeastern Chinese provinces where they were most concentrated decreased from hundreds of thousands in the late 1990s to no more than fifty thousand in 2005, largely due to economic improvement in North Korea. People who return from China to North Korea can face detention, torture, and even execution, especially if they are found to have had contact with westerners or South Koreans, although an increasing number of North Koreans reportedly avoid punishment by bribing border guards. Chinese authorities routinely harass aid workers providing assistance to North Koreans.

Humanitarian groups report persistent problems with the trafficking of North Korean women. Many are abducted or duped into forced marriages, prostitution or outright sexual slavery, while some voluntarily enter such situations to survive or to earn money.

South Korean and Japanese Abductees

According to South Korea's Unification Ministry, a total of 3,790 South Koreans were kidnapped and taken to North Korea between 1953 and 1995, of whom 486 remain detained. Some of the abductees have been used in propaganda broadcasts to South Korea, while others have been used to train North Korean spies. North Korea has rejected repeated requests from families of the South Korean abductees to confirm their existence, to return them, or, in the cases of the dead, to return their remains.

Separately, North Korea has admitted to having abducted thirteen Japanese citizens in the 1970s and 1980s. It allowed five of them to return home in 2002, but said the others had died. This issue remains a source of intense diplomatic dispute between the two countries. North Korea sent to Japan what purported to be the remains of two deceased abductees, but they were found to be remains of other persons.

Key International Actors

The international community's main preoccupation with North Korea over the past decade has been over the country's nuclear ambition. In September 2004 North Korea announced that it had created nuclear weapons "to serve as a deterrent against increasing U.S. nuclear threats." In September 2005 the fourth round of six-party talks involving North Korea, South Korea, the United States, China, Japan, and Russia concluded with North Korea pledging to give up its nuclear weapons program in return for an energy package from the other parties, while the U.S. promised not to attack or invade North Korea. As of this writing, the six parties were holding a fifth round of talks to discuss how to implement the agreement from the previous round.

South Korea's government maintains a policy of engaging North Korea by being its largest trade partner and donor while remaining silent on its human rights record. On the other hand, South Korea continues to recognize all North Koreans arriving in South Korea as southern citizens (about 7,000 North Koreans have resettled in South Korea so far, via China), and provides them with generous resettlement subsidies.

The North Korea Human Rights Act, which the U.S. adopted in 2004, opens up the possibility for North Korean refugees to be admitted for resettlement in the United States. Thus far, however, little action has been taken, and it is unclear how many refugees could benefit or when. The U.N. Commission on Human Rights adopted a resolution for the third straight year calling on North Korea to respect basic human rights. In November 2005, the U.N. General Assembly passed a resolution against North Korea, citing "systemic, widespread and grave violations of human rights."

North Korea has largely shunned talks with U.N. human rights experts, except for a few meetings on children's and women's rights. It has not responded to repeated requests by Vitit Muntarbhorn, special rapporteur on North Korea, to engage in dialogue.

PAKISTAN

Six years after seizing power in a coup d'etat, President Pervez Musharraf's military-backed government did little in 2005 to address ongoing human rights concerns, such as legal discrimination against and mistreatment of women and religious minorities, a rise in sectarian violence, arbitrary detention of political opponents, harassment and intimidation of the media, and lack of due process in the conduct of the "war on terror" in collaboration with the United States. In October a major earthquake in Pakistan's North West Frontier Province and Pakistan-administered Kashmir resulted in at least eighty-five thousand deaths and seventy-five thousand injured, and massive displacement of the local population.

Musharraf continued to tighten his personal grip on power. In October 2004 he secured the passage of "The President to Hold Another Office Act" in order to remain army chief. In 2005 he stated that he will remain army chief as long as "the national interest demands it," and refused to rule out holding on to both the presidency and army chief post beyond elections scheduled for 2007.

Gender-based Violence and Discrimination

As in previous years, violence against women remained rampant in Pakistan. Under Pakistan's existing Hudood Ordinance, proof of rape generally requires the confession of the accused or the testimony of four adult Muslim males who witnessed the assault. If a woman cannot prove her rape allegation she runs a very high risk of being charged with fornication or adultery, the criminal penalty for which is either a long prison sentence and public whipping, or, though rare, death by stoning. The testimony of a woman carries half the weight of a man's testimony under this ordinance. The government has yet to repeal or reform the Hudood Ordinance, despite repeated calls for its repeal by the government-run National Commission on the Status of Women, as well as women's rights and human rights groups. Informed estimates suggest that tens of thousands of cases under the Hudood laws are under process at various levels in Pakistan's legal system.

According to Pakistan's Interior Ministry, there have been more than 4,100 honor killings in the last four years. Nongovernmental groups recorded over 600 honor killings in 2004. Proposed legislation on honor killings drafted in consultation with nongovernmental organizations (NGOs) was sidelined in favor of a far weaker bill. Consequently, provisions of Pakistani law that allow the next of kin to "forgive" the murderer in exchange for monetary compensation remained in force, and continued to be used by offenders to escape punishment in cases of honor killings.

Domestic and international human rights organizations and media drew attention this year to the government's dismissive attitude regarding violence against women. In January 2005 Shazia Khalid, a doctor, was raped by a masked intruder alleged to be an army officer in Balochistan province. Khalid, who subsequently fled to London, accused President Musharraf's principal secretary of acting on behalf of the Pakistan Army in personally coercing her to leave the country. Mukhtaran Mai, who was gang-raped on the orders of a village council in 2002, was denied permission to travel to the United States in June, in order to prevent her from "maligning" Pakistan. The ban was lifted after an international outcry.

President Musharraf subsequently sparked international outrage by publicly stating that rape has become a "money-making concern," and suggesting that many Pakistanis felt it was an easy way to get a foreign visa. He specifically mentioned both Mukhtaran Mai and Shazia Khalid in this context. Despite the international and domestic condemnation, President Musharraf has not apologized for these remarks or withdrawn them.

Sectarian Violence

Sectarian violence continues to increase. Those implicated are rarely prosecuted and virtually no action has been taken to protect the affected communities. While estimates suggest that over 4,000 people, largely from the minority Shi'a Muslim sect, have died in such violence since 1980, the last six years have witnessed a steep rise in incidents. For example, on May 27, 2005, eighteen people were killed and dozens injured in a suicide bombing at the Shi'a Bari Imam shrine near Islamabad, where hundreds had gathered for a religious festival. On May 30, a Shi'a mosque in Karachi was attacked, killing five worshippers and wounding twenty. In retaliatory violence, a Shi'a mob burned down a fast food restaurant, killing six employees.

Sectarian violence also increased in the predominantly Shi'a Northern Areas. In January Agha Ziauddin, a leading Shia cleric, was murdered in the Himalayan city of Gilgit. At least 15 people died in ensuing sectarian violence, and tensions have continued to simmer. Gilgit, Skardu, and other towns in the Northern Areas have remained under intermittent curfew including for twelve days in October in the aftermath of the kidnapping of a local Shi'a activist, allegedly by the paramilitary force Pakistan Rangers. Human rights organizations and independent analysts assert that Pakistan's intelligence agencies are complicit in the sectarian violence in the Northern Areas.

Religious Freedom

Discrimination and persecution on grounds of religion continued in 2005, and an increasing number of blasphemy cases were registered. As in previous years, the Ahmadi religious community in particular was the target for arrests under various provisions of the Blasphemy Law for allegedly contravening the principles of Islam, and attacked by religious extremists. On October 7 Ahmadi worshippers were attacked in a mosque near Mandi Behauddin in Punjab. Eight were killed and at least eighteen were injured. Other religious minorities, including Christians and Hindus, also continue to face discrimination.

"War on Terror"

Since 2001 the conduct of the "war on terror" in Pakistan has involved serious violations of human rights. Suspects arrested and held on terrorism charges frequently were detained without charge and subject to trials without proper judicial process. For example, Zain Afzal and Kashan Afzal, U.S. citizens of Pakistani origin, were abducted from their home in Karachi in August 2004 by Pakistani intelligence agents. They were released on April 22, 2005, without having been charged, after Human Rights Watch intervened. During eight months of illegal detention, the two brothers were repeatedly interrogated and threatened by U.S. FBI agents operating in Pakistan, and were subjected to torture by the Pakistani security services.

Military operations are ongoing in South Waziristan, adjacent to the Afghan border, and previously noted problems persist, including collective punishment, extrajudicial executions, arbitrary detentions, and limited access to prisoners.

Arbitrary Arrest and Detention of Political Opponents

The government continued to use the National Accountability Bureau and a host of anti-corruption and sedition laws to jail or threaten political opponents. Makhdoom Javed Hashmi, of the Alliance for the Restoration of Democracy, began a twenty-three year sentence for sedition, a charge brought against him for reading an anti-Musharraf letter to journalists in April 2004. In April 2005 thousands of opposition Pakistan People's Party (PPP) supporters, including several PPP parliamentarians, were arbitrarily arrested in a countrywide crackdown. Though many of those arrested were subsequently released without charge, cases against hundreds were filed under the Anti-Terrorism Act and under Pakistan's criminal procedure code. Scores continue to face charges and the fear of re-arrest. On May 11 Shahbaz Sharif, president of the Pakistan Muslim League (PML-N), was forcibly deported to Saudi Arabia when he attempted to end three years of involuntary exile. Prior to his arrival at Lahore Airport, scores of PML-N leaders and supporters were arrested and released subsequently.

During the summer of 2005, Musharraf presided over a three-phase local government election marked by brazen intimidation, coercion, and pre-poll rigging. Some forty people died in election-related violence, making this the most violent electoral exercise in Pakistan's recent history. During the campaign, many opposition candidates faced violence and intimidation at the hands of the police and civil administration. Independent observers reported numerous instances of kidnapping, mistreatment, and arbitrary detention of opposition supporters, as well as pre-election and election day irregularities.

Freedom of Expression

Pakistan observed World Press Freedom Day on May 3, 2005, with arrests and beatings of journalists in Islamabad and Lahore. Baton-wielding police violently dispersed a peaceful rally of approximately fifty journalists gathered at the Parliament building in Islamabad. In Lahore, security forces attacked approximately 200 journalists as they rallied peacefully at the Punjab governor's mansion to press for fairer working conditions.

On May 11, 2005, the BBC's highly regarded Islamabad correspondent Zaffar Abbas was detained along with his cameraman as he attempted to cover the abortive return from exile of PML-N leader Shahbaz Sharif. Several other journalists were also mistreated in the incident. On July 18 Pakistani military police arrested Swedish citizens Leon and David Flamholc and Tahir Shah, a British writer of Afghan origin, in Peshawar. The three documentary filmmakers were illegally held in solitary confinement for fifteen days and arbitrarily deported on August 3. Rashid Channa, a reporter with the *Dawn* group of newspapers, was abducted from his home by plainclothes personnel on July 24, held illegally for more than 12 hours, and finally charged with attempted murder, allegedly on the orders of the Sindh provincial government. "Why are you filing anti-chief minister stories?" Channa was reportedly asked as he was arrested. He was released after rights groups intervened.

On March 2, 2005, the BBC World Service was forced to suspend Urdu-language news programs broadcast to the major cities via the radio station Mast FM103. On November 14, the same radio station and two satellite television channels were ordered to cease broadcasting the BBC's special extended bulletins on the earthquake. The government refused to comment on the decision.

Attacks on Human Rights Defenders

On May 14, 2005, human rights defenders organized a "mixed marathon," an event designed to highlight violence against women and to support their right of access to public spaces. The marathon was organized by the Human

Rights Commission of Pakistan and affiliated NGOs. The event was attacked by police; Asma Jahangir, the U.N. special rapporteur on freedom of religion and head of the Human Rights Commission of Pakistan, the country's largest such nongovernmental group, was publicly beaten. The police, under orders, also attempted to strip her naked. Some forty others, including Hina Jilani, the U.N. special rapporteur on the situation of human rights defenders, were also beaten and arrested by the provincial police and the federal Intelligence Bureau. They were released later the same day.

Key International Actors

Pakistan remains heavily dependent on the United States for economic and military aid. The United States has notably failed to press for human rights-related legal reform in the country, in exchange for Pakistan's support in the U.S.-led "war on terror." For its part, the government of Pakistan has excused its failure to uphold human rights and the rule of law by citing domestic political pressure from hard-line religious groups and militant organizations.

Pakistan has still only signed five international conventions. It has signed neither the International Covenant on Civil and Political Rights nor the International Covenant on Economic, Social and Cultural Rights.

PAPUA NEW GUINEA

In 2005, Human Rights Watch conducted research in Papua New Guinea (PNG) for the first time. The summary that follows draws from that research—which focused on police violence against children—and does not purport to offer a comprehensive survey of human rights conditions in the country.

Police Violence

The police routinely use violence, including torture, against individuals in custody. Children are frequent targets. Detainees report being beaten, shot, burned, knifed, gang raped, and forced to have sex with other detainees. Police rarely are held accountable, either internally or in a court of law. Government mechanisms external to the police—the public solicitor's office, the Ombudsmen's Commission, and civil claims against the state—are not effective in diminishing police violence or providing victims with redress. The Ombudsman's Commission, however, has taken useful steps to address government corruption.

In November, police fired into a group of students who had thrown stones as police attempted to arrest and beat their headmaster. Up to three students were reportedly killed and roughly twenty injured, some as young as age nine or ten. The Minister of Police promised to investigate and hold guilty officers accountable.

A 2004 review of the police commissioned by the Minister of Police found that breakdown of discipline and loss of integrity had rendered the force largely ineffective. It recommended urgent and widespread reforms, including the appointment of a Police Ombudsman. Almost none of the reforms recommended by the 2004 review were implemented in 2005, except payment of past due compensation to officers and improvement of police housing.

PAPUA NEW GUINEA

"Making Their Own Rules"

Police Beatings, Rape, and Torture of Children
in Papua New Guinea

HUMAN
RIGHTS
WATCH

"[The police] were kicking my hands, kicking my legs, bouncing me
against the brick wall. They kicked my knees and stepped on my toes.
... I didn't deny it. I said it was me. They brought me to the station and
they belted me again. I think it wasn't the rule of the policeman.
They make their own rules."

FIFTEEN-YEAR-OLD BOY ARRESTED 2004

Detention Conditions

At police stations, detainees are held for weeks or months in squalid conditions that violate basic international standards. Police typically provide no medical care even to seriously injured detainees. In some stations, detainees lack bedding and sufficient food and water. Children routinely are mixed with adults in police lockups, even where separate cells are available.

Girls and Women

Violence against women and girls, including domestic violence, is pervasive. Police often ignore complaints of sexual or domestic violence. Instead of assisting women and girls, some police demand sex from victims. Girls' and women's low status also is reflected in discrimination in education, health care, and access to paid employment; heavy household workloads; and polygamy.

Despite extensive evidence available to the authorities, no officers were prosecuted in 2005 for beatings and gang rape of women and girls arrested in the raid on the Three-Mile Guest House in March 2004.

Juvenile Justice

An interagency working group, with strong support from United Nations Children's Fund (UNICEF), is continuing its efforts to develop a juvenile justice system. As of May 2005, seven juvenile courts were operating in some capacity. In 2004 and early 2005, policies were adopted for police, magistrates, and correctional officials that severely limited the circumstances and conditions under which children could be detained. In April 2005, fifteen volunteer juvenile court officers were commissioned to monitor police treatment of children in police stations. Police inaugurated a single processing center intended for all children detained in the capital. But by September, this center was still not operating. The failure to hold police accountable for implementing the guidelines and for using violence against children threatens to undermine these developments.

HIV/AIDS

Experts believe that at least eighty thousand people—around 3-4 percent of the population in the capital, the highest rate in the South Pacific region—are living with HIV. Some face violence and discrimination in their communities.

Police sexual abuse of males and females increases the risk of HIV transmission. By targeting sex workers and men and boys engaged in homosexual conduct, police violence helps drive these individuals underground and away from lifesaving information on HIV prevention and health services. Public shaming of sex workers as "AIDS carriers" prevents people from seeking HIV-related services for fear of being stigmatized. Police continue to harass persons possessing condoms, including by forcing individuals to chew and swallow condoms and their plastic wrappers. Such responses deter condom use and undermine desperately needed HIV/AIDS prevention work by NGOs and the government.

Education

School fees and related costs pose a significant barrier to children's education and are often linked to non-attendance, dropout, and the entry of children into child labor. School fees are high compared with the average annual income. According to the PNG Department of Labor, caps on school fees in 2004-2005 ranged from 100 kina [US$31.65] through grade two to 1,200 kina [US$379.75] for day students in grades eleven through twelve. Per capita gross national income was U.S.$510 in 2003.

Key International Actors

Australia remains the largest foreign donor by far, reflecting its proximity, colonial history, and continuing special relationship with Papua New Guinea. Much of its aid is directed to the police force. In late 2004 and early 2005, several hundred Australian Federal Police were deployed alongside Papua New Guinea police, but were withdrawn in May, following the Papua New Guinea Supreme Court's decision that the immunity granted to Australian officers was unconstitutional. By November, it was agreed in principle that that some forty officers would be redeployed as advisors only on corruption, training, and prosecutions.

UNICEF has taken the lead on juvenile justice, with AusAID funding several recent reforms. Other donors include the Asian Development Bank, the European Union, Germany, Japan, New Zealand, and the World Bank.

SRI LANKA

The human rights situation in Sri Lanka worsened in 2005. The December 2004 tsunami wrought tremendous destruction, particularly to the areas already most affected by the country's protracted civil war. Thirty thousand people died and up to eight hundred thousand were displaced. Sectarian interests hijacked aid distribution mechanisms, compromising the modest successes of the post-tsunami recovery and rehabilitation effort. Killings, particularly of Tamils in opposition to the Liberation Tigers of Tamil Eelam (LTTE), an armed group advocating a separate homeland for Tamils, reached an alarming rate of one per day by June 2005, and included the assassination of Foreign Minister Lakshman Kadirgamar in August. The LTTE continued to recruit child soldiers. Torture and mistreatment by police continued to be a problem.

Presidential elections were held on November, 17, 2005, with Mahinda Rajapakse, of the ruling party, winning by a slim margin. There was very low voter turnout at the polls in the north and the east after the LTTE discouraged Tamils from voting. Rajapakse's candidacy was backed by hard-line Sinhala nationalist parties.

Political Killings

Since February 2002, when the government and the LTTE signed a ceasefire agreement (CFA), an estimated two hundred Tamils have been killed for apparently political reasons. Most of the killings have been attributed to the LTTE. As of September 2005, the Norwegian-led Sri Lanka Monitoring Mission (SLMM) had received 1,466 reports of abductions for politically motivated reasons, and had certified at least 641 cases of abduction as violations of the CFA.

On February 11, 2005, E. Kaushalyan, the LTTE's Batticaloa-Amparai district political head, was killed together with five other members of his convoy. He was the most senior member of the LTTE to be killed since the CFA.

In May 2005, Dharmeratnam Sivaram, a senior journalist and the outspoken editor of the pro-Tamil news website www.tamilnet.com, was killed by unknown assailants in Colombo. Relanghai Selvarajah, a Tamil radio producer fiercely critical of the LTTE, was shot dead in Colombo on August 13. On October 12, K. Rajadorai, the president of Jaffna Central College, and also a LTTE critic, was shot dead by a suspected LTTE cadre. Rajadorai had close connections with the Eelam People's Democratic Party, an anti-LTTE Tamil party disarmed under the CFA. Numerous EPDP members have been victims of attack allegedly by the LTTE.

On August 13, 2005, unknown gunmen shot and killed Sri Lanka's foreign minister, Lakshman Kadirgamar, at his home in Colombo. Kadirgamar, a Tamil member of the ruling party, the Sri Lanka Freedom Party, had led the campaign to have the LTTE labeled a terrorist organization by several countries. It was widely acknowledged that he topped the LTTE's list of political targets.

President Chandrika Kumaratunga immediately announced emergency rule following Kadirgamar's assassination. In contrast to her past responses to the killings of Tamils, she immediately called for a thorough investigation, deploying thousands of police officers throughout Colombo.

In the context of the political killings, many human rights defenders, particularly Tamils in the north and east, have been forced to either stop their work or go into hiding. Several human rights defenders have had to flee the country over the last year as a direct result of the intimidation generated by the killings.

Child Soldiers

The LTTE has a history of recruiting children to serve in combat. Sri Lanka has ratified the Optional Protocol to the Convention on the Rights of the Child, which prohibits all use of children under eighteen in armed conflict and all recruitment of children by non-state armed groups.

Under a 2003 action plan signed by the LTTE and the Sri Lankan government, the LTTE agreed to release children from its forces. But not only has the LTTE failed to comply, human rights and other groups have reported ongoing child recruitment by the LTTE, which in spite of international condemnation refuses to acknowledge the practice. Recruitment rates dropped during the first half of 2005 following the tsunami, but increased significantly in mid-2005, with numerous reports of child recruitment taking place at temple festivals in the east. During July alone the United Nations Children's Fund (UNICEF) documented 139 cases of child recruitment, the highest level recorded during any single month since late 2003. During the first nine months of 2005 UNICEF documented a total of 483 cases of child recruitment; the true total is believed to be higher, as many cases are never reported. During the same period, 146 children were released from the LTTE.

Those who campaign against child conscription are at risk. On October 11, 2005, the principal of Kopay Christian College in Jaffna, who publicly voiced his criticisms, was shot dead in his home.

Police Torture and Deaths in Custody

In 2003 the National Human Rights Commission (NHRC) and the Police Commission agreed on measures including ensuring that families and lawyers have access to detainees, displaying written summaries of detainees' rights in police stations, and holding officers in command responsible for torture in their stations. In spite of these attempts at reform, the NHRC reported an increase in custodial deaths, with at least nineteen cases reported in 2005 alone, and cases of police torture continue to be reported. For example, on February 2, 2005, D.D. went to visit a friend in Kiriella police custody. While there, two police officers detained and assaulted D.D. They also made him place his fingerprints on an item of evidence, and forced him to sign a false statement. On May 19, twenty-six-year-old H.F. was severely tortured at Panadura police station. He was forced to sit with his head between his knees, and was beaten and kicked all over. The police took him to a doctor who insisted on hospitalizing H.F., but the police refused and returned him to the police station. He was further forced to sign a statement claiming that his injuries had occurred prior to his arrest.

There are reports of police torture of children as well. On June 11, 2005, an eleven-year-old boy accused of stealing money was beaten and sexually tortured in the Kahawatte police station. The police officers squeezed his genitals, tied his legs, and beat him severely in order to extract a confession. In another case, a twelve-year-old boy was severely beaten by police from the Wattegama police station. The police had come to his house to look for his father, and, not finding the father there, assaulted the young boy instead.

The police continue to enjoy great impunity. While some cases of deaths in custody and torture have been investigated, no one has been prosecuted or punished as yet. In May 2005 the Supreme Court acquitted all the defendants in the October 2000 mob killing of twenty-seven Tamil detainees at the Bindunuwewa detention facility. The youngest inmate in the camp was twelve years old at the time of his death. An independent commission of inquiry into the killings faulted the local police commissioners, A.W. Dayaratne and Jayantha Senivaratna, for failure to protect the inmates from the attack despite prior knowledge that a planned demonstration might turn violent. Neither officer has been indicted or even disciplined, and all others who were tried were acquitted.

Tsunami

Reconstruction work is taking place in the communities affected by the December 26, 2004 tsunami, but not at a pace to match the needs. Nearly a year on, government bureaucracies and delays in international financing have left most of the displaced still in temporary shelters.

Since early 2005, minority Tamil and Muslim communities have accused the government of discrimination in the distribution of post-tsunami aid. In an attempt to address some of these concerns, the government of Sri Lanka and the LTTE signed an agreement known as the Post-Tsunami Operational Management Structure (P-TOMS, also known as the "joint mechanism"), intended to ensure fair and equitable distribution of aid to the north and east.

However, the implementation of P-TOMS has stalled due to political parties' quarrels over who has the right to participate in and control the process.

Those opposed to the LTTE, particularly rival Tamil parties, objected to the government-like authority given to the LTTE under the joint mechanism. The Sri Lanka Muslim Congress complained about its exclusion from the joint mechanism, and interpreted it as further evidence of discrimination against its community. The JVP, a Sinhala nationalist party, decried any agreement signed with the LTTE, left the ruling coalition in protest, and launched a legal challenge that led the Supreme Court to issue a stay order on the implementation of sections of P-TOMS.

Key International Actors

The donor community has increasingly spoken out against political killings in the past year, notably in a March 2005 statement by the European Union's commissioner for external relations. The SLMM, which has resisted including human rights monitoring, finally acknowledged that such killings do fall within its mandate. Following the killing of Lakshman Kadirgamar, the international community, and particularly the four co-chairs of the donor conference, stressed the need to re-examine the CFA and to strengthen respect for it by all parties to the conflict. In September the E.U. imposed a travel ban on the LTTE, announcing that its member states would no longer receive LTTE delegations. It also reiterated its condemnation of political killings and child recruitment by the LTTE.

THAILAND

The steady erosion of respect for human rights that has characterized Prime Minister Thaksin Shinawatra's administration reached a new low in 2005 with killings in the south by security forces and insurgents and the introduction of draconian new security legislation. Continuing failure to investigate widespread killings by security forces in the 2003 anti-drug campaign has deepened the culture of impunity, while critical media have come under direct assault.

In this increasingly hostile environment, members of Thailand's once-thriving human rights and media community face serious questions about their ability to continue doing their work.

The Executive Decree on Government Administration in Emergency Situations

The Executive Decree on Government Administration in Emergency Situations, summarily put in place by Prime Minister Thaksin in July 2005 and later ratified by parliament, has undermined or revoked many key safeguards against human rights abuses. The decree gives authorities sweeping powers to declare a state of emergency, arrest and detain suspects, restrict movement and communication, censor the media, and deny access to the Administrative Court and to redress for victims of abuses by government officials and the security forces.

While the emergency law was put in place to address violence in the south, there is no geographical limit on where it can be invoked. The decree allows authorities to detain suspects for an initial period of thirty days in informal places of detention without guarantee of immediate access to lawyers This raises the prospect that detainees will be held in secret, undisclosed, or inaccessible locations where monitoring is impossible and there is no judicial oversight or access to counsel or family. This is an unprecedented and dangerous provision that carries a heightened risk of "disappearances" and is almost certain to lead to abuses. There is no limit to the number of times such detention can be extended, creating the risk of arbitrary, disproportionate, and indefinite limitations on fundamental human rights and freedoms guaranteed under the Constitution of Thailand and the International Covenant on Civil and Political Rights (ICCPR).

Violence in the Southern Border Provinces

Almost 1,000 people have been killed since a new spate of violence began in the southern border provinces of Pattani, Yala, and Narathiwat in January 2004—some at the hands of the security forces and others by insurgent groups. Violence has included arson attacks on government buildings, bombs, beheadings, and assassinations. On October 16, 2005, a Buddhist monk was murdered when Phrom Prasit Temple in Pattani province was burned, marking the first direct militant attack on a Buddhist temple since the spate of violence began in the three southern border provinces last year.

Unrealistic deadlines set by Prime Minister Thaksin to solve cases of insurgent attacks quickly and restore peace in the region have created pressure on the security forces to resort to extrajudicial means and human rights violations. For example, in massive operations to identify and capture those responsible for the January 2004 raid on an army depot in Narathiwat province, a number of people allegedly were arbitrarily arrested and disappeared by the security forces. However, the Thai government has to date refused to include statistics on "disappearances" in official reports released to the public. Promises of investigation and justice appear to be only rhetorical, aiming to defuse criticisms and political pressure. To date, there have still been no criminal persecutions in the Krue Sae Mosque (April 28, 2004) and Tak Bai (October 25, 2004) incidents, in which nearly two hundred Muslims were killed by the security forces.

Growing fear and suspicion of the security forces have caused hundreds of Muslims to seek asylum in Malaysia. At this writing, the United Nations High Commissioner for Refugees (UNHCR) was in the process of determining the status of 131 Thai Muslims who fled to Malaysia in October 2005.

The Anti–Drug Campaign

Prime Minister Thaksin announced a new phase of the war on drugs from October to December 2005. Almost immediately, new reports of suspected drugs dealers shot dead by the police began to appear in many parts of the country.

There remains no significant progress in the investigation of drug-related murders during the first phase of the war on drugs, from February to April 2003. Of 2,598 cases, the police had investigated only 752 at this writing. Arrest warrants were issued in 117 cases, with interrogation of suspects continuing in ninety others. The remaining cases were dropped due to a lack of witnesses and evidence. The unwillingness of the police to investigate these deaths, combined with the unusually high numbers of drug-related murders, has created widespread suspicion that many deaths were due to extra-judicial killings and police brutality.

Human Rights Defenders

Prime Minister Thaksin and government officials continue to publicly denigrate non-governmental organizations (NGOs). At the National Human Rights Commission workshop on August 6, 2005, Prime Minister Thaksin specifically told NGOs not to "sink the boat" by reporting human rights abuses in Thailand to the international community.

There have been reliable reports of surveillance and harassment of some human rights defenders, particularly those working on issues related to violence in the southern border provinces. In March 2004, Somchai Neelapaijit, a prominent Muslim human rights lawyer, was abducted in Bangkok and is now presumed dead. Somchai had been repeatedly threatened after alleging police torture of insurgent suspects in the southern border provinces. Five police officers were arrested in 2004 in relation to his case, but have not been prosecuted for kidnapping or murder.

Another eighteen human rights defenders have been murdered since Prime Minister Thaksin came to power in 2001. Most were killed after raising public concern about economic development activities by individuals or companies. The latest case took place in June 2005 when a renowned conservationist Buddhist monk, Pra Supoj Suwajo, of Suan Bha Metthadharm Temple in Chieng Mai province, was hacked to death after he staged a campaign against the alleged encroachment of forest and public land by a national politician . Prosecutors have largely failed to pursue these cases. As a result, Thailand's once-thriving human rights community now operates in an increasingly tense climate of fear and impunity.

To curry favor with the regime in Rangoon, the Thai government has also cracked down on the work of exiled Burmese human rights defenders monitoring the human rights of refugees and migrant workers.

Restrictions on Media Freedom

The Thai government continues to restrict media freedom by withholding or threatening to withhold advertising contracts, operating licenses, or work permits from media outlets, and by filing defamation cases seeking large monetary damage awards against prominent advocates and independent journalists in order to limit critical coverage.

In September 2005, Prime Minister Thaksin personally filed criminal and civil defamation suits against veteran journalist Sondhi Limthongkul, Sarocha Pornudomsak, and Thai Day Dot Com, Co. The 500 million baht sought in the civil suit represent the largest damages ever pursued by any politician or government official.

Members of Thailand's media, concerned about possible government reprisals, have begun to censor their own work by devoting less attention to human rights abuses and other issues of national importance. As a result, the government has even greater freedom to pursue a range of controversial policy initiatives, including anti-drug campaigns and counter-insurgency operations. Some of the most brutal state-sponsored human rights abuses in the country's modern history have had little or no public discussion.

Refugee Protection

Prime Minister Thaksin continues to backtrack on Thailand's longstanding humanitarian stance toward Burmese refugees in an effort to improve relations with Burma's military junta.

On March 31, 2005, the Thai government enforced a plan requiring all Burmese refugees to move to camps along the Burmese border. According to the Thai authorities, those who fail to register for relocation to the camps—including those officially recognized by the United Nations High Commissioner for Refugees (UNHCR)—will be arrested and deported back to Burma. Those who do not register will no longer be allowed to receive protection or assistance from UNHCR in Thailand and will be barred from resettlement abroad. However, many of the Burmese urban refugees are hesitant to relocate to the border camps, fearing the move may trap them in a detention-like environment without political freedom and access to telephones or other means of communication with the outside world. Others are fearful for their security because of mistreatment by camp officials, cross-border violence, or political and ethnic conflicts within the camps.

Key International Actors

The United States is the key bilateral actor in Thailand. While the U.S. raises human rights concerns on a regular basis with Thailand, activists were disappointed by the White House visit accorded to Prime Minister Thaksin in September 2005 and the failure of President Bush publicly to address the erosion of human rights protections under Thaksin. Bush instead emphasized the two leaders' close friendship.

In June 2005, the United Nations Working Group on Enforced or Involuntary Disappearances expressed "great concern" over missing Muslim human rights lawyer Somchai Neelaphaijit. In July 2005, the United Nations Human Rights Committee expressed concerns over the climate of impunity created by the Executive Decree on Government Administration in Emergency Situations and persistent allegations of extrajudicial killings and other serious human rights violations.

In an apparent response to those concerns, Prime Minister Thaksin gave a speech at the Association of Southeast Asian Nations and United Nations Summit in September 2005 asserting that lack of coordination and inadequate guidelines can draw United Nations agencies into domestic political issues. "This can be a cause of resentment, rejection, and non-cooperation ... and make the United Nations irrelevant," he said.

VIETNAM

With Vietnam's membership into the World Trade Organization pending, the government took some steps in 2005 to counter international concern about its human rights record. The government released some religious and political prisoners, officially outlawed forced recantations of faith, and published a white paper defending its record on human rights.

Despite these gestures, Vietnam's denial of fundamental rights remained largely unchanged during 2005. Authorities continue to persecute members of independent churches, impose controls over the Internet and the press, restrict public gatherings, and imprison people for their religious or political views. Legislation remains in force authorizing the arbitrary "administrative detention"—without trial—for up to two years of anyone suspected of threatening national security.

During 2005 the government released at least twelve political and religious prisoners, but arrested many more. Most of those arrested were minority Christians in the Central Highlands, collectively known as Montagnards, who the government alleged were separatists. The top two leaders of the Unified Buddhist Church of Vietnam remained under house arrest. At least seven Hoa Hao Buddhists were sentenced to prison during 2005.

Controls over Freedom of Expression and the Internet

There is no independent, privately-run media in Vietnam. Domestic newspapers and television and radio stations remain under strict government control, and direct criticism of the Communist Party is forbidden. Foreign media representatives are required to obtain authorization from the Foreign Ministry for all travel outside Hanoi.

The government attempts to control public access to the Internet and blocks websites considered objectionable or politically sensitive. In May 2005, the government blocked the Vietnamese-language website of the British Broadcasting Corporation. A government directive issued in July 2005 prohibits Internet use by "reactionary and hostile forces." In 2004, the Ministry of Public Security established an office to monitor the Internet for unauthorized use and "criminal" content, including disseminating "state secrets." A January 2004 government directive requires Internet café owners to monitor customers' email messages and block access to banned websites.

Several dissidents have been imprisoned for alleged "national security" crimes after using the Internet to disseminate views disliked by the government. They include Pham Hong Son, who is serving five years of imprisonment on espionage charges after he disseminated articles about democracy on the Internet; Nguyen Khac Toan, serving twelve years after being arrested in an Internet café, where he allegedly "vilified" government officials in emails sent abroad; and Nguyen Vu Binh, a journalist who was sentenced to seven years of imprisonment after he posted an article on the Internet criticizing the government.

Freedom of Assembly

Public demonstrations are extremely rare, especially after harsh government crackdowns against mass protests in the Central Highlands in 2001 and 2004. In March 2005, the prime minister signed Decree 38/1005/ND-CP, which stiffened restrictions on freedom of assembly. It bans public gatherings in front of places where government, party, and international conferences are held, and requires organizers of public gatherings to apply for and obtain government permission in advance.

Freedom of Religion

Followers of religions not officially recognized by the government continue to be routinely persecuted. Security officials disperse their religious gatherings, confiscate religious literature, and summon religious leaders to police stations for interrogation.

In 2004, the United States designated Vietnam a "country of particular concern" for its violations of religious freedom. International pressure resulted in a number of prisoner releases in 2005, and the passage of a new ordinance on religion in 2004. A February 2005 decree by the prime minister bans forced recantations of faith and loosens some restrictions on Christian organizations.

However, the government continues to require religious organizations to register with the government in order to be legal, and prohibits religious activities determined to cause public disorder, harm national security, or sow divisions. Local authorities have used the new regulations as grounds to arrest minority Christians suspected of belonging to churches that operate independently. In addition, forced renunciation ceremonies continue despite the new decree banning such practices. Since March 2005, Human Rights Watch has received reports of renunciation ceremonies taking place in Lao Cai, Quang Nai, Ha Giang, and Gia Lai provinces.

Minority Christians

Ethnic Hmong Christians in the northwest and Hre Christians in Quang Nai province have been beaten, detained, and pressured by local authorities to renounce their religion and cease religious gatherings. In February and March 2005, religious repression and a heightened military presence in Lai Chau province caused a number of Hmong Christian families to flee to neighboring China, Burma, and Laos. In March 2005, officials in Dien Bien province launched an official four-month campaign to eradicate Protestantism amongst the Hmong.

In the Central Highlands, the government has continued its persecution of Montagnards, particularly those thought to be following "Dega Christianity," a form of evangelical Christianity that is banned by the Vietnamese government. Since 2001, close to 300 Montagnard Christians have been imprisoned on charges that they are separatists using their religion to "undermine national unity." Similar claims have been made by officials in the northwest, who claim that the Hmong's Vang Chu religion is a front for separatist activity.

The unregistered Vietnam Mennonite Church remains under surveillance and its members continue to encounter conflicts with local authorities. While

Rev. Nguyen Hong Quang, the Mennonite general secretary, was released from prison in 2005, evangelist Pham Ngoc Thach remained in prison.

Buddhists

One monk from the banned Unified Buddhist Church of Vietnam (UBCV), Thich Thien Mien, was released from prison in 2005. However the government continues to persecute UBCV members and withhold any recognition of this group, once the largest organization of Buddhists (the majority religion) in the country. The UBCV's Supreme Patriarch, Thich Huyen Quang, and its second-ranking leader, Thich Quang Do, have been confined without charges to their monasteries for years, under police surveillance. The Foreign Ministry restricts visitors to the monks, including diplomats and journalists, on grounds they are under investigation for possession of "state secrets."

Members of the Hoa Hao sect of Buddhism, while officially recognized by the government, have also been subject to police harassment and surveillance. Two members were arrested in February 2005 for making religious videotapes. In May and June 2005, police disrupted Hoa Hao Buddhist ceremonies and funeral gatherings, reportedly destroying religious banners and an altar. In June 2005 Hoa Hao Buddhists announced a hunger strike to protest lack of government response to a complaint submitted by 500 followers that they were "terrorized and oppressed" by authorities in An Giang.

Two Hoa Hao Buddhists, Vo Van Buu and Tran Van Ut, self-immolated on August 5, 2005, in protest against suppression of their religion and detention of their leaders. Police reportedly used tear gas and water cannons to disperse funeral proceedings for the two, attended by thousands of followers. The Foreign Ministry called Tran Van Ut's immolation "an extremist act of destroying himself." In September 2005, Hoa Hao monk Vo Van Thanh Liem, who had submitted written testimony on human rights in Vietnam for a June 2005 U.S. congressional hearing, was sentenced to nine years of imprisonment. At least six other Hoa Hao members were sentenced to prison during 2005.

In July 2005, nine members of the Cao Dai religion were sentenced to prison for between three and thirteen years for "fleeing abroad to oppose the government." They had been arrested and repatriated from Cambodia in September 2004 when they tried to deliver a letter of protest to international diplomats during a meeting of the Association of Southeast Asian Nations in Phnom Penh.

Arbitrary Arrest, Torture, and Unfair Trials

Hundreds of religious and political prisoners remain behind bars. There is compelling evidence of torture and other mistreatment of detainees. Prison conditions are extremely harsh and fall far short of standards. Human Rights Watch has received reports of solitary confinement of detainees in cramped, dark, unsanitary cells; lack of access to medical care; and of police beating, kicking, and using electric shock batons on detainees, or allowing inmates or prison gangs to carry out beatings of fellow prisoners with impunity.

Police officers routinely arrest and detain suspects without written warrants. Political trials are closed to the international press corps, the public, and often the families of the detainees themselves. Defendants do not have access to independent legal counsel.

Defending Human Rights

No independent or nongovernmental human rights organizations operate in Vietnam. In September 2004, Vietnam denied a visa to U.S. Representative Loretta Sanchez, an outspoken critic of the country's human rights record and co-founder of the Congressional Caucus on Vietnam. In August 2005, Vietnam's Ministry of Foreign Affairs released an eighty-two page white paper entitled, "Achievements in protecting and promoting human rights in Vietnam."

Key International Actors

Vietnam's international donors, who number about fifty bilateral and multi-lateral donors, pledged U.S.$3.4 billion in aid for Vietnam at the December

2004 Consultative Group meeting, a substantial increase over 2004. While donors have publicly focused on economic growth and poverty reduction programs, they have increasingly expressed concerns about the government's imprisonment of dissidents, suppression of freedom of expression and of religion, and its poor handling of the crisis in the Central Highlands.

In 2005 the U.N. Working Group on Arbitrary Detention declared Thich Huyen Quang and Thich Quang Do victims of arbitrary detention. In 2005 officials from the U.N. High Commissioner for Refugees (UNHCR) and foreign diplomats made several visits to the Central Highlands. Among those visited were Montagnard returnees from Cambodian refugee camps. Most of these visits were carried out in the presence of government or party officials. A Memorandum of Understanding (MoU) signed in January 2005 between UNHCR and the governments of Cambodia and Vietnam commits Vietnam not to punish returnees for their illegal departure, but it makes no such promise with respect to punishment or prosecution of returnees for practicing their religion or expressing their political opinions.

Several countries broadened their public support for dissidents in 2005. After repeated requests, the British ambassador and the head of the E.U. delegation to Vietnam received authorization to visit Thich Quang Do in September. The European Parliament held a hearing in September 2005 on human rights in Vietnam, Cambodia, and Laos.

In November 2005, the U.S. embassy praised Vietnam's release of religious prisoners and promulgation of new laws on religion, but continued Vietnam's designation as a "country of particular concern" for religious freedom violations. In June 2005, Prime Minister Phan Van Khai made a state visit to the United States, the highest-level visit by a Vietnamese official since the end of the Vietnam War.

UZBEKISTAN

Bullets Were Falling Like Rain

The Andijan Massacre, May 13, 2005

HUMAN
RIGHTS
WATCH

WORLD REPORT
2006

EUROPE
AND CENTRAL ASIA

ARMENIA

Although the international community continued in 2005 to look favorably on Armenia for its economic performance, the government has failed to improve its human rights record. The crackdown on opposition parties and supporters in 2004 led to fewer public demonstrations in 2005, and, consequently, less overt government pressure on the opposition. However, the authorities continued to use their powers to limit political activity.

In July 2005, after years of failing to meet Council of Europe obligations to amend the constitution to introduce a system of stronger checks and balances among the different branches of government, Armenian authorities secured the approval of Council of Europe legal experts on a raft of constitutional amendments. The opposition (and media freedom activists) were critical, saying that too much power would remain with the executive, and some opposition parties decided to campaign against the amendments, which were to go to a referendum in November. The government made little progress on measures against corruption, a widespread problem in the country, and forced land aquisition by government-backed urban developers resulted in allegations of abuses against homeowners.

Law enforcement authorities restrict freedom of assembly and use torture and other violent and intimidating practices when carrying out their work. The authorities have a history of putting pressure on human rights defenders who are critical of the government. In 2005, such pressure extended to the ombudsperson's office.

Freedom of Assembly

The authorities restrict the right to freedom of assembly, particularly in the case of opposition rallies and demonstrations. May 2005 amendments to the 2004 law on public gatherings resulted in few improvements. On repeated occassions in 2005, nongovernmental organizations and political parties attempted to hold public gatherings at which police or unidentified people interfered, grabbing banners and placards, or triggering disturbances. One such incident occurred on April 20, when the head of the New Times political party, Aram Karapetian, held a public meeting with residents in the town of Sevan. Unidentified people began fighting with rally participants, and one shot and injured in the leg a university student who was participating in the rally. A police investigation concluded that the rally participants had themselves incited the disturbances, and no one was charged in relation to the shooting. In another incident in May, police reportedly threatened to detain people who wanted to attend a rally of the opposition People's Party of Armenia in a village near Yerevan.

State Violence and Intimidation

Torture and ill-treatment in police custody remain widespread in Armenia. Torture usually occurs in pre-trial detention with the aim of coercing a confession or evidence against third parties. Abuse and mistreatment within the army is also widespread, with dozens of suspicious deaths occuring every year.

In May 2005, police allegedly beat supporters of an independent candidate, Artur Shaboyan, in local elections in the town of Hrazdan. According to media reports, police used batons and electric-shock equipment to attack Shaboyan supporters outside several polling stations.

In June, law enforcement authorities arrested Yektan Turkyilmaz, a Turkish scholar who had been carrying out historical research using Armenian archives, for failing to obtain official permission to take old books out of the country. After his arrest, security officers questioned him and his associates about his research and political views. They denied him access to a lawyer for two days and then provided him with a state-appointed lawyer, not of his choice. In August, after significant international pressure, he was released on a two-year suspended prison sentence.

Media

Although Armenia has significant independent and opposition print media, the government continued to restrict full media freedom in the country. Television channels A1+, Noyan Tapan, and Russian NTV, which had aired independent news coverage about Armenia, remained unable to broadcast because the government had taken away their broadcasting frequencies. The proposed constitutional amendments would increase the independence of the National Commission on Television and Radio, the body that issues and revokes broadcasting licenses, by giving parliament the power to appoint half of the members and the president the power to appoint the other half (currently, the president appoints all the members of the commission). Nevertheless, media associations, nongovernmental organizations, and the ombudsperson have criticized the Council of Europe for endorsing the proposed constitutional amendments, which they argue fails to guarantee the independence of the electronic media. They further criticize the authorities' failure to institute changes to increase the independenceof the commission overseeing state-run Armenian Public Television and Radio, set up in 2005 to provide independent public television, one of Armenia's obligations to the Council of Europe.

Freedom of Religion

Despite amendments to the law on alternative service introduced in November 2004, Jehovah's Witnesses continue to be persecuted for their refusal to perform military service. According to the Armenian Helsinki Association, in September 2005 sixteen Jehovah's Witnesses were serving prison terms, and nineteen were awaiting trial, for refusing to perform military service.

On June 9, 2005, according to Forum 18 News Service, a court in Stepanakert, in the unrecognized republic of Nagorno-Karabakh, sentenced Armen Grigorian, an Armenian conscientious objector, to two years in prison for refusing to perform military service. A year earlier, the Armenian military had forcibly taken Grigorian, an eighteen-year-old from a Jehovah's Witness family, from Yerevan to a military unit in Nagorno-Karabakh. His request for alternative civilian service was rejected. When he refused to sing the national anthem and swear the military oath, army officials beat him and later forced him to stand in his underwear in front of about 1,800 soldiers and explain why he refused to perform military service.

Human Rights Defenders

In May 2005, the government successfully applied to the Constitutional Court to curtail the powers of the ombudsperson to access court documents, arguing that the powers breached the principle of the independence of the courts. The decision came after the ombudsperson released her first annual report, which criticized the government for its human rights record. Later in May, security services reportedly confiscated a computer from the office of the ombudsperson that had confidential information about people who had made complaints to the office; ostensibly the computer was seized as evidence against an employee of the office previously arrested and accused of taking a bribe. Larisa Alaverdian, the ombudsperson, claimed that the security services did not have a warrant to take the computer, and that they used information it contained to harass a law firm that had helped two individuals to file complaints to her office.

Key International Actors

Although the Council of Europe continued to engage Armenia to make progress in complying with its membership obligations, local groups criticized the organization for weak monitoring of those obligations and for approving the government-proposed amendments to the constitution. Many of Armenia's obligations to the Council of Europe remain unfulfilled, including resolving the problem of the use of administrative arrests for political purposes, providing plurality in the electronic media, and resolving the issue of alternative service.

In April 2005, the European Union decided to proceed with the European Neighbourhood Policy joint preparations for action plans with the countries of the South Caucasus, including Armenia. This is the first time that the E.U. has offered closer economic, political, and cultural relations in exchange for progress on concrete human rights benchmarks, and therefore marks a significant opportunity for the E.U. to encourage human rights improvements in Armenia. The potential of this opportunity to trigger meaningful reforms will depend, however, on how specific the human rights benchmarks are in the final action plan document, which was being negotiated between the Armenian government and the E.U. throughout the latter half of 2005.

The United States and Russia continued to compete for influence in Armenia. The United States protested over the lack of transparency in the sale of Armenia's electricity grid to a Russian company, which increased Russia's hold over Armenia's energy sector. Russia's withdrawal from its bases in Georgia resulted in Russia relocating part of its military hardware to Armenia. Increasing ties with the United States led to Armenia sending forty-six troops to join coalition forces in Iraq in January 2005. In March, Armenia and the United States signed an action plan regarding Armenia's participation in the Millennium Challenge Account, a multi-million-dollar U.S. aid program. The action plan focuses on development of fiscal policy, banking, corruption, and agriculture.

AZERBAIJAN

Azerbaijan's government has a long-standing record of pressuring opposition political parties and civil society groups and arbitrarily limiting critical expression. In the run-up to the November 2005 parliamentary elections the repressive environment intensified, despite considerable efforts by the international community to encourage Azerbaijan's compliance with international human rights standards. Election day itself fell far short of these standards.

In the elections the government used a variety of tactics that impaired the integrity of the process and ensured that pro-government candidates won the majority of seats. Government policies appear to support an environment in which state officials are free to use violence to achieve their ends without fear of being held accountable. Although the government has released political prisoners, the system of repression against perceived government critics ensures that new politically motivated cases will continue to be generated. Independent and opposition press face major barriers to their work.

Elections and Associated Rights

Azerbaijan has a history of seriously flawed elections. In 2005, repression and harassment of opposition party members, an overwhelmingly pro-government bias in the electronic media, and government control of election commissions ensured that the parliamentary elections would not be free and fair. The government's registration of candidates without party-based bias was an improvement on previous elections but was later overshadowed by other serious violations. Measures taken to improve the election process, such as allowing inking of voters' fingers with invisible ink to prevent multiple voting and lifting the ban on monitoring by foreign-funded nongovernmental organizations (NGOs), proved ineffective because they were introduced late in the election campaign.

During the election campaign period, the government continued to restrict freedom of assembly, despite lifting the absolute ban on opposition gatherings that had existed until June 2005. The authorities refused to allow rallies to be held in city centers, and police carried out mass arrests and beat protesters who attempted to gather for unauthorized meetings or rallies. Officials exerted pressure on government workers, particularly teachers, to attend the ruling Yeni Azerbaijan Party candidates' meetings with voters. At the same time, police detained campaign workers for opposition and independent candidates and warned them to stop their political work. The timing and circumstances surrounding two separate alleged coup d'etats by opposition groups raised serious concerns that the government was using these cases to increase repression against the oppostion and to influence the elections. Based on these two sets of allegations, the government arrested three youth movement members and about a dozen high-level government officials and opposition supporters, and accused them of preparing a coup d'etat.

Election day was marred by numerous irregularities throughout the country. Local and international observers documented serious violations, including ballot box stuffing, repeat voting, and tampering with results of protocols. At the time of writing, the authorities had responded to international calls to rectify falsifications on election day by cancelling the results in several election districts, firing several local officials, and detaining four others.

State Violence

Torture, police abuse, and excessive use of force by security forces are widespread in Azerbaijan. In pre-trial detention severe beating is a common form of torture, although electric shock, threats of rape, and threats against family members are also used, usually to coerce a confession or other information from a detainee. Torture and ill-treatment is less common in post-conviction prison facilities, although a series of incidents were alleged in the context of a February 2005 special operation by Ministry of Interior troops to combat illegal activity in the prisons. Former inmates of prisons number 12 and 13 told Human Rights Watch that security forces beat hundreds of prisoners, forcing some to run through a gauntlet of troops who beat them with batons.

The government has not taken any significant measures to combat the environment of impunity for government officials who commit torture or other forms of ill-treatment. On the contrary, Vilyat Eviazov, the head of the

Organized Crime Unit, a body known for its use of torture, was promoted to deputy minister of interior in April 2005.

Political Prisoners

The existence of political prisoners is a long-standing problem that Azerbaijan committed to resolving when it joined the Council of Europe in 2001. In the eighteen months prior to June 2005 Azerbaijan made progress on this issue, releasing more than one hundred political prisoners. However, according to the Council of Europe, political prisoners remain in custody and Azerbaijan is yet to find a permanent solution to this problem, such increasing the independence of the judiciary. In 2005 opposition supporters continued to be imprisoned and charged in what appear to be politically motivated cases.

Media Freedom

Authorities use a variety of informal measures to prevent or limit news critical of the government from reaching the public. The government pressures opposition and independent media outlets by limiting their access to printing houses and distribution networks, initiating defamation cases resulting in the imposition of crippling fines, restricting access to official information, and harassing journalists. Major television outlets, from which the vast majority of the population gets its news, are either state-owned or affiliated, and the government controls the issuing of radio and television broadcast licenses through a board that consists entirely of presidential appointees. A public television station, set up by the government because of its obligations to the Council of Europe, started broadcasting in August 2005.

Media monitoring carried out by independent monitors during the pre-election campaign showed that the content of all the national television stations' news broadcasts was overwhelmingly pro-governmental.

In one of the worst incidents of violence against journalists in Azerbaijan in many years, on March 4, 2005, an unknown attacker shot dead Elmar Husseinov, founder and editor of the independent weekly magazine *Monitor*.

The magazine regularly published harsh criticism of the government, including allegations of corruption among high-level officials and their families. *Monitor* stopped publication after Husseinov's death.

Human Rights Defenders

The authorities continue to deny registration to many human rights NGOs, usually on minor technical grounds. Human rights defenders are at times subjected to physical and verbal attacks and other forms of pressure and harassment. For example, in March and April 2005, pro-government television channels made harsh and provocative statements against human rights defenders. According to Leila Yunus, the Director of the Institute for Peace and Democracy, in late March a presenter on Lider TV stated, "The whole activity of Leyla Yunus is directed against the statehood of Azerbaijan. And yet she applies to the law-enforcement bodies for protection. Should such people be protected?" On April 2 the authorities refused to allow Ilgar Ibrahimoglu, religious freedom activist, to leave the country to present a statement at the United Nations Commission on Human Rights in Geneva.

Key International Actors

By the end of 2005 construction of the new major oil pipelines routed across Azerbaijan, Georgia, and Turkey had been completed, and a gas pipeline was due for completion in mid-2006. The huge foreign investment in these projects has focused international attention on issues of security and stability in the region, sometimes at the expense of human rights.

United States policy toward Azerbaijan has focused on military cooperation and oil interests. Since 2001, U.S. military aid and cooperation has increased significantly, and Azerbaijan has cooperated in U.S. military operations, sending approximately 150 troops to Iraq. Although the U.S. government criticized the parliamentary elections and put pressure on Azerbaijan to investigate and rectify incidents of falsification on election day itself, its response to pre-election violations was inconsistent and sometimes weak.

In April 2005, the European Union decided to proceed with preparing the European Neighbourhood Policy action plans with the countries of the south Caucasus, including Azerbaijan. This is the first time that the E.U. has offered closer economic, political, and cultural relations in exchange for progress on concrete human rights benchmarks, and therefore marks a significant opportunity for the E.U. to encourage human rights improvements in Azerbaijan. However, the potential of this opportunity to trigger meaningful reforms will depend on the specificity of the human rights benchmarks in the final action plan document, which was being negotiated between the Azerbaijani government and the E.U. throughout the latter half of 2005.

The Council of Europe has played a constructive role in addressing human rights problems in Azerbaijan, pressing for the release of political prisoners, greater pluralism, and a devolution of political power away from the presidency. In 2005, it concentrated on promoting free and fair parliamentary elections, and resolving the issue of political prisoners.

The European Bank for Reconstruction and Development (EBRD) is one of the largest multilateral investors in Azerbaijan, having committed more than ?459 million in projects, approximately half of which goes to the private sector. Although acknowledging many serious shortcomings in Azerbaijan's human rights record and transition to democracy, the EBRD's strategy for Azerbaijan, approved in May 2005, confirmed the government's commitment to the principles of article 1 of the bank's founding document, which includes multiparty democracy, pluralism, and market economics. Despite its conclusion that Azerbaijan's progress in implementing these principles was "slow and uneven," and that "many challenges remain," the Bank did not make use of its political mandate to link further engagement to concrete human rights improvements.

The Organization for Security and Co-operation in Europe (OSCE) was deeply involved in election monitoring for the parliamentary elections, providing 665 election observers from forty-two countries. During the election campaign period and immediately following the elections, the OSCE published three interim reports and a preliminary report that described numerous violations of OSCE commitments and Council of Europe standards for democratic elections.

Belarus

Following pro-democracy uprisings in Georgia, Ukraine, and Kyrgyzstan, the authorities in Belarus focused on preempting similar events during that country's 2006 presidential election. President Alexander Lukashenka tightened his grip on power and maintained an assault on the media, opposition, and human rights groups.

Political Freedoms

After a flawed October 2004 referendum allowed Lukashenka to run for a third term, both the authorities and the opposition began preparing for the March 2006 presidential election. The government continued to prosecute opposition activists, often on spurious grounds. In December 2004, Mikhail Marinich, a leading opposition politician, was sentenced to five years in prison for allegedly stealing computer equipment belonging to a nongovernmental organization (NGO), Dzelavaia Initsiiativa, which he headed. The prosecution was widely criticized as politically motivated, since neither the NGO itself nor the donor of the equipment, the United States Embassy, had complained of theft. Marinich suffered a stroke in prison in March 2005 that, according to relatives, resulted from a denial of treatment for high blood pressure. Later that month, a Minsk court reduced the sentence to three-and-a-half years; a general amnesty in August reduced this sentence by one more year.

On May 15, 2005, the authorities arrested Sergei Skrebets, a former supporter of Lukashenka who had joined the opposition, for bribing a state official. Skrebets denied the charges, maintaining that they were politically motivated, and he twice went on hunger strike, causing him to be hospitalized in September. His trial is scheduled for November.

Opposition activists continued to face jail terms and fines for organizing public protests and meetings. On February 24, 2005, a Minsk court fined Sergei Antonchik, a former Supreme Soviet deputy, the equivalent of U.S.$1,600 for holding an unauthorized gathering at a private apartment. Antonchik had apparently been unable to secure premises for the congress of a humanitarian organization he founded. On May 31 a Minsk court sentenced Nikolai Statkevich and Pavel Severinets to three years' imprisonment—later reduced to two years under the August amnesty—for their role in organizing opposition demonstrations in October 2004. On June 10, opposition politician Andrei Klimov was sentenced to eighteen months' community service for his role in organizing a March 25 demonstration.

In April 2005, the Belarusian Supreme Court closed the Independent Institute of Social, Economic and Political Studies (IISEPS), which was renowned for its objective surveys of public opinion. Observers believed the closure was part of the authorities' attempts to control electoral information in the lead-up to the 2006 ballot.

In October 2005, the opposition organized a National Congress of Pro-Democratic Forces, at which some eight hundred delegates elected Alexander Milinkevich as their candidate for the 2006 presidential election. Previously uninvolved in politics, Milinkevich had held a variety of civil society positions, including as head of a Grodno-based NGO resource centre, Ratusha, which the authorities closed in 2003 for possessing a printing machine without a publishing license.

Media Freedom

The authorities also continued their assault on the independent media. In September 2005, they terminated the national distribution and printing contracts of the independent newspaper *Narodnaia Volia*, forcing it, along with other independent Belarusian newspapers, to print their editions in Smolensk, Russia. Earlier, the newspaper had struggled to pay more than U.S.$50,000—a phenomenal sum for Belarus—in libel damages awarded to a politician in July. The denial of access to the state-owned national distribution network greatly reduced *Narodnaia Volia*'s circulation and viability as a business.

On March 24, 2005, police raided the home of Aleksei Karol, editor-in-chief of *Zhoda*, an independent newspaper, after the paper published several caricatures of Lukashenka. They confiscated materials related to the images and charged Karol and his colleague Zdvizhkou with offending the honor and dignity of the president. A court later found them guilty and ordered them to pay a fine of approximately U.S.$1,500 each.

On October 18, 2005, Vasil Hrodnikau, a freelance journalist who wrote social and political articles for *Narodnaia Volia* for seven years, was murdered at his home. Hrodnikau's death followed the murder a year earlier of Veronika Cherkasova, a journalist with the newspaper *Solidarnost*. Cherkasova had written articles on crime, religion, and a series entitled "The KGB is Still Watching You." At this writing, separate investigations into the two deaths were ongoing. It remained unclear whether the murders were related to the journalists' professional activities.

Interference with NGOs

The government continued to interfere with the work of nongovernmental organizations. In 2005 the authorities particularly targeted the Union of Poles in Belarus (SPB); with approximately ten thousand ethnic Poles (out of a total four hundred thousand in Belarus) estimated to be involved in SPB, it is the largest NGO in the country. It publishes a weekly newspaper, *Glos znad Niemna*, and is reportedly funded by the Polish government. In March the authorities invalidated the results of the SPB's congress, which elected Andzhelika Borys as chair of the organization, maintaining that the previous chair, the allegedly pro-government Tadeusz Kruczkowski, was the organization's legitimate leader. The authorities also prevented the publication of *Glos znad Niemna* and printed bogus editions that criticized Borys and her supporters. Courts imposed fines on six of the newspaper's journalists who publicly protested these developments. The row escalated on July 27 when riot police raided the SPB building, evicted Borys and her supporters, and escorted Kruczkowski inside the building the following day.

Defending Human Rights

Authorities continued to target the Belarusian Helsinki Committee (BHC) and other human rights organizations. In November 2004 prosecutors opened a criminal investigation against BHC lawyer Garry Pogonyailo for allegedly libeling Lukashenka and other senior government officials in an interview with Swedish television. Pogonyailo had accused them of involvement in the "disappearance" of opposition figures. The case was dropped several months later. The BHC was forced to shut down its regional network of offices in January 2005 after the Ministry of Justice alleged violations of the organization's internal membership rules and failure properly to register a regional office.

The Fate of the "Disappeared"

The fate and whereabouts of the four public figures who "disappeared" in Belarus in 1999 and 2000—Viktor Gonchar, Yury Zakharenko, Anatoly Krasovskii, and Dmitry Zavadskii—continued to remain unclear in 2005. The authorities were hostile toward relatives of the four men who sought answers to their fate. On July 7 a riot police officer punched Svetlana Zavadskaia, Dmitry Zavadskii's wife, in the face when the authorities broke up an otherwise peaceful rally marking the fifth anniversary of his "disappearance." Zavadskaia was hospitalized with a concussion. Official investigations continued to fail to address strong suspicions of state involvement in the men's "disappearance" and their likely extrajudicial execution.

Key International Actors

The European Union and the U.S. continued to sharply criticize the Belarusian authorities for their authoritarian rule and maintained a travel ban on top officials imposed in September 2004. On September 29, 2005, the European Parliament strongly condemned "indiscriminate attacks" on opponents of the Lukashenka administration, including against the Union of Poles in Belarus, as well as the government's refusal to permit members of the parliament to conduct a fact-finding mission in Belarus in August.

The E.U. and U.S. continued to provide financial support for Belarus' fledgling civil society. In September the E.U. announced a ?2 million project to broadcast independent television and radio programs from the E.U. to Belarus. The U.S. Agency for International Development (USAID) strategic plan for 2003-2005 focused on assisting the independent media, NGOs, and pro-democracy organizations. In April, USAID launched a two-year U.S.$1 million project to counter human trafficking.

Diplomatic rows erupted in Belarus' bilateral relations with the Czech Republic and Poland. After the Polish government criticized Belarus' interference with the Union of Poles in Belarus, the Belarusian authorities accused the Polish government of interfering in its internal affairs and expelled a diplomat. Poland reciprocated the following day and later recalled its ambassador from Minsk. On January 21, 2005, Belarus expelled Czech diplomat Pavel Krivohlavy amid allegations of sexual liaisons with young boys. State television broadcast footage of Krivohlavy kissing young men in a café, but the footage was accompanied by heavy criticism of the Czech government's support of Belarusian pro-democracy NGOs and the opposition, raising suspicions that the expulsion was politically motivated. The Czech government expelled a Belarusian diplomat in response.

The Organization for Security and Co-operation in Europe (OSCE) presence in Minsk continued to play an active role in monitoring Belarus' adherence to OSCE principles. It issued critical statements in response to attacks on opposition figures and the independent media. In April 2005, the OSCE issued a statement expressing regret at the closure of the IISEPS.

The Lukashenka administration continued to refuse the United Nations special rapporteur on Belarus, Adrian Severin, access to the country. Instead, Severin traveled to Poland, Latvia, and Lithuania to meet with organizations and parliamentarians about Belarus' human rights record. In April the U.N. Commission on Human Rights again adopted a resolution that was strongly critical of the Belarus government's human rights record and extended the special rapporteur's mandate for another year. Among other things, the resolution expressed "deep concern" at the implication of senior officials in the 1999-2000 "enforced disappearance and/or summary execution" of four public figures (see above) and about "persistent reports of harassment and closure" of NGOs, independent media, and the political opposition.

BOSNIA AND HERZEGOVINA

While a number of themes unrelated to the 1992-95 war in Bosnia and Herzegovina—including prison conditions, rights of asylum seekers, and implementation of libel laws—received attention during 2005, war crimes accountability and the return of persons displaced by the war remained the key human rights issues in the country.

War Crimes Accountability

Republika Srpska (the Serb-majority entity) for the first time transferred war crimes indictees to the International Criminal Tribunal for the former Yugoslavia (ICTY). On January 15, 2005, Bosnian Serb authorities transferred Savo Todovic, former deputy commander in a detention camp in Foca, to the tribunal. Gojko Jankovic, also charged in relation to crimes against Bosnian Muslims in Foca, surrendered to Bosnian Serb authorities on March 13. Finally, Sredoje Lukic, charged with crimes against Bosnian Muslims in Visegrad in 1992, surrendered on September 14. Todovic had been in hiding in Serbia, while Jankovic and Lukic had been living in Russia. The circumstances surrounding their surrender in Republika Srpska remain unknown.

On October 9 and 10, 2005, Republika Srpska police raided several buildings in Banja Luka, Kotor Varos and Celinac, ostensibly in an attempt to apprehend war crimes indictee Stojan Zupljanin.

Six war crimes trials took place in Republika Srpska during the year, more than in the entire period since the end of the war. While still insufficient, recent efforts to prosecute war crimes suspects in the Bosnian Serb entity may indicate a change in the decade-long policy of impunity. Two war crimes trials were completed in Banja Luka, the capital of Republika Srpska; three war crimes trials were ongoing in Trebinje and one in Banja Luka at year's end. In all but one trial the defendants were Bosnian Serbs. Republika Srpska also arrested sixteen Bosnian Serb war crimes suspects in June, September, and November 2005, at the request of the Bosnian State Prosecutor and cantonal prosecutors in the Federation of Bosnia and Herzegovina (the Bosniac- and Croat-majority entity).

The Federation of Bosnia and Herzegovina held twenty trials against suspects of various ethnicities during 2005. A major impediment to successful war crimes prosecutions in the Federation was the non-availability of Bosnian Croat and Serb suspects who had fled to Croatia and Serbia after the war and received citizenship there. The constitutions of Croatia and Serbia prohibit extradition of their nationals to other countries.

Availability of the accused is likely to be the greatest challenge to the effective functioning of the newly established special war crimes chamber, based in the Bosnian capital Sarajevo as part of the State Court of Bosnia and Herzegovina. The chamber became operative in 2005, and the first case, against Boban Simsic, a Bosnian Serb, began on September 14.

Return of Refugees and Displaced Persons

With the exception of a few areas in Republika Srpska (Prijedor, Doboj, Janja) and the Federation (Drvar, Bugojno, Stolac), the current figures on the return of refugees and displaced persons in the country appear too small to reverse the effects of the wartime ethnic cleansing. According to the United Nations High Commissioner for Refugees (UNHCR), as of the end of September 2005, just over a million, out of a total of more than two million people forcibly displaced during the war, had returned to their home areas. Of these, 453,464 persons had returned to municipalities where they currently constitute an ethnic minority (so-called "minority returns"). However, both the local authorities in Bosnia and Herzegovina and respected human rights activists argued during the year that the official figures grossly exaggerate the actual number of minority returns, because, according to a field survey by the Bosnian Helsinki Committee for Human Rights, fewer than half of those who repossessed their properties and registered as returnees remained to actually live in their pre-war places of residence.

The return figures were particularly discouraging in 2005. Between January and the end of September, UNHCR registered 5,059 minority returns, a twelve-fold drop compared to the same period in 2002. Continuing attacks and harassment targeting returnees, scarce employment opportunities in places of return, insufficient funding for reconstruction of destroyed properties, and obstacles affecting social and economic needs of prospective returnees, frustrated the return process.

Human Rights Defenders

Human rights activists faced a hostile environment when their activities challenged the dominant attitudes relating to the wartime period. In the Federation, the work of the independent Research and Documentation Center was largely ignored by the government, and met with occasional threats from private actors, because the organization assessed the number of casualties during the Bosnian war at around one hundred thousand. The estimate challenged the widespread belief among the war's principal victims, the Bosnian Muslims, that the number of casualties exceeded two hundred thousand. The Helsinki Committee for Human Rights in Republika Srpska experienced similar responses to its efforts to promote accountability for war crimes and ongoing human rights abuses. The High Representative for Bosnia and Herzegovina, Paddy Ashdown, failed to express strong support for the work of independent human rights groups in the country.

Key International Actors

The focus of the work of the Office of the High Representative (OHR), which oversees civilian aspects of the 1995 Dayton Peace Accords, was police reform. On October 5, 2005, under intensive pressure from the OHR, the United States, and the European Union, the Republika Srpska parliament finally accepted the fundamentals of the proposed reform, which envisage a more unified police force. Between December 2004 and October 2005, the OHR imposed sixteen laws at the state and entity level, and removed eleven officials and public servants from office.

The debate in Bosnia about the proper role for the high representative intensified during the year, with an increasing number of critics arguing that the removals from office under a procedure that allows for no legal remedies, and the practice of imposing laws, did not encourage respect for human rights and the rule of law. In an authoritative report published in March 2005, the Council of Europe's European Commission for Democracy

Through Law (Venice Commission) concluded that the need for wide powers had existed in the early period following the conclusion of the 1995 Dayton Peace Agreement, but that the longer such an arrangement stayed in place, the more it risked becoming incompatible with Council of Europe human rights standards.

On January 17, 2005, a trial chamber of the ICTY sentenced Bosnian Serbs Vidoje Blagojevic and Dragan Jokic to eighteen and nine years in prison respectively, for their role in the killings of some eight thousand Muslim men in Srebrenica in July 1995. The ICTY Appeals Chamber affirmed the sentences of four Bosnian Serbs and two Bosnian Croats guilty of crimes in Prijedor and in central Bosnia.

Three important trials against Bosnian Muslim indictees took place in 2005. On November 16, a trial chamber acquitted the Bosnian Army General Sefer Halilovic, accused of crimes against Bosnian Croat civilians in Herzegovina in 1993. In the trial against Generals Enver Hadzihasanovic and Amir Kubura, both charged with war crimes against Bosnian Croats and Serbs in central Bosnia in 1993-94, the prosecution and the defense presented closing arguments in July 2005. The trial of Naser Oric, commander of Bosnian Muslim forces in the Srebrenica area, for crimes against Serb civilians, continued throughout the year. The spate of trials against Bosnian Muslims somewhat eroded the once unanimous support for the tribunal's work within Bosnia's most numerous ethnic community. At the same time, support for the tribunal increased among Bosnian Croats and Serbs, where the prevailing stance since the war has been one of mistrust.

On November 21, 2005, the day of the tenth anniversary of the Dayton Peace Accords, the E.U. General Affairs and External Relations Council decided to start negotiating a Stabilization and Association Agreement (SAA) with Bosnia and Herzegovina. The Council had previously decided, on October 3, that it was not possible to open the negotiations because of the failure of the Republika Srpska parliament to accept the proposed police reform. The Council emphasized that the establishment of a more unified and efficient police force, free from political interference, was crucial for respect for human rights, the rule of law, and the protection of minorities.

The parliament of Republika Srpska accepted the principles of the proposed reform on October 5.

On December 2, 2004, the E.U.-led peacekeeping force in Bosnia (EUFOR) replaced the NATO-led Stabilization Force (SFOR). For the second consecutive year, international forces in Bosnia and Herzegovina did not arrest a single Bosnian citizen indicted by the ICTY. While most indictees resided in Serbia and were not within the reach of the seven thousand EUFOR troops or a 150-strong contingent of U.S. troops based in Bosnia and Herzegovina, Bosnian Serb wartime leader Radovan Karadzic was believed to be hiding in the eastern parts of the country. The absence of a requisite political will and intelligence resources may account for the failure of the international forces to locate Karadzic and bring about his arrest.

The Council of Europe's European Commission against Racism and Intolerance (ECRI) issued a report in February 2005 faulting ethnically based political parties with nationalist policies that engender "severe problems of racism and racial (including ethnic and religious) discrimination and segregation" and make it difficult for those not belonging to locally or nationally dominant ethnic groups to access rights and opportunities.

CROATIA

In 2005, improved cooperation with the International Criminal Tribunal for the former Yugoslavia (ICTY) earned Croatia a positive decision by the European Union on opening negotiations on membership. There was little progress, however, in the return of Serb refugees. With the majority of defendants continuing to be ethnic Serbs, Croatia has yet to demonstrate that its efforts to pursue war crimes suspects before domestic courts reflect a principled commitment to justice over and above ethnic considerations.

A decade after the 1991-95 war in Croatia, tensions between the majority Croat population and the Serb minority have eased. However, there were some worrying trends in 2005 threatening to reverse the course. In the key multi-ethnic towns of Knin and Vukovar, local boards of the Croatian Democratic Union (HDZ) formed municipal governments in coalition with ultra-nationalist Croat parties following the May 15 local elections, while sidelining the centrist Independent Democratic Serb Party (SDSS). The SDSS nevertheless continues to support the minority HDZ government at the state level. Violent incidents directed at ethnic Serbs were more frequent in 2005 than in previous years.

Refugee Returns

Between three hundred thousand and 350,000 Croatian Serbs left their homes during the 1991-95 war, mostly for Serbia and Montenegro, and Bosnia and Herzegovina. As of September 2005, the government had registered 122,000 Serb returnees. Croatian Serb associations and the Organization for Security and Co-operation in Europe (OSCE) mission to Croatia assessed the actual number of returnees as significantly lower—between 60 and 65 percent of the registered figure—because many Croatian Serbs had left again for Serbia and Montenegro or Bosnia and Herzegovina after only a short stay in Croatia.

There was no tangible progress in 2005 on the issue of lost tenancy rights in socially-owned property. Croatian authorities had terminated the tenancy rights of up to thirty thousand Serb families after they fled their apartments during and after the war. In June 2003, the Croatian cabinet adopted a set of measures to enable former tenancy rights holders in Zagreb and other big cities to rent or purchase government-built apartments at below-market rates. As of early November 2005, only a dozen former tenancy rights holders had benefited from the two-year-old program. The absence of results only exacerbated the skepticism among refugees that the program would eventually deliver benefits. Only 3,628 former tenancy rights holders had filed applications under the program as of September 2005.

The bleak prospects for receiving an adequate substitute for lost tenancy rights made many refugees place their hopes in the European Court of Human Rights (ECtHR). On December 15, 2004, the Grand Chamber of the ECtHR agreed to re-hear a case decided four months earlier, in which the ECtHR upheld Croatian court decisions terminating the tenancy rights of a woman who had left Zadar shortly before the outbreak of hostilities in 1991 and had not returned to her apartment within the six-month period specified by Croatian law at the time. The re-hearing of the case, *Blecic v. Croatia*, took place in September, and a ruling was pending at this writing.

Limited economic opportunities for minority returnees, partly caused by employment discrimination, also greatly impedes return. A December 2002 constitutional law on minority rights obliges the state to ensure proportionate representation of minorities in the state administration and the judiciary, as well as the executive bodies and administration of self-government units. In most areas, there are no Serb returnees in the police, the judiciary, or the regional offices of the state ministries. Private entrepreneurs, although not bound by the law to hire Serbs, have proved to be more willing to do so than government agencies.

Violent acts against ethnic Serbs suddenly increased during 2005. The May 18 killing of eighty-one-year-old Dusan Vidic in his house in Karin, near Benkovac, was particularly shocking. Two months later, on July 19, two elderly Serb returnees were beaten in front of their house in the village of Ostrovica, also near Benkovac. In Pakostani, Benkovac and Zagreb, attackers damaged vehicles with Serbian registration plates. Groups of young men attacked or threatened Serbian bus passengers who were traveling through

Rijeka and Delnice, as well as Serbian train passengers at the railway stations in Vinkovci and Zagreb. Graffiti with the message *"Srbe na vrbe!"* ("[Hang] the Serbs on the willow trees!") appeared in Rijeka and Udbina. Two men broke windows at the entrance of the Serb Orthodox Church in Drnis on November 12. On May 21, a bomb exploded next to the premises of a Serb political party in Vukovar, and the following night, unknown perpetrators threw bombs at the municipal assembly buildings in the majority Serb villages of Borovo Selo and Trpinja, near Vukovar. In all but a few cases the police failed to apprehend the perpetrators.

Accountability for War Crimes

Ante Gotovina, a Croatian army general accused of crimes against Croatian Serbs in 1995, remained at large four years after the issuing of his indictment by the ICTY. Deputy Prime Minister Jadranka Kosor stated in January 2005 that if she came across Gotovina she would not report this to the police because she "would not recognize him." The statement, made during the campaign for the presidential election, was broadly interpreted as an expression of the benevolence with which key officials regarded Gotovina.

ICTY Chief Prosecutor Carla Del Ponte warned on several occasions during the year that Croatia was not doing enough to apprehend Gotovina. However, Del Ponte began to backpedal as the October 3 meeting of the E.U. General Affairs and External Relations Council drew near. The meeting was to decide on whether the European Union would open membership negotiations with Croatia, and the assessment of Croatia's cooperation with the ICTY would be the crucial factor in the decision. In a report submitted to the council on October 3, the ICTY prosecutor concluded that Croatia was fully cooperating. Many observers remained unconvinced that Croatia had indeed made significant progress in the previous months, and interpreted the statement by Del Ponte as a bow to political pressure from some E.U. member states.

The number of war crimes trials against ethnic Serbs (eleven) greatly outnumbered trials of ethnic Croat indictees (six). Trials of ethnic Serbs also tended to involve more defendants, making the contrast between the numbers of individuals standing trial from each ethnic group even starker. Most notable among these were the Miklusevci case and the Lovas case before the Vukovar District Court, and the Branjin Vrh case before the Osijek County Court, all ongoing at this writing.

The absence, for the second consecutive year, of any new indictment against accused Croats raises serious concerns about the sincerity of the Croatian government's accountability efforts. The six trials in 2005 were retrials of cases from the 1990s or the early 2000s: Mihailo Hrastov (originally opened in 1993, now re-tried for the third time); Pakracka poljana (1997); Bjelovar group (2001); Virovitica group (2002); Lora (2002); and Paulin Dvor (2003). Another remaining concern is the ability of the Croatian courts to conduct trials in a fair and effective way, given the high number of reversals of first instance judgments by the Croatian Supreme Court. Much progress is also needed in the protection of witnesses and inter-state cooperation, in spite of certain positive developments in those areas in 2005, related to the Lora retrial.

Key International Actors

On October 3, 2005, the Council of the European Union decided to open formal negotiations on membership with the Republic of Croatia. The all-but-exclusive focus on the issue of ICTY cooperation has in the past prevented the E.U. from using its unique position to vigorously demand greater progress on other pressing issues such as refugee return, treatment of minorities, and domestic war crimes trials. However, on October 9, European Enlargement Commissioner Olli Rehn stressed to his hosts in Zagreb that the issues of refugee return, minority rights, and the rule of law would be critical in the European Commission's assessment of the progress Croatia made in meeting the criteria for E.U. membership. The same issues figured prominently in the Accession Partnership document, issued by the commission on November 9. The new emphasis is welcome, although it has probably come several years too late to have any real impact—the process of refugee return is gradually coming to a halt, the memory of war crimes witnesses is becoming unreliable, and the availability of evidence is becoming increasingly problematic.

The OSCE mission to Croatia has continued to pursue a dialogue with the government, while issuing valuable reports critical of its return-related practices, minority rights record, and progress in domestic war crimes trials. Nevertheless, political considerations have led the mission to sometimes attenuate the criticism of Croatia's human rights record. In a frank assessment of the mission's accomplishments in the past two years, the departing head of mission, Peter Semneby, acknowledged in an April 2005 interview that the return issue was being resolved less successfully than he had expected, because "resistance ... proved to be more difficult than I had anticipated."

On October 7, 2005, U.S. Under Secretary of State for Political Affairs Nicholas Burns reiterated that the U.S. would continue to block Croatia's efforts to join NATO until the capture of Ante Gotovina.

Various Council of Europe bodies—the Committee of Ministers, the European Commission against Racism and Intolerance, and the Advisory Committee on the Framework Convention on National Minorities—concluded during the year that Croatia still needed to make substantial progress regarding the return of refugees, especially in the matter of housing, fairness in the administration of justice, and in tackling ethnic discrimination.

EUROPEAN UNION

The course of integration of the European Union hit a major obstacle in 2005 when voters in France and the Netherlands rejected the new Constitutional Treaty, leaving it endorsed by barely half of the twenty-five member states and prompting some of the undecided states to shelve their own referendum plans. The E.U.'s expansion project nevertheless continues, with human rights conditionality being a point of leverage in the negotiations that led to the opening of formal accession talks with Croatia and Turkey (see separate country chapters).

In matters such as migration and asylum, and counterterrorism, common E.U. approaches as well as policy and practice in individual E.U. states continue to reflect a tendency to circumvent international human rights obligations.

Counterterrorism Measures

The issue of counterterrorism in Europe was dominated in 2005 on the one hand by the terrorist threat taking on characteristics hitherto not experienced in E.U. states, and on the other by further developments in E.U. governments' counterterrorism policy negatively impacting fundamental human rights. The former was shown most vividly when London was struck on July 7 by three simultaneous bomb attacks on its underground train network, and a fourth on a bus, killing fifty-six people (including the four bombers), making it the deadliest attack in modern British history. It also marked the E.U.'s first experience of suicide bombers who were, moreover, British nationals.

On July 21, exactly two weeks later, there was a failed attempt to stage an almost identical attack, involving bombers on three London underground trains and a bus. The next day police shot dead a Brazilian man on a London underground train, having apparently mistaken him for a terrorist suspect. The incident, which raised questions about police surveillance methods as well as about application of a policy authorizing use of lethal force by police, was immediately referred for investigation by the Independent Police

Complaints Commission. At the time of this writing, its report was expected at the end of 2005.

A Spanish court in September sentenced an alleged al-Qaeda leader to twenty-seven years' imprisonment for conspiracy to commit murder by having provided logistical support to the perpetrators of the September 11, 2001, attacks in the United States, and for being the leader of a terrorist organization. Seventeen co-defendants were convicted of belonging to or collaborating with a terrorist group. A terrorism trial opened in Belgium at the beginning of November, with thirteen defendants (all Moroccans or Belgians of Moroccan descent) accused of providing support to the perpetrators of the 2004 Madrid train bombings and the 2003 bombings in Casablanca, Morocco.

At the beginning of November *The Washington Post*, citing U.S. government sources, reported that the U.S. had used secret detention facilities in Europe and elsewhere to illegally hold terrorist suspects without rights or access to counsel. While the article did not identify the locations, its allegations were consistent with Human Rights Watch's own research suggesting the existence of secret detention facilities in Poland and Romania (the former an E.U. member state, the latter an acceding state). Both the European Commission and the Parliamentary Assembly of the Council of Europe immediately announced investigations, and the International Committee of the Red Cross requested access to the alleged facilities.

Indefinite or Prolonged Detention

The U.K.'s highest court, the House of Lords Judicial Committee (commonly known as the "Law Lords") ruled in December 2004 that the indefinite detention without charge or trial of foreigners suspected of terrorism was incompatible with the U.K.'s Human Rights Act (which incorporates the European Convention on Human Rights into domestic law). In response, the U.K. government announced a "twin-track" set of alternatives to indefinite detention. This includes recourse to "control orders" that seriously restrict the movement and activities of any person who is suspected of terrorism-related activities (irrespective of nationality), and the use of "diplomatic assurances" to deport to their home countries foreign nationals who would be at risk of torture or ill-treatment upon return, despite clear evidence that assurances are an ineffective safeguard against such treatment (see below).

Human Rights Watch criticized the legislation introducing control orders on the grounds that there were insufficient procedural safeguards given the serious restrictions on liberty that could be imposed through the orders. The Prevention of Terrorism Act 2005 became law in March 2005.

The U.K. government in September published new draft counterterrorism legislation which included extending the maximum period that terrorism suspects could be detained without charge, to ninety days (from the current fourteen, already the longest in Europe), and adding and a new criminal offense of "encouraging" terrorism (see below). The draft legislation passed in the House of Commons in November, although the government's proposal for the extension to ninety days had been defeated and an amendment approved instead whereby detention without charge for terrorism suspects would be extended to twenty-eight days. Human Rights Watch argued that the case for any extension had not been made, and that detention without charge for up to twenty-eight days could become a form of arbitrary detention, and might infringe the right of an arrested person to be informed promptly of any charge against him. At this writing, the draft legislation was being debated in the House of Lords.

The Italian government introduced a new antiterrorism law in late July 2005, and, after a very brief parliamentary review, it entered into force at the beginning of August. It introduced a number of new offenses, and increased penalties for others. Among its most troubling provisions, it extended the maximum period during which a suspect could be held for questioning without charge and without a lawyer present from twelve to twenty-four hours, and broadened the range of law enforcement authorities empowered to detain and question terrorist suspects. It also allowed authorization of senior police officers to order immediate expulsion of persons residing illegally in Italy who they determined were a threat to national security; appeals against such expulsions would be without suspensive effect.

Draft new antiterrorism legislation in France, presented to parliament in November, included a provision to reclassify "criminal association" in relation to a terrorist offense from a misdemeanour to a felony. The overly vague nature of the offense permits detention on the basis of limited evidence. Its use to detain suspects who are later released without charge has been widely criticized as a form of preventive detention. The reclassification would increase the maximum permissible pre-trial detention period from three years and four months, to four years and eight months. It would also double the maximum possible sentence, to twenty years. The proposed law would also increase the period that police are allowed to detain suspects in terrorism cases from four days to six.

Evidence Obtained under Torture

In October, the U.K. Law Lords began consideration of whether evidence extracted under torture that had been obtained from third countries is permitted in domestic British law. The case was an appeal brought by ten men previously subject to indefinite detention as terrorism suspects against an August 2004 majority decision by the Court of Appeal that the U.K. government was entitled to rely on torture evidence in special terrorism cases, provided that the U.K. "neither procured nor connived at" the torture, a decision contrary to international human rights law. Human Rights Watch was part of a coalition of fourteen human rights and anti-torture organizations that intervened in the House of Lords case. The Law Lords' ruling, expected by the end of 2005, is likely to have profound implications for the worldwide ban on torture.

Refoulement and Diplomatic Assurances

Important rulings were made against individual E.U. governments over their resort to "diplomatic assurances," but governments continue to press ahead with strategies that both challenge head on, and seek to side-step, the absolute prohibition against refoulement—the return of a person to a country where he or she would be at risk of torture or ill-treatment. This alarming trend prompted the Secretary-General of the Council of Europe in

October 2005 to remind European governments that "the prohibition of torture…is absolute and applies in all circumstances. It is not negotiable." In his annual report to the U.N. General Assembly, the U.N. Special Rapporteur on Torture, Manfred Nowak, likewise emphasized that "diplomatic assurances are unreliable and ineffective in the protection against torture and ill-treatment," and called on governments to "observe the principle of non-refoulement scrupulously."

Five E.U. governments were reported to have united in a challenge to the landmark 1996 European Court of Human Rights (ECtHR) ruling *Chahal v. United Kingdom*, affirming the absolute prohibition against refoulement. The U.K., Italy, Lithuania, Poland and Slovakia obtained permission in October to intervene as interested parties in the case of *Ramzy v. Netherlands*, pending before the ECtHR at the time of writing, in which an Algerian man suspected of involvement in terrorism, Mohammed Ramzy, was challenging deportation on the grounds that he would be at risk of torture if returned to Algeria. Reportedly, the governments concerned were seeking to overturn *Chahal* in favour of the position that the right of an individual not to be tortured could be balanced against the national security interests of the state (the essence of the dissenting opinion by a minority of ECtHR judges in *Chahal*).

In May 2005 the U.N. Committee against Torture ruled that Sweden had violated the absolute prohibition on torture by expelling terrorism suspect Ahmed Agiza to Egypt in 2001. Sweden had sought to justify the transfer by saying that it had secured assurances from Egypt that Agiza would be treated humanely, but Agiza credibly alleged that after his forcible return to Egypt he was tortured. The U.N. committee concluded that the assurances Swedish authorities secured from Egyptian officials concerning Agiza could not be trusted as sufficient protection. It noted that Egypt had a well-documented history of torture abuses, especially when dealing with terrorism suspects, and that its routine use of torture, in combination with interest in Agiza by the U.S. as well as Egypt, should have led to a "natural conclusion" that Agiza was at risk of torture upon return.

The transfer of Agiza and another man, Mohammed al-Zari, had been undertaken by U.S. intelligence operatives to whom Swedish officials handed custody of the two men at Stockholm's Bromma Airport, and as such amounted to "extraordinary rendition." In March, a report by the Swedish chief parliamentary ombudsman concluded that the Swedish security service and the airport police "displayed a remarkable subordinance to the American officials" and "lost control of the situation," resulting in the ill-treatment of Agiza and al-Zari, including physical abuse and other humiliation, at the airport immediately before they were transported to Cairo. The U.N. committee said that the ill-treatment at Bromma Airport should have made it clear to Swedish authorities that the men would be at risk of torture if they were returned to Egypt.

An appeals court in the Netherlands ruled in January 2005 against the extradition to Turkey of Nuriye Kesbir, a high-level member of the former Kurdistan Workers' Party (PKK), who was subject to an extradition warrant from Turkey alleging that she had committed war crimes as a PKK military operative in the civil war in Turkey's southeast. In May 2004 a lower court had determined that although Kesbir's fears of torture and unfair trial in Turkey were not completely unfounded, there were insufficient grounds to halt the extradition. The court gave exclusive authority to the government to either grant or reject the extradition request, but advised the Netherlands minister of justice to seek enhanced diplomatic assurances from Turkey against torture and unfair trial. The appeal court concluded that diplomatic assurances could not guarantee that Kesbir would not be tortured or ill-treated upon return to Turkey.

The ECtHR Grand Chamber issued a decision in February 2005 in the case of *Mamatkulov and Askarov v. Turkey*, in relation to which Human Rights Watch and the Advice on Individual Rights in Europe (AIRE) Centre had submitted an amicus curiae brief. The two men had been extradited from Turkey to Uzbekistan in 1999 based on assurances against torture and unfair trial by the Uzbek authorities. It had been anticipated that the Grand Chamber might rule on the reliability and/or sufficiency of diplomatic assurances against torture from the government of Uzbekistan, but the court determined that it did not have sufficient information before it to rule on whether Article 3 of the European Convention on Human Rights (prohibiting torture or ill-treatment) had been violated; the court did not engage in a discussion of the reliability or sufficiency of the assurances. Nevertheless, the decision concluded that Turkey should have been bound by a ECtHR request to delay the men's extradition until the court had an opportunity to review the men's application.

The U.K. government, in August and October 2005, signed memoranda of understanding (MOUs) with Jordan and Libya containing undertakings that people deported to those countries from the United Kingdom would not be tortured or ill-treated there. The U.K. government also confirmed that it was seeking such arrangements with Tunisia, Lebanon and Algeria, and there are credible reports that a similar agreement was being sought with Egypt.

In August, the U.N. special rapporteur on torture expressed "fears that the plan of the United Kingdom to request diplomatic assurances for the purpose of expelling persons in spite of a risk of torture reflects a tendency in Europe to circumvent the international obligation not to deport anybody if there is a serious risk that he or she might be subjected to torture," adding that "diplomatic assurances are not an appropriate tool to eradicate this risk."

The ineffectiveness of diplomatic assurances as a safeguard against torture, and the danger that such assurances pose to the absolute nature of the non-refoulement obligation were extensively documented by Human Rights Watch in an April 2005 report titled, "Still at Risk: Diplomatic Assurances No Safeguard against Torture," as well as in subsequent statements critical of the U.K.'s bilateral agreements based on blanket diplomatic assurances.

Between August and October, more than twenty foreign nationals suspected of involvement in terrorism were detained pending their deportation on the grounds of national security, including persons previously subject to indefinite detention in the United Kingdom. Some of the men, who originate from Jordan, Libya, and Algeria among other countries, had previously been granted asylum in Britain. Four of the Algerians were released on bail in October, but the majority remained in detention at this writing. No deportations had taken place under the agreements at this writing, and it remained unclear what weight the U.K. courts would attach to the promises of humane treatment when evaluating the risk of torture in future appeals against deportation brought by the detainees.

New Offenses of Incitement

The London bombings gave impetus to legislative and other initiatives directed towards confronting terrorist recruitment. Some of the proposed measures had troubling implications for freedom of expression. At the level of common E.U. policy, the tone was set by a September 2005 commission communication on "Terrorist Recruitment: Addressing the Factors Contributing to Violent Radicalization." The European Council was to adopt a strategy on this issue by the end of the year, as part of its action plan on terrorism. A new Council of Europe Convention on the Prevention of Terrorism, adopted in May, requires states to criminalize "public provocation to commit a terrorist offense," whether or not involving direct advocacy of terrorism, when such "provocation" is done with intent.

The draft new counterterrorism legislation published in September by the U.K. government included a new offense criminalizing speech that amounts to "encouragement," including speech that justifies or glorifies terrorism, and the closure of places of worship used to "foment extremism." Human Rights Watch was concerned that such measures would undermine the right to non-violent expression by criminalizing speech even where there is no intention to incite violence. Denmark in September initiated the first case under an antiterrorism law enacted in 2002 that forbids instigation of terrorism or offering advice to terrorists, and carries a penalty of up to six years in prison. The accused, a Moroccan-born Danish citizen, was charged in relation to having downloaded from the Internet and distributed inflammatory speeches and images including beheadings carried out by Iraqi insurgents.

In August the U.K. government announced a list of "unacceptable behaviours" added to the list of national security grounds for the deportation or exclusion of foreign nationals. These included the speech or publication of views deemed to "foment, justify or glorify terrorism," provoke others to commit terrorist acts, or "foster hatred" that might lead to inter-community

359

violence in the United Kingdom. This went further than a July 2004 law in France allowing the expulsion of foreigners who engage in acts that "explicitly and deliberately" incite discrimination, hatred or violence. While expulsions under French law were subject to appeal, an expulsion order was not automatically suspended while the appeal was pending, and there were cases in which persons had been expelled to their countries of origin, only to have the expulsion order overturned on appeal. In Germany, a new immigration law entered into effect on January 1, 2005, allowing authorities to expel those who publicly endorse or promote terrorist acts or incite hatred "in a manner conducive to disturbing public safety."

On November 9, 2005, after thirteen consecutive nights of rioting across France, Interior Minister Nicolas Sarkozy announced that all adult foreigners convicted of involvement in the rioting, including those with residence permits, would be deported.

Asylum Seekers and Migrants

As Human Rights Watch has consistently acknowledged, migration into the E.U. poses clear challenges for European governments, and few would question the legitimacy or urgency of policies to address these. However, common E.U. policy in this area continues its development exclusively in the direction of keeping migrants and asylum seekers out of and away from Europe. Moreover, exclusionary practices stepping beyond the rule of law are seen in at least two E.U. states, Italy and Spain, which have actively engaged in expulsions without respect for the individual right to seek asylum. These and other E.U. states also implement returns with scant regard for whether the receiving countries could offer effective protection.

Common E.U. Immigration and Asylum Policy

The European Commission in September published a proposal for a directive on "common standards and procedures for returning illegally-staying third-country nationals." While the draft directive contains improved language on human rights protection in comparison to the previous iteration of the proposal, a number of concerns remain. The text also falls short of meeting the criteria laid out in a set of common principles of return developed by a coalition of human rights and European refugee nongovernmental organizatrions, including Human Rights Watch. Key concerns include the absence of a mandatory right of appeal against removal with suspensive effect, and the imposition of a re-entry ban that could amount to a double penalty with potentially far-reaching consequences for the principle of non-refoulement. At the time of writing, this directive was pending "co-decision" by the European Council and the European Parliament.

The Asylum Procedures Directive, agreed by the European Council in April 2004, was submitted for consultation with the European Parliament, which in September 2005 expressed "severe reservations" and called for over one hundred amendments to the document. In a reaffirmation of the principle that an asylum seeker should have his/her claim individually assessed, the Parliament argued that any applicant should have the right to "rebut the presumption of safety" associated with the proposal for "safe third country" lists. Human Rights Watch and others had called in March 2004 for withdrawal of the draft directive on grounds that the "most contentious provisions are all intended to deny asylum seekers access to asylum procedures and to facilitate their transfer to countries outside the E.U." The European Parliament's proposed amendments were not binding on the council. At this writing there had been no further movement towards adopting the draft directive.

Readmission Agreements

Human Rights Watch research in countries on the E.U.'s new eastern frontiers confirmed concerns that some of the new E.U. member states do not have systems offering full and fair asylum determination procedures, or policies and practices in place to ensure that no person is sent back to a place where his or her life or freedom is threatened. As documented in the November 2005 Human Rights Watch report, "On the Margins—Ukraine: Rights Violations against Migrants and Asylum Seekers at the New Eastern Border of the Europe Union," border guards in Poland and Slovakia who intercept persons crossing from Ukraine interview and process them generally within forty-eight hours, with no genuine effort to identify them by name, origin or status, and without their having access to lawyers or interpreters or the possibility to challenge a decision by the border guard to return them to Ukraine. Effected under bilateral readmission agreements between the E.U. states concerned and Ukraine, some of these returns lent substance to concerns that, while in theory readmission agreements are not designed to interfere with the right to asylum, in practice those liable to return can include asylum seekers whose protection needs have not been determined.

European Community readmission agreements (applicable to all E.U. member states except Denmark, where an abstention applied) were concluded with Albania and Russia in April and October respectively, and were being negotiated with four other countries including Ukraine and Morocco.

Processing Migrants and Asylum Seekers Outside the E.U.

A communication from the European Commission on Regional Protection Programmes (RPPs) was hailed by the E.U.'s Justice and Home Affairs Council in October as the E.U.'s first step "in improving access to protection needs and durable solutions for those in need of international protection, as quickly and as close to their home as possible." Pilot RPPs were due to be launched before the end of 2005.

In its November 2005 report on Ukraine (located in the region covered by the first pilot RPP), Human Rights Watch noted that RPPs offered the possibility of real improvements to the target countries' protection capacity, but raised concerns that the RPPs might undermine the right to seek asylum in the E.U., by resulting in premature designation of the target countries as "safe third countries," which would then expedite the return of asylum seekers who had transited them without first considering their protection needs. Similarly, the office of the U.N. High Commissioner for Refugees (UNHCR) welcomed the RPP proposal, but stressed the need for guarantees that RPPs would be complementary to existing asylum provisions in E.U. states.

The E.U. continues to press ahead with programs for strict control of access to Europe, and its migration policies towards neighbouring countries emphasize enforcement rather than protection.

By bilateral arrangement with Libya, Italy continue to expel—without a proper assessment of their asylum claims—people who arrive from North Africa and were being held on the island of Lampedusa under Italy's mandatory detention policy for illegal migrants and asylum seekers. In March 2005, nearly five hundred Egyptians were expelled to Libya and sevety-six directly to Egypt, handcuffed and blindfolded for their charter flights. Nearly two hundred persons were expelled to Libya in May and June. The expulsions ignored the evidence that, as a place in which the basic human rights of migrants are frequently violated and that has not ratified the 1951 Convention relating to the Status of Refugees, Libya cannot be regarded as a "safe third country" for return.

The Italian Minister of Interior told the Italian Parliament after the March expulsions that the government's actions were in full compliance with their human rights obligations, but they were criticized by UNHCR, whose officials had been denied access to Lampedusa at that time. A delegation of Members of the European Parliament (MEPs) visiting the Lampedusa facility at the end of June queried the appropriateness of third countries' consular officials being involved in detainee identification procedures there, given the danger this presented to a potential asylum seeker, and were informed that "nobody" had recently claimed asylum, an assertion the MEPs described as "incredible," as this would make Lampedusa "the first centre in Italy where this does not happen."

In early October, faced with mass attempts by undocumented migrants to force entry into Spain's North African enclaves of Ceuta and Melilla, the Spanish government expelled to Morocco at least 73 people who had reached the enclaves, including several who had sought to claim asylum. The expulsions were reportedly carried out without an individual assessment that would have enabled presentation of asylum claims. On October 23, Morocco deported forty-nine Malians from this group to their home country despite the fact that at least two had applied for asylum in Morocco. There are

alarming reports of human rights violations against migrants deported to
Morocco from Spain or detained in Morocco as they tried to enter Ceuta or
Melilla, including expulsions in inhumane conditions to the desert borders
with Algeria and Mauritania. At least eleven people were shot dead as
Spanish and Moroccan troops attempted to block entry to the enclaves.
Morocco admitted that its border guards were responsible for four of the
fatalities, while an internal Spanish inquiry exonerated Spanish forces.
Human Rights Watch called for independent investigation into the deaths, as
did the U.N. Special Rapporteur on the Human Rights of Migrants, Dr.
Jorge Bustamente, who also called on Morocco to end collective deporta-
tions.

GEORGIA

Since the Rose Revolution at the end of 2003, the government has had an uneven record on human rights. In 2005, it continued to prioritize its campaign against corruption and for territorial integrity. Its ambitious reform agenda is supported by the international community. However, at times it carries out reforms hastily, without broad and open consultation and without the thoroughness or detail necessary to eradicate entrenched human rights problems. As a result, human rights abuses continue unchecked in many spheres, following patterns established under former governments.

On a range of issues, including religious and political freedom and independence of the judiciary, government reforms are producing mixed results. Although the media is now relatively free, it has become less critical and there are signs of increasing government influence on media content. The government has taken some positive steps to prevent torture but torture and due process violations continue to be reported. Refugees remain vulnerable to abuse.

Mixed Results on Reform

Constitutional amendments adopted in 2004 increased the president's influence over the judiciary, further eroding judicial independence. In April 2005, after months of uncertainty, a presidential decree changed the Tbilisi court structure and led to the dismissal of significant numbers of judges. The decree, administered by the High Council of Justice, a body headed by President Saakashvili, did not set out criteria for deciding which judges would be removed from their positions. The arbitrary decision-making process heightened the sense of executive prerogative.

The environment for religious freedom has significantly improved since the change in government when violent attacks against minority religions began to subside, suggesting that the attackers were somehow linked to the former government. In a positive move the authorities arrested Vasili Mkalavishvili, the leader of many of the attacks, and in January 2005, he was convicted and sentenced to six years in prison. In another positive step, the parliament

365

passed amendments to the civil code in April 2005 making it easier for religious organizations to be registered. Discrimination against unregistered religious groups had been a major obstacle to religious freedom in Georgia.

Torture

Torture, impunity, and denial of due process remain serious problems in Georgia. By 2005, the government had begun to acknowledge these long-standing concerns and took some steps to combat them.

Legislative amendments to criminal laws in 2005 made out-of-court statements inadmissible as evidence unless confirmed in court and reduced pretrial detention time limits (to take effect from 2006). Further, the authorities prosecuted several police officers for torture or other ill-treatment and helped to set up a monitoring system for police stations under the framework of the Public Defender's Office. According to Georgian nongovernmental organizations (NGOs) and those involved in the monitoring program, by mid-2005 there had been a reduction in the number of complaints of torture in the capital, Tbilisi. They told Human Rights Watch, however, that there had been a corresponding increase in police violence at the time of arrest and during transportation to the police stations. They also said that the widespread problem of torture in other parts of the country remained largely unaffected by government measures, in part because resources were lacking to monitor effectively police stations in the regions.

Media Freedom

Since the Rose Revolution, the government has improved legislative protections for freedom of expression, including by decriminalizing libel, but the media has become more pro-government and less critical than it was during the Shevardnadze era. Newspapers remain relatively free of government pressure. However, major television channels are biased in favor of the government in their news and current affairs coverage. Journalists, NGOs, and representatives of international organizations have told Human Rights Watch that the government uses its influence with the owners of the major television channels to control the content of their programs. The owners give little editorial independence to staff and sometimes censor programs that are critical of the government.

On April 3, 2005, the owner of Imedi television, Badri Patarkatasishvili, ordered the station not to broadcast a story on police corruption on the weekly television program Droeba (Time). The next day, Patarkatasishvili explained why he had refused to allow the program to be broadcast, saying "if I want to tell something to the government, I can tell it personally and directly." NGOs and representatives of international organizations told Human Rights Watch that the presidential administration sometimes directly contacts chief editors, telling them how to cover certain issues. Journalists, however, are reluctant to speak publicly about government interference with or efforts to influence the content of their work. There are reportedly few protections against unfair dismissal, and journalists are rarely willing to risk their positions by speaking out publicly.

Refugees

Chechen refugees remain vulnerable to abuse in Georgia. They lack adequate housing, medical care, and employment opportunities. Refugees are subjected to police harassment and threats of *refoulement*.

In March 2005, two Kists (ethnic Chechens from Georgia), who were Russian citizens, reportedly went to the Ministry of Refugees and Housing in Tbilisi, seeking asylum. Officers from the Ministry of Interior arrested them and took them to the border with Azerbaijan, where Azerbaijani authorities reportedly refused them entry unless they agreed to return to Russia. They spent several weeks in the neutral zone between the Georgian and Azerbaijani borders before returning to Georgia. On May 28, 2005, Russian authorities organized the repatriation of eighteen Chechen refugees from Georgia. Although no force was used, the United Nations High Commissioner for Refugees did not consider the repatriation voluntary due to the lack of access to objective and accurate information about conditions in the country of origin.

Although Georgia passed amendments to its refugee law in April 2005 and has ratified the 1951 Convention relating to the Status of Refugees, its laws and practice in refugee determination and protection do not comply with international standards. For example, pre-screening mechanisms prevent registration of asylum claims, and there are insufficient protections against refoulement for refugees and for those who may have been excluded from refugee status, but who would risk torture or ill-treatment if returned.

Human Rights Defenders

Although the government works closely with a number of human rights NGOs, it has excluded some of the country's most critical human rights defenders from important initiatives, such as the monitoring of prison facilities and police stations. In December 2004, unidentified persons made several threatening calls to the offices of an NGO called "Former Political Prisoners for Human Rights," and in 2005, representatives of the Human Rights Information and Documentation Center told Human Rights Watch that government officials had telephoned their offices and warned them to stop work on particular cases.

Key International Actors

The European Union (E.U.), pursuant to its European Neighbourhood Policy, decided to go ahead with plans to prepare "action plans" for countries of the south Caucasus, including Georgia. This is the first time that the E.U. has offered Georgia closer economic, political, and cultural relations in exchange for measurable human rights progress. As such, it marks a significant opportunity for the E.U. to encourage human rights improvements in Georgia. The potential of the initiative to trigger meaningful reforms will depend, however, on the nature and specificity of the human rights benchmarks included in the final action plan document, which was still being negotiated between the Georgian government and the E.U. at this writing.

In 2005, the Council of Europe extended deadlines for Georgia's compliance with its commitments and obligations, due to the change of government after the Rose Revolution. Council of Europe experts continue to provide opinions on how proposed legal reforms comply with European and international human rights standards. However, the government does not always take into account their recommendations. In June 2005, the Council of Europe recommended that the government address the problem of discrimination against the Azerbaijani minority in Georgia.

U.S. backing of President Saakashvili's government has led to a less critical attitude toward human rights abuses in the country. In a speech during his highly publicized visit to Georgia in May 2005, President Bush claimed that Georgia is a place where free speech flourishes, the rights of minorities are respected, and a vigorous opposition is welcomed, ignoring significant evidence to the contrary. In his speech, Bush did not raise any human rights concerns. The U.S. provides substantial support to Georgia through its assistance and military cooperation programs. In 2005, the U.S. approved U.S.$300 million in aid to Georgia over the next five years under the Millennium Challenge Account. Georgia has 850 troops serving in Iraq.

In 2005, relations with Russia remained difficult due to increased tensions over the breakaway republics of South Ossetia and Abkhazia, Georgia's joint initiatives with Ukraine to promote democracy within the region, and intense negotiations over the withdrawal of Russian military bases, which ended in agreement and a timetable for withdrawal.

KAZAKHSTAN

Government antagonism toward the political opposition created a hostile environment in advance of December 2005 presidential elections. New legislation ostensibly designed to reform the elections process and bolster national security further weakened civil and political rights in the country.

Kazakh authorities continue to interfere with citizens' rights to free assembly and expression, use politically motivated lawsuits to silence independent media, and limit access to opposition and independent Internet sites. While laws that would have severely restricted nongovernmental organizations (NGOs) were struck down in 2005, the government intensified pressure on civil society groups, including foreign NGOs.

Elections

On August 19, 2005, the Constitutional Council of Kazakhstan announced that presidential elections would be held on December 4—a year earlier than some had argued was legally mandated. The decision came after heated debate about the exact length of the president's term of office, as different articles of the constitution appeared to contradict one another on this issue. Opposition politicians complained that holding elections on such short notice placed them at a significant disadvantage.

The current government dominates all political life in the country, limiting the options available to the electorate. At the time of the announcement, only one opposition movement capable of mounting a credible challenge, For a Fair Kazakhstan (ZSK), was registered. In September, international and domestic media overwhelmingly predicted a victory for the incumbent, Nursultan Nazarbaev, who has ruled Kazakhstan since 1989. Opposition activists warned of popular dissatisfaction if the elections were not free and fair.

An election law enacted on April 15, 2005 strictly regulates the actions of foreigners and international organizations. Among other provisions, it bans foreign support of any political movement and external financing of elections. The law also bans public demonstrations from the day before voting until after official election results are announced. A new law on national security, passed on July 8, stipulates heavy fines for international NGOs that become involved in the election process on behalf of any political movement.

Political Opposition

Kazakh authorities dealt harshly with opposition political groups in 2005. Reversing one of the most significant steps toward democratic reform it had taken in recent years, the government filed suit against the leading opposition party. On January 6, 2005, the Special Economic Court in Almaty shut down the Democratic Choice of Kazakhstan (DVK), on the ground that a party statement calling for civil disobedience allegedly posed a threat to national security. Throughout the appeals process, which the DVK lost, the authorities harassed and intimidated party supporters. As of this writing, former DVK leader and co-founder Galimzhan Zhakianov remains in a minimum security facility where he is serving a seven-year sentence on charges of abuse of office. He was convicted in 2002 after a trial that was widely condemned as unfair.

In 2005, supporters of President Nazarbaev attacked the leading opposition candidate for president, ZSK Chairman Zharmahan Tuiakbai, on at least two occasions. On April 9, a brick narrowly missed Tuiakbai at a rally in eastern Kazakhstan and, on May 2, some fifty men stormed a ZSK meeting, declaring their intention to kill Tuiakbai "for Nazarbaev." A police investigation into the incident yielded one arrest, which resulted in probation. On the night of September 25, an arsonist reportedly used Molotov cocktails to destroy the Kostanai office of the ZSK.

Civil Society

Although the Constitutional Council in 2005 struck down two laws that would have substantially circumscribed the activities of NGOs, serious administrative harassment of such groups continues to mar Kazakhstan's rights record. Following political upheavals in other post-Soviet states, Kazakh tax authorities began audits of at least thirty-three international organizations operating in the country. NGO activists viewed these probes as government intimidation.

The rights to free assembly and expression continue to be circumscribed. In one particularly serious incident, police and Special Forces (OMON) officers detained about eighty people on May 1, 2005, in the capital, Astana, after they had participated in a public rally and pop concert in support of a presidential policy initiative. Law enforcement agents detained and beat young people wearing orange scarves and carrying orange balloons as they left the rally. Police told the detainees that wearing orange was a problem because of its symbolic role in the political unrest in Ukraine. Detainees were threatened with expulsion from university or destruction of their businesses. The organizers themselves were charged with holding an "unsanctioned procession" despite the fact that the concert had been approved by the local government.

Press Freedom

The government uses politically-motivated lawsuits extensively to silence independent media. Government agencies use laws making it a crime to insult the "honor and dignity" of the president, legislators, or other authorities (articles 318, 319, and 320 of the criminal code) to punish media outlets that publish information critical of the president or his government. The law does not require that the offending statements be false in order to trigger heavy penalties. In May 2005, the leading independent newspaper, *Respublika*, was ordered closed following a court decision dissolving the company that published it. The decision followed a government lawsuit over the paper's reprint of an interview with a Russian politician who allegedly made disparaging remarks about the Kazakh state and people. Authorities also interfered with the printing of *Set'kz* (Network KZ), the successor to *Respublika*, under the pretext of problems with the paper's license.

In March, the newspaper *Soz* (Voice) lost its appeal against a five-million-tenge (U.S.$40,000) fine levied in an "honor and dignity" lawsuit filed by the National Security Committee (KNB, successor to the KGB). Although *Soz* paid the judgment in full, the KNB pressed the courts to stop publication of the paper, and printing was halted briefly in early June.

The Kazakh government continues to limit access to opposition and independent Internet sites through the government-run provider, Kaztelecom, and another major network, Nursat.

Human Rights Defenders

On March 3, 2005, Kazakhstan's ombudsman, Bolot Baikadamov, accused the country's leading human rights organization, the Kazakh International Bureau of Human Rights and Rule of Law (KIBHR), of publishing biased information and distorting the situation in Kazakhstan in its reports on human rights developments. Baikadamov's comments were made directly to the president, but were later publicized. In mid-August the offices of the KIBHR were burglarized; the organization's staff believed the incident was politically motivated.

Key International Actors

United States

The U.S. government budgeted an estimated $74.2 million in assistance to Kazakhstan in 2004, more than half of which was allocated to security and law enforcement programs. U.S. aid also went to bolstering health care, civil society programs, and market reform. An annual report on human rights released by the State Department's Bureau of Democracy, Human Rights and Labor in February said the Kazakh government "severely limited citizens' right to change their government." In September, members of the Commission for Security and Cooperation in Europe voiced doubts about Kazakhstan's bid for chairmanship of the Organization for Security and Cooperation in Europe (OSCE). The senators pointed to the upcoming presidential election as a test of Kazakhstan's commitment to democracy. In October 2005, U.S. Secretary of State Condoleeza Rice visited Kazakhstan on a tour of Central Asian states and praised the republic as an "island of stability." She held meetings with President Nazarbaev and leading opposition presidential candidate Zharmahan Tuiakbai. Another opposition figure, Tolen Tokhtasynov, was arrested en route to his meeting with Secretary Rice.

European Union

The European Union is currently the single largest source of foreign direct investment in Kazakhstan. It has had a Partnership and Cooperation Agreement (PCA) with Kazakhstan since 1999. During its annual Cooperation Council with Kazakhstan, held in July, and in other public statements, the E.U. "emphasized the need for increased efforts" on the part of the Kazakh authorities to "comply fully with international norms and standards...in particular as regards elections, freedom of media, the ability of political parties to operate freely and the registration of NGOs with the public authorities." The conclusions further expressed the "expectation" that the forthcoming presidential elections would be free and fair, and noted that "any country applying for the chairmanship of the OSCE must exemplify the principles of the Organization." The E.U., however, again stopped short of using the PCA to articulate specific reform steps with a clear timeline for compliance.

Organization for Security and Cooperation in Europe (OSCE)

The OSCE maintains a center in Almaty. During a February visit to Astana, OSCE Chairman-in-Office Dimitrij Rupel urged the government of Kazakhstan to implement substantial political reform and lamented the fact that the parliament was "largely devoid of any opposition party representation." After changes to the election law brought about restrictions on free assembly, the OSCE publicly urged the president to refer the new regulations to the Constitutional Council. The OSCE also voiced concerns about new national security legislation and hosted forums on human rights, the environment, and journalism.

Shanghai Cooperation Organization

Kazakhstan hosted the 2005 summit of the Shanghai Cooperation Organization (SCO) in Astana. The organization's members are Russia, China, Uzbekistan, Kazakhstan, Kyrgyzstan, and Tajikistan. High on the agenda was cooperation in the fight against "terrorism, extremism, and separatism," which was considered especially pressing given the brewing international tension over the government of Uzbekistan's insistence that its neighbors forcibly return Uzbek citizens wanted by Uzbekistan for terrorism. The Uzbek government has claimed that terrorists were responsible for the massacre in Andijan on May 13, 2005. (See Uzbekistan.)

Kazakhstan became involved in an international standoff over the fate of Lutfullo Shamsuddinov, an Uzbek human rights activist who gathered information about government abuses on May 13 and who subsequently fled to Kazakhstan with his family. Shamsuddinov was declared a refugee by the office of the United Nations High Commissioner for Refugees. Nonetheless, the Uzbek government demanded that Kazakh authorities extradite Shamsuddinov on bogus charges of terrorism. The international community strenuously objected to his forcible return. After detaining him for six days, the Kazakh government agreed to release Shamsuddinov and he was flown to safety in another country.

KYRGYZSTAN

Popular demonstrations swept through Kyrgyzstan in March 2005, leading to the ouster and resignation of President Askar Akaev. Echoing the "rose" and "orange" revolutions that brought regime change in Georgia and Ukraine, the country-wide protests and disintegration of the Akaev government dramatically altered the political landscape in Kyrgyzstan.

Following deeply flawed parliamentary elections in February and March 2005, people took to the streets. Outraged by the corruption and repression that characterized the parliamentary vote—including attacks on independent media and the perceived unfair advantage given to candidates who were relatives of the president—protestors in southern Kyrgyzstan and later in the capital took over administrative buildings and defiantly expressed their dissatisfaction with the status quo. A variety of grievances merged into a single demand: the resignation of President Askar Akaev.

Violent clashes between police and protestors flared over several days, and eyewitnesses reported the presence in the crowd of government saboteurs who attacked protestors and police alike, causing chaos and panic. Dozens of people were reportedly injured and government and private property was damaged. However, police dropped their weapons and refused to use violence to suppress the protestors who arrived at the Kyrgyzstan White House on March 24, 2005. The demonstrators forced their way in and took over the seat of government. One of the leaders during the weeks of protest, long-time politician Kurmanbek Bakiev, was named the new president. President Akaev fled the country and later formally resigned his post.

Political prisoner Feliks Kulov was released by protestors on March 24, 2005. On April 6, the Supreme Court overturned his conviction on charges of abuse of power; a second conviction, for embezzlement, was quashed on April 11. Kulov withdrew as a candidate for the July presidential election and President Bakiev, whose leadership was confirmed in that election, later appointed him Prime Minister.

Promises of Reform

In the immediate aftermath of the revolution, the people of Kyrgyzstan had high hopes that the Bakiev government would put a stop to the corruption and repression that had undermined the Akaev administration.

As of this writing, promises of reform made during the early days of the Bakiev administration had not materialized. While Bakiev twice in 2005 announced his support for the abolition of the death penalty in Kyrgyzstan and called for constitutional amendments, no such legislation had been introduced as of late November.

One of the main reforms urged by civil society activists is the creation of a new constitution that would restore freedoms stripped during the Akaev era and would settle important issues regarding the structure of the government, such as whether Kyrgyzstan should be a presidential or parliamentary republic. The Constitutional Committee, set up to draft a new constitution, initially received praise for including civil society representatives in addition to government officials among its members. However, observers later criticized the body as ineffective and marred by infighting and noted that President Bakiev had increased the number of government representatives vis-a-vis representatives of civil society.

Continuing reports of police abuse in 2005, including torture of adult and children detainees, further undermined people's confidence in the government's promises of reform.

In a positive development, local rights groups and media watchdogs reported increased freedom of the media following the change in government.

Human Rights Defenders

During the final months of the Akaev government, as the country geared up for parliamentary elections, human rights defenders suffered intense persecution.

Tursunbek Akun, a prominent human rights defender and leader of the NGO Human Rights Movement of Kyrgyzstan, was kidnapped on November 16, 2004. He was held for fifteen days by men he believed to be associated with police and national security services. Akun was discovered on December 1 at a Bishkek hospital where doctors found he was suffering from "deep psychological trauma." A private doctor later diagnosed him with a brain concussion.

Kyrgyz government officials denied that Akun was the victim of kidnapping or forced disappearance and failed to investigate the possible role of law enforcement agents in the crime. The spokesman for the Ministry of Internal Affairs and the deputy chairman of the National Security Service publicly accused Akun of staging his own disappearance for self-promotion and to discredit law enforcement bodies. Akun claimed that he had been held by members of the security forces in the basement of an unknown house, where his kidnappers allegedly demanded that he stop collecting signatures in support of Akaev's resignation. Prior to his abduction, Akun had been actively advocating for the early resignation of President Akaev. As of September 2005, no one had been held accountable for the kidnapping and police had halted their investigation.

Aziza Abdurasulova, head of the human rights NGO Kylym Shamy (Candle of the Century), was active in the search for Akun while he was missing. On November 26, 2004, a person who identified himself as a police officer tried to force her into his car, claiming she had a stolen cell phone and that she had to be taken to the police station. Her phone had in fact been given to her by the Bishkek office of the U.S.-based organization Freedom House. Abdurasulova fled from the officer. She later received calls on her cell phone from senior police officers asking to meet with her. At a press conference, the spokesman for the Ministry of Internal Affairs accused her of trying to draw public and political attention to herself with allegations that police officers had attempted to abduct her.

With a new government in place, the long-exiled head of the Kyrgyz Committee for Human Rights (KCHR), Ramazan Dyryldaev, was able to return to the country. The KCHR continued to face serious obstacles to its operations, however. During the Akaev government, the KCHR had been stripped of its registration and an alternate group was granted registration under the same name; it is illegal in Kyrgyzstan for two groups with the same name to be registered. As of this writing, the genuine KCHR had not been re-registered.

Key International Actors

The Organization for Security and Cooperation in Europe (OSCE) criticized the former Akaev government for failing to ensure that the February and March 2005 rounds of parliamentary elections complied with international standards. In its report on the July elections that followed President Akaev's ouster, the OSCE noted that the "election marked tangible progress by the Kyrgyz Republic towards meeting OSCE commitments, as well as other international standards for democratic elections."

Following a meeting with then-Foreign Minister Roza Otunbaeva in September, European Commissioner for External Relations Benita Ferrero-Waldner stressed the "unique window of opportunity for the Kyrgyz government to show its political commitment to fully embrace democratic values, develop economic and social policies, which will benefit the Kyrgyz population, and tackle corruption."

With relations already at a low point after Uzbek president Islam Karimov condemned the March "revolution," tensions between Kyrgyzstan and Uzbekistan escalated further when hundreds of Uzbeks sought refuge in Kyrgyzstan following the May 13 massacre of largely unarmed protesters by security forces in the Uzbek city of Andijan. Uzbek authorities pressured the Kyrgyz government to return Uzbek asylum seekers and obtained the handover of four men on June 9. Under strong international pressure, the government of Kyrgyzstan vowed not to return any more of the refugees.

On July 29, 2005, the U.N. High Commissioner for Refugees airlifted 439 Uzbeks from Kyrgyzstan to Romania. One month later, the government of Uzbekistan cancelled its contracts to supply natural gas to Kyrgyzstan. Uzbek authorities went on to implicate Kyrgyzstan in what they claimed was an

Islamic insurgency in Andijan. The state prosecutor's office charged that the "rebels" had trained in southern Kyrgyzstan. The Kyrgyz authorities denied these allegations.

Kyrgyz-Russian cooperation grew closer in 2005 after Kyrgyz authorities allowed Russia to double the number of its troops at the Kant airbase.

Relations between Kyrgyzstan and the U.S. government deteriorated in the final months of the Akaev administration. The U.S. Ambassador to Kyrgyzstan, Stephen M. Young, strongly criticized the government for not allowing free and fair parliamentary elections. During the March unrest in southern Kyrgyzstan, the U.S. government called for dialogue and expressed hope that political changes in Kyrgyzstan would be non-violent. The United States engaged with the newly-installed Bakiev government on issues ranging from the use of the Manas airbase near Bishkek to the Uzbek refugee issue. In April 2005, a group of visiting senators pledged to support the country's political transition. During the fiscal year 2004 (October 1, 2003 through September 30, 2004), U.S. foreign assistance to Kyrgyzstan was U.S.$50.8 million. U.S. expenditures to Kyrgyzstan were expected to increase in 2005.

At a summit of the Shanghai Cooperation Organization (SCO) held in Astana in July 2005, Kyrgyzstan joined Uzbekistan, Kazakhstan, Russia, China, and Tajikistan in signing a declaration on strengthening cooperation in the "fight against terrorism, separatism and extremism." Despite an official SCO statement urging the U.S. to set a date for withdrawal from military bases in Central Asian countries, President Bakiev assured U.S. Secretary of Defense Donald Rumsfeld that the U.S. could use the base in Kyrgyzstan for as long as necessary. At the present time, there are more than nine hundred U.S. troops stationed at Manas airbase.

RUSSIA

Russia slipped deeper into authoritarianism in 2005, as a series of political changes that President Vladimir Putin proposed in the aftermath of the September 2004 Beslan massacre became law. In November, the State Duma took the first step toward approving a draconian law that, if enacted, would substantially curtail the activities of nongovernmental organizations (NGOs) in Russia.

The armed conflict in Chechnya continues unabated. In March 2005, Human Rights Watch concluded that enforced disappearances by Russian forces and their proxies in Chechnya are so widespread and systematic that they constitute crimes against humanity.

The government took modest but important steps in 2005 to resolve some of the country's entrenched human rights problems, including the brutal hazing of conscripts in the armed forces that has claimed dozens of lives and contributed to hundreds of suicides in recent years.

The North Caucasus

Events in 2005 demonstrated the continuing inability of the Russian government to bring peace to Chechnya and its neighboring regions. The conflict continues to claim civilian lives every day.

Enforced disappearances continue to be the conflict's hallmark abuse, with local groups estimating that between two thousand and five thousand people have "disappeared" since 1999 including, according to official figures, more than 140 in the first nine months of 2005. The "disappearances" have followed a clear pattern: the victims are overwhelmingly men between the ages of eighteen and forty, and are always unarmed at the time of apprehension. The perpetrators, in the majority of cases, are clearly identifiable as Russian troops or as belonging to pro-Moscow Chechen commandos. Most "disappearances" have happened in two standards sets of circumstances: in large Russian raids during which troops blocked off and systematically search entire villages or towns, or during targeted raids in the middle of the night.

The Russian government, though long aware of both the frequency and pattern of enforced disappearances, has taken few steps to stop the practice.

As part of Russia's policy of "Chechenization" of the conflict, pro-Moscow Chechen forces under the command of Ramzan Kadyrov have played an increasingly active role in the conflict. In 2004 and 2005, they gradually replaced federal troops as the main perpetrators of "disappearances." They run their own prisons—entirely outside any official penitentiary structure— where they detain, and often ill-treat, hundreds of people. These troops are also responsible for the reprehensible practice of taking hostages among relatives of rebel leaders as a way of forcing the latter to surrender. The Kremlin not only tolerates these practices but has effectively endorsed them by naming Ramzan Kadyrov deputy prime minister of Chechnya and bestowing a Hero of Russia award on him.

Chechen rebels also continue committed egregious violations of human rights. Following the death of rebel leader Aslan Maskhadov in March, they stepped up their campaign against civil servants and regular police both in Chechnya and the neighboring regions of Ingushetia and Dagestan.

Only a few cases against servicemen and police officers charged with abuses against Chechen civilians have reached the courts. In March 2005, a court found police officer Sergei Lapin guilty of abuse of authority for ill-treating Zelimkhan Murdalov and sentenced him to eleven years in prison. In two other cases, juries acquitted servicemen charged with the murder of nine people. In the majority of cases involving serious abuses, however, military and civilian prosecutors have failed to conduct meaningful investigations. In many cases, investigators have failed even to question eyewitnesses. Unable to secure justice within Russia, hundreds of victims have filed applications with the European Court of Human Rights.

Hostilities between law enforcement agencies and insurgents in the Kabardino-Balkaria region dramatically illustrate the increasing instability in the North Caucasus. On October 13, 2005, armed insurgents launched a major attack on police stations, the airport, and government buildings in Nalchik, the region's capital, taking several hostages. The hostilities reportedly resulted in more than 130 deaths, including at least forty-four civilians and local police officers. Although Chechen rebel leader Shamil Basayev claimed responsibility for the attack, most insurgents appeared to have been locals.

Political Rights and Freedoms

In 2005, the government pushed through a package of political changes that increased President Putin's power. New legislation abolished direct elections for governors, ended single constituency voting in parliamentary elections, established new membership requirements for political parties seeking to participate in parliamentary elections, and raised the minimum threshold for entry of these parties into the State Duma from 5 to 7 percent.

Under the new legislation, Russia's president nominates candidates for all regional governorships. Regional parliaments have the right to reject these candidates but if they do so three times, the president can dissolve the parliament. In 2005, President Putin nominated candidates for more than thirty governorships, all of whom were rapidly approved by the regional parliaments.

The changes to election laws are likely to make the next State Duma even more monolithic than today's. The end of single constituency voting will cost most independent deputies their seats. The new rules also require that political parties have at least fifty thousand members in order to be able to compete in parliamentary elections.

When Mikhail Kasyanov, a former prime minister, hinted he might run for president in 2008, law enforcement bodies suddenly opened investigations into alleged wrongdoing during his term in office. The prosecution of Mikhail Khodorkovsky and Platon Lebedev, the former head and a key shareholder of the Yukos oil company, ended in guilty verdicts and an eight-year prison term for each. Many observers believe the men were prosecuted primarily because the Kremlin perceived them as a political threat.

Human Rights Defenders

Pressure on NGOs escalated in 2005. A proposed new law, adopted in the first of three required readings in the State Duma in November, would dramatically increase the government's powers to interfere with their work and would close down foreign NGOs operating in Russia. The law was still pending at this writing.

NGOs that work on human rights issues in Chechnya came under increasing fire in 2005. These groups, the activists who lead them, and the people they work with increasingly faced administrative and judicial harassment, and, in the most severe cases, persecution, threats, and physical attacks. For example, the authorities opened two criminal cases against the Russian-Chechen Friendship Society, accusing it of inciting racial hatred and violating tax laws. If found guilty, Stanislav Dmitrievsky, its director, could face five years in prison.

Although harassment of critical NGOs that do not work on Chechnya was less severe, the working environment deteriorated significantly in 2005. Government officials at both the federal and regional level stepped up their verbal attacks on these groups. In a number of regions, officials used legislation that prohibits extremism to shut down NGOs while in others they selectively used registration procedures or audits to harass groups of which they disapproved.

Entrenched Problems

The government made some modest steps in 2005 toward resolving entrenched human rights problems in large state institutions but still need to take more far-reaching measures to fully address these concerns. Torture and ill-treatment of criminal suspects by police, institutionalization and poor treatment of orphans, and inhumane treatment of persons in psychiatric institutions remain widespread and unaddressed.

The Ministry of Defense signed a memorandum of understanding with the human rights ombudsman that allows for monitoring of human rights condi-

tions in military bases. It also announced that it would start regularly publishing information on deaths in the armed forces. Despite these positive steps, violent hazing continued unabated, with the defense ministry announcing that thirteen conscripts had died as a result of hazing and two hundred others had committed suicide in the first nine months of 2005.

The government's record on combating HIV/AIDS has been mixed. Although high-level officials paid considerably more attention to the problem than in previous years and increased budget allocations to address HIV/AIDS-related concerns, steps to undo a 2004 measure to decriminalize small-scale possession of narcotic drugs threatened to undermine HIV prevention work. Criminalization of small-scale possession of narcotic drugs drives drug users away from HIV prevention services out of fear of police abuse and arrest, and exposes them to health risks in prison that would put them at risk of HIV or exacerbate existing HIV infection.

Key International Actors

While many global leaders in 2005 expressed concern over the post-Beslan political changes, they otherwise continued to signal warm support for the Russian president. German Chancellor Gerhardt Schroeder and President Putin attended each other's birthday parties, and Italian Prime Minister Silvio Berlusconi praised Putin as a "true democrat." The European Union and the United States failed to forcefully address the deteriorating human rights situation in Russia during summits with Russian leaders.

Several international organizations have voiced concern over the shrinking political space in Russia. The Parliamentary Assembly of the Council of Europe criticized the prosecution of Mikhail Khodorkovsky and Platon Lebedev, saying that "the prosecutions went beyond the mere pursuit of justice to include such elements as to weaken an outspoken political opponent, intimidate other wealthy individuals and regain control of strategic economic assets." In its newly adopted country strategy for Russia, the European Bank for Reconstruction and Development noted the continuing concentration of power in the executive and observed that "in the absence of a vibrant civil society and without vibrant political debate in legislature, policy making will fail to benefit from the diversity of views in the electorate."

Criticism of Russia's conduct in Chechnya remains muted. The international community continues to call for a peaceful solution of the conflict without offering a clear vision of how lasting peace could be achieved. In contrast to previous years, in 2005 the European Union failed to table a resolution expressing concern about the Chechnya conflict at the U.N. Commission on Human Rights. Russia continues to refuse access to Chechnya to the U.N. special rapporteurs on torture and extrajudicial executions.

The Parliamentary Assembly of the Council of Europe continues to criticize abuses both by Russian troops and their proxies, and by the Chechen rebels. The Council of Europe Committee for the Prevention of Torture conducted its seventh visit to the region in December 2004, but the Russian government has not allowed the publication of any of its reports on Chechnya. In February 2005, the European Court of Human Rights found the Russian government guilty of violating the right to life and the prohibition of torture with respect to a number of Chechen civilians who had died in 1999 and 2000 at the hands of Russian troops.

SERBIA AND MONTENEGRO

Serbia and Montenegro is a loose union of two republics which face different human rights challenges. In 2005, inadequate official responses to intimidation and violence against ethnic minorities continued to be a problem in Serbia. Cooperation with the International Criminal Tribunal for the former Yugoslavia (ICTY) depended on the government of Serbia, where most of the ICTY indictees resided years after the tribunal brought charges against them. Also in Serbia, treatment of human rights defenders took a marked turn for the worse. In both republics, the judiciary appeared subservient to the executive.

International Criminal Tribunal for the Former Yugoslavia

Serbia and Montenegro's cooperation with the ICTY has improved significantly after the near stalemate for the most part of 2004. Between October 2004 and April 2005, the government transferred fourteen indictees to the tribunal in the Hague. Serbian generals Nebojsa Pavkovic, Vladimir Lazarevic and Sreten Lukic, all indicted for war crimes in Kosovo in 1999, were among those surrendered, although the year before the government had insisted that they should be tried in Belgrade. Serbia also surrendered nine Bosnian Serb former army and police officials charged with genocide and crimes against humanity for the killing of eight thousand Bosnian men in Srebrenica in July 1995.

The change of attitude towards the ICTY resulted more from the willingness of the international community to use a "carrot and stick" approach than from any new-found commitment to justice on the part of the Serbian authorities. The cooperation began only after European Union and United States officials made it clear that closer relations with Serbia were dependent on the latter's full cooperation with the tribunal. In a troubling trend, Serbian government representatives often praised the accused who decided to surrender as "patriotic" and "responsible," without making any reference to the crimes for which they were indicted. On December 30, 2004, Minister of

Interior Vladan Jocic even expressed his conviction that the Serbian army and police generals indicted for crimes in Kosovo were innocent.

Four indictees were believed to remain at large in Serbia and Montenegro as of November 2005, or to travel back and forth between Serbia and Montenegro and Republika Srpska (Bosnia and Herzegovina), including Ratko Mladic, the former commander of the Bosnian Serb army.

Domestic War Crimes Trials

The prosecution of war crimes cases before domestic courts in Serbia is hampered by a lack of political support in the country to establish accountability. The creation of a special war crimes chamber in 2003 appeared to signal an increased seriousness of purpose, but so far the chamber has dealt with only one crime, the November 1991 killing of two hundred Croats near Vukovar, Croatia. Two more indictments involving twelve persons were issued in August and October 2005, relating to war crimes in Bosnia, but the two trials had not started as of mid-November. There were no persons holding positions of seniority in the army or police among the accused.

Judiciary

The executive in Serbia openly encroached upon the independence of the state prosecutor's office in 2005. Invoking his supervisory powers, Minister of Justice Zoran Stojkovic insisted in a newspaper interview in January 2005 that the prosecutors launch criminal proceedings against six individuals who had held positions in the Serbian government between 2001 and 2003. On February 13, Stojkovic repeated a call for the prosecution of former Deputy Prime Minister Cedomir Jovanovic. A municipal prosecutor in Belgrade indicted Jovanovic in September for abuse of official position in 2001, but the municipal court in October rejected the indictment as groundless.

In a newspaper interview published on September 17, 2005, Stojkovic stated that he had asked the competent bodies to look into the legality of certain activities of opposition leader Vladan Batic in 2003, when he had been

Serbia's justice minister. On September 28, police detained Batic for 48 hours and then released him without charge.

The slow and inept handling by the Montenegrin judiciary of a case possibly implicating government officials in commission of a war crime in the 1990s exemplified the longtime concerns about the lack of judicial independence in the republic. The case concerned the handing over of eighty Bosnian Muslim refugees in Montenegro to Bosnian Serb soldiers in May 1992, resulting in the execution of most of the refugees. Dozens of victims' families sued the state for compensation in 2004, but as of October 2005 only four civil proceedings had begun. Under public pressure, in October, the Montenegrin state prosecutor requested the opening of a criminal investigation into the 1992 case. The prosecutor's motion was seriously flawed by including a dozen victims among the potential witnesses and omitting important documents from the evidence. The motion also failed to include any senior official among the suspects.

Ethnic and Religious Minorities

Compared to the previous year, in 2005 incidents of ethnically motivated attacks decreased in the Vojvodina region of northern Serbia, but intensified in other parts of Serbia, often taking the form of anti-Semitic and anti-Muslim graffiti, as well as physical assaults on Roma. Criminal and misdemeanor sentences against the perpetrators of ethnically motivated crimes were light. On July 26, for example, the district court in Nis sentenced eight defendants to prison sentences of between three and five months for their roles in burning down the city mosque in March 2004. On March 23, 2005, a Belgrade misdemeanor court sentenced to ten days' imprisonment three persons who had written graffiti at the entrance to the Jewish cemetery calling for "Jewish parasites" to be expelled from Serbia.

In a positive development, in areas of southern Serbia bordering Kosovo and mainly inhabited by ethnic Albanians, the authorities have made initial steps to include Albanians in the judiciary and to incorporate Albanian culture and history in the local school curriculum. There has also been some progress in providing pre-school education for Roma children in Serbia. However, thou-

sands of Roma continue to face discrimination in most areas of life, and lack basic access to education, health services and housing.

Human Rights Defenders

High-profile government officials expressed hostility towards leading human rights defenders. The head of the State Security Service, Rade Bulatovic, and Minister for Capital Investments, Velimir Ilic, suggested in July and September 2005 that leading human rights organizations in Serbia were working for unspecified foreign powers. In June and July the head of the parliamentary group of Prime Minister Vojislav Kostunica's Democratic Party of Serbia repeatedly expressed contempt for "characters like Natasa Kandic [one of Serbia's most prominent human rights activists]," while Justice Minister Stojkovic accused Kandic of indifference to Serb victims of war crimes. Physical assaults on Serbian Helsinki Committee Director Sonja Biserko and break-ins at her home and at the home of well-known human rights lawyer Biljana Kovacevic-Vuco during 2005 appeared to be the work of Serbian extremists incited by such statements. Verbal harassment of these three leading activists in public places was frequent.

Key International Actors

The U.S. government, which enjoys considerable influence with the authorities in Serbia, took a more uncompromising stance than in previous years on the issue of Serbia's cooperation with the ICTY. In January 2005, for the second consecutive year, the U.S. withheld a portion (U.S.$10 million) of the economic assistance planned for 2005 to Serbia, over its non-cooperation with the tribunal. The aid was released for payment in June, following the transfer of a number of indictees to the Hague in the intervening period. On October 7, Under Secretary of State for Political Affairs Nicholas Burns reiterated that assistance would be again suspended if Serbia did not surrender Ratko Mladic.

The overall perception of the work of the ICTY among the Serbian public remained negative, although it improved somewhat during the year as a result of the improved cooperation by the Serbian authorities and the increase of prosecutions for crimes committed against ethnic Serbs. The trial of former President Slobodan Milosevic, on charges of crimes against humanity and genocide, continued into its fourth year, amidst a lively debate in Serbia and abroad, on the effect the trial has had on the process of coming to terms with the past in Serbia.

The E.U. rewarded Serbia and Montenegro politically for the improved cooperation with the ICTY by deciding in October 2005 to open negotiations on a Stabilization and Association Agreement, following a positive feasibility study by the European Commission in April. The October decision, by the European Council, did not include an explicit "brake clause" that would suspend the negotiations if the E.U. were dissatisfied with the human rights situation in the country, but it put a heavy emphasis on the importance of continued cooperation with the ICTY. The European Parliament adopted a resolution on Vojvodina on September 29, finding that no real progress has been made in reversing the deterioration in the conditions for national and ethnic minorities in Vojvodina, and calling for E.U. monitors to be sent to the province.

Kosovo

The U.N. Security Council's decision in October 2005 to approve the start of negotiations over Kosovo's final status is arguably the most significant development since the United Nations placed Kosovo under international administration in 1999. In the field of human rights, however, the picture remains bleak. Insecurity and lack of free movement for minorities, justice system failures, and widespread discrimination remain serious problems. The return of internally displaced and refugees from Kosovo to their homes continues to be stalled.

Protection of Minorities

Despite improvements in the security situation in Kosovo, members of ethnic minorities, particularly Serbs and Roma, still cannot move about freely. Minorities generally travel with specially provided transport or under military or police escort—and typically from one minority enclave to another.

Due to security incidents and generalized fear, previously disbanded escorts have had to be reinstated in some locations, particularly for transport of children to schools.

While rates of reported inter-ethnic crime fell in 2005, many organizations working with minorities suspect that the decrease simply reflects greater physical separation and lack of interaction between communities since major clashes between majority Albanians and Serbs and widespread rioting in March 2004.

While most minority homes destroyed in March 2004 have been reconstructed, displaced persons trying to visit them have reported continuing threats and intimidation. Ethnic Albanians living in Serb-majority areas or who travel to such areas report similar concerns.

The fragile nature of the security situation was reinforced by a series of incidents in the second half of 2005, including the killing of two young Serbs on the road to Strpce in August; the subsequent destruction of a nearby Albanian war memorial and shooting of an ethnic Serb police officer on duty near the memorial; the shooting of the highest ranking Serb police officer in Gjilan in late September; and confirmed reports of armed masked men (calling themselves "The Army for Kosovo's Independence") operating in the western part of the province in October.

Minorities continue to face persistent discrimination in employment and in the provision of education, social welfare, and health services, and have limited access to administrative offices and courts. The anti-discrimination law remains little more than words on paper.

Among minorities, the situation for Roma is perhaps the grimmest. Their often precarious plight is illustrated by the displaced Roma who have been living adjacent to the Trepca mine in North Mitrovica since 1999. In 2004, the high level of lead contamination in the area led the World Health Organization to recommend an immediate evacuation of children and pregnant women and temporary relocation of all others. At this writing, the Roma remained at the site.

Return of Refugees and Internally Displaced Persons

Fewer than 5 percent of the more than 200,000 displaced Kosovar minorities who fled their homes in the second half of 1999 have returned home. Many are living under makeshift arrangements elsewhere in Kosovo; many others are living as refugees outside Kosovo. The trend of decreasing voluntary minority returns continues. As of September, there had been approximately 1,500 such returns during 2005. By comparison, there were approximately 2,300 returns during 2004 (itself a 37 percent decrease from the previous year).

As in previous years, returns that did take place in 2005 were often incomplete or partial returns, predominately to rural and mono-ethnic areas. The first Serb return to an urban area where there was not already an established Serb presence did not take place until March 2005, with sixteen families returning to Klina.

Progress on the return of the 4,100 persons displaced by the March 2004 riots has been patchy. As of September 2005, more than 1,300 persons remained officially displaced. Among the two-third no longer considered officially displaced, few have returned to reconstructed homes in their former communities, preferring instead to remain in metal containers in Gracanica, in settlements on the outskirts of towns, in unaffected minority enclaves, or outside Kosovo.

In March 2005, UNHCR revised its findings on protection needs of minorities in Kosovo, and concluded that while individual cases should continue to be assessed, there was no longer a security basis for blocking forcible returns of Ashkaelia, Egyptian, Bosniak and Gorani minorities. On that basis, UNMIK relaxed its forced returns policy, which has resulted in an increase in forced returns from western Europe, especially of the first three groups, despite concerns from NGOs in Kosovo about the sustainability of such returns.

Impunity and Access to Justice

While the challenges in establishing a new justice system in Kosovo are considerable, progress to date has been disappointing. The failure to bring to justice many of those responsible for serious crimes has created a climate of impunity that recent efforts have done little to change.

The shortcomings in the justice system, previously identified by Human Rights Watch, include a growing backlog of cases; a shortage of qualified judges; virtually nonexistent mechanisms for witness protection and relocation; poorly-trained and inadequately supported investigators and prosecutors; inadequate defense counsel; perceptions of bias by local judges; and problematic sentencing practices. The problems affect all communities (particularly minorities), undermining confidence in the criminal justice system and the rule of law.

The poor record on prosecuting war crimes and post-war inter-ethnic and political violence continues, especially for offences carried out between 1998 and 2000. The second major trial of former Kosovo Liberation Army (KLA) members only began in October 2004. At writing, the proceedings had been completed and the three accused were awaiting judgment. In September 2005, four Kosovo Serb suspects were arrested on charges of war crimes. Despite some progress on the resolution of outstanding cases of missing persons from Kosovo, more than 2,500 cases remain.

In March 2005, the International Criminal Tribunal for the Former Yugoslavia indicted then-Prime Minister of Kosovo Ramush Haradinaj and two others (Idriz Balaj and Lahi Brahimaj) for their involvement in the "intimidation, abduction, imprisonment, beating, torture and murder" of Serb, Albanian, and Roma civilians while Haradinaj was a KLA commander and the others his subordinates in 1998 and 1999. Haradinaj resigned and surrendered to the Tribunal the same month and was granted conditional release in June 2005.

While the criminal justice response to the March 2004 violence might appear a dramatic improvement in comparison to the dismal rate of prosecutions for offences prior to that date, the reality is more sobering. While 424 people were charged with criminal acts relating to the violence, most were charged only with misdemeanors; by November 2005, only about one-half of the cases had been decided; and the majority of decisions imposed no more than minor penalties or fines, often below those stipulated in Kosovo's minimum sentencing guidelines.

Of fifty-six cases from March 2004 relating to more serious offences—including charges for murder; the incitement of violence or organization of riots; and arson—fewer than one-third had been resolved at this writing. Less than half of the cases had even reached the courts. The vast majority of those that were decided resulted in suspended sentences. The sixteen- and eleven- year sentences imposed on two of the men who murdered a Serb man in Gjilan and brutally attacked his mother were a notable exception.

The problems with the criminal justice system are mirrored in Kosovo's civil courts. An extreme case backlog (up to 60,000 according to some estimates), limited access to the courts for ethnic minorities, and failure to implement court decisions, are among the chief continuing obstacles.

Key International Actors

UNMIK has not recovered from the damage to its already tarnished reputation caused by the March 2004 violence. Neither the appointment of a new special representative and other senior personnel in 2004 nor the ongoing transfer of powers to the Provisional Institutions of Self-Government (set to become Kosovo's interim government),has managed to stem the diminishing credibility of UNMIK among all communities in Kosovo.

In October 2005, the U.N. Secretary-General's Special Envoy to Kosovo Kai Ede submitted a report on Kosovo's progress toward meeting the conditions established by the international community for the start of negotiations on the province's final status. While concluding that talks should commence, the report contained a frank assessment of the international community's human rights failures in Kosovo, including the "climate of impunity" in which "far too few perpetrators of serious crimes are ever brought to justice." The report also made plain that "the overall return process has virtually come to a halt."

Following the Eide Report and the recommendation of the U.N. secretary-general, the Security Council approved the start of status talks, expected at this writing to commence by the end of 2005, emphasizing that "particular and time-conscious attention should be given to protecting minorities...[and] creating the necessary conditions to allow sustainable returns."

The expected transformation of the Ombudsperson office from an international to a local institution at the end of 2005 raised concerns about whether the office would be able to effectively monitor the activities of UNMIK and other international and national bodies, threatening an important mechanism of accountability in Kosovo.

A change of leadership at the E.U. mission helped repair a rift between the mission and the provisional government resulting from the E.U.-led privatization process. E.U. negotiators are likely to play an important role in the status talks.

TAJIKISTAN

Human rights conditions worsened in Tajikistan following political upheaval in neighboring Kyrgyzstan in March 2005 and violence in Uzbekistan in May. Concerned with possible domestic unrest, the government jailed opposition leaders and journalists on spurious charges. Ongoing state persecution of independent media led to the closure of key print and broadcast outlets.

Flawed parliamentary elections also marred Tajikistan's rights record in 2005. Although it noted improvements over previous elections, the Organization for Security and Cooperation in Europe (OSCE) characterized the February 2005 polls as failing to meet international standards.

February Parliamentary Elections

According to the final report of the OSCE observation mission, the February 27, 2005, election for the lower house of parliament failed to meet international and domestic standards. In particular, the OSCE report cited the detention of key political leaders, government domination of the campaign process, and restrictions on independent media as significant obstacles to a free and fair election.

The OSCE report also noted improvements over previous elections in Tajikistan. The polling was peaceful and there was a measure of choice among candidates. Despite the restrictions on independent media, the OSCE determined that state media was "reasonably balanced" in the run-up to elections. However, the report noted that two state-owned newspapers refused to publish the OSCE's preliminary report on the election, even as a paid advertisement.

Observers noted serious problems with the polling process itself. OSCE monitors concluded that the counting process was "poor" or "very poor" at 54 percent of the polling stations they visited. Within five days of the first round of voting, four opposition parties announced that they would not recognize the results of the election, but their protest did not have a significant impact on domestic or international policies.

Political Opposition

As the February elections approached, the government began to pressure members of the political opposition. In August 2004, police raided the offices of the Taraqqiyot (Tajikistan Development) party after its members published an open letter accusing President Emomali Rakhmonov of practicing the "politics of genocide." The authorities seized documents they claimed insulted the president, which is criminalized in Tajikistan, and prosecutors charged the deputy chairman of the party, Rustam Faziev, the letter's author, with violating the lèse majesté law. In June 2005, a court sentenced Faziev to five years and ten months in prison. At this writing, ailing party Chairman Sulton Kuvatov was due to face trial on the same charges pending improvement in his health.

In December 2004, Russian police arrested Mahmudi Iskandarov in Moscow at the request of Tajik authorities. The government had implicated Iskandarov—a vociferous critic of President Rakhmonov, presidential hopeful, and leader of the Tajik Democratic Party—in an attack on two government offices in Tojikobod in August 2004. Russian authorities released him on April 3, 2005, but he disappeared just two days later and eventually turned up in custody in Tajikistan. Iskandarov claimed that he had applied for refugee status after his initial release from Russian custody, but said that Russian police had kidnapped him off the street and transferred him to agents who flew him to Dushanbe. On October 5, 2005, after a trial that lasted more than two months, Iskandarov was found guilty on six counts, including terrorism and illegal possession of weapons. He was sentenced to twenty-three years in prison and fined 1.5 million soms (approximately U.S.$470,000).

Prosecutors also charged a group of individuals, including Iskandarov's former driver, in connection with the attack. One of the defendants, Bakhtior Saidov, claimed at trial that investigators had tortured him and the other members of the group and forced them to plead guilty to the August 2004 attack. On October 4, 2005, all the men were found guilty and received sentences ranging from eleven to twenty-two years in prison.

After the uprising in Kyrgyzstan and public demonstrations in Uzbekistan, the government broadened its repression of dissident political activists. A court convicted Nizomiddin Begmatov and Nasimjon Shukurov, who ran as Social Democratic Party (SDP) candidates in the February 2005 parliamentary elections, on charges of hooliganism and sentenced them to twelve and eighteen months in prison, respectively. They were contesting the election on behalf of the party when they allegedly addressed a judge with foul language during a court hearing. The SDP leadership decried their conviction as political persecution.

The government also charged Saifiddin Faizov of the Islamic Renaissance Party with hooliganism for allegedly using foul language in a mosque. IRP leaders contend that the charges were meant to discredit their image in the majority-Muslim country and to punish Faizov for his work as an active campaigner in the February polls. Police briefly detained another IRP member, Abdulvose Abdujalilov, in July on charges of teaching Islam to minors without legal authorization.

Nongovernmental Organizations

In the wake of popular upheavals in a number of post-Soviet states, the Tajik government has become increasingly concerned about foreign sponsorship of civil society groups. On April 14, 2005, the Tajik foreign ministry announced that foreign embassies and aid organizations would have to report to the government their contacts with local political and civic activists. Under the new regulations, diplomats and international organizations are required to give Tajik authorities advance notice of any meetings with local activists.

Press Freedom

The Tajik government uses a range of administrative methods to crack down on freedom of the press. In August 2004, for example, the government shut down Jionhon printing house, which published *Ruzi Nav*, another independent paper. Prosecutors have since charged the paper's editor, Rajabi Mirzo, with insulting the president. The paper remains out of print.

Tajikistan's practice of targeting the printing houses that publish opposition newspapers continued in 2005 with the January closure of the printing house that published *Nerui Sukhan*. Authorities also charged the paper's editor-in-chief, Mukhtor Bokizoda, with tax evasion, but eventually dropped the charges. In July, the government allowed the newspaper to reopen, but tax authorities shut it down again after only one issue.

Tajik regulatory authorities shut down two private broadcasters in April 2005, leaving the capital with no alternative to state television. The government ordered closure of TV Somonian because its license had apparently expired. TV Gul-i-Bodom was taken off the air over accusations that it had violated regulations on election coverage, but it was allowed to resume operations in July. Free press advocates regarded both closures as politically motivated.

In May 2005, the Institute for War and Peace Reporting (IWPR) reported allegations that the license applications of some thirty print and other media outlets were still pending. Some of these delays were due to the lack of a statute on broadcasting. A draft statute introduced by authorities in April 2005 was strongly opposed by independent broadcasters who believed the proposed legislation would open the door to Soviet-style censorship.

The state also engaged in repression of individual journalists. On April 24, 2005, authorities arrested independent reporter Jumaboi Tolibov in Aini on charges of hooliganism and resisting arrest. Free press advocates suspected he was detained for his criticism of the district prosecutor. The public outcry at this arrest was so great that, on June 8, a crowd of more than 120 people demonstrated in support of him. In July, a court in Shahristan sentenced Tolibov to two years in prison for drunken behavior and abusing his government post as head of the legal department of a district administration.

In June 2005, the deputy editor-in-chief of *Nerui Sukhan*, Vahhob Odinaev, was accused of violating Tajikistan's press law in connection with a story that allegedly contained a libelous statement about a university professor. He was ultimately convicted, however, under a negligence statute. The court sentenced him to a year in prison and ordered the confiscation of 30 percent of his wages.

Key International Actors

On October 16, 2004, Russia and Tajikistan signed a bilateral agreement revising their security relationship. Under the terms of the agreement, Russia will maintain an important military base in the country. Most significantly, Russia agreed to hand over control of the Tajik-Afghan border entirely to Tajikistan. Russian troops abandoned the last border post on July 12, 2005, marking a substantial shift in the Russian-Tajik relationship. Russian forces had remained on the border after Tajik independence in 1991, ostensibly to stem the flow of drugs from Afghanistan.

The United States continues to weigh in on Tajik policy, expressing concern about detentions of dissident politicians and the lack of free press in the country. It is also an important source of foreign aid. In FY 2005, the United States disbursed an estimated U.S.$43.6 million in assistance to Tajikistan. The State Department's Bureau of Democracy, Human Rights, and Labor characterized Tajikistan's human rights situation as "poor" in its 2004 report on the country, citing unfair elections, the use of torture, and poor prison conditions. Secretary of State Condoleeza Rice visited Tajikistan in October and held talks with President Rakhmonov on the U.S. military presence in the region.

The European Union has been a major donor to Tajikistan since 1992. Tajikistan has received more aid per capita from the E.U. than any other Central Asian country during this period. In October 2004, Tajikistan and the E.U. signed a Partnership and Cooperation Agreement (PCA), which formalized closer ties between the two parties. An interim agreement governing trade was signed at the same time.

The Organization for Security and Cooperation in Europe (OSCE) maintains an office in Dushanbe that serves as a base for its monitoring and development activities. In addition to monitoring the 2005 parliamentary elections, the OSCE also has weighed in on governance and rights issues. OSCE chairman Dimitrij Rupel visited Tajikistan in April 2005, meeting with President Rakhmonov and urging the government to lift media restrictions and punish corruption. In September 2005, Miklos Haraszti, the OSCE

Representative on Freedom of the Media, expressed concern that nothing had been done to address the closure of several independent newspapers by the Tajik government.

In September 2005, the United Nations High Commissioner for Refugees (UNHCR) criticized the Tajik government for breaking a pledge to the United Nations when it forcibly deported an Afghan woman and four of her children.

TURKEY

Human rights developments in Turkey were mixed during 2005. The government shows some commitment to reform, but is clearly inhibited by anti-reform elements within the judiciary, police, and army. The main achievement of the year was sustained progress in combating torture, with the number of reports of ill-treatment in police stations continuing to fall. Little progress was made, however, toward guaranteeing language freedoms and freedom of expression. In an alarming development, there were episodes of police using unwarranted lethal violence during street disturbances. Political violence by the Kurdish Workers' Party (PKK) flared during the year, increasing tension and provoking heavy-handed responses, including human rights violations, by state forces.

In October Turkey began negotiations for full membership of the European Union—a process expected to take a decade or more, during which time the E.U. will continue to monitor Turkey's protection of human rights and respect for minorities.

Freedom of Expression and Religion

As of November 2005 no individuals were known by Human Rights Watch to be serving prison sentences for the non-violent expression of their opinions. However, scores of people were charged with speech-related offenses and threatened with imprisonment, most being indicted under provisions criminalizing insults to the president, the flag, and state institutions. The government failed to eliminate these provisions from the revised criminal code, introduced in June.

In October 2005 writer Cemal Tokpınar was sentenced to a year's imprisonment for an article suggesting that Turkey's 1999 earthquake was a divine punishment inflicted upon the military. The newspaper article contained no advocacy of violence, but Tokpınar was convicted under criminal code article 216 for "incitement to religious hatred ... in a manner liable to threaten public order." Novelist Orhan Pamuk faced charges for "insulting Turkishness."

His supposed crime was his statement in a magazine interview, that "thirty-thousand Kurds and one million Armenians were killed in these lands."

Women who wear the headscarf for religious reasons continue to be excluded from higher education, the civil service, and political life. Female lawyers who wear the headscarf are not permitted to enter courtrooms, and in July the Ankara Bar took disciplinary action against a lawyer who wore a head-scarf while carrying out her duty to a client in a bailiff's office.

Respect for Minorities

Turkey's courts and state officials repeatedly obstruct language freedoms. As of November 2005 not a single private broadcaster had been given permission to broadcast in Kurdish. In March state television channel TRT stated that "regulations" did not permit it to show musician Birol Topaloğlu singing in the Laz language. In June the Ankara governor refused to authorize the Kurdish Democracy Culture and Solidarity Association (Kürt-Der), claiming that the organization's program "to secure the social and individual rights of Kurds" was unconstitutional. In July the Bingöl governor imposed a U.S.$800 "administrative fine" on local Human Rights Association (HRA) President Rıdvan Kızgın for printing the association's letterhead in Kurdish as well as Turkish, supposedly a breach of the Associations Law requirement that correspondence be exclusively in Turkish.

Extrajudicial Execution

In November 2005, grenades thrown into a bookshop in Şemdinli, Hakkari province, killed one man and wounded eight. Local people captured two gen-darmes and a "confessor" (a former PKK member now working for the secu-rity forces) in the vicinity, together with a grenade and a map showing the bookshop. Gendarmes in an armored vehicle fired on a crowd gathered at the scene of the crime, killing another man. The "confessor" and the armored vehicle commander were arrested but the other two gendarmes were released.

Freedom of Assembly

Police repeatedly used unwarranted force to break up peaceful demonstrations in 2005. In March, Istanbul police assaulted demonstrators who had gathered for International Women's Day. Male and female demonstrators were beaten and sprayed with pepper gas. Prime Minister Recep Tayyip Erdoğan briefly condemned the police violence, but upbraided the press for bringing the incident to public notice.

Still more alarming, the police frequently used lethal force when public gatherings gave way to disturbances. In various incidents, eight demonstrators were shot dead by police. For example, in November, police shot and killed five demonstrators in Hakkari province who were protesting the Şemdinli attack.

Torture and Ill-treatment in Police Stations and Psychiatric Hospitals

Reports of ill-treatment continue to decline thanks to improved safeguards for detainees, including the right to see a lawyer from the first moments of detention. Police compliance with laws and regulations is generally good, even in remoter areas of the southeast. In some provinces, delegations from local human rights boards, including bar association and medical chamber representatives, made unannounced monitoring visits to police stations and gendarmeries. There were, however, still some reports of beating and torture in police stations. For example, in October 2005, four minors reported they had been tortured at police headquarters in Ordu, where no monitoring visits had been conducted. The boys said police officers had stripped and beaten them, squeezed their testicles, and threatened them with rape. The medical reports showed that the boys, released without charge, suffered extensive bruising.

In January 2005, the Turkish parliamentary human rights commission reported that, during a visit to Saray Rehabilitation Center, a psychiatric institution in Ankara, it had discovered children tied to their beds and imprisoned naked in cold rooms. Mental Disability Rights International reported in September that psychiatric hospitals in Istanbul and Izmir were inflicting electroconvulsive treatment (ECT) on patients without muscle relaxants and anesthesia. The Council of Europe's Committee for the Prevention of Torture had already condemned this painful and dangerous practice in a 1997 visit to Turkey. The report also described how children were subjected to ECT, and had their hands and feet bound to their beds for long periods.

Internal Displacement

Most of the 378,335 Kurdish villagers forcibly displaced by security forces during the conflict of the 1980s and 1990s are still unable to return to their homes in the southeast. The government's Return to Village and Rehabilitation Project has failed to provide even the most basic infrastructure, and villagers are unwilling to return to settlements that do not have electricity, telephone service, or a school. Implementation of a 2004 law to compensate the displaced has been uneven, with some villagers receiving appropriate sums while others' claims were unfairly dismissed.

The threat of violence from village guards—paramilitaries armed and paid by the government to fight the PKK—remains an important obstacle to return. Some returning villagers were attacked by village guards during the year. In March 2005, a village guard shot and killed thirteen-year-old Selahattin Günbay, near Nusaybin in Mardin province, because he was allegedly grazing animals on the guard's pasture.

Human Rights Defenders

The government took some steps to recognize the value of human rights organizations, and invited them, together with other Turkish civil society groups, to a consultation about reform and the E.U. process in September 2005. Nevertheless, human rights defenders were once again threatened with physical violence and subjected to numerous criminal prosecutions as well as efforts to discredit them as unpatriotic or treacherous. In May, speaking at the funeral of a soldier killed by a mine, Gen. Hürflit Tolon reproved human rights organizations for their absence. The widely reported comment alarmed defenders, as similar statements by the military preceded the near-fatal shooting of HRA President Akin Birdal in 1998. In June 2005, Istanbul HRA President Eren Keskin and two board members, who had narrowly survived an attack by a lone gunman in 2001, received death threats from the Turkish Revenge Brigade, the extreme right-wing group that had assumed responsibility for the Birdal attack.

Key International Actors

In October 2005, the attention of Turkey and the international community was focused on the E.U.'s decision, after extended discussion, to open membership negotiations. The E.U. maintains a strong and effective engagement with the Turkish government on human rights issues. Confronted with media reports of the police attack on the International Women's Day demonstration in March, visiting E.U. troika representatives declared that they were "shocked by images of the police beating women and young people demonstrating in Istanbul." In September E.U. Enlargement Commissioner Olli Rehn expressed "serious concern" about the prosecution of Orhan Pamuk and visited the writer in his home.

In February 2005, the European Commission against Racism and Intolerance (ECRI) in a report on Turkey mentioned non-Muslim minorities' difficulties, including administrative barriers to building places of worship and training clergy. Noting persistent suspicion of minorities of any kind, ECRI urged the government to establish an agency to combat racism and intolerance.

In January 2005, the U.N. special representative on human rights defenders published a report on her 2004 visit to Turkey. She expressed concern about the harassment of human rights defenders, and called on state officials and the media to refrain from stigmatizing human rights defenders as "enemies." She also urged that human rights defenders be given full access to places of detention. In May, during an informal visit to Turkey, the U.N. special representative on internal displacement highlighted emerging problems in the implementation of the law on compensation.

The European Court of Human Rights issued scores of judgments against Turkey concerning torture, unfair trial, arbitrary detention, and extrajudicial execution. In July 2005, the court found the Turkish government responsible for violations of the right to life concerning twenty-two people shot dead by police during disturbances in Istanbul in 1995 (Şimşek and others v. Turkey).

TURKMENISTAN

Headed by president-for-life Saparmurat Niazov, Turkmenistan remains one of the most repressive and closed countries in the world. Regressive government policies in education, culture, and health care caused increasing concern in the international community. In an attempt to mollify international critics, Niazov conceded to soften registration rules for religious groups, revoked the notorious law providing for a U.S.$50,000 fee for registering a marriage with a foreigner, and granted citizenship to over sixteen thousand refugees and stateless persons. Despite these small positive steps, the overall human rights situation in Turkmenistan remains dismal.

During the first ever review of Turkmenistan by the U.N. Committee on the Elimination of Racial Discrimination (CERD) in August, the government came under heavy criticism on numerous counts of rights violations, including its policy of forced assimilation; restrictions on national and ethnic minorities in access to employment; forcible internal displacement and other restrictions on freedom of movement; closure of minority cultural institutions and of schools teaching in minority languages; limitations on access to foreign culture and art, as well as to foreign media and the Internet; impediments on Turkmen students wishing to study abroad; and the dominant role played by the *Ruhnama* in school curricula.

Persecution of "Internal Enemies"

In June 2005, several defendants were brought to trial in closed court on charges of conspiring to assassinate the president in November 2002. One of them, Begench Beknazarov, was sentenced to life imprisonment, while the rest received lengthy prison terms. The fate of more than fifty others convicted in previous years for the 2002 assassination attempt remains unknown, as they are still denied visits by and correspondence with relatives. There are unconfirmed reports that some may have died in custody or are seriously ill.

Nearly incessant reshuffles initiated by Niazov in the central government and regional administrations are frequently accompanied by arrest and internal exile, confiscation of property, and persecution of the dismissed officials' family members. In July two influential government figures, Rejep Saparov, the former head of the Presidential Administration, and Yelly Kurbanmuradov, the former Deputy Prime Minister in charge of gas and petroleum, were sentenced to prison terms of twenty and twenty-five years respectively on charges of corruption and links with foreign intelligence services. As in many other cases, a brief and closed court hearing only served to rubber stamp harsh verdicts that had apparently been decided by the president before the trial even started.

Authorities persisted in their refusal to drop charges brought in 2004 against seventy-eight-year-old writer Rakhim Esenov, who stands accused of the unauthorized publication abroad of a novel on medieval India, and of smuggling eight hundred copies of it into Turkmenistan. In March 2005 state security officials denied Esenov permission to travel to Russia for medical treatment.

The law equating any criticism of presidential policy to high treason is still in place, making any open dissent impossible. In July, Niazov called on the police to identify and fine persons who "spread false rumors." Dissident Gurbandurdy Durdykuliev remains in a psychiatric hospital in a remote region, having been confined there after asking the president to allow a peaceful demonstration. Relatives of political émigrés openly criticizing Niazov continue to face persecution.

Regression in Education and Culture

Study of *Ruhnama*, a "new holy book" written by president Niazov, is taking the dominant position in school and university curriculum and is gradually replacing other disciplines. By late 2005, Russian-language instruction in grade school had been severely curtailed, and teaching in the languages of other ethnic minorities had ceased altogether. For many children, access even to education within the diminished curriculum is seriously impeded because authorities continue, despite legal prohibition, to widely employ child labor in agriculture.

In February, President Niazov declared his intention to close all libraries with the exception of the central library and those attached to universities. Although this directive has not been fully implemented, over a hundred libraries were closed, including all district and most city libraries.

Civil Society and Media

Despite the October 2004 decriminalization of membership in unregistered nongovernmental organizations (NGOs), independent NGOs were unable to resume activities, or to register. Their activists remained under security police surveillance, and they frequently found themselves effectively confined to their homes ahead of planned meetings with visiting senior international officials.

In February 2005, Victor Panov, one of the few Russian journalists officially accredited in Turkmenistan, was arrested on false espionage charges and three weeks later was deported to Russia. Also in February, Nikolai Gerasimov, a former correspondent for the *Neutralny Turkmenistan* newspaper, was forced to leave the country following threats he received after having given an interview to Radio Liberty's Turkmen service.

Internet access remains severely restricted, and the last remaining Internet club in Turkmenistan was shut down in April. That same month import of foreign periodicals was banned.

Religious Freedom

Despite a certain loosening of religion-related legislation, all confessions faced difficulties registering, which is essential for lawful activities in Turkmenistan. According to official data, as of August only 118 mosques and churches were registered, several times less than the number registered in the mid-1990s.

President Niazov not only banned the construction of new mosques (several old ones having been demolished or transferred to other uses in 2004), but in June also liquidated the theological faculty of Ashgabat State University, the only educational establishment authorized to teach Islam. Niazov ordered that religious practices be unified, through publication of a list of approved Islamic rites and launch of a campaign against those who independently interpret Islam. Under this campaign two Muslims were arrested in Dashoguz in July as "Wahhabis."

Authorities were delaying registration of twelve parishes and a convent of the Russian Orthodox Church, and denied visas to several priests who were assigned to Turkmenistan. At the same time, Niazov suggested that the Moscow Patriarch should separate Turkmen parishes from the Central Asian Diocese, which was seen by observers as a step towards an "independent Orthodox church" controlled by the Turkmen authorities.

Although under United States pressure authorities registered five protestant congregations in 2005, many religious minorities still cannot obtain registration (among them Shia Muslims, Roman Catholics, Lutherans, and the Armenian Apostolic Church). In some cases even registered congregations continue to face harassment and restrictions. Police questioned religious activists, obstructed religious meetings, and confiscated religious literature. Some believers, including Jehovah's Witnesses, were beaten and intimidated by the police for "rejecting the Muslim faith." In December 2004 and February 2005, two Jehovah's Witnesses were given prison terms for evading military service on religious grounds. Two others, convicted in May and June 2004, continued to serve their sentences.

Key International Actors

In December 2004 and again in November 2005, the Third Committee of United Nations General Assembly adopted resolutions on Turkmenistan expressing concern about serious human rights violations and lack of progress in key areas mentioned in the U.N. Commission on Human Rights resolutions of 2004 and 2005. In an apparent response to international criticism, Turkmenistan acceded to several U.N. instruments in 2005, including the optional protocol to the Convention on the Rights of the Child on the sale of children, child prostitution, and child pornography, and the Convention on the Elimination of all Forms of Discrimination against

Women. It also submitted its initial report to the CERD, the first ever report submitted by Turkmenistan to any U.N. treaty body, which was examined by the Committee in August 2005.

Relations between Turkmenistan and the Organization for Security and Co-operation in Europe (OSCE) remained tense. OSCE experts were denied visas to observe the December 2004 parliamentary elections. However, in early 2005, Niazov agreed to resume dialogue with the OSCE and, as reported, even went as far as to promise OSCE Chairman-in-Office Dimitrij Rupel to give up his presidency for life and retire in 2009. In May OSCE High Commissioner on National Minorities Rolf Ekéus was allowed to visit the country, and September marked the first time that a representative of the Turkmen government participated in the OSCE human dimension implementation meeting in Warsaw.

U.S. pressure contributed to further softening of the legislation on religion and simplified procedures for registration of religious minority groups. Despite the U.S. Commission on International Religious Freedom's recommendation, however, the U.S. State Department again failed to make full use of the leverage at its disposal and designate Turkmenistan a "country of particular concern" under the terms of the International Religious Freedom Act. The European Union's Partnership and Cooperation Agreement with Turkmenistan remained frozen. Russia, in contrast, has muted its criticism of Niazov even on the controversial issue of Turkmenistan's unilateral abolition of dual Russian-Turkmen citizenship.

UKRAINE

Presidential elections in November 2004, which were neither free nor fair, sparked a popular uprising in support of presidential candidate Viktor Yushchenko. In what became known as the Orange Revolution, thousands of Ukrainian citizens took to the streets to peacefully protest the government's manipulation of the elections in favor of Prime Minister Viktor Yanukovich. Yushchenko secured a victory over Yanukovich in repeat elections on December 26 and was sworn in as president in January 2005.

While the new government enjoyed relative stability for the first nine months of 2005, many government agencies remained unformed and economic indicators deteriorated. Following a wave of resignations by senior presidential administration and other officials amid mutual recriminations of corruption, Yushchenko fired Prime Minister Yulia Timoshenko, his closest ally in the Orange Revolution, on September 8, 2005. Yurii Yekhanurov was sworn in as prime minister on September 21 following a political compromise brokered between Yushchenko and his former rival Yanukovich to secure parliamentary approval.

The popular uprising that helped sweep Yushchenko to the presidency was rooted in the belief among many Ukrainians that a Yushchenko administration would improve the government's record in economic, social, and political spheres and demonstrate greater respect for human rights and political liberties. For years, under the leadership of President Kuchma, the government had imposed strict controls on media coverage, manipulated electoral processes, and ignored widespread discontent.

Upon taking office, the Yushchenko government announced its intention to protect and promote human rights and to rectify the abuses of the previous government. While some important measures were taken in 2005, numerous serious human rights problems remain.

UKRAINE

On the Margins

Rights Violations against Migrants and Asylum Seekers
at the New Eastern Border of the European Union

HUMAN
RIGHTS
WATCH

Media Freedom

Under the Yushchenko government, state manipulation of television and other media rampant in previous years appears to have ceased, although major television and radio stations remain under the control of either the state or a few wealthy business owners, rendering media outlets vulnerable to political pressures. Attempts to pass legislation that would establish independent public television and radio outlets have failed despite the new government's stated support for reform of the media sector.

Upon entering office, Yushchenko pledged to make the investigation into the unsolved kidnapping and murder of investigative journalist Georgy Gongadze in 2000 a priority. Many considered progress on this front a political litmus test of the seriousness with which the new authorities were pursuing the restoration of the rule of law in Ukraine. In September 2005, a parliamentary commission accused former President Kuchma and three senior officials, including the current Parliamentary Speaker, Vladimir Litvin, of masterminding the murder and recommended that the Prosecutor General's Office open criminal cases against the men. At this writing, the Prosecutor General's Office still had not done so. In August, the Prosecutor General's Office identified and charged three police officers with Gongadze's murder, but closed the investigation without finding and charging senior Interior Ministry official Olixy Pukach, who allegedly led the group that killed Gongadze, and without identifying those who ordered the crime.

Torture and Conditions in Detention

The national human rights ombudsman has campaigned vocally to end the practice of torture and ill-treatment in Ukrainian police detention facilities and prisons, but the problem persists. In its December 2004 report on Ukraine, the Council of Europe's Committee for the Prevention of Torture noted that detainees are at high risk of being physically ill-treated at the time of their apprehension and while in police custody, particularly when being questioned. Those responsible for crimes against detainees are very rarely investigated or prosecuted. Serious problems in detention facilities include overcrowding, substandard conditions of detention, high rates of tuberculosis and other infectious diseases, as well as inadequate food, medical, and other provisions.

Migrants hoping to enter E.U. countries increasingly attempt to transit through Ukraine. Ukraine, however, fails to comply with its international obligations related to migration management and the right to seek asylum. Police and border guards regularly detain undocumented migrants, including asylum-seekers, in appalling conditions in border guard and police detention facilities, often for many months. Migrants rarely have access to interpreters or legal counsel and are unable to challenge their detention. Government officials often refuse to accept applications for asylum, and the migration service is ill-equipped to handle the applications it does receive. Refoulement is also a serious concern. In the first four months of 2005, 1,500 migrants were deported from Ukraine. UNHCR estimates that of these, four hundred persons (mostly from Afghanistan and Chechnya) should have been granted access to asylum procedures. Despite having ratified the 1951 Convention relating to the Status of Refugees and the 1967 protocol, Ukrainian legislation fails to provide adequate protection to persons who risk persecution if deported.

Human Rights Abuses Fueling the HIV/AIDS Epidemic

As many as five hundred thousand people are living with HIV/AIDS in Ukraine, and Ukraine is believed by many to be home to the world's fastest growing HIV/AIDS epidemic. The epidemic is fueled by a wide range of human rights abuses against those at greatest risk of HIV/AIDS: injection drug users, sex workers, men who have sex with men, and prisoners. As a result of their HIV status, these vulnerable groups face discrimination in access to health and social services and violations of their right to privacy. In addition, they often face discrimination in the workplace and ill-treatment by police.

The government has enacted a body of legislation and policies designed to protect the rights of people living with and at high risk of HIV/AIDS. However, drug and law enforcement officials regularly prevent people living with or at high risk of HIV/AIDS from obtaining critical services, often subjecting them to violence or other ill-treatment. Proposed changes in drug policies to criminalize possession of small amounts of narcotics, pending at this writing, threaten to further accelerate HIV infection rates by driving those most vulnerable to HIV infection away from HIV prevention services and exposing many to health risks in prison that would put them at risk of contracting HIV or exacerbate existing HIV infection. Methadone and buprenorphine, widely recognized as among the most effective means to treat opiate dependence, are critical to prevent HIV among injection drug users (IDUs) and to support antiretroviral treatment adherence for HIV-positive IDUs. Ukraine began to provide buprenorphine on a limited basis, but law enforcement opposition to methadone has thus far prevented its use.

Racism

Racism and xenophobia remain entrenched problems in Ukraine. Police regularly target minorities for so-called "document checks," which almost always result in bribes or illegal detention accompanied by beatings or other ill-treatment.

Numerous anti-Semitic attacks were reported in 2005, but police have been reluctant to label the incidents as hate crimes. In January, ten Orthodox Jewish children and three adults were assaulted by skinheads near a synagogue in Simferopol. A group of young men yelling anti-Semitic insults attacked and repeatedly stabbed Yeshiva student Mordechai Molozhenov in Kyiv in August. Two weeks later, also in Kyiv, a group of eight young people attacked and beat Rabbi Mikhail Menis and his fourteen-year-old son. In all cases, police again denied that anti-Semitism had anything to do with the attacks.

Roma in Ukraine continue to suffer frequent and unremedied police abuse, despite repeated appeals by Romani organizations to the police, prosecutors, and the Ombudsperson calling for effective investigations and punishments. In a positive development, the Parliament's Human Rights Committee held its first ever hearing on "The Situation of the Romani People," on April 12, 2005.

Discrimination against Women and Trafficking in Persons

Women in Ukraine do not enjoy equal access to employment opportunities as a result of discriminatory attitudes among both public and private employers, including blatantly discriminatory recruitment practices. Men hold a disproportionate number of senior government and managerial positions and receive better pay than women in comparable jobs. Women are forced into the low-paying and unregulated informal economy or remain unemployed. A large number of women opt to seek better economic opportunities abroad, rendering them vulnerable to trafficking. According to the Interior Ministry, up to four hundred thousand women under the age of thirty have left Ukraine in the last decade.

Ukraine remains a primary source country and an important transit country for the trafficking of women, men, and children to Europe, the Middle East, and Russia for sexual exploitation and forced labor. Anti-trafficking legislation, prosecutions of those complicit in trafficking, and implementation of rehabilitation programs for victims remain inadequate.

Key International Actors

International organizations continue to monitor closely Ukraine's human rights record. The Council of Europe's Parliamentary Assembly has maintained its monitoring procedure on Ukraine and issued a report in October 2005 which noted the first achievements of the new leadership but reiterated statements from previous reports regarding Ukraine's failure to meet many key human rights obligations.

The European Court of Human Rights took a number of key decisions in cases related to Ukraine in 2005. In the case of the *Ukrainian Media Group vs. Ukraine*, the Court ruled that there had been a violation of freedom of expression when domestic courts ruled in favor of two politicians in defamation cases against a Kyiv newspaper. In the case *Gongadze vs. Ukraine*, the Court ruled that Ukrainian authorities failed to protect the life of slain journalist Georgii Gongadze, failed to conduct an effective investigation into his death, treated Gongadze's wife, Myroslava Gongadze, in an inhuman and

degrading manner during the course of the investigation, and failed to provide Myroslava Gongadze with an effective remedy. The court awarded
Myroslava Gongadze, who fled to the United States after her husband's
death, 100,000 euros (U.S.$118,000) in damages.

The European Union offered Ukraine no immediate prospects for accession,
but signed a three-year Action Plan with Ukraine that deepened cooperation
and includes requirements that the government further strengthen human
rights guarantees. The European Bank for Reconstruction and
Development's Country Strategy for Ukraine noted that women face employment discrimination.

The U.S. continues to maintain close ties with Ukraine, but in its June 2005
Report on Human Trafficking criticized the government for not taking sufficient action to combat the problem.

UZBEKISTAN

Uzbekistan's disastrous human rights record worsened further in 2005 after a government massacre of demonstrators in Andijan in May. The government committed major violations of the rights to freedom of religion, expression, association, and assembly, and such abuses only increased after the May massacre. Uzbekistan has no independent judiciary, and torture is widespread in both pre-trial and post-conviction facilities. The government continues its practice of controlling, intimidating, and arbitrarily suspending or interfering with the work of civil society groups, the media, human rights activists, and opposition political parties. In particular, repression against independent journalists, human rights defenders, and opposition members increased this year. Government declarations of human rights reform, such as an announcement that the government will abolish the death penalty and the president's declaration of support for habeas corpus, had no practical impact.

The Andijan Events

On May 13, 2005, Uzbek government forces killed hundreds of unarmed protesters as they fled a demonstration in Andijan, in eastern Uzbekistan. To date the government has taken no steps to investigate or hold accountable those responsible for this atrocity. Instead it denies all responsibility and persecutes those who seek an independent and transparent investigation.

In the early hours of May 13, gunmen attacked government buildings, killed security officials, broke into the city prison, took over the local government building (hokimiat), and took hostages. The trigger for the attacks was the trial of twenty-three respected local businessmen for religious extremism, charges widely perceived as unfair. Towards dawn, the instigators began to prepare for a large protest in a public square, in front of the hokimiat, and mobilized people to attend. By mid-morning, as word spread, the protest grew into the thousands, as people came of their own will and vented their grievances about poverty and government repression. When government forces sealed off the square and started shooting indiscriminately, the protesters fled. Hundreds of them were ambushed by government forces and were gunned down without warning. This stunning use of excessive force has been documented by the United Nations and other intergovernmental organizations.

The Aftermath of Andijan

Since the Andijan massacre, the government has engaged in a concerted campaign to re-write the history of the events. Government authorities deny responsibility for the deaths, blaming them instead on Islamic extremists who were intent on overthrowing the government and creating an Islamic state in the Fergana valley. Foreign journalists were forcibly ejected from the city, and had their notes and equipment confiscated. Local law enforcement and mahalla (neighborhood) committee members went door to door warning residents not to speak with journalists or foreigners or to discuss the events of May 13. The Uzbek government detained hundreds—perhaps thousands—of people in Andijan and coerced testimony from them about the events. On September 20 a trial of fifteen defendants charged with more than thirty crimes relating to the Andijan events began in the Supreme Court. The trial fell far short of international standards and gave rise to concerns that the defendants could have been subjected to torture or coercion. All of the defendants confessed to the charges; although defense lawyers were present at the trial, they did not mount an active defense of their clients. All witnesses supported the government's version of events except for one woman who gave detailed testimony of soldiers firing on civilians. All fifteen defendants were convicted and sentenced to prison terms ranging from fourteen to twenty years. Following the announcement of the verdicts, U.N. Commissioner for Human Rights Louise Arbour issued a statement voicing concern over the convictions, saying the trial had been "marred by allegations of irregularities and serious questions remained about its fairness." A series of trials of approximately one hundred more defendants was expected to take place in the lower courts.

UZBEKISTAN

Burying the Truth

Uzbekistan Rewrites the Story of the Andijan Massacre

HUMAN

RIGHTS

WATCH

Persecution of Human Rights Defenders and Independent Journalists

The crackdown on civil society following the Andijan events focused particularly on human rights defenders. Since the Andijan massacre, human rights defenders have faced increased harassment, surveillance, house arrest, interrogation, arbitrary arrest, criminal charges, and interference with their work. Some human rights defenders have faced public Soviet-style denunciations and hate rallies, and eviction from their homes. At least thirteen defenders and journalists were forced to flee the country fearing persecution. Authorities arrested or detained at least forty-seven defenders and journalists; thirteen remain in detention pending criminal charges related to their work, five have been charged and released pending trial, and two have been tried and sentenced to terms of imprisonment of six months and ten years.

Human rights defenders who attempted to document the Andijan events, called for accountability, or spoke publicly about the government's role in the massacre were particularly vulnerable. For example, Saidjahon Zainabitdinov, chairman of the Andijan human rights group Appeliatsia ("Appeal") whose accounts of the Andijan events appeared widely in the foreign press, was arrested on May 29, 2005, and charged with slander, terrorism, and preparation or distribution of information threatening public security and public order. On August 26 a court sentenced Radio Liberty journalist Nosir Zokir to six months' imprisonment for insulting a security officer. Seven activists from the human rights organizations Ezgulik ("Goodness"), the Human Rights Society of Uzbekistan, and the International Human Rights Society and the Birlik ("Unity") opposition party in Andijan province were arrested for attempting to conduct an inquiry into the Andijan events and for possession of a Birlik party statement about the massacre, and at this writing awaited trial.

On August 27, 2005, authorities arrested Elena Urlaeva, a tenacious human rights activist with the Society for Human Rights and Freedoms of the Citizens of Uzbekistan and a member of the unregistered Ozod Dekhon ("Free Peasants") political party. Police charged Urlaeva with desecrating national symbols for attempting to distribute a caricature of the Uzbek national emblem and forcibly committed her to a psychiatric hospital for observation and evaluation. In September an expert psychiatric commission concluded that Urlaeva did not require treatment, but the police transferred her to a different hospital where a second commission concluded that she was "insane" and required compulsory psychiatric treatment. In October Urlaeva was committed by court order to a psychiatric hospital and forcibly treated with psychotropic drugs. She was released on October 27, but was still compelled to undergo outpatient treatment.

Also in October 2005, police arrested Mukhtabar Tojibaeva, an outspoken critic of the government and chairwoman of the Burning Hearts human rights club in Margilan, on the eve of her departure for an international conference for human rights defenders at risk. Tojibaeva had been actively involved in defending the rights of the group of twenty-three businessmen whose trial had sparked the Andijan events. She was charged with extortion and fraud, and, at this writing, awaited trial.

Restrictions on Nongovernmental Organizations (NGOs)

The authorities continue to interfere with civil society groups and refuse to register any independent human rights groups. The government also continues to tighten restrictions on local groups, taking steps to close hundreds of NGOs in cities around Uzbekistan. It severely limits the work of others by requiring groups to receive advance permission to carry out events, demanding participant lists for activities, and restricting the transfer of grant money from international donors. The government also took steps in 2005 to expel or restrict international NGOs. In September, a court in Tashkent ordered the liquidation of Internews, a media support organization. The Ministry of Justice initiated suspension proceedings against other international NGOs, including the International Resources and Exchanges Board (IREX) and Freedom House, for alleged violations of administrative regulations. A court ordered IREX to suspend its activities for six months, and a criminal investigation was initiated against IREX staff for providing internet services without a license. Proceedings against Freedom House were ongoing. The government revoked or refused to grant accreditation to the staff of several international NGOs, including IREX and the International Republican Institute.

Religious Persecution

For years the government has imprisoned on "fundamentalism" charges individuals whose peaceful Islamic beliefs, practices, and affiliations fell outside strict government controls. Approximately seven thousand people are believed to have been imprisoned since the government's campaign against independent Islam began in the mid-1990s. The government justifies this campaign by referring to the "war on terror," failing to distinguish between those who advocate violence and those who peacefully express their religious beliefs; it used the May 2005 events in Andijan to give new validation to the campaign. By November, Human Rights Watch had documented 194 religious believers convicted in 2005 with at least sixty-nine more awaiting trial; the true numbers are believed to be much higher.

Conditions in Uzbekistan's prisons are poor, and religious and political prisoners suffer particularly harsh treatment. According to testimony by relatives, prisoners are forced to sign statements begging President Islam Karimov for forgiveness, renouncing their faith, and incriminating themselves as terrorists. Prisoners who refuse are punished with beatings, time in punishment cells, and even new criminal prosecutions.

Torture

The government has made no visible progress on ending the use of torture in practice, and only minimal progress on implementing the recommendations made by the U.N. special rapporteur on torture after his visit to Uzbekistan in 2002. Human Rights Watch continues to receive credible allegations of torture during investigations and pre-trial custody, as well as in prisons. Police use torture and other illegal means to coerce statements and confessions from detainees, and investigators routinely block defense attorneys from visiting their clients, a critical safeguard against torture in pre-trial detention. President Karimov made a statement supporting habeas corpus, but as of this writing, this key protection against torture had not been implemented.

Courts ignored defendants' claims at trial that they had confessed under torture and accepted such confessions into evidence (despite an instruction by the Supreme Court to judges to exclude any evidence obtained under illegal means). In trials such as those of religious believers, defendants were routinely sentenced to long prison terms based solely or predominantly on such confessions.

Key International Actors

International actors such as the European Union, the United States, the U.N. and the Organization for Security and Cooperation in Europe (OSCE) played a key role in calling for an independent investigation into the Andijan massacre and for accountability for government officials found responsible, calls that the Uzbek government rejected. Representatives from embassies and the OSCE Office for Democratic Institutions and Human Rights (ODIHR) monitored the trials.

The close strategic partnership between the United States and Uzbekistan cooled considerably after the Andijan massacre. On July 30, 2005, the Uzbek government notified the U.S. embassy in Tashkent that the United States had 180 days to withdraw its forces from a military base in southern Uzbekistan that it had used since 2002 to support operations in Afghanistan. In the fall of 2005, the U.S. Commission on International Religious Freedom formally recommended that the State Department designate Uzbekistan a "country of particular concern" for religious freedom, pursuant to the International Religious Freedom Act. In its subsequent decision issued in November, however, the Department of State failed to heed this recommendation.

In a landmark decision in October, the E.U. partially suspended its Partnership and Cooperation Agreement with Uzbekistan—the first time it has ever done so with any country. The E.U. also imposed sanctions, including an embargo on arms sales to Uzbekistan and a visa ban on top Uzbek officials directly responsible for the massacre. The E.U. issued an initial list of twelve government officials subject to the ban in mid-November, with Minister of Interior Zokirjon Almatov topping the list. In blatant violation of the spirit of this ban, Germany granted a visa on humanitarian grounds to Almatov for medical treatment at a clinic in Hannover just days before the list of names was formally announced. Germany also maintained troops in Termez in southern Uzbekistan.

The European Bank for Reconstruction and Development adopted a new country strategy for Uzbekistan in July, in which it upheld its unprecedented decision of 2004 to suspend public sector lending over human rights concerns. In addition, the Bank conditioned its further engagement with the private sector on there being no direct or indirect link to the government or specific government officials. It also made clear that it would be monitoring its existing portfolio in Uzbekistan, both in the private and public sphere. The World Bank and the Asian Development Bank were both revising their strategies for Uzbekistan as this report went to press.

The U.N. called for an independent inquiry into the Andijan killings. Requests for access to Uzbekistan by a number of U.N. special mechanisms, including the special rapporteur on extrajudicial executions and the special representative for human rights defenders, remained unanswered. In November 2005, the Third Committee of the General Assembly adopted a strongly-critical resolution on Uzbekistan expressing grave concern about the human rights situation in the country and calling on the government to agree to an international commission of inquiry into the Andijan massacre.

Russia and China stood out among nations for publicly supporting Uzbekistan after the Andijan massacre. At the July 2005 summit of the Shanghai Cooperation Organization (SCO), of which Uzbekistan, Russia, and China are members, the heads of state signed seven agreements aimed at the fight against "terrorism, separatism and extremism." The summit framed the Andijan events as part of a wider threat of destabilization rather than as an excessive government response to a largely peaceful demonstration. At the meeting, Russia, China, and the SCO reiterated the Uzbek government's core assertions regarding Andijan. Russia announced joint maneuvers with

Uzbek troops, and both Russia and China declared that they would continue arms sales to Uzbekistan. Russia and Uzbekistan signed a new partnership agreement.

ⵝⵉⵎⴰⵣⵉ ⵥⵓ ⵝⵉⵎⴰⵥⵉ ⵥⵙ ⵝ | ⵥⵙⴲⵥⵒⵉⵔ

MOROCCO

Morocco's Truth Commission

Honoring Past Victims during an Uncertain Present

HUMAN
RIGHTS
WATCH

WORLD REPORT
2006

MIDDLE EAST
AND NORTH AFRICA

EGYPT

Many aspects of Egypt's poor human rights record came in for unprecedented public criticism in 2005 as Egyptian democracy activists challenged President Hosni Mubarak's quarter century of authoritarian rule and the U.S. administration pressed the Egyptian leader to promote basic political rights such as freedom of expression and freedom of assembly. President Mubarak easily won a fifth presidential term in the country's first-ever contested presidential election in early September, which took place largely without incident, but the first rounds of nationwide parliamentary elections in November were marked by extensive irregularities and, in some cases, violence by pro-government forces. Serious issues like routine torture remain unaddressed. Emergency rule continued to provide the basis for arbitrary detention and trials before military and state security courts. Approximately fifteen thousand people remain in prolonged detention without charge under the terms of the Emergency Law, according to the Cairo-based Human Rights Association for Assistance to Prisoners. Several car bomb attacks on tourist sites since October 2004 led to additional mass arrests, arbitrary detentions, and credible allegations of torture.

Emergency Rule

The government last renewed the Emergency Law (Law No. 162 of 1958) in February 2003, and must do so again by May 2006 or allow it to expire. The law, with its prohibition on demonstrations and public rallies, remained in effect during the presidential election campaign, but the government did not interfere with opposition rallies linked to the campaign. President Mubarak indicated he would suspend the law or allow it to expire, but only after instituting what he termed "a firm and decisive law that eliminates terrorism and uproots its threats." Egyptian human rights defenders fear that such legislation would perpetuate many objectionable features of Law 162/1958.

Political Violence and Internal Security

A large car bomb explosion on October 7, 2004, at the Taba Hilton hotel, on the border with Israel, killed more than thirty persons and wounded more than a hundred. The government announced on October 25 that it had identified nine persons responsible, of whom five were in custody, two were killed carrying out the attack, and two remained at large. Nevertheless, over the following months the State Security Investigation (SSI) arm of the Ministry of Interior carried out mass arbitrary arrests in and around al-`Arish, the North Sinai commercial and administrative center, detaining an estimated 2,500-3,000 persons. In April 2005 the government-appointed National Council for Human Rights (NCHR), in its first annual report, stated that at least two thousand persons remained in detention without charge.

On July 23, 2005 three suicide car bombers struck a hotel and tourist markets at Sharm al-Shaikh, at the southern tip of the Sinai Peninsula, killing sixty-seven persons. Three previously unknown groups claimed responsibility. Although security forces arrested several suspects in the days following the attack, in late August they detained an estimated 500-600 persons in a sweep of the mountainous Jabal Halal area of northern Sinai. As of late October 2005 the government had not provided information about whether any of the hundreds arrested had been released or charged in connection with the attack.

In April, three separate shooting and small explosives attacks in Cairo resulted in the deaths of three tourists, as well as the attackers, and injured more than a dozen persons, mostly Egyptian.

The U.S. military command in Iraq said in October that 78 Egyptians, the largest number from any single country, were among the 312 foreign fighters captured thus far while allegedly taking part in the insurgency there.

Torture

Security forces and police routinely torture and mistreat detainees, particularly during interrogations. Torture in the past was used primarily against political dissidents, but in recent years it has been rife in police stations as well, affecting ordinary citizens. In 2004 the Egyptian Organization for Human Rights (EOHR) reported 292 known torture cases between January 1993 and April 2004, 120 of which resulted in the death of the suspect or prisoner. According to EOHR, there were at least seventeen additional cases of deaths in police or security force custody between May 2004 and July 2005. Human Rights Watch and Egyptian human rights organizations documented credible allegations of torture during interrogation from many persons detained following the Taba bombing (see above). A high-level Ministry of Interior official confirmed to Human Rights Watch in February 2005 that the government had not conducted a single criminal investigation of SSI officials for torture or ill-treatment in the past nineteen years, or imposed any disciplinary measures, despite numerous credible allegations of serious abuse in SSI custody.

Restrictions on Freedom of Association and Freedom of Expression

Egypt's law governing associations, Law 84/2002, severely compromises the right to freedom of association, giving the government unwarranted control over the governance and operations of nongovernmental organizations (NGOs). The law provides criminal penalties for "unauthorized" activities, including "engaging in political or union activities, reserved for political parties and syndicates," as well as for carrying out activities prior to an NGO's official authorization and for receiving donations without prior approval from the Ministry of Social Affairs.

Egypt maintains strict controls over political associations as well. In July 2005, the parliament passed government-sponsored revisions to the Political Parties Law (Law 40/1956) providing that new parties be legally registered automatically unless the Political Parties Affairs Committee (PPC), headed by the chair of the National Democratic Party (NDP), rejects the application. The revised law also empowers the PPC to suspend an existing party's activities if it judges this to be "in the national interest" and to refer alleged breaches of the law to the Prosecutor General.

EGYPT

Reading between the "Red Lines"

The Repression of Academic Freedom in Egyptian Universities

HUMAN
RIGHTS
WATCH

The government also revised the Law on Political Rights (Law 73/1956), introducing criminal penalties for journalists and publications convicted of publishing "false information" intended to affect election results. The government took no steps to follow through on President Mubarak's public commitment of February 2004 to revise the 1996 Press Law to eliminate, among other things, criminal penalties for offenses such as libel and defamation. According to Egyptian human rights monitors, the Prosecutor General in the first eight months of 2005 summoned 22 journalists and writers for questioning on alleged defamation charges after they wrote articles critical of public officials.

Ill-treatment of Street Children

The government periodically conducts arrest campaigns of homeless or truant street children who have committed no crime. In custody many face beatings, sexual abuse, and extortion by police and adult suspects, and police deny them access to food, bedding, and medical care. The authorities do not routinely monitor conditions of detention for children, investigate cases of arbitrary arrest or abuse in custody, or discipline those responsible. In many cases, the police detain children illegally for days before taking them to the public prosecutor on charges of being "vulnerable to delinquency."

Women's Rights

Despite recent reforms of Egypt's family and nationality laws, additional steps are needed to amend laws that discriminate against women and girls, to prosecute gender-based violence, and to grant women and girls equal citizenship rights. Discriminatory personal status laws governing marriage, divorce, custody, and inheritance have institutionalized the second class status of women in the private realm and undermined their legal standing. The penal code does not effectively deter or punish domestic violence, and police are routinely unsympathetic to the concerns of battered women and girls.

Religious Intolerance and Discrimination against Religious Minorities

Although Egypt's constitution provides for equal rights without regard to religion, discrimination against Egyptian Christians and intolerance of Baha'is and unorthodox Muslim sects remains a problem. Egyptian law recognizes conversions to Islam, but not from Islam to other religions. Muslims who convert to Christianity face difficulties in getting new identity papers and some have been arrested for allegedly forging such documents. Baha'i institutions and community activities are prohibited by law.

Key International Actors

The U.S. has long been Egypt's largest provider of foreign military and economic assistance, amounting to U.S.$1.3 billion in military aid and U.S.$535 million in economic assistance in 2005. Early in 2005 Deputy Secretary of State Robert Zoellick reportedly warned visiting Egyptian officials that U.S.$200 million of the annual assistance would be withheld until opposition leader Ayman Nour was released from jail. In September Egypt hosted the six-week Bright Star joint military exercise involving 8,600 U.S. troops as well as some 8,000 troops from ten other countries.

President George Bush said in May 2005 that he "embraced" President Mubarak's decision to allow for a contested presidential elections, and he criticized the widely-publicized May 25 beatings of dissidents by ruling party vigilantes. Secretary of State Condoleeza Rice cancelled a planned February visit to Egypt to protest Ayman Nour's jailing. When she visited Cairo in June she expressed concern that in Egypt "peaceful supporters of democracy…are not free from violence. The day must come when the rule of law replaces emergency decrees." Both Bush and Rice endorsed publicly the need for international election monitors, but the Egyptian government remained opposed to their presence during the September voting.

The Association Agreement between Egypt and the European Union, which came into force in June 2004, is premised on "respect for human rights and democratic principles," but Egypt's human rights violations do not seem to have disturbed its operation. In late 2005 Egypt and the European Commission commenced negotiations on an Action Plan under the European Neighbourhood Policy, but progress was uncertain as Egypt reportedly resisted inclusion of numerous human rights-related commitments.

In September, the United Kingdom quietly began efforts to deport three Egyptian Islamists, trying to secure Egyptian diplomatic assurances that the three would not be mistreated if returned to Egypt, even though efforts to get such assurances from Cairo in 1999 regarding one of the men, Hani al-Seba`i, had failed. The British Embassy approached the government-appointed NCHR to play a monitoring role, but the NCHR declined. As of November 2005 there were credible reports that the U.K. was seeking to conclude a memorandum of understanding with Egypt containing a blanket undertaking that people deported there from the U.K. would not be tortured or ill-treated.

Egypt failed to respond to a request from the U.N. special rapporteur on torture for an invitation to visit the country, a request that has been outstanding since 1996. The U.N. Committee against Torture, in a May 2005 ruling that Sweden had violated the absolute prohibition on torture by expelling terrorism suspect Ahmed Agiza to Egypt in 2001, noted that Egypt had a well-documented history of torture abuses, especially when dealing with terrorism suspects (for further details see European Union chapter).

IRAN

Respect for basic human rights in Iran, especially freedom of expression and opinion, deteriorated considerably in 2005. The government routinely uses torture and ill-treatment in detention, including prolonged solitary confinement, to punish dissidents. The judiciary, which is accountable to Supreme Leader Ali Khamenei, has been at the center of many serious human rights violations. Abuses are perpetrated by what Iranians call "parallel institutions": paramilitary groups and plainclothes intelligence agents violently attack peaceful protesters, and intelligence services run illegal secret prisons and interrogation centers. President Mahmoud Ahmadinejad, elected in June 2005, appointed a cabinet dominated by former members of the intelligence and security forces, some of whom are allegedly implicated in the most serious human rights violations since the Islamic Republic of Iran was established twenty-six years ago, such as the assassination of dissident intellectuals.

Freedom of Expression and Opinion

The Iranian authorities have systematically suppressed freedom of expression and opinion since April 2000, when the government launched a campaign involving closure of newspapers and the imprisonment of journalists and editors. Consequently, very few independent dailies remain, and those that do self-censor heavily. Many writers and intellectuals have left the country, are in prison, or have ceased to be critical. During 2005 the authorities also targeted websites and Internet journalists in an effort to prevent online dissemination of news and information. Between September and November of 2004, the judiciary detained and tortured more than twenty bloggers and Internet journalists, and subjected them to lengthy solitary confinement. The government systematically blocks websites with political news and analysis from inside Iran and abroad. On February 2, 2005, a court in the province of Gilan sentenced Arash Sigarchi to fourteen years in prison for his online writings. In August 2005, the judiciary sentenced another blogger, Mojtaba Saminejad, to two years in prison for "insulting" Iran's leaders.

Torture and Ill-treatment in Detention

With the closure of independent newspapers and journals and the suppression of reporting on human rights abuses, treatment of detainees has worsened in Evin prison as well as in detention centers operated clandestinely by the judiciary and the Islamic Revolutionary Guard Corps. The authorities have subjected those imprisoned for peaceful expression of their political views to torture and ill-treatment. Judges often accept coerced confessions. The authorities use prolonged solitary confinement, often in small basement cells, to coerce confessions (which are videotaped) and gain information regarding associates. Combined with denial of access to counsel, prolonged solitary confinement creates an environment in which prisoners have nowhere to turn to seek redress for their treatment in detention.

The judiciary issued an internal report in July 2005 admitting serious human rights violations, including widespread use of torture, illegal detentions, and coercive interrogation techniques. However, the judiciary failed to establish any safeguards, follow up on its findings, or hold any officials responsible.

Impunity

There is no mechanism for monitoring and investigating human rights violations perpetrated by agents of the government. The closure of independent media in Iran has helped to perpetuate an atmosphere of impunity.

In recent years, public testimonies by numerous former prisoners and detainees have implicated Tehran's public prosecutor Saeed Mortazavi and his office in some of the worst cases of human rights violations. Despite extensive evidence, Mortazavi has not been held responsible for his role in illegal detentions, torture of detainees, and coercing false confessions. The case of Iranian-Canadian photojournalist Zahra Kazemi, who died in the custody of judiciary and security agents led by Mortazavi in June 2003, remains unresolved. Lawyers representing Kazemi's family revealed that in addition to signs of torture including fractures to her nose, fingers, and toes, Kazemi received heavy blows to her head, once during her initial detention by the head of the intelligence unit at Evin prison on June 23, 2003, and another blow during an interrogation led by Mortazavi three days later. According to autopsy reports, Kazemi died of severe blows to her head. The judiciary had accused a low-ranking Intelligence Ministry official, Reza Ahmadi, of Kazemi's unintentional homicide, and had proceeded with a hastily organized trial held in May 2004 which cleared Reza Ahmadi of the charges. Following an appeal by lawyers representing Kazemi's family, an appeal hearing was convened in July 2005, in which the lawyers demanded that the judiciary launch an investigation into charges of intentional homicide, but the judge refused their request. The judiciary has taken no further steps to identify or prosecute those responsible for Kazemi's killing.

Human Rights Defenders

In 2005, the authorities intensified their harassment of independent human rights defenders and lawyers in an attempt to prevent them from publicizing and pursuing human rights violations. The judiciary summoned Noble Peace Prize winner Shirin Ebadi in January 2005 without specifying charges against her. After she challenged her summons as illegal, and following an international outcry, the judiciary rescinded its order. In July, the authorities once again threatened to arrest Ebadi after she publicized several high-profile human rights cases. On July 30, the judiciary detained Abdolfattah Soltani, a lawyer and member of the Center for Defense of Human Rights, after Soltani and Ebadi protested the judiciary's inaction in Zahra Kazemi's case. No formal charges have been filed against Soltani; the judiciary appears to be using his illegal detention as a way to intimidate and silence other human rights defenders and lawyers. Prominent dissident and investigative journalist Akbar Ganji, who exposed the role of high-ranking officials in the murders of writers and intellectuals in 1998, remained imprisoned for a sixth year.

Minorities

Iran's ethnic and religious minorities are subject to discrimination and, in some cases, persecution. The Baha'i community continues to be denied permission to worship or engage in communal affairs in a public manner. In April 2005, protests erupted in the southern province of Khuzistan, home to nearly two million Iranians of Arab descent, following publication of a letter allegedly written by Mohammad Ali Abtahi, an advisor to then-President Mohammad Khatami, which referred to government plans to implement policies that would reduce the proportion of ethnic Arabs in Khuzistan's population. After security forces opened fire to disperse demonstrators in Ahvaz, the confrontation turned violent and spread to other cities and towns in Khuzistan. The next day, Abtahi and other government officials called the letter a fake. During the clashes, security forces killed at least fifty protestors and detained hundreds more.

In July 2005, security forces shot and killed a Kurdish activist, Shivan Qaderi, in Mahabad. In the wake of this incident protests were held in several cities and towns in Kurdistan demanding that the government apprehend Qaderi's killers and put them on trial. Government forces put down the protests, killing at least seventeen people and detaining several prominent Kurdish journalists and activists. In October 2005, they were released on bail.

Key International Actors

In 2005 the policy of the European Union towards Iran was dominated by negotiations over Iran's nuclear programs, with human rights concerns a secondary matter. The European Union has pledged to tie Iranian respect for human rights to progress in co-operation on other issues, but so far with little impact. Australia and Switzerland also have "human rights dialogues" with Iran but have not made public any relevant benchmarks for assessing progress.

Against strenuous Iranian objections, the United Nations General Assembly adopted a resolution in November 2004, noting serious violations and the worsening of the human rights situation in Iran. However, in 2005, unlike in previous years, no resolution was introduced at the U.N. Commission on Human Rights concerning the human rights situation in Iran. Under a standing invitation issued in 2002 from Tehran to the thematic mechanisms of the U.N. Commission on Human Rights, the Working Group on Arbitrary Detention and the special rapporteur on the promotion and protection of the right to freedom of opinion and expression visited the country and subsequently issued reports critical of government practices. However, the government has failed to implement their recommendations, and in some cases there were reprisals, such as re-arrest, against persons who testified to the experts. In January 2005 the special rapporteur on violence against women visited Iran, and the special rapporteur on adequate housing made a visit in August. Iran has not responded to requests by the U.N. special rapporteurs on torture and on extrajudicial executions to visit the country.

Relations between the United States and Iran remain poor. President Bush in August 2005 said that U.S. military action against Iran was an "option on the table," but the administration reportedly remains divided on this point.

IRAQ

The human rights situation in Iraq deteriorated significantly in 2005, with a continuing rise in the number of armed attacks by insurgent groups, including the deliberate targeting of civilians and violent attacks such as suicide bombings. The level of abductions of Iraqis, in many cases for ransom, has remained high, while those of foreign nationals has decreased – reflecting in part the departure of foreign personnel working with humanitarian agencies, media outlets and others as a result of deteriorating security conditions.

Counterinsurgency attacks by U.S.-led international and Iraqi forces further aggravated the human rights situation, resulting in the killing of civilians in violation of the laws of armed conflict. There was also continuing concern about the absence of basic precautions by the U.S. military to protect civilians, including at checkpoints, brought to the fore by the killing of an Italian intelligence officer in March 2005. The subsequent U.S. military investigation exonerated all U.S. military personnel involved in the shooting, but showed that the army had failed to implement lessons learned during two years of manning checkpoints.

Evidence of the torture and other mistreatment of detainees held in the custody of U.S. forces in 2003 and 2004 has continued to emerge in the wake of the Abu Ghraib revelations in April 2004. Some of the evidence is based on accounts by U.S. military personnel, who have described routine and severe beatings of detainees, including subjecting them to forced stress positions, sleep deprivation, extremes of hot and cold, denial of food and water, and the application of chemical substances to detainees' skin and eyes. The accounts show that abuses have resulted from civilian and military failures of leadership and confusion about interrogation standards and the application of the Geneva Conventions. They contradict claims by the Bush administration that detainee abuses by U.S. forces abroad have been infrequent, exceptional and unrelated to policy.

Efforts to boost economic reconstruction and the rebuilding of Iraq's devastated infrastructure continue to be hampered by general instability in the country and the level of violence caused by insurgency and counterinsur-

IRAQ

The New Iraq?

Torture and ill-treatment of detainees in Iraqi custody

HUMAN
RIGHTS
WATCH

gency attacks. This is despite progress made in the political process, including the holding of general elections in January 2005, the convening of the Transitional National Assembly in March, the formation of the Iraqi Transitional Government in April and the holding of a referendum on a draft constitution in October.

The Governing Authority and the Political Process

Elections were held on January 30, 2005 for twenty government bodies, including a Transitional National Assembly. The U.N.-assisted elections took place amid conditions of extreme insecurity and political turmoil, limiting the ability of all eligible voters to participate. Following prolonged delays, the successor Transitional Government, headed by prime minister Ibrahim al-Ja'fari, was formed on April 28.

On October 15, a draft constitution was adopted by national referendum. According to official results, 63 per cent of eligible voters participated, with over 78 percent voting in favor. The drafting process was fraught with difficulties amid efforts to secure the participation of Sunni political groups that had boycotted the January elections and to achieve consensus on key issues including the role of religion and federalism. The constitution contained key fundamental principles and individual rights, but left many of them subject to implementing legislation. A mechanism was established for further review of the constitution following parliamentary elections, scheduled for December 15, 2005.

Attacks against Civilians by Insurgent Groups

Insurgent groups perpetrated widespread attacks against civilians throughout 2005, claiming the lives of hundreds of Iraqis and other nationals. Among the groups responsible for these abuses are al-Qaeda in Iraq, Ansar al-Sunna and the Islamic Army in Iraq, which have all targeted civilians for abductions and executions. The first two groups have repeatedly boasted about massive car bombs and suicide bombs in mosques, markets, bus stations and other civilian areas.

IRAQ

A Face and a Name

Civilian Victims of Insurgent Groups in Iraq

HUMAN
RIGHTS
WATCH

These abuses took place in the context of the U.S.-led invasion of Iraq and the ensuing military occupation that resulted in tens of thousands of civilian deaths and sparked the emergence of insurgent groups. Chief among the justifications insurgent groups use is that the U.S. illegally invaded Iraq and killed thousands of Iraqi civilians since March 2003.

The victims of targeted assassination by insurgent groups include government officials, politicians, judges, journalists, humanitarian aid workers, doctors, professors and those deemed to be collaborating with the foreign forces in Iraq, including translators, cleaners and others who perform civilian jobs for the U.S.-led Multi-National Force in Iraq (MNF - I). Insurgents have directed suicide and car bomb attacks at Shi`a mosques, Christian churches and Kurdish political parties with the purpose of killing civilians. Claims that these communities are legitimate targets because they may support the foreign forces in Iraq have no basis in international law, which requires the protection of any civilian who is not actively participating in the hostilities.

Torture and Killings by Iraqi forces

The torture and ill-treatment of detainees in Iraqi custody remains a serious concern, with the level of reported incidents rising. The vast majority of allegations concern forces of the Iraqi Ministry of Interior, as well as members of the Iraqi armed forces under Ministry of Defense authority. Detainees in pretrial detention on security-related offenses, in particular, are subjected to various forms of torture or ill-treatment, including routine beatings, sleep deprivation, electric shocks to sensitive parts of the body, prolonged suspension from the wrists with the hands tied behind the back, deprivation of food and water for prolonged periods, and severely overcrowded cells. Former detainees held by Ministry of Interior forces in connection with alleged terrorist offenses linked to insurgent activity report other forms of torture, including having weights attacked to their testicles, or having a string tied tightly round their penis and then being forced to drink large amounts of water.

Iraqi government officials have publicly committed to investigating the abuse of detainees and to holding criminally responsible those found guilty of the torture of detainees and the killing of civilians. At this writing, neither the Ministry of Interior nor the Ministry of Defense had established an effective mechanism for the monitoring of abuses by law enforcement personnel or the armed forces, nor set up a system for bringing those accused of such offenses to justice. In addition to assistance provided by MNF-I personnel, other training programs through the European Union and NATO to train personnel from the Iraqi police, armed forces, the judiciary and penitentiary personnel were ongoing during 2005, but with little focus on issues related to monitoring and accountability.

Accountability for Past Crimes

The Statute of the Iraqi Special Tribunal, established in December 2003 to try members of the former Iraqi government for genocide, crimes against humanity and war crimes, was amended and adopted by Iraq's Transitional National Assembly in October 2005, one week before the first trial was scheduled to begin on October 19. The Assembly renamed the tribunal the "Supreme Iraqi Criminal Tribunal" (SICT).

Serious doubts remain about the capacity of the Tribunal, as constituted, to conduct fair trials that meet international human rights standards for the prosecution of the crimes in its Statute. Reliance on Iraqi criminal law, which does not adequately ensure protection of the rights of accused, could further undermine the legitimacy of the Tribunal. There remain inadequate protections against self-incrimination, an inappropriate standard of proof, and inadequate procedural and substantive measures to ensure an adequate defense, including the right to confront and examine witnesses. Defense counsel for some of the accused claim that their ability to mount an effective defense has been hampered by lack of adequate access to the accused and to the court's evidence against them. Additionally, prejudicial comments by senior public officials, the politicization of control of the Tribunal and the susceptibility of judges to dismissal seriously undermine the court's appearance of independence and impartiality. After the opening of the first SICT trial on October 19, two defense counsel were assassinated, highlighting the grave risks faced

IRAQ

'Ali Hasan Al-Majid and
the Basra Massacre of 1999

HUMAN
RIGHTS
WATCH

by all who participate in the trials. The defense counsel killings intensify concerns about the accused's right to a competent and effective defense.

As of October 2005, the MNF retained physical custody of over 90 "high value detainees", most of whom remained held at Camp Cropper near Baghdad International Airport, and include members of the former Iraqi government awaiting trial before the Iraqi Criminal Tribunal. U.S. forces began granting these detainees family visits starting in July 2005, in some cases more than two years after arresting them. It is unclear how many continue to be held without access to defense counsel.

Key International Actors

As of July 2005, the United States retained approximately 140,000 military personnel deployed in Iraq as part of the United Nations Security Council-authorized MNF-I. The mandate of the MNF-I, under Security Council resolution 1546, adopted in June 2004, was scheduled for review in December 2005. The United Kingdom remains the key military and political partner to the United States in the MNF-I, retaining approximately 8,300 troops in Iraq, deployed primarily in the south-eastern governorates. Other countries with a military presence in Iraq include Poland, Italy, Ukraine, Denmark, Romania and Japan, totaling some 12,700 troops.

In a report to the U.S. Secretary-General in September 2005, the United Nations Assistance Mission in Iraq (UNAMI) said the human rights situation in Iraq continued to give rise to serious concern. The report cited "ongoing insurgent attacks and acts of terrorism, including kidnapping and torture", as well as 'continuing concern about military operations conducted by the Multinational Force in the north and north-west of Iraq, resulting in civilian deaths, injury and displacement from excessive or apparently indiscriminate use of force."

Israel/Occupied Palestinian Territories (OPT)

Following the death of Palestinian leader Yasser Arafat in November 2004, Palestinians held their second-ever national elections on January 9, 2005. The main contender, Mahmoud Abbas (Abu Mazen), became the second Palestinian president with 62.52% of the vote. The Palestinian Authority (P.A.) postponed Legislative Council elections, which were due to take place in 2005, until January 2006, but held first-ever municipal elections in four stages across the West Bank and Gaza, with Hamas gaining a substantial leadership role in local politics, especially in Gaza. The P.A. has postponed a fifth and final round of voting, which includes fifty-nine local councils, until 2006.

On February 8, 2005 Mahmoud Abbas and Israeli Prime Minister Ariel Sharon met in Sharm el-Sheikh for the first Israeli-Palestinian summit in four years. The summit ended in a loose ceasefire agreement "that all Palestinians will stop all acts of violence against all Israelis and at the same time Israel will cease its military activity against all Palestinians everywhere." While Islamic Jihad and Hamas said they were not bound by the ceasefire, they did commit to respecting a mutual period of calm.

As part of the ceasefire, Israel agreed to release nine hundred Palestinian prisoners, which it did in February and June. Approximately eight thousand Palestinian political and security prisoners remain imprisoned by Israel. Israel also currently holds more than six hundred Palestinians under administrative detention (detention without trial or charge, which can be indefinitely renewed).

In August and September 2005, Israel unilaterally withdrew approximately eight thousand settlers, along with military personnel and installations, from the Gaza Strip and four small settlements in the northern West Bank near Jenin. While Israel has since declared the Gaza Strip a "foreign territory" and the crossings between Gaza and Israel "international borders," under international humanitarian law (IHL), Gaza remains occupied, and Israel retains its responsibilities for the welfare of Gaza residents. Israel maintains effective control over Gaza by regulating movement in and out of the Strip as well as the airspace, sea space, public utilities and population registry. In addition, Israel declared the right to re-enter Gaza militarily at any time in its "Disengagement Plan" Since the withdrawal, Israel has carried out aerial bombardments, including targeted killings, and has fired artillery into the northeastern corner of Gaza.

While the total number of Israeli and Palestinian casualties fell in 2005 following the February ceasefire, the overall human rights situation in Israel and the OPT remained grave. Since the beginning of the current intifada in September 2000, Israel has killed nearly three thousand Palestinians in the West Bank and Gaza, including more than six hundred children. During the same period, Palestinian fighters have killed more than nine hundred Israelis inside Israel and in the OPT. Most of those killed on both sides were civilians.

The Israeli authorities continue a policy of closure, imposing severe and frequently arbitrary restrictions on freedom of movement in the West Bank, Gaza Strip, and East Jerusalem, contributing to a serious humanitarian crisis marked by extreme poverty, unemployment, and food insecurity. The movement restrictions also have severely compromised Palestinian residents' access to health care, education, and other services. As of August 1, 2005, the U.N. Office for the Coordination of Humanitarian Affairs (OCHA) reported 376 closure obstacles, down from 605 in February. However, this decrease, a result of the Sharm summit and the subsequent decrease in fighting, is offset by an increase in the number of "flying checkpoints" (currently an average of sixty each month), which usually consist of a military jeep blocking a road and checking all traffic for an undisclosed period of time; an increase in concrete military towers and "road protection barriers", which block Palestinian traffic from entering settler-only roads through the OPT; and the increased movement restrictions associated with the "separation barrier" or "wall" that Israel is building mostly inside the West Bank.

During 2005, Israel continued with its construction of the wall, notwithstanding the International Court of Justice's Advisory Opinion declaring the construction of the wall inside the OPT a violation of IHL, and demanding that Israel cease further construction inside the OPT. While the stated Israeli security rationale for the wall is to prevent Palestinian armed groups from carrying out attacks in Israel, 85 percent of its route extends into the West Bank, facilitating the eventual annexation to Israel of most of the large illegal Jewish settlements constructed over the past several decades as well as some of the most productive Palestinian farmlands and key water resources.

In July 2005, the Israeli Knesset approved legislation that effectively bars Palestinians from the OPT from suing Israel for death, injury or damages caused by Israeli security agents. The amendment to the Civil Wrongs (Liability of State) Law, 5712-1952 further strips Palestinians of an effective remedy for serious human rights abuses, which is required under international human rights law. The Knesset passed the bill at a time when the Israel Defense Forces (IDF) had criminally investigated fewer than ten percent of the Palestinian civilian deaths since September 2000, and have convicted only a handful of IDF soldiers for causing death or injury. In August, an Israeli court handed down an eight year sentence, by far the longest of the past five years, to the soldier found responsible for lethally shooting Briton Tom Hurndall in Gaza in 2002. The IDF maintains the policy that killings of Palestinians will be investigated only under "exceptional circumstances," which neither the IDF nor the government has ever defined. The Israeli authorities' failure to bring perpetrators to justice fosters a culture of impunity.

The Knesset also passed legislation in July 2005 barring family reunification between Israeli citizens (mostly Palestinians) and their Palestinian spouses from the OPT, except in certain age categories. Since 2002 Israel has frozen family reunification and forced thousands of married couples and their children to live apart or live together illegally. This law violates the right not to be subjected to arbitrary interference with one's family as set out in international human rights treaties ratified by Israel.

In the OPT, despite Abbas' pledges of restored law and order and his reorganization of the security services, including firing long-standing officials who P.A. authorities deemed inept or corrupt, control of the Palestinian Authority over Palestinian population centers is frequently nominal at best, and conditions of lawlessness have increased in the Gaza Strip and parts of the West Bank in 2005. Palestinian gunmen carried out several assassinations against persons alleged to have collaborated with Israeli security forces, and fighting between various Palestinian factions, security services and armed groups has led to armed clashes on the streets, vigilante killings and even the kidnapping of foreigners on several occasions in Gaza.

Since taking office, Abbas has overseen the execution of five death row inmates. At least twenty-two people remain on death row, many of them tried in the notorious Palestinian security or military courts where minimum standards of due process are not met. On June 22 Abbas ordered that the Palestinian justice system retry those whom the State Security Court had sentenced to death. It is unclear whether this process has begun.

Unlawful Use of Force

The Israeli army and security forces continued to carry out daily arrest raids and military operations in Palestinian areas during 2005. There have been over two thousand IDF incursions into Palestinian population centers this year. The IDF often carried out the operations in a manner that failed to demonstrate that it had used all feasible measures to avoid or minimize harm to civilians and their property. In one such incident, an August 24 arrest raid in the Tulkarem refugee camp, the IDF shot and killed five unarmed Palestinians, including three seventeen-year-olds. This incident reflects a growing pattern of IDF "arrest operations" in which security forces kill the target of arrest or bystanders rather than seeking to apprehend the target. More than 20 Palestinians were killed in assassinations or extra-judicial killings in 2005.

In 2005, the number of Palestinian suicide bombings and similar attacks targeting civilians inside Israel reached their lowest point since the beginning of the current intifada in 2000. Palestinian armed groups carried out three lethal suicide bombing attacks inside Israel in 2005, killing fifteen Israelis and injuring scores more. Armed groups also carried out several roadside shootings and bomb attacks in the OPT, killing several Israeli civilians. In addition, on several occasions, Palestinian armed groups in the Gaza Strip fired home-made rockets, known as Qassams, and mortar shells into Israel and at

Jewish settlements in the Gaza Strip (up until the withdrawal in August), which killed several Israelis, Palestinians, and foreign workers. These weapons are inherently indiscriminate and are generally fired at civilian areas, in contravention of IHL. Abbas publicly denounced such tactics and called for an end to the armed uprising. Yet the Palestinian Authority appeared unable to stop those who have ordered or organized such attacks.

The Wall

On February 20, 2005 Israel modified the planned route of the wall. While the new route runs closer to the Green Line in some areas, such as the southern West Bank, in other areas it will run far inside the West Bank in order to capture key Israeli settlements such as Ariel (twenty-two kilometers inside the West Bank), the Gush Etzion bloc (with fifty thousand settlers) near Bethlehem and the Maaleh Adumim settlement east of Jerusalem. The new route is 670 km, twice the length of the "Green Line" (the 1949 armistice line between Israel and Jordan which served as the de facto border between Israel and the West Bank after Israel's 1967 occupation); only about one-fifth of the route follows the Green Line itself. During 2005 Israel still failed to make the case why a wall constructed entirely on the Israeli side of the Green Line would not have been at least as effective in providing security inside Israel. Instead, the current wall will bring over three hundred thousand West Bank and East Jerusalem settlers and a minimum of 135,000 acres of West Bank territory over to the Israeli side. Despite Israel's contention that the wall is a "temporary" security measure, it captures settlements that Israel has vowed to hold onto permanently. On July 21 Sharon said that the Ariel bloc of settlements "will be part of the State of Israel forever."

The construction of the wall and settlement expansion essentially have cut off East Jerusalem from the rest of the West Bank. In June the Israeli cabinet approved the final details of the 60-kilometer fence around Jerusalem that will cut off some fifty-five thousand Palestinian Jerusalem residents from their city. Israel also has announced plans to build in the three thousand acre piece of West Bank land between Jerusalem and the West Bank settlement of

Maaleh Adumim, known as E-1, and to surround the entire area with the wall. This will effectively sever the northern and southern West Bank.

Key International Actors

In April 2005, after meeting with Prime Minister Ariel Sharon, U.S. President George Bush "reiterated that the United States supports the establishment of a Palestinian state that is viable, contiguous, sovereign and independent." Yet while the Bush administration expressed displeasure at Israel's decision to build in the E-1 area of the OPT, and paid lip service to the call for a freeze in settlement expansion, it provided no political or economic sanctions on Israel's continued building. Sharon publicly vowed to continue building despite U.S. displeasure.

Israel remained the largest recipient of U.S. military and economic aid, receiving almost U.S.$3 billion in 2005. In contrast, after a May meeting between Bush and Abbas, Bush pledged U.S.$50 million in aid to the P.A. for housing and other construction following the Israeli withdrawal from Gaza. However Congress later earmarked part of this money to be used to beef up "border crossings" along the wall, which are mostly located on occupied West Bank land. In September 2005, following the Israeli withdrawal, the United States approved disbursement of a U.S.$3 million supplemental grant to the P.A. security services.

Also in September, the Quartet (the United Nations, Russia, the European Union and the United States) foreign ministers met to welcome the successful conclusion of the Israeli withdrawal and call for renewed efforts to return to the Road Map (a performance-based plan with three phases which is supposed to build confidence in preparation for final status negotiations to end the conflict). Their final statement read: "The Quartet reaffirms that any agreement on final status issues must be reached through negotiations and that a new Palestinian State must be truly viable, with contiguity in the West Bank and connectivity to Gaza." The Quartet also called for an end to settlement expansion and expressed concern regarding the route of the wall.

JORDAN

King Abdullah II is invested with extensive executive and legislative powers under Jordan's constitution. He issues decrees and dismisses and appoints key government officials, including a new prime minister and cabinet in April and a new chief of intelligence in May 2005. The government and the king have announced their intention to anchor the right to freedom of expression in law, but in practice the exercise of basic rights such as freedom of expression, association and assembly remains restricted. Security forces carry out arbitrary arrests and detain people without charge in the name of counterterrorism. A lack of determined government action against "honor" crimes and discrimination continues to circumscribe women's political, civil and economic rights.

Human Rights Defenders

In its first annual report, issued in 2005, Jordan's National Center for Human Rights, a government-regulated body, painted an unflattering picture of the state of political and civil rights and transgressions by security forces. Established by law in 2002, the center has a mandate to follow up on individual human rights violations, but many victims complain that it does not expend serious effort on their cases, especially when sensitive issues such as torture, unfair trials, or redress for victims are involved. The center has fostered public debate on prison conditions in the country following the release in October 2004 of a report documenting one case of torture in detention.

Jordan's independent human rights organizations do not systematically investigate abuses, publish reports, or assist victims. They cite a lack of resources, or a preference for work on training and capacity building.

Freedom of Expression

Jordanians are not entirely free to express their opinions. Criticisms of the king and the intelligence forces are strictly taboo and carry serious penalties. Articles of the Penal Code criminalize speech slandering public officials, criticizing the king and his family, and harming relations with other states. High government officials have indicated that the authorities will no longer enforce these laws, and criticism of the government (as distinct from the king), as well as Israeli, other Arab states, and United States' policies, or voicing support for Islamist causes, is tolerated, but within limits. For example, Ali Hattar and Riyadh Nuwaisa, two prominent political activists, were arrested on slander charges after they criticized the U.S. at a conference in Amman in December 2004. A court sentenced Hattar to three months in prison; Nuwaisa was acquitted.

The government has barred over 150 clerics from preaching in recent years. Around forty have been banned since the beginning of 2004, according to one of their lawyers, despite the fact that courts had cleared them of charges under the Law on Preaching and Guidance in Mosques.

The government censors printing houses, especially those used by smaller circulation weekly newspapers. Intelligence officers have stopped print runs, and demanded changes in or cancellation of articles, most recently on September 19, 2005, concerning an article in the weekly *Al-Wahda*. Managers of newspapers, as well as editors, can be held criminally liable for content in breach of the law, such as alleged slander.

King Abdullah in February convened a National Agenda Committee to undertake a comprehensive review of legislation and propose amendments for political reform, including laws governing elections and political parties. In the area of free expression, the committee has reportedly proposed lifting the requirement that working journalists must belong to the Jordanian Press Association. In July, the Cabinet submitted to parliament a draft Journalism and Publications Law that would prohibit forcing journalists to reveal sources or arresting journalists in the course of their work. It would abolish pre-publication censorship, and a decision to ban a publication would require a court ruling, not merely an administrative decision.

Freedom of Association and Assembly

In March, then Prime Minister Faisal al-Fayez's government introduced a bill that would regulate the 120,000 members of Jordan's twelve professional associations under one law, and that would restrict discussion at association gatherings to purely professional and internal matters, prohibiting political discussion. Most disturbingly, the government proposed to appoint two-thirds of the members of each association's disciplinary committee, which was empowered to punish infractions of the new law with suspension from work for up to one year.

In April, the king replaced al-Fayez with Prime Minister Adnan Badran. The new government has not sought parliamentary approval of the law on professional associations. It also appears to have withdrawn another draft bill of the al-Fayez government, the Welfare Societies bill, that reportedly would have imposed strict regulation and Ministry of Interior supervision over non-governmental organizations—requiring, for example, ministerial approval for every foreign-funded project, and giving ministry officials the right to confiscate NGO documents.

In 2004, parliament ratified a 2001 temporary Law on General Assemblies, under which organizers of public gatherings must seek permission from the relevant governor three days in advance. A governor is not bound to consider only public safety concerns when deciding whether to give or withhold permission, and the authorities have used the law to withhold permission for demonstrations and other public gatherings, especially those in support of the uprising in the Occupied Palestinian Territories. For example, the governor of Amman in late August 2005 banned a festival in support of Palestinians organised by the Islamic Action Front in Amman's 2nd District.

Arbitrary Detention and Torture

Jordan's General Intelligence Department (GID) arrests Jordanian Islamists and detains them at its own detention facility for prolonged periods, often without charge or on baseless charges. The GID routinely denies detainees access to legal representation, and grants requests for family visits with considerable delay, if at all. Some security detainees allege torture and ill-treatment during interrogation, the alleged abuse almost invariably taking two forms. One is severe beatings on the lower legs and feet with a metal or bamboo stick, with some victims allegedly then being forced by GID officers to walk with lacerated and bruised feet on a mixture of vinegar and salt. The other form is solitary confinement for periods of months at a time with little or no exposure to daylight.

Provincial governors and their deputies have the authority to detain persons they deem a "danger to society" but who have not committed any crime. Such persons, who usually have committed prior offenses, remain in detention until they can meet a personal, material or monetary bail guarantee. If they breach conditions of bail, such as daily reports to the police station, or if no guarantor comes forward, they remain imprisoned for up to one year.

Women's Rights

The arbitrary detention on a governor's orders of people deemed a "danger to society" also applies to women who are detained in order to protect them from threats of harm from family members as a result of alleged "honor" offenses. In Jordan's second largest province, Zarqa', there were some eleven such cases in September 2005. Honor crimes continue to remain a serious problem in Jordan. Laws provide lax penalties for murders committed "in a fit of fury"—a defense frequently invoked in so-called "honor killings." Family members reportedly killed twelve women in the ten months of 2005 for alleged sexual misconduct.

There is an ongoing debate over the future of a women's quota in parliament, first introduced in 1997. In the 2003 elections, allotted seats went to the six women candidates with the highest percentages of votes, although none won a seat outright. Some women's rights activists favor a requirement for parties to reserve candidate places for women in order to increase their representation, rather than increase the quota of women's seats in parliament.

Political Reform

The 110 deputies in Jordan's lower house of parliament cannot initiate legislation or exercise effective control over government actions, but they debate national issues and ratify laws and international agreements. They can issue a vote of no confidence in the government and overrule a royal veto of legislation. The king appoints the upper house's forty members, who also must ratify laws, and he can dissolve parliament. During 2001-03, when the king delayed elections after dissolving parliament, the government passed over 150 laws by decree, which parliament may now review.

Key International Actors

U.S. assistance in 2005, at $660 million, constitutes over one-fifth of Jordan's annual budget, according to the IMF (the European Union, by comparison, promised to give ?63 million in assistance to Jordan for 2006). The country's dependence on U.S. assistance increased after it lost access to subsidized Kuwaiti oil in early 2005, leading the king to pressure parliamentarians to approve a bilateral immunity agreement sought by the U.S. The agreement would obligate Jordan not to surrender to the International Criminal Court U.S. citizens (and non-citizens working for the U.S. government) under Jordanian jurisdiction, even if they are accused and sought by the ICC for genocide, war crimes, or crimes against humanity (U.S. legislation in late 2004 conditioned foreign economic assistance for ICC states parties on countries' ratifying such an agreement). The king signed the immunity agreement in December 2004 during a visit to Washington, but the lower house of parliament refused to ratify it in July 2005. The king is expected to resubmit it.

Following the July 7 London bombings, the United Kingdom concluded a Memorandum of Understanding with Jordan under which Jordan undertakes not to torture or mistreat persons the U.K. deports to Jordan. Abu Qatada, a Jordanian residing in the U.K., currently faces deportation hearings under these new arrangements.

Libya

Human rights conditions in Libya improved slightly in 2005 as the country continued its slow international reintegration, but serious problems remain. The government severely curtails freedom of expression and association, banning political parties and independent organizations. It continues to imprison individuals for criticizing Libya's unique political system, the government, or its leader Col. Muammar Qaddafi. Due process violations and torture remain concerns, as do disappearances from past years.

Political Prisoners

Dozens and probably hundreds of individuals are in prison for engaging in peaceful political activity. Many were imprisoned for violating Law 71, which bans any group activity based on a political ideology opposed to the principles of the 1969 revolution that brought Qaddafi to power. Violators of the law can be put to death. Among the prisoners are eighty-six members of the Muslim Brotherhood, a non-violent political and social organization, who have been in prison since 1998 after trials that violated Libyan and international law. The court sentenced its two leaders to death, and they remained on death row throughout 2005. In a positive development, the Supreme Court ruled in October that the brotherhood members should get a new trial, which will proceed in 2006.

In September, the government released five long-term political prisoners who had been serving prison terms up to life for participation in a banned political group. Later that month, a government committee recommended that 131 political prisoners be released because they no longer posed a threat to society, among them the eighty-six imprisoned members of the Muslim Brotherhood. As of December all 131 people remained in prison.

The most prominent political prisoner is Fathi al-Jahmi, a former government official, who strongly criticized Qaddafi in interviews with international media in March 2004. The Internal Security Agency held al-Jahmi, his wife and son for about six months in 2004, ostensibly for their own protection. They released the family members late that year, but continued to hold al-

Jahmi without a trial at a special facility throughout 2005, denying him regular visits from a doctor and his family. According to the family, the government denied them visits since early June.

The fate of dozens of political prisoners remains unknown. According to one Libyan group based abroad, more than 250 political prisoners have disappeared. Libyan officials told Human Rights Watch that one of these men, Ahmad 'Abd al-Qadir al-Thulti, arrested in 1986, had died of natural causes in prison, but the government has not officially informed the family or returned the body.

Freedom of Expression

Freedom of expression is severely curtailed, although Libyan lawyers, academics and journalists are slowly beginning to address topics previously taboo. A pervasive security service monitors the population, and self-censorship is rife.

There are no private radio or television stations, and government authorities or the Revolutionary Committees Movement, a powerful ideological organization, control the country's main newspapers. The state-run media glorifies the government and its leaders and rarely, if ever, presents alternative or critical views. The only access to uncensored news comes via the Internet and satellite television, which is widely viewed.

The Internet is spreading quickly in Libya, with dozens of opposition or independent websites based abroad. The government has occasionally blocked some Internet sites. In January 2005 the government arrested writer `Abd al-Raziq al-Mansuri, who worked with a United Kingdom-based website, apparently due to his critical work. In October, a court sentenced him to one-and-a-half years in prison for the illegal possession of a handgun.

On May 21, unidentified men abducted Daif al-Ghazal, who had been active in the Revolutionary Committees Movement and had written for the movement's newspaper, *al-Zahf al-Akhdar*. He reportedly was disenchanted with the movement and had been writing critical articles for a website based abroad. The authorities found al-Ghazal's decomposing body with signs of torture and a gunshot to the head on June 2. The government denied responsibility and said it had arrested two men in relation to the crime.

Freedom of Association

Libya has many professional organizations and associations but no truly independent nongovernmental organizations. Some lawyers complained that the Law on Associations (Law 19) needed amending to facilitate the process of registration by a non-political body. In June 2005 the head of the official journalists union resigned from his post because, among other reasons, the government had refused to allow an independent journalists organization. In November the official lawyers union issued an unusually strong protest statement because the government did not allow them to appoint their own union heads. Law 71, described above, and other restrictive legislation severely limits the right to establish independent groups, with violators punished by death.

Two human rights groups exist in Libya, most prominently the human rights program at the Qaddafi International Foundation for Charity Associations, run by Muammar Qaddafi's influential son Seif. In 2005 the foundation ran campaigns against torture and called for the release of political prisoners. A quasi-official institution, it is also the most vocal domestic critic of the government.

Torture and the Death Penalty

Five Bulgarian nurses and a Palestinian doctor remained on death row for infecting 426 Libyan children with HIV, despite credible claims that they were tortured to extract confessions. On June 7, 2005, a Tripoli court acquitted ten Libyans accused of using torture against the defendants. The Supreme Court will review the case on January 31, 2006.

Despite government claims that it will not execute anyone until a new penal code comes into effect (see below), the state continues to execute persons on death row, most recently two Turks and four Egyptians sentenced to death for murder.

Detention of Women and Girls in "Social Rehabilitation"

Women and girls suspected of transgressing moral codes may be detained indefinitely in "social rehabilitation" facilities—portrayed as "protective" homes for wayward women and girls or those whose families reject them. There, the government routinely violates women's and girls' human rights, including those to due process, liberty, freedom of movement, personal dignity, and privacy. Many women and girls detained in these facilities have committed no crime, or have already served a sentence. Some are there because they were raped and are now ostracized for staining their family's honor. There is no way out of these facilities unless a male relative takes custody of the woman or girl or she consents to marriage.

Treatment of Foreigners

Libya has no asylum law or procedure. It has not signed the 1951 Refugee Convention and it has no formal cooperation agreement with the United Nations High Commissioner for Refugees. Throughout the year, the government continued to deport thousands of foreigners, mostly sub-Saharan Africans, who had entered the country without authorization, sometimes back to countries where they could face persecution or torture. Foreigners reported beatings and other abuse throughout the deportation process.

Signs of Reform

The government initiated some important reforms in 2005, but promises of change lagged behind implementation. In January, the government abolished the People's Court, a body that had tried most political cases without adequate due process guarantees. The cases before the court at the time of closure were transferred to the regular courts, but many of the people already imprisoned by the People's Court remain in prison.

Throughout the year, the government reviewed many Libyan laws and, according to the secretary of justice, there is an "ambitious plan to reform legislation to bring it into line with international human rights standards." Legal experts drafted a new penal code and code of criminal procedure, and officials said the main legislative body, the General People's Congress, would review the drafts by the year's end. The goal of the new penal code, the secretary of justice said, is to reduce both the death penalty and imprisonment as a punishment. The death penalty would remain, he said, for the "most dangerous crimes" and for "terrorism."

The most recent version of the penal code draft is unknown, but a review of a 2004 draft suggests the government will accept a very broad definition of terrorism, which it might then use to imprison people who are expressing peaceful political views. The government used to imprison opponents because of their "anti-revolutionary behavior," but today the government uses the rhetoric of anti-terrorism to silence dissent.

The government pledged itself to examine some human rights abuses of the past, notably the 1998 deaths of prisoners in Abu Selim prison at the hands of guards. The government says that guards responded properly to a revolt and attempted escape. Former prisoners and Libyan human rights groups abroad say the guards executed hundreds of prisoners after they had regained control of the prison. In 2005, the government said it had established a committee to investigate the incident, but it remains unclear how the committee will conduct its work or when it will produce its findings.

Libya periodically opened itself to scrutiny from human rights groups after years of denying them entry. Physicians for Human Rights sent a doctor in February to examine the political prisoner Fathi al-Jahmi. In April-May, Human Rights Watch conducted research in the country for the first time.

Key International Actors

The United States and European governments steadily improved their relations with Libya throughout 2005. In part this was driven by energy companies who are eager to tap Libya's vast oil reserves, but Western governments are also drawn to Qaddafi's cooperation in the global war on terror. In addition to renouncing weapons of mass destruction in 2003, Libya has provided valuable intelligence on militant Islamic individuals and groups. In return, countries like the U.S. and U.K. have added the Libyan Islamic Fighting

Group (LIFG), fighting to overthrow Qaddafi since the late 1990s, to their lists of terrorist groups.

In October 2005, the British government signed a Memorandum of Understanding with Libya that allows the U.K to deport individuals to Libya if the Libyan government gives diplomatic assurances the deportees will not be subjected to torture. As of November deportation proceedings were under way for five members of the LIFG.

Libya's secretary of foreign liaison and international cooperation (foreign minister) met U.S. Secretary of State Condoleeza Rice in New York in September 2005, the highest bilateral meeting between the two countries in more than twenty years. Full diplomatic relations are stymied because Libya remains on the U.S. government's list of countries that sponsor terrorism. The U.S. government at times criticized human rights abuses in Libya, notably in the State Department's 2004 human rights report. In October President Bush called on Libya to free the five Bulgarian nurses sentenced to death in the HIV-infection case.

MOROCCO

Morocco continues to present a mixed picture on human rights. It has made great strides in addressing past abuses and allowed considerable space for public dissent and protest in recent years. But authorities, aided by complaisant courts, continue to use repressive legislation to punish peaceful opponents; and the police use excessive force to break up demonstrations, especially in outlying areas.

Arrests of suspected Islamist extremists eased in 2004 and 2005. However, several hundred who had been arrested in the weeks after the Casablanca bombings of May 2003 remained in prison at this writing in late 2005. Many of these had been held in secret detention for days or weeks and subjected to mistreatment, and sometimes torture, while under interrogation, and then convicted in unfair trials of having links to terror cells. Reports of such mistreatment have been more sporadic among those arrested since 2004.

On April 14, 2005, King Mohamed VI freed forty-four Islamists in a royal grace. But hundreds more remained in prison, including more than twenty sentenced to death after the 2003 Casablanca attacks. (Morocco has not applied the death penalty since 1993.) In May, Islamist prisoners staged a large hunger strike to demand better conditions and their retrial or release. Royal graces in August and November freed seventy-seven and 164 Islamist prisoners, respectively.

Reforms to the family law, enacted in 2004, have raised the minimum age of marriage for women from fifteen to eighteen, made the family the joint responsibility of both spouses, rescinded the wife's duty of obedience to her husband, and placed the practice of polygyny under strict judicial control. Concerns remain about the judiciary's lack of familiarity with the reforms and about a legal loophole that allows judges to use religious principles to decide matters not covered in the text.

Morocco has one of the highest child labor rates in the Middle East and North Africa. Its school attendance rates for working children are among the lowest for any country outside sub-Saharan Africa. An estimated 11 percent of children (about six hundred thousand) age seven through fourteen work. In 2004 Morocco raised the minimum age of employment to fifteen, the minimum school-leaving age, but thus far has done little to enforce the ban on underage workers or prosecute those who otherwise abuse working children.

The Justice System and Legal Reforms

Amendments to the code of criminal procedure that took effect in October 2003 have enhanced the rights of defendants. Articles 396-415 strengthen the right of appeal and resulted in decisions by appeals courts in 2005 that reduced sentences for many defendants convicted under the anti-terror law.

Nevertheless, in cases with a political color, courts routinely deny defendants a fair trial, ignoring requests for medical examinations lodged by defendants who claim to have been tortured, refusing to summon exculpatory witnesses, and convicting defendants solely on the basis of apparently coerced confessions. Prosecutions of state agents for abusing persons in their custody are rare.

The trial of journalist Ali Mrabet in 2005 illustrates the lack of judicial independence. A hitherto obscure association sued the outspoken reporter for libel because he had used the term "refugees" to characterize Sahrawis living in camps in Tindouf, Algeria, rather than the officially preferred characterization of them as "captives" of the Polisario organization, which seeks independence for the Western Sahara. On April 12, 2005, a Rabat court found this remark sufficiently libelous to fine Mrabet and ban him from practicing journalism for ten years.

Freedom of Association and Assembly

The right to freedom of association, guaranteed by the constitution, is curbed in practice. According to a 2003 decree, an association's founders need only inform authorities of its creation. But authorities sometimes subvert this process by refusing to issue a receipt affirming that the requisite notice has been given.

Most types of public assemblies require authorization from the Interior Ministry, which can refuse permission if it deems them liable to "disturb the public order." This discretion is exercised more often when the demonstrators' agenda is critical of government policies. Public protests are frequent in the capital of Rabat, and usually are not disturbed. On occasion, however, police wielding batons break them up with force and brutality.

Repression of demonstrations is harsher in outlying regions. On May 11, the government arrested three who organized a march in the Rif region to demand earthquake relief on charges of "insulting civil servants and elected officials" and "encouraging others to revolt." Eight days later, when thousands of local residents marched to protest their arrest, security forces, assisted by helicopters, used force and tear gas to disperse the demonstrators. Thirty-five were arrested and nine were sentenced to terms of six to nine months. In November, those who had not already completed their sentences were freed by a royal grace.

In the Western Sahara, authorities continue to prosecute advocates of independence and are quick to put down protests. In late May and early June, pro-independence demonstrations erupted in Lâayoune and spread to other cities. In some cases, the participants threw stones and Molotov cocktails at police. Amnesty International said it had received "consistent reports" of the security forces using "excessive force when dispersing protesters and when carrying out arrests." In some cases, Amnesty stated, security force officers allegedly beat "demonstrators on the spot to 'punish' them for their political beliefs." Authorities arrested more than one hundred persons; twenty-one were sentenced to up to six years in prison, on charges that included "participation in a criminal gang," "use of weapons," "destruction of public property," and "violence toward state agents in the exercise of their duty."

Press Freedom

Media criticism of the authorities is often quite blunt, but is nevertheless circumscribed by a press law that provides prison terms for libel and for expression critical of "Islam, the institution of the monarchy, or the territorial integrity" of Morocco (a phrase understood to mean Morocco's claim to the Western Sahara).

On November 25, 2004, Parliament adopted a law liberalizing broadcast media. However, it requires foreign media seeking licenses for stations inside Morocco to "scrupulously respect the values of the monarchy and its heritage in terms of Islam and territorial integrity."

According to Reporters without Borders, at least ten journalists were assaulted, detained, or expelled while attempting to cover tensions in the Western Sahara between April and June 2005. It was hardly the first time that Morocco mistreated journalists as part of efforts to control coverage of this region.

On June 28, 2005, Nadia Yassine of the Justice and Charity Islamist movement appeared in court to answer charges of "attacking the institution of the monarchy" after the weekly *Al-Ousbouyia Al-Jadida (The New Weekly)* quoted her as saying that the monarchy was ill-suited for Morocco and would soon collapse.

On August 15, a Casablanca court convicted Ahmed Reda Benchemsi and Karim Boukhari of the weekly *TelQuel* to a suspended prison term and a heavy fine for having libeled a parliamentarian in an unflattering profile of her career. Their appeal was still in progress as this report went to press. Also convicted of criminal libel in 2005 was Ali Mrabet (see above).

Acknowledging Past Abuses

In 2005, Morocco's Equity and Reconciliation Commission (ERC), launched in 2004 by the king, continued its research into grave human rights violations committed between 1956 and 1999, stimulating taboo-breaking discussions of past repression. Between December 2004 and May 2005, it took testimony from some 20,000 victims and their beneficiaries, and organized seven public hearings for victims—sometimes before television cameras. It was due by the end of 2005 to complete a report documenting the history of repression in Morocco and determine how much compensation the state is to pay victims.

Critics have pointed out that the ERC cannot publicly name or sanction individual perpetrators, and thus will contribute little to ending impunity. A few of those suspected of committing grave abuses during the period under study continue to hold high posts or serve as deputies.

In October 2005 the ERC announced that it had found the bodies of fifty "disappeared" persons near a former secret prison, it was the first announcement concerning its efforts to locate the hundreds of Moroccans who "disappeared" between the 1960s and 1980s after being picked up by security forces.

Human Rights Defenders

Authorities largely tolerate the work of the many human rights organizations active in Rabat and Casablanca. Harassment is more common in remote regions and smaller towns. In June and July, police arrested six Sahrawi human rights defenders, accusing them of having instigated violent disturbances in Lâayoune. According to the Moroccan Human Rights Association (AMDH) and Amnesty International, two of them, Hussein Lidri and Brahim Noumria, were tortured during interrogation. They belong to the AMDH's Lâayoune section.

Key International Actors

Morocco is an important ally of the United States because of its cooperation in fighting terrorism, the 2004 signing of a bilateral free-trade agreement, and its generally pro-West policies. In June 2004, the United States designated Morocco "a major non-NATO ally," thus easing restrictions on arms sales.

In its *Country Reports on Human Rights Practices* for 2004, the U.S. State department referred to allegations of torture and mistreatment of persons arrested as suspected militants. This did not prevent the United States from repatriating five suspected militants, who had been held at the Guantanamo Bay detention center, into Moroccan custody in August 2004.

The U.S. Embassy wrote to Human Rights Watch in September 2005, stating: "It is U.S. policy to seek assurances from countries concerning the treatment of the returnees prior to their repatriation. The U.S. has followed the legal proceedings for the five returnees and is not aware of any abuse carried out against them, nor have such charges been made." However, U.S. officials acknowledged that they did not speak to any of the five since their release from detention in Morocco. They said they followed their cases through third parties. It is not clear whether U.S. authorities assessed the likelihood that fear of reprisal prevented the detainees from speaking truthfully.

An association agreement has been in effect between Morocco and the European Union since 2000. Morocco is the leading beneficiary of funds from the E.U.'s Meda program, having received 1.25 billion euros in grants over the past decade. The program for 2005-2006 is budgeted at 275 million euros. E.U. public comments on Morocco's human rights situation are rare.

France is Morocco's leading trade partner and the leading provider of investments and public development aid. French officials made almost no public comments on human rights in Morocco during 2005.

SAUDI ARABIA

Human rights violations are pervasive in Saudi Arabia, an absolute monarchy. Despite international and domestic pressure to implement reforms, improvements have been halting and inadequate. King Abdullah's succession to the throne after King Fahd's death in August inspired some hope among Saudi citizens for future reform. King Abdullah quickly pardoned three prominent reformers who had earlier been sentenced to long prison terms for voicing criticism of the government, and announced a new labor law promising increased rights for women and migrant workers, but overall human rights conditions in the kingdom remain poor.

Saudi law does not protect many basic rights. The government does not allow political parties, and places strict limits on freedom of expression. Arbitrary detention, mistreatment and torture of detainees, restrictions on freedom of movement, and lack of official accountability remain serious concerns. The kingdom carried out some seventy-three executions as of late September 2005, more than double the thirty-two executions in the whole of 2004. Saudi women continue to face serious obstacles to their participation in the economy, politics, media, and society. Many foreign workers face exploitative working conditions; migrant women working as domestics often are subjected to round-the-clock confinement by their employers, making them vulnerable to sexual abuse and other mistreatment. The government continued to harass independent Saudi Arabian human rights defenders and stifle their efforts to establish independent rights monitoring groups.

Political Violence and Internal Security

A December 6, 2004 attack on the United States consulate in Jeddah killed nine people; al-Qaeda in the Arabian Peninsula clamed responsibility. A series of car bomb attacks on Saudi security installations in Riyadh occurred on December 29, 2004. In late June 2005 the government issued a list of thirty-six Saudi and foreign terror suspects wanted domestically. Throughout 2005 Saudi security forces carried out raids, killing or capturing wanted men including five suspects on the June 2005 list and all but one on a previous

December 2004 list of twenty-six suspects; the government gave no information on those captured. Interior Minister Prince Nayif in February said that fighting between militants and security forces over the past two years had killed 221 people, including ninety-two suspected militants. In April, the Saudi government executed three convicted militants in al-Juf, the first executions for political crimes, according to officials.

At least several hundred Saudis have reportedly traveled to Iraq to take part in insurgent activities. The Associated Press reported that on May 30, 2005, Syrian authorities deported more than thirty Saudis who allegedly had sought to join the Iraqi insurgency. Since early 2005 Saudi border patrols reportedly apprehended sixty-three Saudis seeking to illegally enter Iraq.

In August 2005, the Saudi government released from detention five Saudis formerly detained by the U.S. at Guantanamo Bay; they had been transferred to Saudi Arabia in May 2003. In July, the U.S. transferred three more Saudis from Guantanamo Bay to Saudi Arabia, where at least one, Salih al-Awshan, remains in detention. As of October the U.S. was negotiating with Saudi officials over the transfer into Saudi Arabian custody of some or all of the 121 Saudis still at Guantanamo Bay.

Political Reform

Saudi Arabia's political reform movement focused in 2005 on the release of three prominent advocates of constitutional reform who had been in detention since March 2004 after they refused to sign a pledge to cease all public activism. A Saudi court on May 15, 2004, had sentenced the three—Matruk al-Falih, Abdullah al-Hamid, and Ali al-Dumaini—to between six and nine years in prison for calling for a constitutional monarchy and parliamentary elections. Their lawyer, Abd al-Rahman al-Lahim, was arrested on November 6, 2004, after publicly criticizing the trial of the three as unfair. In August 2005 King Abdullah pardoned the four, as well as Dr. Sa'id Mubarak al-Zu'air, jailed since April 2004 for remarks he made on the al-Jazeera TV channel, and the king later met with some of them.

Municipal Elections

The first elections since the 1960s, for half of the country's municipal council seats, went ahead in three stages between February and April 2005 after having been postponed from 2004. The government has reportedly nominated the remaining councilors, but the councils have yet to begin work. Election regulations forbade candidates from uniting in electoral lists, and limited the two-week campaigns to printed materials and meetings in private homes. The election sparked intense debate between conservatives and liberals, especially after both Sunni and Shi'a religious sheikhs endorsed groups of candidates, so-called "golden lists," which were widely circulated by mobile telephone text messaging, in contravention of regulations.

Women's Rights

Women in the kingdom continued to suffer from severe discrimination in the workplace, home, and the courts, and from restrictions in their freedom of movement and their choice of partners. The religious police enforce strict gender segregation and women's public dress code of head-to-toe covering. Women were not allowed to vote or stand as candidates in the municipal elections. Women are also excluded from the weekly *majlis* (council), where senior members of the royal family listen to the complaints and proposals of Saudi citizens.

Women cannot work, study, or travel without explicit permission from a male relative. Their freedom of movement is further restricted by a law prohibiting them from driving. While a new labor law passed in late September 2005 reportedly expands the professional fields where women are eligible for work, they continue to be barred from jobs that are deemed "not suitable to their nature."

Migrant Workers

The estimated 8.8 million largely South and Southeast Asian and Arab foreign workers in Saudi Arabia comprise a third of the country's population, according to Minister of Labor Ghazi al-Gosaibi. Many face exploitative working conditions, including sixteen-hour workdays, no breaks or food and drink, and often remain confined to locked dormitories during their time off. Security forces deported tens of thousands of illegal immigrants in 2005. Arrested foreign workers face torture and prolonged incommunicado detention.

Nongovernmental organizations in several Asian countries and those countries' diplomatic missions in Saudi Arabia documented hundreds of abuses of migrant workers in Saudi Arabia, such as unpaid wages, long working hours, and physical and sexual abuse. The isolation of women domestic workers in private homes, and the lack of legal protection, puts them at risk of serious abuse. For example, in April 2005 Indonesian maid Suniati Binti Nibaran Sujari barely survived burn injuries she alleged her employer inflicted on her. The Saudi court system offers little or no redress. Nur Miyati, another Indonesian maid, in March accused her employers of torture. While they remained free, she was detained successively in a hospital, a prison, and a women's rehabilitation center before being released into the custody of the labor attaché of the Indonesian embassy.

Indonesia suspended sending unskilled labor to Saudi Arabia from March until August 2005, when the two countries concluded a bilateral agreement on standard employment contracts, regulated weekly and annual time-off, and minimum wages. The Saudi government issued a new labor law in September 2005 that continues to exclude domestic workers, although a special annex promises to regulate their relations with employers. The law entitles non-domestic migrant workers to one day of rest per week and twenty-one vacation days annually. On July 24 the Ministry of Labor announced the creation within the ministry of a new Department for the Protection of Domestic Workers, to receive complaints and impose penalties. Deputy Minister Ahmed al-Zamil warned that employers would be barred from hiring expatriates and transferring employment sponsorships if they violate the law, and that they may be prosecuted. There was no information available on how the government applied these sanctions.

Human Rights Defenders

The Prosecution and Investigation Department (*mabahith*) detained and interrogated human rights defenders during the year. As a condition for their release, the authorities forced activists to pledge to refrain from speaking to the media or human rights organizations and to cease their human rights advocacy. The government also maintained travel bans on several human rights activists.

International—especially U.S.—media attention to Saudi reform and rights initiatives has not led to changes in restrictive practices or measurably enhanced public access to information about rights violations. A nongovernmental national society for human rights began work in 2004, but it lacks independence, expertise, and determination to investigate and publicize sensitive human rights abuses. The society visited prisons and deportation centers, but failed to monitor the trial of the three reformers mentioned above. The society remains dependent on the good will of members of the royal family to provide redress. In September 2005, the government announced the formation of a governmental human rights commission, reporting directly to the prime minister (a position held by the king), with a remit to bring Saudi Arabia's government practices into line with human rights standards.

Key International Actors

The U.S. is a key ally of Saudi Arabia and a major trading partner. The strain in bilateral relations in the aftermath of the September 11, 2001 attacks eased considerably in 2005. The U.S. agenda in its relations with Saudi Arabia appeared to prioritize measures to reduce crude oil prices, boost counterterrorism cooperation, and open Saudi markets to foreign investment and goods through Saudi Arabia's accession to the World Trade Organization (WTO), which took place in November..

U.S. officials praised the Saudi municipal elections. In April, then-Crown Prince Abdullah visited President Bush's ranch in Texas. They discussed educational reform in addition to oil prices and counterterrorism cooperation. Secretary of State Condoleezza Rice visited Riyadh in June, where she highlighted the detention of the constitutional reformers. Undersecretary of State for Public Diplomacy Karen Hughes visited Riyadh in September, where she raised the prohibition on Saudi women driving.

In November 2005, the U.S. State Department's annual International Religious Freedom Report designated Saudi Arabia as "a country of particular concern" for the second year in a row. In June, the State Department's annual report on human trafficking downgraded Saudi Arabia from tier II to III – i.e., countries that "do not comply with the minimum standards for the elimination of trafficking and are not making significant efforts to do so." Responding to each of the reports, the White House announced that President Bush had chosen not to impose sanctions on Saudi Arabia.

SYRIA

Syria's human rights situation is poor, and showed little or no improvement in 2005. Emergency rule, imposed in 1963, remains in effect, despite public calls by Syrian reformers for its repeal. In June, a state security court acquitted Aktham Na`issa, president of the Committees for the Defence of Democratic Liberties and Human Rights in Syria, of charges that he opposed "the objectives of the revolution" and disseminated "false information" aimed at "weakening the State," but the authorities continue to harass and imprison other human rights defenders and non-violent critics of government policies. The government strictly limits freedom of expression, association, and assembly. Thousands of political prisoners, many of them members of the banned Muslim Brotherhood and the Communist Party, remained in detention. Syrian Kurds, the country's largest ethnic minority, continued to protest their treatment as second-class citizens. Women face legal as well as societal discrimination, and have little means for redress when they are victims of sexual abuse or domestic violence.

The February 2005 assassination of former Lebanese Prime Minister Rafik Hariri sharply intensified international pressure on the Syrian government. Bowing to this as well as Lebanese popular pressure, Syria withdrew its troops from Lebanon on April 26.

Arbitrary Detention, Torture, and "Disappearances"

In March 2005, the government released 312 political prisoners. They included Muhannad al-Dibs and Muhammad `Arab, Damascus University students, whom the Supreme State Security Court (SSSC) had just sentenced to three years in jail for organizing a protest against the suspension of two Aleppo University students; they were convicted of "resistance" and "support of goals contrary to the revolution." On November 2, the government freed a further 190 political prisoners as part of its "overall reforms." Among those released in the second group were `Ali Abdullah, a member of the Atasi political discussion forum, and Muhammad Ra`dun, president of the Arab Organization for Human Rights (AOHR), as well as members of "Islamist organizations." Security forces had arrested Abdullah on May 16 for his suspected ties to the Muslim Brotherhood and Ra`dun on May 22 for his affiliation with the AOHR and for allegedly publishing false information.

Dr. `Arif Dalila, a prominent economics professor and a proponent of political liberalization, continues to serve a ten-year prison term imposed in July 2002 for his non-violent criticism of government policies. Ma'mun al-Humsi, a democracy activist and former member of parliament, is serving a five-year jail term for "attempting to change the constitution." The London-based Syrian Human Rights Committee (SHRC) estimates that about four thousand political prisoners remain in detention in Syria. The authorities refuse to divulge information regarding numbers or names of people in detention on political or security-related charges. Moreover, 2005 passed without any government acknowledgement that its security forces had "disappeared" an estimated seventeen thousand persons—Lebanese citizens and stateless Palestinians— in Lebanon in the early 1990s. Many of these people are known or believed to be imprisoned in Syria.

In recent years, dozens of people suspected of being connected to the Muslim Brotherhood have been arrested upon their voluntary or forced return home from exile. Syrian authorities arrested `Abd al-Sitar Qattan, for example, on November 23, 2004, upon his return from Saudi Arabia, and reportedly prosecuted him before the SSSC under Law 49 (1980), which states, in part, that affiliation with the Muslim Brotherhood is punishable by death.

The government also targeted students whom it suspected of having ties with Islamist groups. In March 2005, the government arrested over forty students of Tishrin University, in Latakia, for being affiliated with an Islamist movement called Sunna` al-Hayat (Makers of Life). At least some of the detained students were reportedly tortured, according to the Damascus-based Human Rights Association in Syria.

An unprecedented coalition of political reform activists, on October 16, publicly issued the "Damascus Declaration for Democratic and National Change," which calls for establishing a democratic system that respects citizens' rights, ensures freedom of speech and association, and ends discrimination based on religious or political beliefs. As of November the government's reaction was unknown.

New Arrests of Human Rights Activists

Human rights activists continue to be frequent targets of government harassment and arrest. Among those arrested in the past year and still in detention are Salim al-Salim, an activist from Homs in the Society of Human Rights in Syria, arrested on February 24; Nizar Rastawani, from Hama, arrested on April 18; the writer and activist `Ali al-Abdullah, arrested on May 15 for having publicly read a letter written by `Ali Sadr al-Din al-Bayanuni, London-based leader of the Muslim Brotherhood, about the group's agenda; and Habib Salih, arrested on May 29 in response to his writings and his appearance on satellite television channels. In the case of Rastawani, security agents refused to admit he was in their custody until his missing car was spotted at one of their security branches ten days after they arrested him.

The government prevented many human rights activists from traveling. According to the SHRC, the authorities are presently preventing over 190 activists from traveling outside the country.

Discrimination and Violence Against Kurds

Kurds are the largest non-Arab ethnic minority in Syria, comprising about 10 percent of the population of 18.5 million. Activists have long called for an end to systematic discrimination, including the arbitrary denial of citizenship to an estimated 120,000 Syria-born Kurds.

Since the March 2004 clashes between Kurdish demonstrators and security forces in Qamishli that left more than thirty dead and four hundred injured, tensions in that city and surrounding areas have remained high. A prominent Kurdish cleric, Muhammad Ma`shuq al-Khaznawi, disappeared during a visit to Damascus in May 2005; the Interior Ministry denied having al-Khaznawi in its custody, and authorities found his body in eastern Syria three weeks after his disappearance. His sons and Kurdish activists blamed state security for the abduction and murder, stating that there were signs of torture on his body. After the announcement of al-Khaznawi's death, more than five thousand protesters gathered in Qamishli to condemn the killing. The protest escalated when looters, allegedly local Arabs, pillaged more than eighty Kurdish shops.

In September 2005, police beat a Syrian Kurdish woman to death when she attempted to stop the demolition of illegally built homes outside Damascus. According to defense lawyer and human rights activist Anwar Bunni, residents were primarily poor Kurdish workers.

On November 2, Syrian authorities freed seven Kurds, including three women, who had been arrested earlier in the year for belonging to a "secret organization aiming to annex part of Syrian territory to a foreign country."

Discrimination against Women

Syria's constitution guarantees gender equality, and many women are active in public life, but personal status laws as well as the penal code contain provisions that discriminate against women. The penal code allows a judge to suspend punishment for a rapist if the rapist chooses to marry his victim, and provides leniency for so-called "honor" crimes, such as assault or killing of women by male relatives for alleged sexual misconduct. Wives require the permission of their husbands to travel abroad, and divorce laws remain discriminatory.

Key International Actors

The United Nations Security Council passed Resolution 1559 on September 2, 2004, calling for the complete withdrawal of all foreign—i.e. Syrian—troops from Lebanon, and reiterating support for Lebanon's sovereignty and independence. The Security Council on April 7, 2005, adopted Resolution 1595, launching an investigation into the February 14 assassination, in Beirut, of former Lebanese Prime Minister Rafik Hariri. Lebanese authorities arrested four senior pro-Syrian Lebanese intelligence and security officers in August on suspicion of involvement in the Hariri assassination, but the preliminary report of chief U.N. investigator Detlev Mehlis, submitted to Secretary-General Kofi Annan on October 20, implicated senior Syrian security officials as well. On October 31, the Security Council unanimously adopted Resolution 1636 threatening "further action" against Syria if it did not fully cooperate with the investigation.

France, the United Kingdom, and the United States were among states which pressed Syria to implement Resolution 1559 and fully withdraw its forces from Lebanon. The European Commission and Syria initialed an Association Agreement in October 2004, but U.K. Foreign Secretary Jack Straw said on July 12, 2005, that the signing would likely not take place in 2005. The text stipulates that Syria must implement all international non-proliferation accords, and that "respect for human rights and democratic principles" constitutes "an essential element of the agreement."

TUNISIA

President Zine el-Abidine Ben Ali and the ruling party, the Constitutional Democratic Assembly, dominate political life in Tunisia. The government uses the threat of terrorism and religious extremism as a pretext to crack down on peaceful dissent. Government critics are frequently harassed or imprisoned on trumped-up charges after unfair trials. Over four hundred political prisoners remained incarcerated, nearly all of them suspected Islamists. There are continuous and credible reports of torture and ill-treatment being used to obtain statements from suspects in custody. Sentenced prisoners also face deliberate ill-treatment. However, during 2005 authorities allowed the International Committee of the Red Cross to start visiting prisons, and ended the practice of placing certain political prisoners in prolonged and arbitrary solitary confinement.

Human Rights Defenders

Authorities have refused legal recognition to every truly independent human rights organization that has applied over the past decade. They then use the pretext of an organization's "illegal" status to hamper its activities. On September 3, police encircled the Tunis office of the non-recognized National Council on Liberties in Tunisia (CNLT) and, as they had done many times before, prevented members from meeting. Authorities also prevented the non-recognized Tunisian Journalists' Syndicate from holding its constitutive assembly on September 7.

In 2005 the independent Tunisian Human Rights League (a legally recognized group) was beset by lawsuits filed by dissident members over procedural matters. The broader context shows that these suits are part of a larger pattern of repression; the courts ruled systematically in favor of these plaintiffs, providing a legal veneer for swift and large-scale police operations to prevent League meetings, including its general assembly scheduled for September. The government has continued to block grants issued by the European Union to the League, and Tunisia's mainstream press obliges with a blackout on criticism by the League and other human rights organizations of Tunisia's rights record.

Authorities tried to undermine another legally recognized organization, the Tunisian Association of Magistrates, after it elected a leadership calling for more judicial independence. In July judges close to the ruling party attempted to oust that leadership in a special vote. In August authorities evicted the leadership from the association's headquarters on the disputable grounds that it had been repudiated in the July vote.

Human rights defenders, like dissidents generally, are subject to heavy police surveillance, sporadic travel bans, dismissal from work, interruptions in phone service, physical assaults, harassment of relatives, suspicious acts of vandalism and theft, and slander campaigns in the press. In early May CNLT spokesperson Sihem Bensedrine was the target of an especially vulgar series of articles in at least four pro-government newspapers.

Police arrested lawyer and dissident Mohamed Abou on March 1, 2005— the day after he published an article online comparing President Ben Ali unfavorably to Israeli Prime Minister Ariel Sharon. To disguise that this was the real reason for Abou's arrest, authorities prosecuted him instead for an article he had written in August 2004 deploring Tunisian prison conditions and on a second, trumped-up charge of assaulting a woman lawyer in 2002. He received a three-year prison sentence.

The Justice System

The judiciary lacks independence. Investigative judges often question defendants without their lawyers present. Trial judges frequently turn a blind eye to torture allegations and procedural irregularities, convicting defendants solely or predominantly on the basis of coerced confessions. Civilians are sometimes tried on terror charges in military courts, verdicts of which carry no right of appeal.

In political cases lawyers are frequently hobbled in their attempts to mount an effective defense of their clients. They sometimes encounter obstacles to obtaining their clients' complete court file or gaining access to their clients in detention before trial.

Media Freedom

Tunisia's press remains largely controlled by the authorities. None of the print and broadcast media offers critical coverage of government policies, apart from a few low-circulation independent magazines. The private dailies are all loyalist, often slandering government critics in a manner that is deemed too base for the official media. In 2005 Tunisia got its second private radio station and first private television station, but here too private ownership was not synonymous with editorial independence.

The government blocks certain political or human rights websites that focus on critical coverage of Tunisia. As of September 2005, the government was blocking access to more than thirty such sites, although censorship had been lifted on other sites, such as those of *Le Monde* and *Liberation* and of various international human rights organizations.

In light of Tunisia's record on freedom of expression, human rights organizations criticized Tunisia's designation as host of the World Summit on the Information Society (WSIS) in November 2005. During that event, authorities prevented Tunisian and international human rights organizations from organizing an alternative "Citizens' Summit" in Tunis.

Counterterrorism Measures

Tunisian authorities claim that they have long been in the forefront of combating terrorism and extremism, alluding to their long-running crackdown against the once-tolerated Islamist Nahdha movement. In December 2003 Tunisia adopted the "Law in Support of International Efforts to Fight Terrorism and the Repression of Money-Laundering." It contained a broad definition of terrorism that could be used to prosecute persons for peaceful exercise of their right to dissent.

Since 1991, the one deadly terrorist attack to occur in Tunisia was the April 2002 truck bomb that targeted a synagogue on the island of Djerba. Al-Qaeda claimed responsibility for the attack.

Since April 2005, "anti-terrorism" arrests increased as authorities rounded up scores of young Tunisians in cities around the country, accusing most of them of planning to enlist in jihadist movements abroad. As of this writing, to Human Rights Watch's knowledge, authorities had charged none of them with committing, or plotting to commit, a specific act of violence, or of possessing arms or explosives. Those brought to court claimed uniformly that the police had extracted their statements under torture or threat of torture. In 2005, a Tunis court convicted eleven youths who had been arrested in similar circumstances during 2004. The conviction of the so-called "Bizerte group" was based almost entirely on confessions to the police that they contested as having been made under torture. In July 2005, an appeals court acquitted five of them but sentenced five others to between ten and twenty years in prison.

Key International Actors

Concerned by Tunisia's curbs on free expression and nongovernmental organizations, the E.U., the United States, and eleven other countries co-signed a sharp statement on September 30 in advance of the WSIS in Tunis in November 2005. It stated, "the Summit envisages an important and inclusive role for ... civil society, international organizations [and] editorially independent media both for the preparations and in the final summit itself. We expect Tunisia ... to ensure that arrangements for the Summit take account of and guarantee the unhindered participation of nongovernmental organizations and their members. This is the only way to make sure that this will be a Summit in Tunisia, not a Summit on Tunisia."

In his speech at the inauguration of the Summit on November 16, Swiss President Samuel Schmid declared, "It goes without saying that here in Tunis, within these walls as well as outside them, everyone should be able to speak with complete freedom." Tunisian state television censored his remarks.

The United States enjoys good relations with Tunisia and frequently praises its role in "stabilizing" the region and combating terror. The United States also actively monitors human rights conditions in Tunisia, sending observers to political trials. On November 4, 2004, after President Ben Ali pardoned some political prisoners, the U.S. State Department spokesman urged him to extend the amnesty "to all political prisoners convicted or detained for activities not linked to violence or terrorism." On November 18, 2005, the closing day of WSIS, the U.S. delegation to the summit expressed "disappointment that the government of Tunisia did not take advantage of this important opportunity to demonstrate its commitment to freedom of expression and assembly in Tunisia."

In its report, "Supporting Human Rights and Democracy" for 2004-05, the State Department noted that the government of Tunisia had blocked "several programs that the U.S. Government funded indirectly, including an attempt by a U.S. NGO to train Tunisian election monitors prior to the Tunisian election."

The E.U.-Tunisia Association Agreement continued in force, despite the government's human rights record and its blocking of E.U. grants to some NGOs, including the Tunisian Human Rights League and the Tunisian Women's Association for Research and Development.

The United Kingdom E.U. Presidency issued a statement on September 13 voicing concern about the plight of the Tunisian Human Rights League. The European Parliament adopted a resolution on September 29 that praised social and economic progress while urging the release of Mohamed Abou and other political prisoners.

France remained Tunisia's largest trading partner, and President Jacques Chirac a staunch supporter of President Ben Ali. Public statements about human rights were infrequent and cautious. However, on November 15, on the eve of the WSIS, the spokesperson of the French foreign ministry urged Tunisian authorities "to do everything possible to guarantee freedom of information and that journalists can work in freedom." The remark followed incidents where police prevented French and Belgian crews from filming in

Tunis, and the suspicious stabbing of French journalist Christophe Boltanski on a Tunis street on November 11.

France made diplomatic representations, "on a humanitarian basis," on behalf of a few political prisoners, selected because they had relatives who were French citizens or who resided in France. Tunisian authorities freed one of these, Lotfi Farhat, in July.

In 2004, France returned to Tunisia Taher Belkhirat, despite strong evidence that he would face persecution there. Tunisian authorities arrested him upon his arrival and, in 2005, sentenced him in an unfair trial to ten years in prison (reduced to five years on appeal) on charges of membership in, and recruiting for, a terrorist organization operating abroad. In January 2005, the French Council of State issued a ruling voiding Belkhirat's expulsion order—months after he had been expelled to and jailed in Tunisia.

United Arab Emirates (UAE)

The UAE is a federation of seven emirates: Abu Dhabi, 'Ajman, Al Fujayrah, Sharjah, Dubai, Ra's al Khaymah, and Umm al Qaywayn. The president and vice president are elected by the Federal Supreme Council, which is composed of the rulers of each emirate. The UAE has experienced rapid economic development and growth during the past several decades, but it lags in the development of its civil society: the country does not hold elections for any public office, and political participation is limited to the ruling family in each emirate. The government has not signed most international human rights and labor rights treaties. Migrant workers, comprising nearly 90 percent of the workforce in the private sector, are particularly vulnerable to serious human rights violations.

Freedom of Association and Expression

A major obstacle to monitoring and reporting human rights violations in the UAE is the lack of independent nongovernmental organizations. The government actively discourages formation of such organizations. In July 2004 a group of lawyers and activists led by prominent lawyer Mohammad al-Roken filed an application with the Ministry of Labor and Social Welfare under the Association Law to form the Emirates Human Rights Society. In April 2005 another group of thirty activists headed by human rights campaigner Khalifa Bakhit al-Falasi also filed application for a human rights association. According to the Associations Law, the Ministry of Labor and Social Welfare should reply to these requests within a month of their filing, but as of October 2005 the ministry had not responded to these applications.

For the past five years, the government has barred twelve prominent UAE commentators and academics from disseminating their views. In June 2000 the government sent a letter to Abu Dhabi Television stating that "based on information from the administration we urge all producers to refrain from hosting the following [twelve] individuals in programs for the Abu Dhabi channel and the Emirates channel." The ban effectively applies to the print media as well as radio and television broadcasts. Otherwise, the media is rela-

495

tively free from official censorship, but is susceptible to heavy self-censorship due to pressures from officials and influential business interests.

Migrant Labor

Nearly 80 percent of the UAE's population are foreigners, and foreigners account for 90 percent of the workforce in the private sector, including as domestic workers. The UAE's extensive economic growth has attracted large sums in domestic and foreign investment, and a recent construction boom is one of the largest in the world. There are persistent credible reports of abuses committed by employers, especially in small firms and against low-skilled workers. A main factor is the immigration sponsorship laws that grant employers extraordinary control over the affairs of migrant workers.

Abuses committed against migrant workers include nonpayment of wages, extended working hours without overtime compensation, unsafe working environments resulting in death and injury, squalid living conditions in labor camps, and withholding of passports and travel documents by employers.

In 2005 the UAE witnessed an increasing number of public demonstrations by migrant workers protesting nonpayment of wages. During a protest on September 24 (one of at least three that month), 800 workers blocked a main highway in Dubai. They were part of a group of six thousand workers employed by Al Hamed Development and Construction of Abu Dhabi, and had not been paid for more than five months. In an unprecedented development, the minister of labor and social welfare, Ali bin Abdullah al-Kaabi, required the company to pay all overdue wages within twenty-four hours, and prohibited it from hiring migrant workers for the next six months.

Since becoming minister in November 2004, al-Kaabi has introduced a number of promising reforms that have met stiff resistance from the business community. Following a surge in heat-related illness and injuries at construction sites in July 2005, the ministry directed construction companies to give their workers an afternoon break from 12:30 p.m. to 4:30 p.m. during the months of July and August. However, a number of companies defied this order and publicly stated that they prefer to pay fines rather than comply.

Women domestic workers are often confined to their places of work, and may be at particular risk of abuse including unpaid wages, long working hours, and physical or sexual abuse.

Trafficking

According to the U.S. State Department, human trafficking to the UAE is an endemic problem. Large numbers of young boys are annually trafficked to the UAE to be trained as camel jockeys, and in 2005 the UAE government estimated the number of children working as camel jockeys to be between 1,200 and 2,700; international organizations have put the numbers much higher, at between five thousand and six thousand. Responding to the international criticism, UAE President Sheikh Khalifa bin Zayed al Nahyan issued a federal decree in July 2005 requiring that all camel jockeys must be eighteen years of age or older. The law stipulated that violators will be jailed for up to three years and/or fined a minimum of Dh50,000 (U.S.$13,600). The government's ability to institute mechanisms of enforcement will be tested in the coming year.

Key International Actors

The UAE has emerged as a major business and trading hub in the Middle East, attracting substantial foreign investments. The U.S., Japan, and the European Union are among the UAE's main trading partners. In April 2004 the UAE signed a Trade and Investment Framework Agreement (TIFA) with the U.S., and the two countries in November 2004 began negotiations toward a Free Trade Agreement (FTA).

In its 2005 annual report on human trafficking, the U.S. State Department downgraded the UAE to the third tier, including it among "countries whose governments do not fully comply with the minimum standards for the elimination of trafficking and are not making significant efforts to do so." In September 2005 the White House, in a memorandum to the secretary of state, said that the UAE had taken actions that averted the need for the president to make a decision to impose or waive sanctions under the Trafficking

Victims Protection Act of 2000. According to this memorandum, the UAE's efforts to combat trafficking would be re-evaluated in six months.

The UAE in October 2004 acceded to the Convention on the Elimination of All Forms of Discrimination against Women. However, it is not a signatory to other major international human rights instruments such as the International Covenant on Civil and Political Rights, the International Convention on the Protection of the Rights of All Migrant Workers and Members of Their Families, and the Convention against Torture.

The Rest of Their Lives

Life without Parole for Child Offenders
in the United States

HUMAN
RIGHTS
WATCH

WORLD REPORT
2005

UNITED STATES

UNITED STATES

The United States government has been widely condemned for violating basic human rights in the fight against terrorism. Since 2001, the Bush administration has authorized interrogation techniques widely considered torture, including by its own Department of State in its annual human rights reports. It has held an unknown number of detainees as "ghosts" beyond the reach of all monitors, including the International Committee of the Red Cross. And it has become the only government in the world to seek legislative sanction to treat detainees inhumanely.

In addition to focusing on U.S. counterterrorism practices, Human Rights Watch in 2005 continued to work on other pressing human rights concerns in the United States, including abysmal prison conditions, continued use of the death penalty, racial disparities (brought to public consciousness in 2005 by Hurricane Katrina and its aftermath), and increasingly restrictive asylum and other immigration policies.

Guantanamo Bay and Military Commissions

Approximately 505 men remain in long-term indefinite detention at Guantanamo Bay, Cuba. The United States continues to assert authority to hold "enemy combatants" without charges and without regard to the laws of armed conflict as long as the war on terror continues.

In March 2005, the Pentagon completed a one-time administrative review of each detainee at Guantanamo to determine whether he should be considered an "enemy combatant." The proceedings were stacked against the detainees: they were presumed to be enemy combatants, were denied the assistance of counsel, were not able to bring in outside witnesses, and were not able to see all of the evidence against them. All but thirty-eight of the detainees were deemed enemy combatants (most of the thirty-eight are believed to be Uighurs from China). The Pentagon is also conducting annual reviews to determine if an enemy combatant is no longer a threat or useful for intelligence-gathering purposes and can be released. Neither U.S. domestic law nor international laws of war authorize such grounds for indefinite detention.

A total of nine detainees have been charged with crimes, including a Canadian citizen who was fifteen years old at the time of his arrest in Afghanistan. These detainees would be tried by military commissions, but commission proceedings are halted until the U.S. Supreme Court rules on their legality. The Court's ruling is not expected until mid 2006.

Responding to a consistent critique of the commissions by human rights groups and others, the U.S. Senate passed legislation—not yet approved by the full Congress at this writing—that would permit civilian appellate court review of military commission rulings. Following a 2004 U.S. Supreme Court ruling that the Guantanamo detainees must have a meaningful opportunity to contest their detention before a neutral decision-maker, habeas corpus cases for some seventy-four detainees have been filed in U.S. courts. In a frontal attack on the detainees' use of habeas proceedings, the Senate passed legislation in November 2005 to curtail their access to the courts to challenge indefinite detention or torture. The full Congress was expected to approve the legislation by year's end.

At least 131 detainees began a hunger strike in August 2005 to protest their indefinite confinement, pledging to starve themselves to death unless they were brought to trial or released. Two dozen have been kept alive by force-feeding.

In October, the United States responded to a three-year-old request by a team of independent United Nations experts to visit Guantanamo, but denied them the ability to meet privately with the detainees. The experts refused the invitation, because having access to detainees is a requirement for all their prison visits.

Torture Policy

The Bush administration asserts that it does not use or condone torture. Its definition of torture, however, remains unclear. At the end of 2004, the Department of Justice (DOJ) issued a memorandum repudiating earlier policies that had permitted a broad range of brutal interrogation tactics by, among other legal sleights-of-hand, redefining torture to exclude all techniques that did not inflict pain "equivalent in intensity to the pain accompanying serious physical injury, such as organ failure, impairment of bodily function or even death." The Department has not, however, ever revealed what its definition currently is.

Authorized Central Intelligence Agency (CIA) interrogation techniques apparently include a notorious method the administration has renamed "waterboarding" (when practiced by Latin American dictatorships, it was called "the submarine")—forcefully submerging a suspect's head in water or otherwise making him believe he is about to drown. The director of the CIA has stated that waterboarding is a "professional interrogation technique."

As noted above, the Bush Administration asserts that U.S. treaty obligations to refrain from cruel, inhuman and degrading (CID) treatment do not apply to the conduct of nonmilitary U.S. personnel interrogating non-U.S. citizens outside of the United States.

Led by Vice President Cheney, the Bush administration strongly resisted efforts by Congress to strengthen the legal ban against torture. A measure proposed by Republican Senator John McCain to prohibit torture and other ill-treatment of detainees anywhere by the U.S. military and the CIA passed 90-9 in the Senate but at this writing had not been approved by the full Congress at least in part because of administration objections.

Detainee Abuse

Reports of abuse of detainees in U.S. custody in Afghanistan, Iraq, Guantanamo Bay, and at secret detention facilities continue to mount. Since 2002, over three hundred specific cases of serious detainee abuse have surfaced. At least eighty-six detainees have died in U.S. custody since 2002, and the U.S. government has admitted that at least twenty-seven of these cases were criminal homicides.

The abuse did not end after Abu Ghraib became public; U.S. military personnel have revealed new cases of abuse in 2004 at forward-operating bases in Afghanistan and Iraq, where prisoners are kept temporarily. Detainees at the Guantanamo Bay detention center, scores of whom now have access to legal counsel, have made new allegations of prisoner mistreatment.

The United States continues to hold incommunicado at least twenty-five— and possibly as many as one hundred—"ghost detainees" at secret detention facilities around the world, without any rights and without access to legal counsel or to the International Committee of the Red Cross. New evidence emerged in 2005 suggesting that some "ghost" facilities may have operated at least through 2004 in Eastern Europe and in several Middle Eastern countries.

Additional evidence also emerged in 2005 about cases of "extraordinary rendition," in which the United States sent detainees to third countries for interrogation, including countries with records of torture, such as Morocco, Jordan, and Egypt. Several current and former prisoners in Guantanamo claim they were taken to Jordan or Morocco for interrogation, and tortured, before being sent to Guantanamo.

Despite the unequivocal international prohibition on return of people to situations where there is a risk of torture, the Bush administration openly claims the right to send counterterrorism detainees to countries where there is such a risk so long as it obtains guarantees—so-called "diplomatic assurances"— from the authorities in the country concerned that the detainee in question will not be tortured. A growing number of cases—such as that of Mahar Arar, a Canadian-Syrian citizen who was transiting through John F. Kennedy airport on his way home to Canada when he was detained by U.S. authorities, sent to Syria via Jordan, and allegedly tortured—suggest that such diplomatic assurances are routinely violated.

The Bush administration has done little to address government policies or actions that may have led to abuse of detainees, continues to deny that widespread abuse has occurred, and resists calls for detention policy reforms.

Despite a number of investigations, the United States has not robustly prosecuted cases of alleged detainee abuse or homicide. In the majority of cases involving alleged abuse, military commanders have taken potential prosecutions before administrative hearing boards for non-judicial punishments, such as "reprimands," "admonishments," rank reductions, and discharges, instead of bringing them for criminal prosecutions before courts martial.

At this writing, the military had prosecuted only about forty cases of abuse or prisoner mistreatment. Although a few tough sentences have been handed down, most prosecutions have resulted in relatively light sentences—confinement for less than one year. Virtually all of those prosecuted have been lower-ranking military personnel, not officers. With civilians implicated in prisoner abuse, the record is even worse: despite extensive evidence that CIA personnel and civilian contractors were involved in several homicides, the DOJ has not prosecuted a single agent in a federal court for abuse, except for one CIA contractor, who was charged with assault in connection with a homicide committed in Afghanistan in 2003.

Al-Marri and Padilla

For most of 2005, the United States continued to detain in a U.S. navy brig two men whom President Bush has designated "enemy combatants" because of alleged links to al Qaeda. Both men were arrested in the United States and have been held for over three years, mostly in solitary confinement.

On November 22, one of the men, Jose Padilla, who is a U.S. citizen, was indicted on criminal charges. The Bush administration decision to bring Padilla into the civilian criminal justice system means that the Supreme Court likely will no longer hear Padilla's challenge to an appellate court ruling that the president may subject American citizens to indefinite military detention without criminal charge or trial.

The other suspect, Qatari student Ali Saleh Kahlah al-Marri, was denied a writ of habeas corpus by a federal court in 2005 on grounds that President Bush has the authority to detain as enemy combatants non-citizens residing in the United States. Lawyers for al-Marri have also filed suit against U.S. Secretary of Defense Donald Rumsfeld, challenging the harsh conditions, including virtually complete isolation and denial of reading material, under which he initially was held.

Material Witnesses

Another form of arbitrary detention used by the United States since September 11, 2001, is the indefinite jailing of suspects without charges under a federal "material witness" law. Although there were no known cases at this writing, the Department of Justice has used this law to detain at least seventy men living in the United States and suspected of links to terrorism. The law was created to allow prosecutors to detain important witnesses to a crime who might flee to avoid testifying in a criminal proceeding.

Many of those detained were held for two months or more, and almost half were never brought to testify before any court or grand jury. Few proved to have any information about, much less links to, terrorism. The U.S. government has since apologized to thirteen for wrongly detaining them. It refuses to reveal how many material witnesses it has detained in connection with its post-September 11 efforts.

Incarceration

The United States incarcerates people at a greater rate than any other country, 724 per one hundred thousand residents. Seven million people—or one in every thirty-one persons—is in prison, or on probation or parole. Black men between the ages of twenty-five and twenty-nine are seven times more likely than their white counterparts to be in prison or jail. More than six hundred thousand people annually leave prison, most of them to return to distressed minority neighborhoods, facing formidable barriers to successful reentry, including laws that limit their access to education, housing, and jobs.

Prison overcrowding coupled with budget cuts leave prisoners without the programs and services they need and without adequate correctional staff to maintain safety and security. Adult and juvenile inmates confront sexual assaults and violence—by each other as well as by staff. With poor supervision and discipline, staff in many facilities can engage in excessive or malicious use of force with near impunity.

According to a report by the federal Bureau of Justice Statistics, prison officials reported they had received 8,210 allegations of staff or inmate sexual violence in 2004; one-third of those allegations were substantiated following investigations. The number of reported incidents is smaller than the actual number, because distrust of staff, fear of reprisal from perpetrators, personal embarrassment, and a sense of futility keep many prisoners from reporting abuse to correctional authorities. The National Prison Rape Elimination Commission established by Congress held three hearings in 2005, receiving testimony of inmate and staff sexual violence from victims, officials, and advocates.

Across the country, medical and mental health care in prisons ranges from mediocre to terrible. Correctional systems lack adequate funds to hire and retain qualified personnel and fail to institute procedures to ensure proper treatment of inmates. In California, a federal judge placed the entire state prison healthcare system under a receivership after determining that the state killed one inmate per week through medical incompetence or neglect. Poor mental health care can also be fatal. For example, a paranoid schizophrenic jail inmate hanged himself in May 2005 after not having received any anti-psychotic or antidepressant medication for seven days.

The Death Penalty and Other Cruel Sentences

As of November 4, forty-eight people had been executed in 2005. Evidence of the arbitrariness and procedural flaws in the imposition of the sentence continue to grow. Since 1973, 121 people have been released from death row with evidence of their innocence, including one in 2005.

In February, the Bush administration said it would comply with the 2004 ruling of the International Court of Justice (ICJ) that the United States should review and reconsider the cases of fifty-one Mexican citizens on death row because it had failed to give the Mexicans access to diplomatic officials after they were arrested. This victory was a Pyrrhic one. In March, Secretary of State Condeleeza Rice sent a letter to the United Nations formally withdrawing from the Optional Protocol to the Vienna Convention that the United States had violated—a protocol under which the ICJ could hear disputes

about consular rights in the Convention that the United States itself proposed in 1963 and ratified in 1969.

In March, the U.S. Supreme Court ruled that the execution of child offenders, i.e., those who were under age eighteen when they committed their
crimes, constituted unconstitutionally cruel and unusual punishment.
According to the Court, the immaturity and irresponsibility of children, their
susceptibility to negative influences and peer pressure, and their greater
capacity for change make them categorically less culpable than adults. The
Court acknowledged that its ruling was influenced by the overwhelming
international consensus against the sentence and the fact that it violates international human rights law.

While U.S. child offenders no longer face the death penalty, they do face the
possibility of life without parole sentences. There are at least 2,225 child
offenders sentenced to spend the rest of their lives in prison in the United
States, an estimated 59 percent of whom received the sentence for their first
criminal conviction. The United States is one of fourteen countries in the
world known to permit such sentences and research suggests that there may
be no more than twelve child offenders outside the United States serving life
sentences without possibility of release. The Convention on the Rights of the
Child, ratified by every country in the world except the United States and
Somalia, forbids sentencing child offenders to life without parole.

HIV/AIDS

The California legislature introduced a bill permitting condom distribution
in state prisons, which passed the Assembly but died in the Senate. Prisons
in Mississippi and Vermont, and jails in New York, Philadelphia,
Washington, D.C., San Francisco, and Los Angeles have taken measures to
ensure the health and human rights of inmates by permitting condom distribution. California also made some progress on the provision of needle-
exchange services to injection drug users at risk of HIV infection from the
sharing of syringes. Los Angeles re-issued a directive ordering police officers
not to interfere with the activity of sanctioned needle-exchange programs,

and the California Assembly passed legislation that would make it easier for counties to legalize these programs.

Katrina

The Gulf Coast suffered the nation's worst natural disaster in August, when Hurricane Katrina killed over one thousand people, displaced millions, and shut down public services for more than a month. When the mayor of New Orleans called on residents to evacuate in anticipation of the storm, those with automobiles or financial resources left. Those who were too poor to leave stayed behind, most of them African American. Media coverage of the hurricane tore away national blinders on the enormous class and racial divide in the country: no one could ignore the significance of poor people of color trapped on rooftops asking for help in the days following the storm.

The thousands of people incarcerated in local jails were among those most at risk when the storm hit. Inmates locked in the New Orleans jail spent several days in flooded buildings without light, food, water, or sanitation facilities before they were evacuated. Four hundred of those inmates were taken to a former prison facility in Jena, Louisiana that was hastily reopened to receive them. Inmates at Jena allege they were kicked, beaten, and taunted with racial and sexual slurs.

Hurricane Katrina also caused the collapse of the legal system, including the courts, in the affected areas. One consequence was that an unknown number of inmates, who should have been released in the days and weeks after the hurricane because their sentences had ended, remained incarcerated. Other inmates, who had been arrested before the storm for minor offenses, e.g., public intoxication, remained incarcerated because there were no courts to hear the charges against them and to sentence or release them.

Immigration

A law passed this year amends U.S. asylum policy in ways that violate international legal standards. Asylum seekers in the United States must now prove their persecutor's reasons for harming them, i.e. they must show what their persecutor was or would be thinking. Judges may now require asylum seekers to obtain corroborating evidence (which is often difficult to obtain) for their claims. Any inconsistency between asylum seekers' statements is now a valid reason to withhold protection, even if the inaccuracy is not relevant to the claim. The legislation also severely restricts opportunities for non-citizens ordered removed to have their cases reviewed by a federal judge.

Anti-immigrant hostility, and especially hostility to undocumented immigrants, prompted two states, Virginia and Arizona, to require state and local officials to verify an individual's immigration status before providing certain non-emergency public benefits. In several southwestern states, vigilante groups are "patrolling" the borders for undocumented immigrants. Immigrants' rights groups believe vigilantes may be responsible for four unsolved murders in the border region.

In late October, Congressional leaders announced their intentions to forge compromise guest-worker legislation in early 2006. It remained unclear whether the compromise would address the widespread human rights violations suffered by low-wage immigrant workers across the country. For example, immigrants in the meatpacking industry work in hazardous conditions without basic protections for their rights to a safe workplace, to medical care for workplace injuries, to organize labor unions, or to protection from exploitation and discrimination based on their vulnerable status as immigrants.

International Treaty Obligations

The United States submitted two human rights reports this year, one to the Committee against Torture (CAT) on its compliance with the Convention against Torture and one (eight years overdue) to the Human Rights Committee on its compliance with the International Covenant on Civil and Political Rights. Unfortunately, the reports are little more than a compendium of laws and selected federal legal proceedings. The Bush administration says little in either report about its counter-terrorism detention and interrogation policies or about other U.S. actions—whether by federal, state, or local authorities—inconsistent with U.S. treaty obligations.

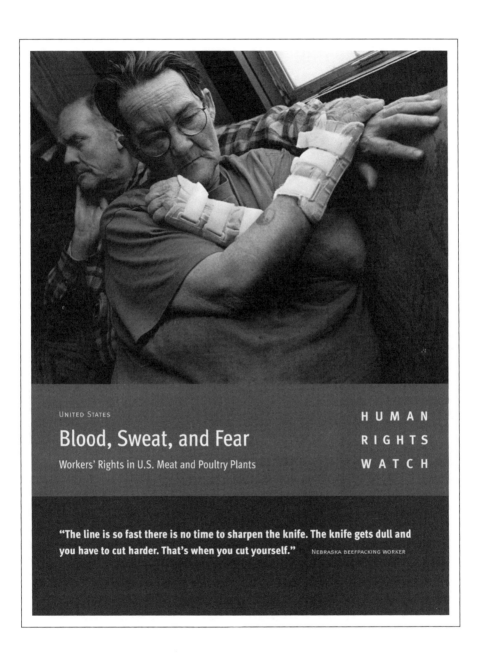

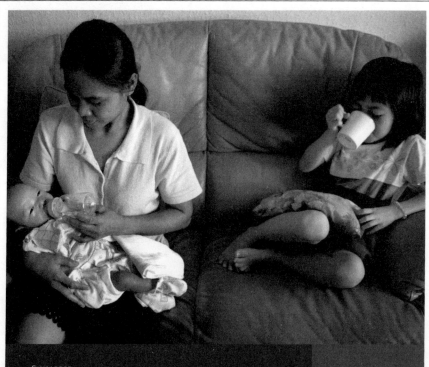

SINGAPORE

Maid to Order

Ending Abuses against Migrant Domestic Workers
in Singapore

**HUMAN
RIGHTS
WATCH**

WORLD REPORT
2006

2005
HUMAN RIGHTS WATCH
PUBLICATIONS

BY COUNTRY

Afghanistan

AFGHANISTAN ON THE EVE OF PARLIAMENTARY AND PROVINCIAL ELECTIONS, 09/05, 27pp.

CAMPAIGNING AGAINST FEAR: WOMEN'S PARTICIPATION IN AFGHANISTAN'S 2005 ELECTIONS, 09/05, 29pp.

BLOOD-STAINED HANDS: PAST ATROCITIES IN KABUL AND AFGHANISTAN'S LEGACY OF IMPUNITY, 07/05, 135pp.

Algeria

IMPUNITY IN THE NAME OF RECONCILIATION, 9/05, 23pp.

Angola

COMING HOME: RETURN AND REINTEGRATION IN ANGOLA, 03/05, 39pp.

Argentina

DECISIONS DENIED: WOMEN'S ACCESS TO CONTRACEPTIVES AND ABORTION IN ARGENTINA, 06/05, 87pp.

Azerbaijan

PARLIAMENTARY ELECTIONS 2005: LESSONS NOT LEARNED, 10/05, 28pp.

AZERBAIJAN AND THE EUROPEAN NEIGHBORHOOD POLICY, 06/05, 13pp.

Bangladesh

BREACH OF FAITH: PERSECUTION OF THE AHMADIYYA COMMUNITY IN BANGLADESH, 06/05, 45pp.

Bosnia and Herzogovina

"Safe Areas" for Srebrenica's Most Wanted: A Decade of Failure to Apprehend Karadzic and Mladic, 06/05, 25pp.

Brazil

In the Dark: Hidden Abuses Against Detained Youths in Rio de Janeiro, 06/05, 49pp.

Burma

"They Came and Destroyed Our Village Again": The Plight of Internally Displaced Persons in Karen State, 06/05, 69pp.

Burundi

Missteps at a Crucial Moment, 11/05, 18pp.

Canada

Transfer of Maher Arar to Torture, 06/05, 36pp.

Chad

The Victims of Hissène Habré Still Awaiting Justice, 07/05, 43pp.

Sexual Violence and its Consequences among Displaced Persons in Darfur and Chad, 04/05, 18pp.

China

"We Could Disappear At Any Time": Retaliation and Abuses Against Chinese Petitioners, 12/05, 89pp.

Restrictions on AIDS Activists in China, 06/05, 59pp.

Devastating Blows: Religious Repression of Uighurs in Xinjiang, 04/05, 114pp.

Colombia

Displaced and Discarded: The Plight of Internally Displaced Persons in Bogotá and Cartagena, 10/05, 60pp.

Smoke and Mirrors: Colombia's Demobilization of Paramilitary Groups, 8/05, 64pp.

Letting Paramilitaries Off The Hook, 01/05, 17pp.

Côte d'Ivoire

Country on a Precipice: The Precarious State of Human Rights and Civilian Protection in Côte d'Ivoire, 05/05, 35pp.

Youth, Poverty and Blood: The Lethal Legacy of West Africa's Regional Warriors, 03/05, 66pp.

Cuba

Families Torn Apart: The High Cost of U.S. and Cuban Travel Restrictions, 10/05, 69pp.

Democratic Republic of Congo

Democratic Republic of Congo: Civilians attacked in North Kivu, 07/05, 36pp.

The Curse of Gold, 06/05, 159pp.

Seeking Justice: The Prosecution of Sexual Violence in the Congo War, 03/05, 52pp.

Ecuador

PETITION REGARDING ECUADOR'S ELIGIBILITY FOR ATPA DESIGNATION, 09/05, 23pp.

COMMENTS TO USTR ON ECUADOR'S ATPDEA ELIGIBILITY, 03/05, 17pp.

Egypt

FALSE FREEDOM: ONLINE CENSORSHIP IN THE MIDDLE EAST AND NORTH AFRICA, 11/05, 144pp.

FROM PLEBISCITE TO CONTEST? EGYPT'S PRESIDENTIAL ELECTION, 09/05, 14pp.

MARGINS OF REPRESSION, 06/05, 48pp.

READING BETWEEN THE "RED LINES": THE REPRESSION OF ACADEMIC FREEDOM IN EGYPTIAN UNIVERSITIES, 06/05, 109pp.

BLACK HOLE: THE FATE OF ISLAMISTS RENDERED TO EGYPT, 05/05, 64pp.

MASS ARRESTS AND TORTURE IN SINAI, 02/05, 48pp.

Ethiopia

SUPPRESSING DISSENT: HUMAN RIGHTS ABUSES AND POLITICAL REPRESSION IN ETHIOPIA'S OROMIA REGION, 05/05, 46pp.

TARGETING THE ANUAK: HUMAN RIGHTS VIOLATIONS AND CRIMES AGAINST HUMANITY IN ETHIOPIA'S GAMBELLA REGION, 03/05, 64pp.

Georgia

GEORGIA AND THE EUROPEAN NEIGHBOURHOOD POLICY, 06/05, 11pp.

UNCERTAIN TORTURE REFORM, 04/05, 27pp.

India

AFTER THE DELUGE: INDIA'S RECONSTRUCTION FOLLOWING THE 2004 TSUNAMI, 05/05, 47pp.

Indonesia

ALWAYS ON CALL: ABUSE AND EXPLOITATION OF CHILD DOMESTIC WORKERS IN INDONESIA, 06/05, 78pp.

Iran

FALSE FREEDOM: ONLINE CENSORSHIP IN THE MIDDLE EAST AND NORTH AFRICA, 11/05, 144pp.

CLERICAL LEADERS FORECLOSE FREE ELECTIONS, 06/05, 17pp.

NO EXIT: HUMAN RIGHTS ABUSES INSIDE THE MOJAHEDIN KHALQ CAMPS, 05/05, 29pp.

Iraq

THE FORMER IRAQI GOVERNMENT ON TRIAL, 10/05, 20pp.

A FACE AND A NAME: CIVILIAN VICTIMS OF INSURGENT GROUPS IN IRAQ, 10/05, 142pp.

ALI HASSAN AL-MAJID AND THE BASRA MASSACRE OF 1999, 02/05, 32pp.

THE NEW IRAQ?: TORTURE AND ILL-TREATMENT OF DETAINEES IN IRAQI CUSTODY, 01/05, 94pp.

Israel/Occupied Palestinian Territories

PROMOTING IMPUNITY: THE ISRAELI MILITARY'S FAILURE TO INVESTIGATE WRONGDOING, 06/05, 125pp.

Kenya

LETTING THEM FAIL: GOVERNMENT NEGLECT AND THE RIGHT TO EDUCATION FOR CHILDREN AFFECTED BY AIDS, 10/05, 59pp.

Liberia

JUSTICE IN MOTION: THE TRIAL PHASE OF THE SPECIAL COURT FOR SIERRA LEONE, 11/05, 46pp.

Malaysia

DETAINED WITHOUT TRIAL: ABUSE OF INTERNAL SECURITY ACT DETAINEES IN MALAYSIA, 09/05, 34pp.

Morocco

INSIDE THE HOME, OUTSIDE THE LAW: ABUSE OF CHILD DOMESTIC WORKERS IN MOROCCO,12/05, 60pp.

MOROCCO TRUTH COMMISSIONS: HONORING PAST VICTIMS DURING AN UNCERTAIN PRESENT, 04/05, 50pp.

Nepal

CLEAR CULPABILITY: "DISAPPEARANCES" BY SECURITY FORCES IN NEPAL, 03/05, 86pp.

Nigeria

"REST IN PIECES": POLICE TORTURE AND DEATHS IN CUSTODY IN NIGERIA, 07/05, 76pp.

REVENGE IN THE NAME OF RELIGION: THE CYCLE OF VIOLENCE IN PLATEAU AND KANO STATES, 06/05, 75pp.

RIVERS AND BLOOD: GUNS, OIL, AND POWER IN NIGERIA'S RIVERS STATE, 02/05, 22pp.

Papua New Guinea

"MAKING THEIR OWN RULES": POLICE BEATINGS, RAPE, AND TORTURE OF CHILDREN IN PAPUA NEW GUINEA, 08/05, 121pp.

Russia

POSITIVELY ABANDONED: STIGMA AND DISCRIMINATION AGAINST HIV-POSITIVE MOTHERS AND THEIR CHILDREN IN RUSSIA, 07/05, 43pp.

WORSE THAN A WAR: "DISAPPEARANCES" IN CHECHNYA—A CRIME AGAINST HUMANITY, 03/05, 57pp.

MANAGING CIVIL SOCIETY: ARE NGOs NEXT?, 11/05, 26pp.

Serbia and Montenegro

DANGEROUS INDIFFERENCE: VIOLENCE AGAINST MINORITIES IN SERBIA, 10/05, 54pp.

Sierra Leone

JUSTICE IN MOTION: THE TRIAL PHASE OF THE SPECIAL COURT FOR SIERRA LEONE, 11/05, 46pp.

YOUTH, POVERTY, AND BLOOD: THE LETHAL LEGACY OF WEST AFRICA'S REGIONAL WARRIORS, 03/05, 66pp.

Singapore

MAID TO ORDER: ENDING ABUSES AGAINST MIGRANT DOMESTIC WORKERS IN SINGAPORE, 12/05, 115pp.

South Africa

LIVING ON THE MARGINS: INADEQUATE PROTECTION FOR REFUGEES AND ASYLUM SEEKERS IN JOHANNESBURG, 11/05, 64pp.

Spain

SETTING AN EXAMPLE: COUNTERTERRORISM MEASURES IN SPAIN, 01/05, 67pp.

Sudan

SEXUAL VIOLENCE AND ITS CONSEQUENCES AMONG DISPLACED PERSONS IN DARFUR AND CHAD, 04/05, 18pp.

TARGETING THE FUR: MASS KILLINGS IN DARFUR, 01/05, 22pp.

Syria

FALSE FREEDOM: ONLINE CENSORSHIP IN THE MIDDLE EAST AND NORTH AFRICA, 11/05, 144pp.

TRANSFER OF MAHER ARAR TO TORTURE, 06/05, 36pp.

Tunisia

FALSE FREEDOM: ONLINE CENSORSHIP IN THE MIDDLE EAST AND NORTH AFRICA, 11/05, 144pp.

CRUSHING THE PERSON, CRUSHING A MOVEMENT, 04/05, 39pp.

Turkey

"STILL CRITICAL": PROSPECTS IN 2005 FOR INTERNALLY DISPLACED KURDS IN TURKEY, 03/05, 29pp.

Uganda

UPROOTED AND FORGOTTEN: IMPUNITY AND HUMAN RIGHTS ABUSES IN NORTHERN UGANDA, 09/05, 78pp.

THE LESS THEY KNOW, THE BETTER: ABSTINENCE-ONLY HIV/AIDS PROGRAMS IN UGANDA, 03/05, 80pp.

Ukraine

ON THE MARGINS: RIGHTS VIOLATIONS AGAINST MIGRANTS AND ASYLUM SEEKERS AT THE NEW EASTERN BORDER OF THE EUROPEAN UNION, 11/05, 77pp.

United Kingdom

BRIEFING ON THE TERRORISM BILL 2005, 11/05, 16pp.

COMMENTARY ON THE PREVENTION OF TERRORISM BILL 2005, 03/05, 11pp.

United States

THE REST OF THEIR LIVES: LIFE WITHOUT PAROLE FOR CHILD OFFENDERS IN THE UNITED STATES, 10/05, 125pp.

LEADERSHIP FAILURE: FIRSTHAND ACCOUNTS OF TORTURE OF IRAQI DETAINEES BY THE U.S. ARMY'S 82ND AIRBORNE DIVISION, 09/05, 30pp.

BACK IN BUSINESS? U.S. LANDMINE PRODUCTION AND EXPORTS, 8/05, 16pp.

TIME TO TAKE STOCK: THE U.S. CLUSTER MUNITION INVENTORY AND THE FY 2006 DEPARTMENT OF DEFENSE BUDGET, 07/05, 20pp.

BRIEFING PAPER ON U.S. MILITARY COMMISSIONS, 07/05, 13pp.

WITNESS TO ABUSE: HUMAN RIGHTS ABUSES UNDER THE MATERIAL WITNESS LAW SINCE SEPTEMBER 11, 06/05, 103pp.

GETTING AWAY WITH TORTURE? COMMAND RESPONSIBILITY FOR THE U.S. ABUSE OF DETAINEES, 06/05, 95pp.

TRANSFER OF MAHER ARAR TO TORTURE, 06/05, 36pp.

STILL AT RISK: DIPLOMATIC ASSURANCES NO SAFEGUARD AGAINST TORTURE, 04/05, 94pp.

BLOOD, SWEAT, AND FEAR: WORKERS' RIGHTS IN THE MEAT AND POULTRY INDUSTRY, 01/05, 175pp.

Uzbekistan

BURYING THE TRUTH: UZBEKISTAN REWRITES THE STORY OF THE ANDIJAN MASSACRE, 09/05, 73pp.

"BULLETS WERE FALLING LIKE RAIN": THE ANDIJAN MASSACRE, MAY 13, 2005, 06/05, 63pp.

TORTURE REFORM ASSESSMENT: UZBEKISTAN'S IMPLEMENTATION OF THE RECOMMENDATIONS OF THE SPECIAL RAPPORTEUR ON TORTURE, 03/05, 21pp.

Vietnam

KEY HUMAN RIGHTS ISSUES IN VIETNAM, 06/05, 10pp.

PERSECUTION OF MONTAGNARDS CONTINUES, 05/05, 16pp.

TORTURE, ARRESTS OF MONTAGNARD CHRISTIANS, 01/05 25pp.

Zimbabwe

"CLEAR THE FILTH": MASS EVICTIONS AND DEMOLITIONS IN ZIMBABWE, 09/05, 42pp.

NOT A LEVEL PLAYING FIELD: ZIMBABWE'S PARLIAMENTARY ELECTIONS IN 2005, 03/05, 38pp.

Worldwide

LANDMINE MONITOR REPORT 2005: TOWARD A MINE-FREE WORLD, 11/05, 1,071pp.

STILL AT RISK: DIPLOMATIC ASSURANCES NO SAFEGUARD AGAINST TORTURE, 04/05, 94pp

BY THEME

Arms Issues

STATES PARTIES' RESPONSES TO "INTERNATIONAL HUMANITARIAN LAW AND ERW" QUESTIONNAIRE: MEMORANDUM TO CCW DELEGATES, 11/05, 10pp.

LANDMINE MONITOR REPORT 2005: TOWARD A MINE-FREE WORLD, 11/05, 1,071pp.

BACK IN BUSINESS? U.S. LANDMINE PRODUCTION AND EXPORTS, 8/05, 16pp.

TIME TO TAKE STOCK: THE U.S. CLUSTER MUNITION INVENTORY AND THE FY 2006 DEPARTMENT OF DEFENSE BUDGET, 07/05, 20pp.

WORLDWIDE PRODUCTION AND EXPORT OF CLUSTER MUNITIONS, 04/05, 16pp.

Business and Human Rights Issues

COMMENTS ON THE OECD'S DRAFT RISK MANAGEMENT TOOL FOR INVESTORS IN WEAK GOVERNANCE ZONES, 11/05, 10pp.

COMMENTS ON THE INTERNATIONAL FINANCE CORPORATION' DRAFT SUSTAINABILITY POLICY AND PERFORMANCE STANDARDS, 11/05, 8pp.

ECUADOR: PETITION REGARDING ECUADOR'S ELIGIBILITY FOR ATPA DESIGNATION, 09/05, 23pp.

THE CURSE OF GOLD, 06/05, 159pp.

THE UNITED STATES-DOMINICAN REPUBLIC-CENTRAL AMERICA FREE TRADE AGREEMENT FALLS SHORT ON WORKERS' RIGHTS: WRITTEN TESTIMONY SUBMITTED TO THE U.S. HOUSE OF REPRESENTATIVES COMMITTEE ON WAYS AND MEANS, 04/05, 8pp.

COMMENTS TO USTR ON ECUADOR'S ATPDEA ELIGIBILITY, 03/05, 17pp.

FOX'S LABOR REFORM PROPOSAL WOULD DEAL SERIOUS BLOW TO WORKERS' RIGHTS: LETTER TO MEXICO'S CHAMBER OF DEPUTIES, 02/05, 5pp.

RIVERS AND BLOOD: GUNS, OIL, AND POWER IN NIGERIA'S RIVERS STATE, 02/05, 23pp.

BLOOD, SWEAT, AND FEAR: WORKERS' RIGHTS IN U.S. MEAT AND POULTRY PLANTS, 01/05, 185pp.

Children's Rights Issues

INSIDE THE HOME, OUTSIDE THE LAW: ABUSE OF CHILD DOMESTIC WORKERS IN MOROCCO,12/05, 60pp.

COLOMBIA: DISPLACED AND DISCARDED: THE PLIGHT OF INTERNALLY DISPLACED PERSONS IN BOGOTÁ AND CARTAGENA, 10/05, 62pp.

THE REST OF THEIR LIVES: LIFE WITHOUT PAROLE FOR CHILD OFFENDERS IN THE UNITED STATES, 10/05, 167pp.

LETTING THEM FAIL: GOVERNMENT NEGLECT AND THE RIGHT TO EDUCATION
FOR CHILDREN AFFECTED BY AIDS, 10/05, 59pp.

FAILING OUR CHILDREN: BARRIERS TO THE RIGHT TO EDUCATION, 09/05, 61pp.

"Making Their Own Rules": Police Beatings, Rape, and Torture of Children in Papua New Guinea, 09/05, 128pp.

Positively Abandoned: Stigma and Discrimination Against HIV-Positive Mothers and Their Children in Russia, 07/05, 43pp.

Always on Call: Abuse and Exploitation of Child Domestic Workers in Indonesia, 06/05, 78pp.

In the Dark: Hidden Abuses Against Detained Youths in Rio de Janeiro, 06/05, 51pp.

Youth, Poverty, and Blood: The Lethal Legacy of West Africa's Regional Warriors, 04/05, 69pp.

The Less They Know, the Better: Abstinence-Only HIV/AIDS Programs in Uganda, 03/05, 81pp.

Counterterrorism Issues

U.K.: Briefing on the Terrorism Bill 2005, 11/05, 16pp.

Leadership Failure: Firsthand Accounts of Torture of Iraqi Detainees by the U.S. Army's 82nd Airborne Division, 09/05, 30pp.

Detained Without Trial: Abuse of Internal Security Act Detainees in Malaysia, 09/05, 34pp.

Witness to Abuse: Human Rights Abuses under the U.S. Material Witness Law since September 11, 06/05, 103pp.

Transfer of Maher Arar to Torture: Human Rights Watch Report to the Commission of Inquiry on Maher Arar, 06/05, 36pp.

Black Hole: The Fate of Islamists Rendered to Egypt, 05/05, 64pp.

Getting Away with Torture? Command Responsibility for U.S. Abuse of Detainees, 04/05, 95pp.

Still at Risk: Diplomatic Assurances No Safeguard Against Torture, 04/05, 94pp.

Egypt: Mass Arrests and Torture in Sinai, 04/05, 49pp.

U.K.: Commentary on Prevention of Terrorism Bill 2005, 03/05, 11pp.

The New Iraq?: Torture and Ill-treatment of Detainees in Iraqi Custody, 01/05, 96pp.

Setting an Example?: Counterterrorism Measures in Spain, 01/05, 65pp.

HIV/AIDS Issues

Letting Them Fail: Government Neglect and the Right to Education for Children Affected by AIDS, 10/05, 55pp.

Restrictions on AIDS Activists in China, 06/05, 57pp.

Positively Abandoned: Stigma and Discrimination against HIV-Positive Mothers and their Children in Russia, 6/05, 41pp.

The Less They Know, the Better: Abstinence-Only HIV/AIDS Programs in Uganda, 03/05, 80pp.

A Dose of Reality: Women's Rights in the Fight against HIV/AIDS, 03/05, 10pp.

International Justice Issues

Justice in Motion: The Trial Phase of the Special Court for Sierra Leone, 11/05, 45pp.

The Former Iraqi Government on Trial, 10/05, 20pp.

Memorandum to the International Criminal Court on the Draft Regulations of the Registry, 8/05, 18pp.

The Victims of Hissène Habré Still Awaiting Justice, 07/05, 43pp.

The Meaning of "the Interests of Justice" in Article 53 of the Rome Statute, 06/05, 25pp.

Refugees/Displaced Persons Issues

On the Margins: Rights Violations Against Migrants and Asylum Seekers at the New Eastern Border of the European Union, 11/05, 77pp.

Living on the Margins: Inadequate Protection for Refugees and Asylum Seekers in Johannesburg, 11/05, 66pp.

Colombia: Displaced and Discarded: The Plight of Internally Displaced Persons in Bogota and Cartagena, 10/05, 62pp.

Burying the Truth: Uzbekistan Rewrites the Story of the Andijan Massacre, 09/05, 75pp.

Uprooted and Forgotten: Impunity and Human Rights Abuses in Northern Uganda, 9/05, 78pp.

Burma: "They Came and Destroyed Our Village Again": The Plight of Internally Displaced Persons in Karen State, 06/05, 69pp.

"Bullets Were Falling Like Rain": The Andijan Massacre, May 13, 2005, 06/05, 65pp.

Vietnam: Persecution of Montagnards Continues: Dega Christians Targeted in Latest Crackdown, 05/05, 16pp.

Sexual Violence and its Consequences among Displaced Persons in Darfur and Chad, 4/05, 18pp.

Coming Home: Return and Reintegration in Angola, 03/05, 39pp.

STILL CRITICAL: PROSPECTS IN 2005 FOR INTERNALLY DISPLACED KURDS IN TURKEY, 03/05, 38pp.

VIETNAM: TORTURE, ARRESTS OF MONTAGNARD CHRISTIANS: CAMBODIA SLAMS THE DOOR ON NEW ASYLUM SEEKERS, 01/05, 25pp.

Women's Rights Issues

MAID TO ORDER: ENDING ABUSES AGAINST MIGRANT DOMESTIC WORKERS IN SINGAPORE, 12/05, 115pp.

CAMPAIGNING AGAINST FEAR: WOMEN'S PARTICIPATION IN AFGHANISTAN'S 2005 ELECTIONS, 08/05, 29pp.

DECISIONS DENIED: WOMEN'S ACCESS TO CONTRACEPTIVES AND ABORTION IN ARGENTINA, 06/05, 87pp.

INTERNATIONAL HUMAN RIGHTS LAW AND ABORTION IN LATIN AMERICA, 6/05, 22pp.

A DOSE OF REALITY: WOMEN'S RIGHTS IN THE FIGHT AGAINST HIV/AIDS, 03/05, 10pp.